Issues in 21st Century World Politics

Issues in 21st Century World Politics

Edited by Mark Beeson
and
Nick Bisley

First published 2010 by
PALGRAVE MACMILLAN
100662 576x
Palgrave Macmillan in the UK is an imprint of Macmillan Publishers Limited,
registered in England, company number 785998, of Houndmills, Basingstoke,
Hampshire RG21 6XS.

Palgrave Macmillan in the US is a division of St Martin's Press LLC,
175 Fifth Avenue, New York, NY 10010.

Palgrave Macmillan is the global academic imprint of the above companies
and has companies and representatives throughout the world.

Palgrave® and Macmillan® are registered trademarks in the United States,
the United Kingdom, Europe and other countries.

ISBN-13: 978-0-230-59451-7 hardback
ISBN-13: 978-0-230-59452-4 paperback

This book is printed on paper suitable for recycling and made from fully
managed and sustained forest sources. Logging, pulping and manufacturing
processes are expected to conform to the environmental regulations of the
country of origin.

A catalogue record for this book is available from the British Library.

A catalog record for this book is available from the Library of Congress.

10   9   8   7   6   5   4
19   18   17   16   15   14   13   12   11

Printed in China

Contents

List of Contributors

Mark Beeson is Winthrop Professor in Political Science and International Relations, at the University of Western Australia. His most recent books are *Institutions of the Asia-Pacific: ASEAN, APEC, and Beyond* (2009) and *Securing Southeast Asia: The Politics of Security Sector Reform* (with Alex Bellamy) (2008).

Alex J. Bellamy is Professor of International Relations and Executive Director of the Asia-Pacific Centre for the Responsibility to Protect at the University of Queensland, Australia. His most recent book is *Responsibility to Protect: The Global Effort to End Mass Atrocities* (2009).

Nick Bisley is Associate Professor in International Relations and Convenor of the Politics & International Relations Program at La Trobe University and is a Senior Research Associate at the International Institute for Strategic Studies. His most recent book is *Building Asia's Security* (2009).

Shaun Breslin is Professor of Politics and International Studies at the University of Warwick. He is a co-editor of *The Pacific Review* and is the author of *China and the Global Political Economy* (2009).

Mely Caballero-Anthony is an Associate Professor at the S. Rajaratnam School of International Studies (RSIS) at Nanyang Technological University, Singapore, and Head of the RSIS Centre for Non-Traditional Security (NTS) Studies. She is also the Secretary-General of the Consortium on Non-Traditional Security Studies in Asia (NTS-Asia).

Neil Carter is Professor of Politics at the University of York. He is the author of *The Politics of the Environment: Ideas, Activism, Policy*, 2nd edition (2007), and the joint editor of the journal *Environmental Politics*.

William Case is Professor in the Department of Asian and International Studies and Director of the Southeast Asia Research Centre (SEARC) at City University of Hong Kong. His research interests include comparative politics and the politics of Southeast Asia.

Philip G. Cerny is Professor Emeritus of Government at the University of Manchester (UK) and is currently Professor of Politics, International Studies and Global Affairs at Rutgers University-Newark (New Jersey, USA). He has published several books, the most recent of which is *Rethinking World Politics:*

A Theory of Transnational Neopluralism (2010), and a number of academic articles and book chapters.

Anne Hammerstad is a lecturer in International Relations at the University of Kent in Canterbury, and an ESRC Global Uncertainties Fellow.

Richard Higgott is Professor of International Political Economy and Pro Vice Chancellor at the University of Warwick. He has been Editor of *The Pacific Review* since 1995 and his latest work, with Shaun Breslin, is *The International Relations of the Asia Pacific* (2010, 4 volumes).

Ray Kiely is Professor of International Politics at Queen Mary University of London. His books include *Rethinking Imperialism* (2010), *The New Political Economy of Development* (2007) and *Industrialization and Development: A Comparative Analysis* (1998).

Matt Killingsworth is an Associate Lecturer in International Relations at La Trobe University, Australia. Matt primarily researches the former Communist regimes of Central and Eastern Europe, specialising in opposition and dissent under Communism, democratic transition and accession to the European Union.

Richard W. Mansbach is Professor of Political Science at Iowa State University. He is the author or editor of 14 books on international relations theory, including *A World of Polities*, *Remapping Global Politics*, *The Elusive Quest Continues: Theory and Global Politics* and *Polities: Authority, Identities, and Change*, as well as numerous articles and book chapters.

Andrew Phillips is Lecturer in International Relations at the University of Queensland. He is the author of *War, Empire and the Transformation of International Orders* to be published in 2010.

Laura J. Shepherd is Lecturer in International Relations at the Department of Political Science and International Studies, University of Birmingham. Recent publications include *Gender, Violence and Security: Discourse as Practice* (2008), and articles in *International Studies Quarterly*, *Review of International Studies* and *Political Studies Review*.

Timothy J. Sinclair is Associate Professor of International Political Economy at the University of Warwick. He received his Ph.D from York University, Toronto, in 1995. Sinclair is an expert on the international capital markets, especially the major American credit rating agencies, Moody's Investors Service and Standard & Poor's.

Frank Umbach is an independent consultant on international energy security and an official advisor on international energy security to the Lithuanian government.

Issues in Twenty-first Century World Politics: An Introduction

MARK BEESON AND NICK BISLEY

On a sunny September morning early in the twenty-first century, 19 middle class men from Saudi Arabia and Egypt hijacked four commercial airliners and used the craft as ballistic missiles in an attack on symbols of American power and prestige with devastating psychological effect. Seven years later, although with less terrifying immediate effect, Lehman Brothers, a venerable financial house of almost unquestionable solidity, collapsed, triggering the worst financial and economic crisis since the 1930s. These two events are, in many respects, the two great international events of the new century and bookmark its first phase. They represent not only the utter centrality of the US and more particularly its most global city, New York, to the international system, but more importantly they reveal the unpredictable dangers of a globalising world. On the one hand, religious fervour mixed with a profound sense of grievance has found an extremely fertile field, thanks to the opportunities opened up by globalisation. On the other, questionable banking practices in the backwaters of the American property market, when combined with lax regulation and murky financial instruments, can wreak havoc on the economic prospects of the entire planet.

If these two events display the new kinds of challenges with which states and peoples have to cope – exposure to new risks delivered with novel means and remarkable power – other issues may have less immediacy, but they are equally novel and potentially even more devastating. The prospects of changes in the natural environment, and their consequences for agricultural systems, water supplies, indeed the habitability of crucial parts of the planet, appear more real now than at any time since the issue was first raised at the international level in the 1960s. While changes in the natural environment are fundamental in effect, their slow movement and the absence of a singular televisually compelling moment to say nothing of the difficulties of understanding such complex metabolic mechanisms militate against the kind of action which financial crisis and transnational terrorism have prompted.

Elsewhere in world politics the sense of the novel and the unexpected is evident. The richest and most powerful country the world has ever seen, one endowed with unparalleled cultural, technological and educational advantages, has managed not only to get itself bogged down in two seemingly intractable wars in Southwest Asia, it is also largely responsible for the economic catastrophe of the

Global Financial Crisis. Elsewhere, Asia is on the brink of a different unparalleled historical circumstance: the contemporaneous wealth and prosperity of the region's three great powers China, India and Japan. The growing affluence of Asia's massive societies is beginning to make humanity acknowledge the environmental consequences of rapid, widespread industrialisation. This is not to downplay the environmental impact of earlier periods of industrialisation – the devastations caused during Britain's Industrial Revolution or the Stalinist modernisation programmes were stark – rather it is to emphasise that the scale of development in Asia makes the stark realities of environmental constraint unarguably clear-cut. The sustainability of the way human beings currently arrange their lives, especially in the West, appears to be under very real threat (see Homer-Dixon 2006). Of equal novelty are the sources of insecurity which peoples the world over face. For most states and societies the most pressing threats to their sense of security and well-being no longer come from neighbours threatening their interests and resources; rather they stem from more unusual origins, most particularly infectious diseases, transnational criminality, such as drug smuggling, money laundering, people trafficking and transnational political movements, particularly those which use terrorist methods.

All of these seem to imply that world politics in this new century will, in many respects, represent a distinct break with the past. Yet for many, politics – or at least its international manifestations – has been driven by the same forces for thousands of years, and this century will be no different. The self-proclaimed 'realist' branch of international relations theory, for example, sees world politics as a perennial game of power in the competition for survival and advancement. Whether the game is played on horseback or with thermonuclear weapons is, from this perspective, immaterial to the underlying rules. For realists, therefore, the twenty-first century will look much like every other that has been; it will be characterised by rivalry, competition and only very limited forms of instrumental cooperation between international actors (see, e.g., Ross 2006; Waltz 2000). In the rise of China and India and the challenge they represent to American dominance one sees only the latest variation in the endless drama of great power politics (Mearsheimer 2001). Others see continuity in the larger themes of world politics, but for different and somewhat more optimistic reasons. At the close of the Cold War, Francis Fukuyama (1992) declared that the victory of liberal democratic capitalism over its challengers – first fascism and latterly Soviet-led communism – had brought about the end of history. By this he meant that the long-running contest about the optimum way of arranging human societies, both politically and economically, had come to an end as liberal democratic capitalism was embraced around the world. A related liberal view saw the emergence of globalisation – a global process binding societies ever closer in a network of finance, trade, cultural, political and strategic linkages – as not only reinforcing the trend of democratisation, but also expanding the reach of global capitalism and doing so in ways that improved the lot of people the world over. Globalisation was touted as driving a convergence of political and economic systems and through this dramatically reducing the differences among states and societies and improving the welfare of all, most especially the worst off (Ohmae 1990). From this liberal perspective, world politics in the new century appeared to be marked for a good deal of continuity with the last, understood as the continuation of the twin trends of globalisation and democratisation. Yet the sobering reality is that much of the world remains locked in seemingly inescapable poverty, and the prospects for genuine democracy remain as elusive as ever for most of the world's people (Diamond 2008a). In short, for all the talk of globalisation, the declining importance of national borders and of the potential for convergence on some sort of Western template of economic and political order, the world remains a heterogeneous place. Paradoxically there is continuity, but it is not necessarily the progressive spread of liberalism that many had expected in the 1990s. On the contrary, one of the most depressing features of the contemporary international system is the perpetuation of structured disadvantage, exclusion and conflict of a sort that was a hallmark of much of the last century's international affairs (Collier 2007).

The aim of this book is to identify the issues that are, and look likely to remain, significant influences on the international system, and to provide some sense of context for the widely held proposition that the new century presents a set of novel challenges that in many ways break with the pattern of the past. Where the twentieth century opened as largely a continuation of the nineteenth's preoccupations – colonial rivalries, rising nationalism and complex diplomatic manoeuvring around marginal shifts in the balance of power – the twenty-first appears to have a set of threats and risks that are as frightening as they are unprecedented. For this reason, it has become commonplace to talk about a 'new' security agenda (Brown 2003). And yet, notwithstanding the novelty and risk of climate change, pandemics, energy security and violent transnational terrorism, world politics is, in many ways, driven by many of the same forces as in the past. States seek security and prosperity in an uncertain and anarchic political environment. The uneven distribution of power and resources prompts rivalry, fear and ambition among states and peoples. The manifest material inequalities among and between states continue to be a determinant of the prospects of people the world over. The hopes and dreams of people to remake the world in ways which they believe to be more just, more moral or simply their own continue, as ever they did, to disrupt the plans, maps and power structures of the established order. One of the central aims of this book, therefore, is to help students, scholars and policymakers to make informed assessments of the points of change and continuity in the international system.

At the outset, therefore, we need to recognise that some issues really are global, and that they present novel problems and require distinctive solutions. For example, we have always had a natural environment whose state has profoundly shaped human development, but it is only recently that we have begun to think about it as something that needs to be managed. Even more significantly, the all-encompassing nature of 'the environment' is something that no state or political community acting alone can hope to address: if the human race is to maintain the basic necessities of life, let alone the quality of life many in the West assume is their birthright, then cooperation that transcends national borders would seem to be essential (Elliott 2004).

But while we might agree in principle that our own times seem to necessitate some form of collaborative action if we are to address issues like climate change, it is far from clear what form this should take, which countries should lead it or what the underlying rationale for such actions should be. One thing that is clear is that, far from becoming irrelevant, there are continuing differences in the ways problems are understood, prioritised and addressed. Ideas matter and the competition among ideas will be a central driving force in world politics (Blyth 2002; Williams 2004). The possibility that ideas may have a major influence on the conduct of policy and determine how – indeed, if – problems are to be addressed has led to the development of new theoretical approaches in international relations. Unlike realists who focus on material power, 'constructivists' pay a great deal of attention to the formation of ideas, their competition and the ways in which particular ways of thinking about the world actually shape political practice (Reus-Smit 1999; Ruggie 1998).

The environment and our response to it is not only one of the most pressing problems of our times, but it also serves as a reminder of the enduring nature of some underlying realities. Karl Marx (1913) suggested that men – his word, not ours – make their own history, but 'under circumstances existing already, given and transmitted from the past'. Marx's ideas have become rather unfashionable, an ironic reminder of the importance and indeterminacy of non-material forces, but his basic insight into the 'dialectical' nature of our collective relationship with material reality continues to resonate: if the planet were a little larger, if there were more resources to distribute and if our impact on the environment was not as great as it is, the contemporary world might look rather different. As economists are right to point out, the scarcity of desirable goods *does* remain a profound influence on human beings' acquisitive behaviour. Whether we take such behaviour to be learned or innate, beneficial or harmful or ultimately subject to change are rather different questions, of course.

But even if we agree that the pursuit of wealth, be it at the individual, corporate or state level, is still one of the central dynamics of the international system, it is not obvious how such activities are to be organised or legitimated. The financial crisis that erupted in 2008 served as a powerful reminder of both the cyclical nature of economic crises and the different ways people think economic activities should be regulated. The crisis highlighted a number of issues that are worth bearing in mind when thinking about the contents of this book. First, this has been a crisis of capitalism, and a particular form of 'Western' capitalism at that. Not only are there different ways of organising broadly capitalist economic activities, there are alternatives to capitalism itself. While we may all inhabit nation-states of one sort or another these days, the domestic political systems within those states, the ideologies that populations may subscribe to and the very capacity of the states themselves vary tremendously and continue to throw up different answers to the basic questions of social organisation, economic development and political stability (see Hollingsworth and Boyer 1997).

Such possibilities are implicit in the language we use to describe some of the most important features and fissures in the international system: neoliberalism, the north–south divide, failed states and hegemony, to name but a few of the most prominent that will appear in the pages that follow. The point to re-emphasise at the outset, however, is that the world continues to be characterised by major disparities of political and economic power, and major divisions in thinking about the way the international system should be organised. These differences have been thrown into sharp relief by the recent crisis because it is entirely possible that the dominant distribution of power and influence in the international system is about to change before our eyes. The old order established under the auspices of American power in the aftermath of the Second World War has been profoundly challenged by the apparent economic fragility of the US itself and by the emergence of a serious competitor in the form of a resurgent and increasingly powerful China, as well as that of other Asian behemoth, India.

The 'rise of China' is such an important development that it is worth making a few observations about it at the outset. Like the environment, China's rise seems a definitively contemporary issue, but like environmental problems, China's long history is a reminder of both how much things can change and how some seem to remain the same. After all, what we think of as 'China' is, in fact, the world's most enduring civilisation, but one that has experienced major historical fluctuations in its power and influence. After being marginalised by European imperialism, and the impact of internal and external conflict, China is back at, or at least very close to, the centre of world affairs and is seemingly intent asserting itself on the international stage. Such an outcome would not surprise realist scholars, of course, and there is a substantial literature that discusses the prospects for 'power transition' and competition between the US and China for global leadership (see, e.g., Beeson 2009; Chan 2008). Indeed, many influential observers – especially in the US – think that inter-state competition is the inescapable consequence of changes in the relative standing of major powers (Mearsheimer 2006). As China becomes more powerful relative to the US, it will inevitably want to challenge the dominance of the US, so the argument goes. However, other scholars argue that China's policy-making elites are being 'socialised' into different forms of behaviour, and as they become more familiar with the international system and its rules and procedures, they will begin to adopt the habits of normal members of the system (Johnston 2003). Yet another long-standing strand of theory has been developed by liberals who argue that greater economic and even political interdependence will change the calculation of national interests, and through this China's leaders recognise their own growing stake in the existing order (Keohane and Nye 1977).

When we look at the massive expansion in the size of China's economy and the growing and increasingly complex links it has to the rest of the world, such an interpretation of events seems persuasive. The fact that China is developing increasingly cordial relations with Taiwan suggests that economic considerations may indeed be on the verge of becoming more important than strategic concerns in the minds of policymakers in precisely the way liberals would expect.

If the implacable logic of economic interdependence seems to be influencing state behaviour at the local level, there is little doubt that states are being profoundly influenced by changes at both the international and the transnational level.

One of the biggest and most distinctive changes about the contemporary international system is the emergence of a plethora of new transnational actors that have appeared on the international stage. Multinational corporations (MNCs) are recognised as some of the world's most important economic entities. It is not hard to see why many feel that ExxonMobil, Goldman Sachs or Microsoft are more important than many states. Unsurprisingly, perhaps, some of these corporations are able to exercise a good deal more influence over the behaviour of states in particular and the operation of the international political economy more generally than many individual states do. It was equally predictable that the regulatory and legal framework that governs the activities of MNCs would begin to reflect the interests of such powerful actors, as the emergence of issues like intellectual property law seems to confirm (Braithwaite and Drahos 2000).

But MNCs are not the only new forces that are shaping economic and political outcomes. The massive expansion of international financial markets has placed constraints on the autonomy of even the most powerful states, as it seems policymakers must tailor their decisions with one eye on 'the markets'. And yet the current crisis is a reminder of how rapidly apparent certainties can change. The balance of power between broadly conceived market and political power remains fluid: if policymakers have the requisite will and motivation, it is apparent that they can quite quickly legislate to change the nature of the international political economy and the key relationships of which it is constituted – especially if they act in concert.

A key question in this context is which countries should initiate such changes and which institutions should implement them. This is another aspect of the contemporary international scene that appears to be indispensible: international institutions have become major, functionally necessary parts of what has increasingly come to be known as 'global governance'. While there are some enduring theoretical and practical problems about the way we think about and operationalise global governance (see, e.g., Murphy 2000; Rosenau 1995), it does draw our attention to the array of new inter-governmental organisations that have become such prominent parts of international life. The so-called Bretton Woods institutions – the International Monetary Fund, the World Bank and the World Trade Organisation (WTO) – created after the Second World War are the most important and enduring organisations of this sort. But there are many others, including those that represent the interests of the private sector such as business lobby groups, and those that represent civil society.

A further recent development has been the idea that civil society – or that sphere of collective action that exists outside the family and the state – has become transnational (Keane 2003). The expectation or hope that 'global civil society' could give political expression to issues that are either not taken seriously by national elites or are inherently transnational and thus outside the realm of national politics seems intuitively persuasive. Some of the most high profile actors on the international stage these days are, after all, organisations like Greenpeace or the myriad anti-globalisation groups that have become prominent features of most conventional international political gatherings. Civil society groups are, however, not all liberal, progressive and making up the shortfall of western states. They include such decidedly illiberal entities as Hezbollah and Al Qaeda. While there are major questions about the legitimacy of unelected actors that may represent single issues, there is a growing sense among many scholars and participants that only unconventional politics can actually achieve the political outcomes they desire, whether that means action on climate change, human rights advancement or a caliphate in Southeast Asia (O'Brien et al. 2000). They may have a point: would we take environmental issues as seriously as we do if it had not been for the tireless efforts of non-governmental organisations that have agitated about their importance for so long? Would the much invoked but rather nebulous 'international community' have got around to banning the use of landmines if this cause had not been championed by civil society groups? Indeed, are such groups any less legitimate than the unelected technocratic elites that populate the Western-dominated international financial institutions (IFIs)?

Even if the extent and implications of globalisation are overstated and less precise than we might wish, the idea that some issues are beyond the capability of individual states to deal with has become firmly established. The fact that some states have no desire to deal with certain issues is also clear. Consequently, one of the defining issues of the twenty-first century is deciding how – perhaps even whether – certain problems and challenges are even capable of being addressed with the sorts of political mechanisms and processes that we have developed collectively thus far. Even the organisations or institutions that have been created with a specific mission in mind – like the World Bank or the WTO – often seem incapable of furthering their central goals, be it poverty reduction or trade liberalisation (Woods 2000). Adding to the problem is the fact that the goals themselves may be contentious and not representative of the interests of the 'international community'. All of these should caution us against using unspecific phrases like the 'international community' in the first place. While some scholars might like to promote the idea of a 'cosmopolitan' future shaped by collectively derived, universally applicable notions of justice and equality (Pogge 2002), achieving such noble goals remains depressingly elusive; wishful thinking will not make it so.

None of this should be taken to mean that we should abandon hope about our ability to bring about change. Indeed, how could it be otherwise? Paradoxically, change is the one certainty in international life. But we need to think about who 'we' are and whether 'our' views and thinking even accurately reflect the reality that we experience as individuals, much less that of the planet's population as a whole. This is where international relations theory offers some hope, but also some inevitably dashed expectations. The very fact that there are a number of competing perspectives about the apparently fundamental realities of international life is a reminder of how much remains uncertain, contested and unknowable. This may seem a strange observation for the editors of a book about the key issues of the twenty-first century to make, but experience dictates that we assume a little intellectual modesty as we try to pick a way through the foothills of this still new century. What we can do is to try to identify the key issues and recognise that the way that we feel about them will reflect our geographical position, our gender, our age, our class and ultimately, perhaps, that idiosyncratic amalgam of memories, impressions and experiences that make us who we are as individuals. We cannot tell you what to make of all this, but we can introduce you to the forces and actors that will shape your world and ours.

Overview of the book

The chapters in this book attempt to provide a detailed introduction to 17 of the major issues that influence the dynamics of world politics and over which there is considerable social and political contestation in the contemporary world. Of course we cannot hope to provide exhaustive coverage of every issue that matters; rather we have selected what we feel are the most important of these issues at present and which are likely to remain of considerable salience in the coming years. The book is presented in two main parts. The first focuses its attention on issues which have implications for the structure of the international system and the dynamics of international order, that is, with the foundational elements of world politics. The second examines issues that relate to conflict, crises and questions of authority. Here the focus is on more immediate concerns – which themselves may have longer-run structural consequences in the future – that relate to the changing nature of conflict and security, shifting attitudes towards social roles and obligations and the ongoing problems that stem from the absence of a central authority over global systems of finance, production and distribution. The book's aim is to provide a comprehensive overview of the key issues in contemporary world politics. To some degree many of these issues are inter-connected, for example, climate change is contributing to the increasing politicisation of security questions, such as resource and food security, while globalisation is amplifying the rate, incidence and consequences of financial crises. However, each is sufficiently discrete as to warrant specific treatment.

In Chapter 1, Philip Cerny examines what has become one of the central questions in contemporary politics: the relationship between globalisation and the state. States are the foundation stones of the international system, and many have argued that the powerful transnational forces of globalisation threaten not only the power of states but the very functioning of the international system itself. Cerny observes that the state faces a crisis in its traditional function and that this is prompting a transformation of governance and authority structures which will produce a much more complex and multilayered system of world politics over the coming years. The chapter examines the origins of this crisis, its contemporary manifestations and the place of globalisation in this process. Cerny argues that the state will increasingly be hamstrung as webs of authority networks increasingly limit its ability to fulfil its traditional governance function. Shaun Breslin then examines one aspect of the process that Cerny has identified: the growing role of regional cooperation in world politics. In Chapter 2, he argues that geographically constrained forms of inter-governmental cooperation are a central feature of the current order and are likely to remain so for many years to come. They will not, however, supersede the state and often operate in an uneasy and sometimes antagonistic relationship with global multilateral mechanisms. The chapter charts the emergence of regionalism in the twentieth century and particularly the centrality of the European experience in shaping both the theory and practice of regional cooperation, its transformation in response to changing circumstances and its likely future trajectory.

Climate change, and the diplomatic and institutional dealings that try to cope with or mitigate it, has become one of the most important issues in world politics. In Chapter 3, Neil Carter examines the efforts to respond to climate change, assesses their strengths and weaknesses and reflects on the extent to which environmental questions have transcended their traditional location as 'low' politics and have now become a major national interest concern. He argues that central to the, so far, inadequate response to the profound challenge presented by environmental transformation is the predominance of territorial conceptions of sovereignty. Until such time as this is overcome, prospects for ameliorating the worst consequences of climate change remain slim. Chapter 4 examines the prospects of a shift in the basic pattern of power distribution among states and its implications for the structure of world politics. Nick Bisley provides an overview and assessment of the arguments that the rise of China and India, alongside the hydrocarbon-fuelled wealth of Russia and a number of other powers, is presaging a shift in power and influence from the North Atlantic to the Asian continent. He overviews the origins of the West's dominance and the different ways in which relative power seems to be changing. While he argues that Western decline can be overstated, and has been in the past, on balance he concludes that there are good reasons for thinking that world politics will be shaped by the interplay of a larger number of closely inter-related major powers than in the past 60 years. This is likely to make world politics a more unstable, complex and unpredictable place.

Chapter 5 takes up issues directly related to the dramatic economic success of China, India and others. Here, Mark Beeson argues that experiences of the past 10–15 years have put paid to the idea, so dominant in the 1990s, that an Anglo-American liberal vision of capitalist economic development was the only plausible way in which societies could structure their economies. Not only has the Global Financial Crisis of 2008 seriously undermined arguments in favour of deregulation, privatisation and lower social spending, the dramatic resurgence of a number of developing economies, most notably China, has shown that there is a wide variety of forms of capitalism that can be successful, in some cases spectacularly so. Thus circumstances in the twenty-first century might be decidedly more conducive to less liberal ones than many had thought. The chapter examines the different types of economic systems, their interaction and concludes with a consideration of the implications of the recent crisis on economic and political systems. The predominance of neoliberal capitalism in the economic realm was matched by the apparent victory of liberal democracy in the light of Soviet Communism's demise. In Chapter 6, William Case considers the current state of democracy and democratisation and the implications for world politics of the stuttering expansion of democratic systems of political rule. The chapter examines the preconditions for democracy that have been identified in the literature as well as the substantive aims of those who seek to bring about democratic change. It assesses the extent to which democratic systems of government affect human welfare and the extent to which democracy is able to bring about the improvements that many of its supporters seek. Case argues that some of the shortcomings of democracy relate not simply to the problems of particular countries and their elites but to the transfer of power away from statist forms and thus away from participatory systems of authority. The chapter concludes with a consideration of the recent democracy 'recession' whereby authoritarian governments are increasingly able to resist democratising impulses and democratic standard bearers, such as the US, have plummeted in popularity.

In the final chapter of the first part of the book, Richard Mansbach analyses the role of nationalism and ethnicity in world politics. He considers the extent to which these remarkably powerful forces of particularism are able to find such traction in an era when states and societies are increasingly deeply inter-connected. Mansbach provides an overview of theories of nation, nationalism and ethnicity and the historical development of these ideas in practice in the political as well as the economic realm. He draws attention to the way in which these ideas have always been subversive of existing practices but shows that they can play out in both positive and negatives ways: they can unify disparate peoples into a functioning society or equally be the source of strife and conflict. He concludes that in spite of the unifying tendencies of globalising forces, the politics of identity as manifested in nationalism and ethnicity is likely to continue to drive conflict and contestation well into the twenty-first century.

The first four chapters of Part II consider different aspect of the changing nature of conflict and security. Chapter 8 examines the changing nature of war and reflects on the extent to which organised violent conflict in world politics is qualitatively different from that which has traditionally been the norm and the consequences of these changes for world politics. Matt Killingsworth first sets out the traditional understanding of the nature of war and then assesses this in light of recent arguments that globalisation is producing war which is different both in its purpose and in its conduct. He then examines the US-led conflicts in Afghanistan and Iraq and concludes that they bear out many of the claims made about the transformation of war, particularly as they relate to violence, especially to civilians, the predominance of irregular combatants and asymmetric conduct. In Chapter 9, Andrew Phillips considers a phenomenon that encapsulates many of the changing facets of contemporary world politics: transnational terrorism. Having distinguished terrorism from other forms of irregular organised violence, and emphasising its distinctly transnational character, Phillips traces transnational terrorism's historical origins and then assesses its contemporary significance.

Terrorism is of particular importance, he shows, not because of its strategic threat but because of the destabilising consequences that reaction to it has brought about and, of course, the intellectual jolt that transnational terrorism caused to the academic discipline of International Relations. He concludes by arguing that terrorism is likely to remain an important factor in shaping international order, albeit an indirect one, as the structural circumstances of world politics, whereby the interaction of the major powers with zones of the world where terrorism is particularly appealing shows no sign of changing.

As Alex Bellamy explains in Chapter 10, the increasing sense that international society should breach the core non-intervention norm for humanitarian reasons presents a serious challenge to world politics. Since the creation of the United Nations (UN) in 1945, international society has increasingly devised military means to try to manage international conflict and its consequences. The chapter charts this practice and particularly focuses on the emergence of peace operations during the Cold War and the turn to more coercive interventionism of the post-Cold War period. The chapter then examines the emerging principle that state sovereignty implies a responsibility to provide a minimum level of protection to citizens, of which the failure to provide warrants international action. This principle is not uniformly accepted and has yet to prompt more effective humanitarian action; however, key policymakers at the UN and elsewhere are trying to work out the best way in which this principle can reduce the frequency and impact of humanitarian catastrophe. Mely Caballero-Anthony then examines the changing way in which security is conceived and its implications for inter-state cooperation. Chapter 11 charts the growing perception of new sources of insecurity in the post-Cold War world, many of which relate to the broader changes associated with globalisation, and the way in which non-traditional security challenges are shaping the policy landscape. It focuses particularly on Asia as a region that is especially illustrative of the issues of non-traditional security, the challenge they pose to traditional policy tools and considers the extent to which they have been a spur to better international cooperation.

Chapter 12 looks at gender as a central issue in world politics. Here, Laura Shepherd argues that conceptions of gender roles, both masculine and feminine, profoundly shape not only our understanding of how world politics operates, but influence outcomes of concrete policy choices as well. Shepherd shows that gender matters to the workings of world politics by examining its place in the processes of foreign policy-making, policies relating to the international economy and in international development theory and practice. In each of these she explores different theoretical perspectives which all share the common commitment to the basic proposition that gender is a vital component of both the theory and practice of international relations even if it is not often a self-conscious focus of thinking, whether academic discourse or that which informs governmental policy. In Chapter 13, Ray Kiely examines the staggering material inequality of states and societies, one of the most enduring features of the contemporary world. The chapter assesses the competing arguments about the causes of the perpetuation, and for some, the ever-widening gap between rich and poor. It focuses particularly on the debate between those who feel that globalisation provides reason to be optimistic about the prospect of the poor being able to improve their lot and those who are more sceptical of this position. After examining a wide range of views, Kiely concludes that, on balance, the evidence seems to support a more pessimistic interpretation. He argues that globalisation is, if not exacerbating, then not doing anything to redress the structures of inequality, particularly in power relations that have produced the current setting. This is likely to remain a central organising principle of the world economy.

In Chapter 14, Frank Umbach focuses on global and regional energy security. He provides an overview of the worldwide energy environment and its impact on security issues and then examines the issue by way of more specific analyses of the situation in the European Union (EU) and China. The acute and highly political sensitive character of the question of energy means that the traditional division between economics and politics that dominates so much policy thinking, particularly in Europe, has to go by the wayside. He argues that energy is set to become a point of particularly heated political contestation and international cooperation will be needed to damp down the more negative consequences of this competition. In the recent past the incidence, consequences and numbers of people affected by financial crises have grown exponentially. In Chapter 15, Timothy Sinclair examines first the differing way financial crises are understood and explained and then considers the reasons for the increasing volatility of global finance following the breakdown of the Bretton Woods monetary order. He then examines the origins of the 2008 Global Financial Crisis and concludes by reflecting on the prospects of regulatory reform of the global financial system. Sinclair argues that while it is not necessarily inevitable, the political reality is that we are unlikely to see the kind of governmental cooperation and coordination as well as shifts in attitude that would be necessary to ensure a significant reduction in the scale and severity of financial crises.

Richard Higgott's subsequent chapter takes up this theme directly with a consideration of the origins and current state of multilateral economic institutions. The penultimate chapter charts the rise of multilateralism in world politics and particularly the emergence and transformation of the Bretton Woods system. It then examines the emergence of a range of newer multilateral organisations, such as the G20, as well as the way in which these institutions have been increasingly questioned about the legitimacy and efficacy of their policy-making. The chapter then considers the prospects of improved economic governance and overviews a number of changes that policy advocates have put forward to make the global economy function more efficiently and more fairly. He is, however, reasonably sober in the prognostications for change noting that the prospects for greater governance are subject to the willingness of the powerful to concede the need to change. In the book's final chapter, Anne Hammerstad considers the impact of population movement on the broader dynamics of world politics. Her chapter considers why population movement is thought to be such a contentious issue in so many polities. It does so first by investigating whether perceptions that the present is an unparalleled 'great age' of migration, as some have claimed, is true. It then looks at what is old and what is new about migration trends, and argues that today's population movements do pose some distinctive challenges, particularly as they relate to the way in which globalisation is blending questions of identity with often acute problems of security. She concludes that the hard realities of demographic change are likely to ensure that migration continues to occur, but that with it will come continued political and cultural contestation and resistance.

Part I

Evolution of the International System

Chapter 1

Globalisation and Statehood

PHILIP G. CERNY

States and statehood in world politics

States have been the fundamental building blocks of modern world politics. They have formed a dualistic structure reminiscent of the role of the Roman god Janus. Statues of Janus were placed at the gates to the city. The god had two faces, one looking inwards to guard the social, economic and political life of the city, to give it unity and a sense of the common good and public interest. The second face looked outwards, to protect the city from external threats and predators, to pursue the city's interests in a hostile world and to interact with other cities. In today's collective choice literature, the first face or function of the state is said to be an 'arena of collective action' among its inhabitants and citizens. The second face or function was to permit the state to make – or break – 'credible commitments' to other states, what Kenneth Waltz, in his magisterial *Theory of International Politics*, called 'like units' (Waltz 1979). The capacity of a set of political institutions to play such 'two-level games' (Putnam 1988) effectively – that is, to do both things successfully at the same time – is called 'statehood' (Brenner 2004).

'Statehood', therefore, is defined as the capacity to fulfil these two different and sometimes conflicting functions simultaneously. It is the central *problématique* or analytical puzzle of the modern world system itself. States frequently cannot do either of these tasks very well, much less do them both successfully at the same time. States have always been consolidating, fragmenting, experiencing both domestic conflict and upheaval and international weakness and subordination throughout what historians label the 'modern' period – that is, from (broadly speaking) the seventeenth century to the mid-twentieth century – as well as the 'contemporary' period – that is, from the late twentieth century until today. Today, a process of adaptation to what are sometimes loosely called 'global realities' has presented a challenge both to older post-feudal and quasi-states that have been absorbed into larger units, as in eighteenth–twentieth century Europe, and today to 'new' and 'postcolonial' states.

More powerful older nation-states like Britain, France, Germany and, more recently, the United States have normally been seen to have a comparative institutional advantage in terms of embodying 'statehood'. This advantage is said to be rooted in the association of several factors, including their long-term

17

historical development, their relative wealth and power in an industrialising world, their governments' increasing bureaucratisation and state intervention and regulation to promote economic growth, prosperity and welfare – or what French social philosopher Michel Foucault called 'biopolitics' (Foucault 2008; Gallarotti 2000) – and their inhabitants' sense of common sociological or ideological identity or belonging, whether instilled and indoctrinated from above or spontaneously emerging from below. In contrast, states that have *not* had strong centralising institutions, political processes, economic development and/or cultural identity – 'weak' states generally, especially what are today called 'failed' or 'collapsed' states – are seen as failing to fulfil the fundamental requirements of statehood (Badie and Birnbaum 1983; Migdal 1988).

Thus the way most academic analysts as well as policymakers and mass publics conceive of 'modern' world politics has centred on the roles of states as the core political–organisational units. These have often been called 'nation-states', on the assumption that some sort of social and economic *grass roots* 'nation' had either pre-existed or been constructed from above or below and justified through nationalism to underpin and empower state institutions and political processes. Yet that very form of organisation has been problematic from the start, and it is becoming even more problematic in an age of globalisation, from the mid-to-late twentieth century to today. In the twenty-first century, what is often called 'globalisation' presents a particular challenge to this modern – 'multifunctional' – conception of the state and statehood through a range of top-down and crosscutting structural transformations, from the integration of global markets and production chains to rapid technological innovation, the growth of complex 'multi-level governance' surrounding and cutting across the state, the convergence of economic policies around varieties of 'neoliberalism', the increasing influence of transnational interest groups and social movements, the emergence of a 'global village' linking societies and identities across borders and the like. This process is at an early stage, but 'statehood' is being stretched, relocated, broken up and put back together in new, often experimental, ways.

In the twenty-first century, then, the capacity of traditional nation-states to act in effective 'state-like' fashion is increasingly being challenged by a range of factors. The transnational and global nature of the most pressing problems being faced by policymakers and publics, from globalised financial markets to endemic economic crises to the challenges of the environment, makes it difficult for state actors to make coherent and effective policy at the nation-state level. The transnationalisation of technology, from the Internet to transport to flexible production techniques, creates and strengthens all sorts of cross-border economic, political and social linkages and processes. Changing political attitudes towards the human and economic costs of traditional interstate wars, from the rapid exhaustion of domestic public support to the rise of ethnic and religious conflict, including terrorism, means that the nature of warfare is undermining traditional state-based military hierarchies and methods.

Furthermore, growing awareness of the complexity of political and social identities, from ever-increasing migration and multiculturalism to the capacity of groups to maintain and intensify cross-border social and political linkages (e.g., through the Internet and the growing ease of international travel), challenges the fundamental sense of national identity and belonging that is essential to the social coherence and effectiveness of the 'nation' that the nation-state relies upon for stability, accountability and legitimacy. Transnational economic stresses, from factory closings and job losses seen to stem from the globalisation of multinational firms and production chains to trade and financial flows, particularly in the current environment of financial crisis and recession, highlight the interdependence of economic processes across borders and make it more and more difficult to make effective economic policy in isolation. Lifestyle issues from consumerism and the media 'global village' (McLuhan 1964) to today's 'green' consciousness make ordinary people, as well as elites, increasingly aware of the global and transnational significance and consequences of these challenges. And a fundamental shift is taking place from mindless patriotism and jingoistic nationalism to an awareness of the need for transnational and global responses to a whole range of other issues that were traditionally seen to be the job of nation-states to tackle.

Indeed, the problem of statehood itself is at the centre of political debate, as various kinds of 'multi-level governance' crystallise and proliferate in a globalising world. More formal international regimes, institutions and quasi-supranational bodies have been set up and are increasingly influential, if still in somewhat fragmentary form, from the United Nations and the International Monetary Fund, the World Bank, the World Trade Organisation, the Bank for International Settlements and the like to regional institutions like the European Union, as well as urban and other subnational or cross-national regions sometimes reaching across borders (Brenner 2004).

A range of less formal transnational processes are also emerging, including the crystallisation and intertwining of 'transgovernmental networks' among national regulators, legislators and legal specialists whose cross-border links increasingly take priority in terms of policy development over domestic hierarchies (Slaughter 2004), the development of 'global civil society', especially with regard to non-governmental organisations (NGOs), and the growing role of 'summits' and other *ad hoc* or semi-formal intergovernmental negotiating fora like the G7/8 and especially the G20, so much in the news at the time of writing (Beeson and Bell 2009). 'Issue areas' are increasingly globalised, like the question of whether an 'international financial architecture' is developing, especially in the context of the current global financial crisis, including the recent transformation of the Financial Stability Forum into the Financial Stability Board, the convergence of public policies across borders through imitation, policy learning and 'policy transfer' (Evans 2005).

Thus there is a crisis of statehood in today's world. Some see the solution in resurrecting the nation-state – whether through religious identity (Israel, Iran), 'nation-building' or 'state-building' (Fukuyama 2004), the reinvention of various forms of 'state capitalism' and the 'return of the state' (Plender 2008), or the renewal of American hegemony through 'soft power' or economic leadership

(Cerny 2006; Gallarotti 2009; Nye 2004). Others look to a range of more specific organisational alternatives:

- strengthening existing international institutions such as the United Nations (United Nations Commission of Experts on Reforms of the International Monetary and Financial System 2009);
- working through regional organisations like the European Union (de Larosière 2009);
- encouraging the development of a new multilateralism of 'civilian states' (Sheehan 2008) or a more pluralistic 'society of states' (Hurrell 2007);
- the creation of new forms of transnational 'regulatory capitalism' (Braithwaite 2008);
- the spread of such intermediate levels of urban, sub-national and cross-border regional governance (Brenner 2004);
- 'global civil society' (Edwards 2004);
- the spread of democratisation and cosmopolitanism (Archibugi 2008; Held 1995;); and/or
- the 'bottom up' development of new forms of social globalism based on translocal initiatives or 'glocalisation', that is, crosscutting local initiatives (Sassen 2007).

There are also more pessimistic interpretations that argue that we are entering a world of greater volatility, competing institutions, overlapping jurisdictions and greater instability reflecting a general 'disarticulation of political power' and statehood in a more open-ended, destabilising way sometimes referred to as 'neomedievalism' (Cerny 2000a).

Therefore the future of statehood itself – not merely of states or nation-states – is increasingly uncertain and *contested* at a number of levels in a world characterised by increasing transnational and global problems, crosscutting political alliances and the emergence of more complex forms of awareness and expectations that new kinds of political action and policy making are necessary. This chapter will examine the background to this development – the growth and decline of the states system and of states themselves – and reinterpret the *problématique* of statehood in the light of the central challenges facing World Politics (*not* 'International Relations') in the twenty-first century. I will argue that future structural and organisational developments will depend on the kinds of political coalitions that can be built to confront and deal with those challenges, especially those involving cross-border networks. The result is likely to be a more complex form of world politics that is not only *multi-level* but also *multi-nodal* (Cerny 2010). States are enmeshed in increasingly dense webs of power and politicking, as well as economic and social connections, that – in the continued absence of a world government or a world state – diffuse 'statehood' unevenly through differently structured points of access and decision making. This process sometimes leads to conflict and stalemate, and sometimes to new, innovative forms of governance and a kind of multi-dimensional statehood within an ongoing process of construction and evolution.

The distorted development of the nation-state and the states system

The state has been the predominant organisational unit for political, social and economic life in the modern world. Paradoxically, the development of the modern state has historically gone hand in hand with the long-term globalisation of world politics and the international economy. Globalisation itself, in its earlier mani-festations, was primarily organised and structured by and through the division of the world into states. The effective division of Europe into the first post-feudal states in the sixteenth and seventeenth centuries stemmed from a territorial stalemate among competing monarchs. Since that time, ambitious national elites have sought not only to consolidate their rule domestically but also to keep up with other states, especially their neighbours, both politically and economically, through imperialism, trade and other forms of outward expansion and linkages. The development of the leading states has been inextricably intertwined with their imperial expansion and global reach.

From the first European colonial empires in the fifteenth century to the spread of globalisation in the late twentieth century, the development and institutionali-sation of states as such and the states system has been inextricably intertwined in a range of profound transformative changes at various levels:

- the spread of international trade and finance;
- the promotion of industrialisation, economic growth and technological change;
- underdevelopment and development;
- the construction of social identity;
- the establishment of international institutions; and
- political modernisation, including democratisation.

Until the late twentieth century, therefore, the very organisation of world politics itself and the global political economy was rooted in the emergence, consolidation and interaction of nation-states. Those states still remain. Despite the flaws in the system, which will be dealt with in more detail below, it must be stressed that states also have deeply entrenched sources of institutional and organisational strength. The legacy of the states system is embedded in both perception and practice. Nevertheless, contemporary forms of globalisation are challenging the predominant role of the state and transforming it in numerous ways.

In long-term historical perspective, of course, the nation-state is only one of a wide range of alternative political–organisational forms, including village soci-eties, tribal societies, city states, multilayered feudal- and warlord-dominated societies, federations and confederations of various kinds, and empires. These other forms have characterised most historical epochs. Nevertheless, the nation-state form is inextricably linked with the concept of *modernity* and thus with an evolutionary conception of political change leading to 'higher' forms of organisational, institutional and socio-economic development. However, with the emergence of new forms of complex interdependence in the late twentieth and early twenty-first centuries – including global markets, networks of firms, transnational pressure groups (NGOs), international regimes, the rise of world cities and urban regions and the like – states have found themselves increasingly enmeshed in crosscutting or 'transnational' political, social and economic structures and processes. Rather than constituting the natural 'container' for social life, as much modern social and political theory and ideology has suggested, the nation-state today is highly contingent and in flux (Brenner et al. 2003).

Social and political bonds, once rooted in fixed concepts of social status and kinship hierarchies, were increasingly seen from the seventeenth century onwards to derive from a 'social contract', and such contracts were embodied in and constituted through the state (Barker 1962). In turn, political actors representing both old and new socio-economic forces sought to construct new institutional forms to replace the failed feudal system. This process has been called 'institutional selection' (Spruyt 1994). Foucault sees it as representing a particular 'governmentality' or 'governmental rationality' rooted in what in France is called *raison d'État* or what others have called a 'shared mental model' (Roy et al. 2007) that takes the state for granted as the normal way to organise social life, effectively the only option (Burchell et al. 1991; Foucault 2007 and 2008). Powerful new European state elites – monarchs, bureaucrats and lower-level administrators and politicians, increasingly allied to the new wealthy classes called *bourgeoisie* (city-dwellers) – increasingly defeated attempts to set up alternative organisational forms such as city states and city leagues.

These increasingly centralised states had, or appeared to have, a 'differentiated' organisational structure – that is to say, each had its own set of relatively autonomous officeholders outside other socio-economic hierarchies, with its own rules and resources increasingly coming from taxes rather than from feudal, personal or religious obligations. State actors were able collectively to claim 'sovereignty' (Hinsley 1966). Sovereignty, originally rule or supreme power and authority from above, was a more legalistic, centralised, formal and normative version of what is here called statehood. The original European states derived key aspects of their power from the 1648 Peace of Westphalia. This treaty, which ended decades of religious warfare in the wake of the collapse of feudalism and the Holy Roman Empire, indirectly enshrined the twin principles of (a) the territorial integrity of the state and (b) non-intervention in the internal affairs of other states. Together these principles have become the fundamental organising doctrine of an international system rooted in the *de jure* sovereignty and *de facto* autonomy of states. Sovereignty in the ideal type sense has therefore been more a political objective than a fact on the ground, and the ideology of the sovereign nation-state has been called a form of 'organised hypocrisy' (Krasner 1999).

Nevertheless, the principle of national (or state) sovereignty has been at the heart of both domestic state building and international relations throughout the modern era (James 1986).

Nation-states had to be consciously *constructed* precisely because they did *not* constitute self-evident 'natural containers'. Rather they were complex, historically contingent playing fields for political, social and economic power struggles. They were products of discourse, manipulation and institutionalisation – the cornerstone of a wider project of political modernisation. In this process, European states and later the United States and Japan turned themselves into 'Great Powers' that together dominated world politics and the international political economy, whether through imperial expansion, political influence, economic clout or social imitation. Britain and France were the first effective nation-states (Kohn 1955); much of their strength later came from their worldwide empires. Germany and Italy were only unified in the late nineteenth century but sought to become empires thereafter. Russia remained a loose, quasi-feudal empire until the Soviet era and retained many of its characteristics thereafter. The United States saw itself originally as a quasi-democratic continental empire that needed to avoid 'foreign entanglements' and had a complex federal structure, but it increasingly expanded outwards and centralised from the end of the nineteenth century. Japan moved rapidly from an isolationist empire to an expansionist empire in the twentieth century.

Therefore imperial expansion was crucial in providing a resource base for 'core' states to spread the states system around the world through both imposition, on the one hand, and a mixture of resistance and emulation, especially by national liberation movements, on the other. In turn, the most dramatic phases of the global extension of the states system came with decolonisation – the end of Spain's empire in Latin America in the 1820s and the dismantling of the British and French Empires from the end of the Second World War through the mid-1960s. Leaders of independence movements and postcolonial governments tried to emulate the European nation-state model as the road to progress and modernity, what has been called 'nation-building' (Bendix 1964), although this process often did not include democratisation.

In this context, attempts at post-independence democratisation merely opened the way for zero-sum social and economic struggles to be introduced into the core of the institutionalised political process without sufficient capacity for conflict resolution or pursuit of the common good, leading to predatory politics, corruption and authoritarian takeovers (Cerny 2009a). Only a few postcolonial states (especially India) stayed democratic for long, although since 1990 most former Communist states have become democratic and attempts to spread democracy in Asia, Latin America, Africa and the Middle East have also multiplied in that time, all too often unsuccessfully. Nevertheless, by the end of the 1960s virtually the entire world was divided up into supposedly sovereign states, democratic or not. International arrangements reinforced this trend, as the membership and institutional structures of United Nations and other formal international organisations are essentially composed of sovereign states. Ironically, it was at this time that the system of states started to decay as the first shoots of a new, transnational form of globalisation emerged in the mid-to-late twentieth century.

The state as a contested organisation

The capacity of the state to embody and exercise effective statehood rests on two analytically distinct but inextricably intertwined foundations. In the first place, the state, as an *organisation or institution*, is embodied in particular factors including: (a) a set of generally accepted 'rules of the game'; (b) the distribution of resources in a particular society; (c) a dominant ideology; and (d) the capacity of the state to use force, whether 'the monopoly of legitimate violence' (Max Weber) or a range of legal, economic and social sanctions, to impose particular decisions and ways of doing things upon both individuals and the society as a whole. In the second place, the state, like other organisations and institutions, is populated by a range of actors within and around the state apparatus. These 'state actors' make decisions and attempt to impose outcomes on non-state actors. In other words, the state is both a structured field of institutionalised power, on the one hand, and a structured *playing field* for the exercise of social or personal power, on the other.

The most important organisational characteristic of states is that they are – ostensibly at least – so-called differentiated organisations. In other words, ideal type states are organisationally distinct from families, churches, classes, races and the like; from economic institutions like firms or markets; and indeed, from non-state political organisations such as interest and pressure groups or social movements. They are in legal and philosophical principle (and to some extent in practice) both discrete and autonomous, in that they are not subordinate to, nor incorporated within, nor morphologically determined by (structurally sub-sumed into) other organisations, institutions or structures. The state, in theory at least, stands on its own. Nevertheless, both conceptually and in practice, the 'state' is also a deeply contested category. The modern state, as it has evolved in recent centuries, is often taken as a 'given' of political, social and economic life. However, the very notion of the state can be thought of as what philosophers call a 'reification' – that is, seeing an abstract concept as if it were a material thing. But states, like ideas, have real consequences. The state can be seen as contested on at least three levels.

First, the state is an *economically* contested organisation. As noted above, it is organised around relationships of power as well as political ideas such as fairness and justice, whereas economic organisations like firms and markets are organ-ised in principle at least around material criteria and relations of profit, exchange and economic efficiency. Nevertheless, firms and markets also involve inherent *de facto* relationships of power. In particular, states and state actors have been increasingly involved historically in trying to promote economic growth and mod-ernisation. This deeply embedded organisational relationship between state and economy has been the subject of intense debates and conflicts, both academic and political, private and public.

Second, the state is a *socially* contested organisation. States are not natural, spontaneous emanations from a taken-for-granted, pre-existing 'society', 'people' or 'public'. States are political superstructures that are historically constructed by real people and political forces around and over often deep divisions such as class, clans and extended families, ethnicity, religion, geography, gender and ideology, usually in an attempt precisely to mitigate, counteract or even violently repress those divisions. People are regularly forced or indoctrinated into acquiescing to the rules, ideas, power structures and policy decisions of the state. 'Citizens' are made, not born. This often entrenches deep conflicts of identity and interest actually *within* the state itself, whether right at the apex or on different levels of the state apparatus.

And finally, the state is a *politically* contested organisation. States are constructed in the first place and controlled and/or fought over by political, social and economic actors – from absolutist monarchs and national revolutionaries to various bureaucrats, officials, patrons and clients, from corporate elites to popular movements and from religious movements to corrupt and even criminal gangs. States can be organisationally 'strong' in the sense that they can be rooted in widely accepted social identities and bonds, or that their institutions are effective and efficiently run or that their 'writ' runs throughout the territory. They can also be powerful internationally. However, states can also be weak on both levels. All states have particular strengths and weaknesses along various dimensions, often cutting across the so-called inside/outside distinction (Walker 1992).

Nevertheless, as noted earlier, what is distinct about states in the modern world is that the state form of political organisation has at least until recently prevailed historically over *other* forms, which have been relatively weak and vulnerable in comparison. The combination of hierarchical power inside the state and the spread of the state form of organised governance across the globe – along with the rise of modern political ideologies and the strategic and tactical focus of political, economic and social actors on gaining power and influence within the state – has led to the widespread assertion and belief that states are, and should be, genuinely 'sovereign'. Whether that sovereignty is thought to start from the top down, as in 'the divine right of kings', or from the bottom up, as in 'popular sovereignty', state organisations in the final analysis are said to represent a holistic concentration and centralisation of generalised, overarching and legitimate political power that is unique among organisations – what the political philosopher Michael Oakeshott called a 'civil association', as distinct from an 'enterprise association' that has specific purposes and a limited remit (Oakeshott 1976).

State sovereignty is also Janus-faced, as noted at the beginning of this chapter. At the international level of analysis, there is supposedly no international 'state' or authority structure that has the kind of legal, political, social, economic or cultural reality, claim to primacy or legitimacy that the state possesses. The international system of states – that is, the claim that the international system itself is composed of and constructed by (*and for?*) states above and beyond any other institutions or structures – is seen as the norm. The international balance of power, the territorial division of the world and international law are therefore in theory all constituted by and through relations among states. Each state is in principle, in international law, founded upon a unique base – a specific geographical territory, a specific people or recognised group of citizens, a specific organisational structure or set of institutions, a specific legal personality and a specific sociological identity. Such distinctions, however, have historically often been constructed upon shaky foundations. More importantly for this book, however, is that the inside/outside distinction rests on foundations that are increasingly problematic in the context of globalisation.

Contemporary challenges to the organisational capacity of the state

Both dimensions of the inside/outside distinction are rooted in the organisational capacity of states – that is, the ability of states and state actors to act autonomously and simultaneously both in domestic politics and in the external states system. This is problematic in two main ways. On the one hand, various international, transnational and global structures and processes have competed with, cut across and constrained – as well as empowered – states and state actors throughout modern history. As noted earlier, the most successful European states throughout the early modern and modern periods were ones whose power and prosperity were rooted in international trade and imperial expansion as well as domestic consolidation, including the United States once it had expanded across the American continent. Indeed, globalisation itself has often been seen as the externalisation of a mix of hegemonic British and later American patterns of open capitalism, trade liberalisation and monetary and financial hegemony, not to mention military success in defeating more authoritarian and state corporatist states like Germany and Japan and even the Soviet Union in the Cold War. But in working to expand and extend such patterns globally, state organisational power has paradoxically boxed itself in by promoting its own subsumption in the globalisation process.

States and the states system thus do not exist in a vacuum, but are increasingly cut across by a range of 'complex interdependencies' (Keohane and Nye 1977). Globalisation theorists suggest that these interdependencies constitute a rather different infrastructure of the international or global. This structure is based on crosscutting linkages that states have both ridden on the back of and struggled to control – whether multinational corporations, international production chains, the increasing international division of labour rooted in trade interdependence, globalising financial markets, the spread of advanced information and communications technologies (Marshall McLuhan's 'global village'), rapidly growing patterns of migration and diasporas and the emergence of diverse forms of 'global governance' and international regimes, not to mention the rapidly evolving field of international law.

For example, the core of domestic state power – what is called in legal terms the 'police power – is becoming more problematic in this world, where borders are often helpless in controlling the movement of people, information, goods and ideas (Mostov 2008). These highly structured linkages and patterns of behaviour have encompassed and shaped the ways states are born, develop and operate in practice – and they are becoming increasingly institutionalised. They have their own organisational characteristics, power structures and agents that shape the world in ways even apparently strong governments must work harder and harder to catch up with. They may not exhibit the same holistic, hierarchical institutions and processes that developed states do, but they are often more structurally mobile and organisationally flexible than states. In the twenty-first century, states are increasingly seen as the organisational Maginot Line of global politics.

On the other hand, states are rapidly evolving in their role as domestic or endogenous arenas of collective action in ways that also are inextricably intertwined with complex interdependence and globalisation rather than holistic autonomy. Paradoxically, as stated earlier, the world as a whole was only finally divided up into nation-states in the mid-to-late twentieth century, just as globalisation was starting to change the organisational parameters of the world: in the 1950s and 1960s, when the British and French empires shed their final colonies; and in the 1980s and 1990s, when the Soviet Union lost its Eastern European empire and itself dissolved into the Russian Federation and other post-Soviet states. However, many newer states, as well as older states that had in the past been part of quasi-imperial spheres of influence like that of the United States in Latin America or of Britain and France in Africa, have not 'developed' into bureaucratically effective, politically unified, socially homogeneous or economically more prosperous and/or fairer societies. Some have thrown in their lot with regional organisations like the European Union, while others have stagnated and become more corrupt, for example, suffering from the 'resource curse' or the 'aid curse' (Moyo 2009), and some have become 'failed' or 'collapsed' states, descending into quasi-anarchy, like Somalia.

States are also exogenously diverse and highly unequal. Some are relatively effective, efficient and/or powerful, while others are weak, collapsed or failed. But even in relatively developed and powerful states like the United States, a combination of economic problems and the increasing difficulty of controlling external events has led to what the historian Paul Kennedy called 'imperial overstretch' (Kennedy 1987). These developments involve not only the lack of capability to project military and economic power abroad, but also what in the Vietnam War was symbolised by the 'body bag syndrome', that is, the unwillingness of the American public to see American soldiers die for either unwinnable or inappropriate foreign adventures – a syndrome that has been revived by today's wars in Iraq and Afghanistan. Indeed, historian James Sheehan has argued that precisely because of its extreme experience of war in the twentieth century, Europe, the cauldron of international imperialism in the modern era, has simply lost its taste for war and evolved into a grouping of 'civilian states', more concerned with promoting transnational economic prosperity than seeing their survival and success as bound up in warfare and the external projection of power (Sheehan 2008).

In this context, states are also endogenously – domestically – diverse. They consist of a bewildering variety of institutions and practices – democratic, authoritarian, egalitarian or exploitative – that have very different consequences both for their inhabitants or citizens, on the one hand, and for other states and their inhabitants/citizens, on the other. No state can fail to be ensnared in the global web in one way or another. Each state combines with and internalises globalising trends in somewhat different ways (Soederberg et al. 2005). Sometimes this enables them to exploit the opportunities presented by the opening up of particular international markets, for example, the so-called BRICs (Brazil, Russia, India and China), but sometimes they find their international linkages exacerbating domestic problems by aggravating social or ethnic conflicts, hindering or even reversing economic development, or undermining political stability and leading to violent conflict, civil wars and terrorism.

Of course, to paraphrase Churchill on democracy, states are still the central and predominant political organisation of the modern era – compared with all the others. Markets and other economic organisational structures are concerned with material outcomes, not basic social or political organisation. Ethnic groups pursue their own cultural goals, whether inside or outside existing political structures and processes. Only in theocracies do religious organisations claim political sovereignty, and even in the leading theocracy of the twenty-first century, Iran, religious claims to political authority are contested at various levels. International institutions and regimes are fragmented and lack sanctioning power, although a certain neoliberal hegemony increasingly pertains. Nevertheless, as a result of variables discussed here, the role of the state is increasingly contested both inside and outside. States are the conventional product of history and social forces, not a 'given' or 'natural' phenomenon, and statehood is continuing to evolve in a more open and interdependent world.

Key issues in the relationship between globalisation and statehood

It is possible to identify a range of organisational issues crucial to any understanding of how states work both internally and externally (and in between) in this more complex environment. The first of these is what traditional 'Realist' International Relations theorists call 'capabilities'. This term originally covered mainly military resources but has been extended more and more to social and economic organisation. States that could marshal concentrated military power to defend their national territory and, especially, to conquer or exercise effective influence over other states and/or power sources have, over the course of modern history, been likely to exercise disproportionate influence over outcomes at the international as well as the domestic level. Such powerful states could use their organisational capacity to control other states and the evolution of the international system in general, whether through alliances or through more direct forms of domination or hegemony. However, these states were also very vulnerable to complex shifts in the 'balance of power' and often found that others could 'balance' against them by forming alliances as well. Technological changes can also upset such existing balances or relations of capabilities. And diplomacy or international bargaining and politicking among states could also constrain or effectively alter existing balances (Little 2007).

Although the possession of such capabilities has been the main underpinning of national strength or power in the modern era, today it is often seen that other forms of capacity or effectiveness are far more important. As noted above, people, especially in liberal democratic states, are more aware, particularly because of the development of the 'global village', of the downside of military involvement in other parts of the world. Paradoxically, this globalisation of awareness has led to a growing unwillingness to get involved in military operations abroad unless they are relatively costless. Historians usually see the Tet Offensive by the Vietcong against American military forces in Vietnam starting in January 1968 as the cultural watershed here, when, for the first time in history, images of battles apparently being lost (although historians disagree on who won or lost Tet) were viewed over the breakfast table by ordinary people and fed into a mass movement against the war.

More importantly, the costs of war, like the costs of empire in the 1950s, are increasingly seen by economists to be counterproductive of economic development, growth and prosperity – in other words a drain on the state (and the country) rather than a benefit. Debates are raging over whether the costs of the war in Iraq, often estimated at 2–3 trillion US dollars, have in turn prevented the United States from tackling a range of other problems, both domestic (health care, rebuilding infrastructure, social security, employment and so on) and foreign (development aid, fighting disease and so on) (Bilmes and Stiglitz 2008). In this context, the maintenance or expansion of military and military-related capabilities are increasingly seen as having negative consequences for state, society and economy. The implications of this shift for the organisation of the state are enormous, both in opening the state up to new international economic and institutional opportunities and constraints and in expanding the economic regulatory/domestic state. The current financial crisis has accelerated awareness of these issues at all levels across the globe.

The second major organisational issue facing the state in the twenty-first century involves the internal coherence and hierarchical effectiveness of states in both domestic and foreign policy-type decision making. States that are internally divided, bureaucratically weak, torn asunder by civil conflict and/or subject to the influence of special interests of various kinds may either be ineffective and inefficient in pursuing so-called national interests and may even be themselves the cause of destabilisation processes that limit or even destroy state capacity and therefore undermine statehood itself. All states are facing analogous pressures, including the strongest. Competing domestic interests have often been at odds with the 'national interest' in the modern era, and in the age of globalisation, that conflict of interests is expanding rapidly.

The competition of interests has previously been analysed primarily at domestic level but it is becoming increasingly transnationalised (Cerny 2010). Some critical analysts have identified the formation of a 'transnational capitalist class' – or at least a 'transnational elite' linked with multinational corporations, global financial markets, various transnational 'policy networks' and 'epistemic communities' and the like, and further associated with hegemonic opinion formers – especially in developed states (Gill 2003; Sklair 2000; van der Pijl 1998). These groups are more than mere competing actors. Indeed, they are said to have a common interest in the spread of a neoliberal model of globalising capitalism. Not only do they have common goals across borders, they also have resource power and a set of institutional bases and linkages that go from the local to the global (sometimes called 'glocalisation'), not to mention the kinds of personal connections traditionally associated in domestic-level political sociology with class and elite analysis. Even if they do not, in fact, possess this kind of organisational coherence and instead are seen as a set of competing pluralistic interests, their common concern with developing transnational power bases – cross-border sources of income and influence – gives them a kind of political muscle collectively that parochial domestic groups cannot match.

The most powerful interest groups are increasingly those who can mobilise resources transnationally and not just internally – multinational corporations, global financial market actors, social networks that cut across borders like ethnic and/or religious diasporas and even consumers who don't care where particular goods are made provided the price and quality are right for the means at their disposal. The nation-states represent sociological 'nations' less and less and are more like associations of consumers (Ostrom et al. 1961) trying to get the best product at the best price in the international marketplace. They are characterised by domestic fragmentation and cross-border linkages – what Rosenau calls 'fragmegration', or transnational integration alongside domestic fragmentation (Rosenau 2003). In this context, neoliberal globalisation has become the 'common sense' of a wide range of otherwise competing interests and factions (Cerny 2010).

The third major organisational issue of the twenty-first century concerns whether the state itself is increasingly becoming 'splintered' or 'disaggregated'. In studies of bureaucracy in the twentieth-century tradition of Max Weber, the key to effective rule was said to require a hierarchically organised state in which officials knew their roles and functions in the larger structure. Although a full command hierarchy in the authoritarian or Soviet planning modes was seen to be counterproductive, the state required a great deal of centrally organised institutional coherence and administrative efficiency in order to develop and prosper. Today, that logic has been turned on its head. The most effective bureaucratic structures and processes are those that link officials in particular issue areas with their counterparts in other countries, in order that they might design and implement converging international standards, whether for global financial market regulation, trade rules, accounting and auditing standards and the like. Expanding 'transgovernmental networks' among regulators, legislators and legal officials are effectively transnationalising such issue areas, red-lining them from domestic protectionist interests, dominating policy-making processes and globalising the most important parts of the state in order to promote economic growth and other key policy goals (Slaughter 2004).

A fourth level of internal organisational change concerns the so-called competition state (Cerny 2000b, 2009b). Modern nation-states, in the pursuit of the public interest or the general welfare', have traditionally sought to 'decommodify' key areas of public policy – to take them out of the market through some form of direct state intervention – in order to protect strategic industries or financial institutions, bail out consumers or investors, build infrastructure, counteract business cycles and integrate workers into cooperating with the capitalist process through unionisation, corporatism, the welfare state and the like. This process in the twentieth century was linked with the growing social and economic functions of the state – the industrial state and the welfare state – and tended to come about through the expansion of what have been called 'one-size-fits-all' bureaucracies for the delivery of public and social services.

Today governments are more concerned not with decommodification of social and economic policy but with the 'commodification of the state' itself (Cerny 1990). This has two goals. The first is to promote the international competitiveness of domestically based (although often transnationally organised) industries. Domestic sources of inputs and domestic markets for products are too small to be economically efficient. Only competitiveness in the international marketplace will do. The second is to reduce the costs of the state – what is called 'reinventing government' – or 'getting more for less' (Osborne and Gaebler 1992). These two processes are aimed both at streamlining and marketising state intervention in the economy and at reorganising the state itself according to organisational practices and procedures drawn from private business. The welfare state is increasingly under cost pressure in the developed world, and developing states are often not able to provide meaningful welfare systems at all. The current financial crisis is only exacerbating this trend, despite Keynesian stimulus policies, which are seen as short-term remedies intended to 'save capitalism from the capitalists' (Cerny 2009c). Economic growth in general is today more the result of global economic trends and developments than of state policies.

This combination of the transformation of capabilities through complex interdependence, the transnationalisation of interests, the disaggregation of the state and the coming of the competition state has fundamentally transformed how the state itself works – eroding, undermining and making 'end runs' around the traditional Weberian state. Of course, different states have distinct institutional (or organisational) 'logics'. Each is subject to a form of 'path dependency' in which historical developments create both specific constraints and specific opportunities that become embedded in the way states work. Nevertheless, there is a rapidly growing trend towards the erosion of national varieties of capitalism and the rise of a new neoliberal hegemony rooted in globalisation (Cerny 2010; Soederberg et al. 2005).

Conclusion: statehood as the predominant *problématique* of twenty-first century world politics

Statehood is not a given, the exclusive property and distinguishing feature of modern nation-states, but a *problématique* or analytical puzzle, the parameters of which are continually evolving. Organisationally strong states may, to some extent, be able both to internalise and to resist the pressures of economic, social and political globalisation, although that capacity is increasingly hedged around by complex interdependence. Organisationally weak states are undermined by globalisation and crisis becomes endemic. Most states are in between these two extremes, with state actors and various kinds of interest groups – crucial players in the international system of states as well as the expanding globalisation process – seeking to alter, reform or completely restructure states in order to cope with the challenges of a globalising world. In this context, effective statehood is becoming more and more difficult to achieve at the level of the nation-state, while multi-level and multi-nodal politics are creating new and complex forms of latent, embryonic and, indeed, emergent forms of statehood that have increasingly come to dominate politics in the first decade of the twenty-first century. The statue of Janus increasingly resembles a kind of Gulliver, pinned down by the Liliputians of globalisation, while people cast about for new ways of organising their relationships and going about their business.

Guide to further reading

These issues are covered more comprehensively in Cerny (2010). A classic work developing concepts like 'transnational networks' and 'complex interdependence' is Keohane and Nye (1977). Foucault (2008) provides a highly insightful discussion of concepts like 'neoliberalism' and 'governmentality', that is, how statehood changed fundamentally in the twentieth century. Hurrell (2007) is an excellent contrasting perspective from a leading member of the 'English School' of International Relations, while Gallarotti (2009) shows how attempts by states to develop traditional power capabilities in a context of growing interdependence can backfire – the 'power curse'. A range of key public policy issues are analysed in innovative ways in Evans (2005). Sassen (2007) looks at micro level developments that underpin the kind of transformation of statehood addressed here; Slaughter (2004) shows how governments themselves are increasingly inextricably intertwined with each other; and Soederberg et al. (2005) argue that 'globalisation' is increasingly 'internalised' in the domestic politics of states, interest groups and other actors – that is, it is not an 'outside in' or 'top down' phenomenon, but one that shapes daily life and politics at all levels, leading to a new, variegated statehood that transcends and absorbs the nation-state.

Chapter 2

Regions and Regionalism in World Politics

SHAUN BRESLIN

In the aftermath of the Second World War, George Orwell published his classic novel, *Nineteen Eighty-Four* (Orwell 1949). He envisaged a world dominated by three massive regional powers – Oceania, Eurasia and Eastasia – that were in ever-changing alliances and a constant state of war. At the same time in France, Jean Monnet developed a plan to create 'a common High Authority' to oversee coal and steel production in Europe. This cooperation would ensure that 'war between France and Germany becomes not merely unthinkable, but materially impossible' and in the longer term would establish 'a true foundation for ... economic unification' (Schuman 1950). So the publication of *Nineteen Eighty-Four* in 1949, and the articulation of Monnet's ideas in the Schuman Declaration in 1950 established two contrasting views of the role of regions in a future world order: Orwell's dystopian warning of the potential for the emergence of authoritarian super states and global conflict on the one hand, and Monnet's and Schuman's almost utopian vision for peace and prosperity on the other.

Some six decades later, the world has of course moved on. Among the changes, perhaps the single greatest achievement of the European project (and a major concern for both Monnet and Orwell) tends to be overlooked the more it becomes accepted as the 'normal' state of affairs. But viewed through a historical lens, the lack of war in (North)West Europe after 1945 stands in stark contrast to the almost permanent state of Franco-German conflict which was all but the 'normal' situation in the previous century and a half. With the end of the Cold War, the possibility of global conflict and the spectre of a world of rival military–political 'blocs' have also declined, and the nation-state has failed to wither away to be superseded by higher regional authorities. But while the comparison between the world today and an Orwellian world of regions should not be pushed too far, at least some of the hopes, fears and desires that informed thinking in the late 1940s still resonate today. For example, a world of regional blocs is still a vision that causes alarm. That the nation-state might yet be usurped and replaced by a regional sovereign entity also remains salient in many parts of Europe. Conversely, proponents of regionalism continue to echo these earlier

assumptions about the economic benefits of regional coordination and cooperation. And making conflict 'impossible' by tying national economic fates together
in a coordinated regional effort remains one of the justifications for regional
projects beyond just Western Europe.

Another enduring issue is that Europe still remains the primary focus of both
political and academic interest in regional projects. To be sure, there has been a
steady growth of interest in regional integration in other parts of the world. Particularly since the 1980s, there has been an upsurge in the number of regional
projects being negotiated and enacted; regionalism has become a truly global
issue rather than just a European one. Nevertheless, Europe remains by far the
most studied and debated case of regional integration. Indeed, the 'success' of the
European Union (EU) acts as something of an impediment towards the emergence
of a truly comparative (and holistic) scholarship that allows us to understand the
real significance of regionalism in contemporary world politics. Perhaps somewhat strangely, this emerges from both the dominance and the exceptionalism of
the European case.

On one side, observations of the European project spawned expectations about
the end-point of regional projects elsewhere – for a number of analysts, there is
an expectation that regional integration in Africa or Asia or wherever will end
up looking something like the EU in the long run. On the other side, the study of
Europe has also all but generated its own academic sub-discipline – specialist journals, conferences, book series and associations that locate the study of European
regionalism as separate from the study of regional integration *per se* (Rosamond
2007). Here there is a focus on major concerns within Europe that are a consequence of long term and deep integration – the potential for a federal Europe
superseding the state, the move towards a common foreign and security policy,
how to handle enlargement, the democratic deficit and the relationship between
different agencies. Both positions have made it difficult to develop theoretical perspectives that elucidate the salience of regionalism as a challenge to the current
global order beyond the European case.

Of course, Europe is not the only case of a relatively long-standing regional
organisation – the Association of Southeast Asian Nations (ASEAN), established
in 1967, is also a good example. But even though ASEAN has shared some of
the experiences of the EU – most notably expansion to include former communist
party states – ASEAN has always been characterised by looser linkages than the
more legally formalised European project. Its operating principle, the 'ASEAN
way', is defined in terms of consensus building rather that formal rules and a
strict acceptance of the ultimate sovereignty of member states (Henry 2007).
Moreover, much of the current discussion over the future of Asian regionalism
is concerned with the formation of a larger East Asian region of which ASEAN
is only one constituent part. So with the possible exception of ASEAN, for the
majority of students of regionalism beyond Europe, the focus is not on consequences of regionalism, but on causes – what makes a region come into existence,
cohere and have longevity. Or even more fundamentally, it is often on the prior
question of 'what is the region'?

Bearing in mind both the importance of Europe as a generator of ideas, theories and experiences, but also that there is much more to regional integration than just the European case, the study of regionalism in world politics today can be divided into seven sub-groups:

1. Theory building. This work considers how we define a region, how and why regional integration takes place and what forces a region to cohere, consolidate/institutionalise and survive (and the counterfactual question of why regional integration does not occur or has not occurred in some places).

2. The study of Europe. An isolated and discrete sub-discipline, this includes theories of European integration, analyses of the consequences of regionalism, studies of the machinery and processes of EU policy-making, the relationship between the regional and national levels of governance and prospects for future integration. These studies might have significance for the wider study of regionalism *per se*, but are conceived of as being part of the EU studies sub-discipline.

3. Case-specific studies of individual regions. Conducted by specialists in those regions, these case studies are informed by wider theoretical understandings of regional integration and often explicitly seek to contribute to theory and comparative understandings, rather than simply being concerned with events in the region under discussion.

4. Comparative studies of different regional processes. These typically focus on different types or levels of institutionalisation of regional cooperation and there is a tendency in these for the EU to be the constant against which other regional forms are compared. Non-European regions are much more rarely compared to each other. These comparisons often imply that Europe is the norm that others diverge from, rather than perhaps Europe being the exception and informality and shallow integration the norm in most of the world.

5. The relationship between regionalism and world order. Here the main focus is on the relationship between regionalism and global multilateralism. The question is whether regional forms of cooperation are a 'building block or stumbling block' to global solutions, particularly in terms of regional free trade arrangements and global free trade agendas – an arena where some of the relevance of the Orwellian dystopia of competing regional blocs sometimes reappears. There is also a strong focus on the extent to which regions can provide forms of economic supervision and regulation that either protect the region from unregulated global capitalism or provide regional alternatives to global regulatory forms and developmental strategies.

6. Regions as actors in international relations (IR). Perhaps really a sub-set of considerations of global order, this work focuses on how, if at all, regions can develop and promote a common/single interest in IR – the 'actorness' of regions. The majority of this work unsurprisingly focuses on the actions and self-identity of the EU which has done more than most to promote itself as an actor, for example, through adopting a single EU position in trade negotiations and by promoting international 'strategic partnerships'.

✗ There is also increasing interest in how regions interact with each other – inter-regionalism.

7. Regions and security. Ensuring security in Europe was a key impulse in Monnet's original thinking, and the extent to which economic interactions decrease the possibility of conflict remains important in explaining regional initiatives in other parts of the world. To this extent, security issues have always been at the heart of theories and processes of regional integration. But there is also a strand of research that focuses specifically on regional security alliances, communities and cultures that has become a separate strand of the study of regionalism – a sub-sub discipline that is not covered in any detail in this chapter.

These categories are not always mutually exclusive. Work on security regions, for example, may well also fit in one or more of the first four categories. But while the boundaries might be sometimes a little blurred, this typology nevertheless provides a rough overview of the different ways in which regionalism impacts on international politics today.

Rather than run through each of these different categories in turn, this chapter shows how the balance of interest in these seven areas has changed over time by tracing the evolution of approaches to studying regions since the end of the Second World War. This exercise partly shows how actual changes in region building in various parts of the world often generated the need for new theories to explain these changes. But it also acts as a device that illuminates a number of common concerns that run through the different waves of regionalism and the different waves of theoretical innovations. The extent to which the development of a regional identity matters (and among whom) is one such common thread. What regions mean for the future of the nation-state is a second. The importance of hegemony and hegemons in driving or blocking regional processes is also rarely wholly absent. But the single most important reoccurring concern is the way in which the region emerges as a result of (or response to) the internationalisation of economic activity beyond the national scale, and beyond the ability of individual national governments to control on their own.

Contextualising the study of regionalism: historical perspectives and precedents

Although interest in regionalism in political science and IR is dominated by the study of the post-1945 global order, the world of regions did not simply begin with the Treaty of Paris in 1951 – indeed, there is a much longer history of regional integration projects in Europe itself. The Napoleonic 'continental system' (1806–14) established a common customs policy of sorts in French-controlled Europe and Russia in the form of a blockade against goods from Britain or British colonies. Partly to restore the protection from cheap imports that the continental system had provided, in 1834 the majority of the 39 then independent German states formally established the Zollverein – an economic Union that removed internal customs barriers and established a common external position (see Pollard 2006).

These early European experiences are important here for three reasons. First, they show us that the sovereignty of states is sometimes replaced by a 'common High Authority'. In these cases they became what we now know as nation-states, but at the time started out as processes of regional integration among sovereign states. Not only did the Zollverein play a role in laying the foundations for the establishment of the German state in 1871, but the creation of the United States of America can also be read as a process of continental regional integration (List 1827 [1909]). Of course this does not mean that states will be superseded by 'higher' regional entities in the future – it simply means that it can happen.

Second, as was the case with the Napoleonic continental system, many processes of regional integration have been achieved through military conflict and occupation – or regionalism as empire. This was the case not only in Europe in the nineteenth century, but many scholars argue that this occurred in Southeast Asia (as opposed to the larger understanding of Asia as a whole) which did not exist as an idea before French imperial colonisation created coherent strategies across the different occupied territories, and later through the establishment of the Allied South-East Asia Command to fight Japan in 1943 (Charrier 2001). More recently, the creation of both security and economic regions in East Europe – the Warsaw Pact and Council for Mutual Economic Assistance (COMECON) – owed more than a little to the military activities of the Soviet Red Army.

Region as empire retains some importance – but more in terms of the consequences of colonial rule and decolonisation than as a force for regional integration in itself. For example, the two Franc Zones that created shared currencies (and fixed exchange rates with first the Franc and now the Euro) in Western and Central Africa have their origins in French colonial rule in Africa. After the dissolution of the Soviet Union, a number of regional organisations were established to try to coordinate political and economic relations between the newly independent states: the Commonwealth of Independent States, the Organisation of Central Asian Cooperation, the Eurasian Economic Community and the proposed Common Economic Space (Kubicek 2009). The idea of something called 'Latin' America also has its origins in the commonalities of colonial experiences on the continent that continue to exercise some influence over region-building projects today (Mignolo 2005).

Contextualising the study of regionalism: identifying regions and regional identities

The third area of importance relates to how we conceptualise and identify regions – and perhaps more importantly, how those who are engaged in processes of regional integration identify what region they think they (should) belong to. This might sound a little strange. Surely we can identify regions simply by looking at a map. But while continents are formed by nature, regions are formed by people; they are politically and socially constructed. And these political constructs are as likely to sub-divide continents as they are to work on continent-wide levels.

For example, although there are (at the time of writing) ongoing attempts to build a continental-wide Free Trade Area of the Americas, the majority of region-building projects on the Americas have been at the sub-continent level. And notwithstanding the above comments about a shared history of colonisation (of sorts) in Latin America, the question of what countries constitute the 'region' is yet to be fully resolved. For example, Mexico might be part of Latin America in terms of culture and a history of Spanish colonisation, or Central America/Mesoamerica in terms of the population settlements that spanned this part of the continent before the arrival of the colonial powers. But largely because of its position as a major producer of goods for the US market, Mexico became part of a different region in the shape of the North American Free Trade Agreement (NAFTA) in 1994. Further south, the continent is further divided by different conceptions of region – perhaps most importantly, the Andean Community of Nations and Mercosur.

Similar observations can be made about Africa, where continent-wide regionalism in the form of the African Union coexists with numerous sub-continental projects, for example, the South African Development Community (SADC), the Economic Community of West African States (ECOWAS), the East African Community (EAC) and so on. If anything, identifying the Asian region (or regions in plural) is even more problematic; for example, does the region called 'East Asia' include India and Australasia as it does in the form of the East Asia Summit, or exclude them as it does in ASEAN Plus Three meetings (ASEAN plus China, Japan and South Korea)? Or should the region actually be something else; the idea of Asia-Pacific as embodied by Asia-Pacific Economic Cooperation (APEC) – a definition that brings together countries like Russia, Papua New Guinea and Peru, but which excludes India.

To add an extra level of complexity, regions change over time. The most obvious example is the expansion of Europe from the six founder members of the European Coal and Steel Community (ECSC) to the 12 members of the European Economic Community by the late 1980s, through to the expansion of the EU to 27 member states in 2007. Similarly, ASEAN expanded to add Vietnam, Burma/Myanmar, Laos and Cambodia to the original six member states in the 1990s. Regions also change as members leave – for example, Venezuela's withdrawal from the Andean Community in 2006 – and occasionally as regional organisations fail and/or dissolve. For example, the Central American Common Market dissolved in 1969 (but reformed in 1991) and regional cooperation between the Soviet Union and Eastern Europe did not survive the end of Communist Party rule.

Perhaps what comes across most clearly from this short discussion is the potentially bewildering array of organisations – and an even more bewildering array of acronyms of organisations! It is not always easy to identify what is a regional organisation – for example, is APEC a regional organisation, or an arena where other regions come together to cooperate? Occasionally linguistic (Portuguese, French and the Union of Latin Speaking States) or religious (Islamic states) communities are included in lists of regional organisations even though they have members from across the world. There are also a number of regional development banks that play a role in promoting regional integration, but which have members from across the world and therefore occupy something of a blurred space between being regional and/or global organisations. If we ignore these groups (but include those regional organisations subsequently subsumed into the EU), a total of 76 regional organisations can be identified as being in operation since the Second World War (each with its own acronym).

So both regional identities and regional formations are fluid. What is Europe and who is European does not have to be defined by membership of the EU, but the idea of 'Europe' as a political entity in the guise of the EU has gained currency – and as we have seen, the membership of this idea of 'Europe' has changed considerably over time. Moreover, multiple identities are common and do not always map with the boundaries of formal regional organisations. So if we go back to the example of Mexico and ask if Mexicans are part of North America, Mesoamerica or Latin America, the answer is probably all three at different times depending on the issue at hand that requires people to think of their identity (and against which 'other' this identity is constructed).

There is a relatively strong consensus that a shared regional identity helps a region cohere – a feeling of being part of the region knits people and thus economies and societies together, and makes the regional sphere of governance legitimate (see Adler 1997). However, there is less unanimity over what is cause and what is effect. Does the existence of a shared identity lead to people coming together in a shared regional effort? Or does the creation of a region for other reasons establish common laws and borders and facilitate the flow of goods and people that subsequently leads to the emergence of a regional identity? For the first generation of students of European regionalism, the creation of new regional identities was an essential part of the transition from national to regional levels of political activity. Crucially, however, this was a shift that was conceived to first take place in the minds and actions of key political and economic elites rather than in the general population.

So are popular identities important? Or put another way, whose identity matters? These questions are not only important for understanding how regions emerge and/or consolidate, but also for highlighting arguably the single most important political significance of regionalism (when calculated by newspaper column inches at least). The feeling that the regional project is being driven by business and political elites in opposition to the more national(ist) identities and aspirations of the general public has long become part and parcel of political debates in many European states, and one component of voting behaviour in not just European, but also national and local elections. But it is not just a one-way process – the anti-European stance of some political parties has also been blamed for poor electoral performances in some European countries. While the focus in this chapter is on regionalism and world politics, it is also important to acknowledge that conflicting identities have become a major reason why region-alism is now a major domestic politics issue in European states, and to think how this might affect domestic political configurations as regional projects evolve in other parts of the world.

Contextualising the study of regionalism: the long shadow of Europe

There is a case for arguing that the creation of what we now know as the United States of America is the most successful case of region building that the world has seen to date. There is also a case for saying that military might is one of the most effective ways of bringing states together into new regional orders. But the dominant driver of interest in integration has been the European experience (or experiences) in the post-War era. Europe is not just important in its own right, but has also generated theories of regional integration and expectations for regional projects elsewhere that continue to dominate the wider study of region-alism beyond Europe. As we shall see, for a number of scholars (including this one – see Breslin et al. 2002) the European experience is perhaps too dominant and has skewed the study of 'different' projects and processes; but, nevertheless, it remains the starting point for the study of regionalism in the modern world. And if Europe is the starting point for the study of regions, then there are perhaps two starting points for studying the European experience (and thus two main lega-cies for the study of regionalism today) – the possibility of the nation-state being replaced by a higher regional sovereign authority and the related shift in identities from the national to the regional level.

Transcending the state: regional identities and regionalising institutions

In the above-mentioned debates in domestic polities over European regionalism, a recurring concern is that the authority of the state might be eroded. But rather than fearing the reduced power of nation-states, in the early post-War years the erosion of state sovereignty was considered a good thing. The state, after all, had been the key source of instability and war in Europe in the 1930s and 1940s – or more correctly, competition between states and nationalism had been the cause of the problem. Moreover, once the early experiment in collaboration in the form of the ECSC seemed to be a success, the ceding of some state authority to a higher authority seemed sensible from an economic as well as security viewpoint.

The idea that the state was being transcended was an important component in the emergence of 'functional' interpretations of IR that have become firmly embedded as means of understanding regional integration in Europe and else-where. Most often associated with the work of David Mitrany, functionalists assumed that the common transnational issues that states faced, combined with an increase in scientific knowledge about the nature of these problems and how to deal with them, would result in cooperation. Territorial organisation (states) would be transcended and replaced by functional organisation (transnational bodies) with competence in specific areas – for example, one dealing with finance, another for education and another specialising in trade. With competence in regulation transferring from the national scale to supranational specialist agencies, national-based identities and nationalism would decline resulting in what Mitrany (1943) called 'a working peace system'.

While sharing the basic assumption about the need to cooperate beyond national borders, the functional division of authority was questioned by neofunctionalists. Most closely associated with the early work of Ernst Haas (perhaps most famously Haas 1958), neofunctionalists concentrated on the idea that functional cooperation on technical issues would 'spillover' into other forms of integration. For example, it is simply impossible to deal with issues relating to coal and steel production without considering wider trade and investment rules, and the domestic social and economic policies of the states involved in this functional collaboration. Thus, cooperation on narrow functional areas would inevitably lead to the new organisations extending their reach into other areas of authority and governance. So for neofunctionalists, it was essential to have an institution above the state level supported by a regional elite that could take the lead in pushing the regional project forwards. In the early years of the European project, for example, the ECSC was assumed to fulfil this role and the Europeanisation agenda of people like Robert Schuman and Jean Monnet personified the idea of regionalising elites.

As with earlier functional understandings, the shift of identification from the national to the regional scale is seen as a crucial dynamic. Integration occurs and as the political sphere of action moves from the national to the regional level – individuals and groups increasingly realise that national governments are unable to meet their demands and so instead move the focus of their action and allegiances to new regional bodies. For Walter Mattli (1999), integration is most likely to occur and cohere when the supply of supranational institutions by regionalising political elites meets the demand for regional-level coordination and action by primarily economic elites – for example, as nation-states simply cannot, on their own, manage the ever-increasing complexity of international financial and trade flows. The logical end point of this process is that the state is ultimately replaced by a new locus of power at the regional level – a single holistic regional organisation that becomes a single political union.

States, intergovernmentalism and national interests

By the mid-1970s, it had become clear that the early expectations that Europe would be the prototype for other regional cooperative efforts were misplaced. Rather than wither away, states had maintained their own individual and competitive IR with extra-regional actors, but also remained the key units of authority within the European project itself. They might decide to cooperate at the European level on certain issues if they were deemed to be in their national interest, but the national level remained not only the key unit of authority and political action, but also overwhelmingly the dominant source of identity. Indeed, Haas (1975) proclaimed that his own theory was now out of date and inapplicable. To add insult to injury, the rest of the world had stubbornly resisted following the European model of even this level of integration.

Nevertheless, some of the core concerns that informed the original neofunctional approaches not only remain, but were reinvigorated by the shift in the pace of European integration from the mid-1980s. The emergence of an activist European Commission under Jacques Delors appeared to provide the regionalising institutions and elites that were necessary for the promotion of further integration (Ross 1995). The possibility of spillover into a new federalist Europe was enhanced when the Maastricht Treaty of 1992 established the transition from a European Economic Community to a European Union, laying the foundations for monetary union, and theoretically at least creating the basis for a common foreign and security policy. With more and more regulation and legislation occurring at the regional level, an additional regional level of political activity, such as lobbying, was added to existing national foci.

But there are two important differences between these two phases. First, while some still think of Europe as the blueprint that other regional projects will follow, there is a growing acceptance that Europe is not THE model of regional integration, but simply A model (albeit an extremely important case study). In the late 1980s and early 1990s, a slew of new regional organisations either came into being or reformed themselves with new agendas that increased the pool of case studies for students of regionalism – for example, the creation of the Southern Cone/MERCOSUR (1991) and the North American Free Trade Area (signed 1992, enforced 1994) in the Americas; the resurgence and expansion of the ASEAN and the creation of the Pacific Islands Forum (1995) in Asia and the Pacific; and the transition of the Southern African Development Community in 1992 from an organisation designed to resist South Africa into a development community all are important examples of new 'non-European' forms of regional integration projects.

Second, the residual role of states as the key locus of authority and action in IR has been re-imposed on debates over regionalism. This has included attempts to reconcile neofunctional assumptions of the inevitability of 'spillover' with an understanding of how states mediate, manage and, in some ways, govern these processes of spillover (Cameron 1991). For others, the significance of regional institutions and elites in promoting integration has been replaced by a more singular focus on the region as a political space occupied by states. For those scholars who come to regionalism from a broadly liberal perspective, thinking about how states act at the regional level is relatively straightforward. What happens at the European level, for example, is intergovernmental bargaining by different national governments, with each government's position on any given issue primarily a consequence of bargaining within the national political sphere. Regionalism creates rules of the games and other mechanisms that make coming together to negotiate less costly and more predictable, and over time, the success of the regional level in solving problems grants further legitimacy to the regional level as an arena for problem solving (Moravcsik 1993).

But for those from other traditions, cooperation in Europe and in particular the move towards monetary union 'pose a serious challenge to neorealist arguments about international institutions' (Grieco 1995: 24). The solution was to find ways of explaining why assumptions that states act to maximise their national interests were not contradicted by the reality of cooperation and even the pooling of sovereignty at the regional level. One of the earliest attempts to do so entailed a synthesis of sorts between realist and liberal positions through the idea of 'complex interdependence' (Keohane and Nye 1977), where cooperation at the regional level was seen as just one means deployed by states to rationally manage their interests through varieties of intergovernmental cooperation. Thus, regionalism is seen as a statist response to an increasingly complex world where the activities of non-state actors (primarily companies) operating beyond the national sphere mean that national-level legislation and action alone cannot control (Keohane 1988).

Regionalism beyond Europe: common enemies, common responses?

While the relative importance of states and national interests remains hotly debated in the European case, the focus on the role of states promoting their interests through regional cooperation becomes stronger when analysis moves away from Europe. For example, China's promotion of regional integration in East Asia has been depicted as a process of 'cooperating to compete' (Moore 2008) – establishing good relations with neighbours in an attempt to align them to Chinese interests and to undermine support for Japan and the US in the region. In short, regionalism is promoted by those states who have most to gain from it. Indeed, different powers will promote different understandings of what the region is (or should be) based on how this understanding of the region maximises the national interest. Returning to the case of competing understandings of what the Asian region is or should be outlined towards the beginning of the chapter, we see the US's preferred understanding of region as the Asia-Pacific (as embodied by APEC); China's preferred understanding of region as ASEAN Plus Three (China, Japan and Korea); and a third Japanese alternative that adds India, New Zealand and Australia to the Chinese understanding to provide checks and balances to putative Chinese regional power.

Alternatively, states might choose regionalism as a means of serving the national interest by combining to fight a common enemy. This common foe is often conceived in terms of a common military threat (or potential threat). Examples include ASEAN's role as a mutual defence against communism, the Gulf Cooperation Council (GCC) as a means of resisting Iran and the Southern African Development Coordination Conference's role as a bulwark against apartheid-era South Africa. But this does not always have to be a common defence against military power. For example, after the Asian financial crisis of 1997, there was a relatively strong feeling in East Asia that the west was imposing unfair and inappropriate reforms on the region designed to serve Western interests. The solution was to build a regional level of regulation – the Chiang Mai Initiative through which Asian states agree to support each others' currencies in any future financial crisis. So a regional identity and regional cooperation can be built on a shared understanding of what 'we' are not; an identification that requires an 'other' to be different from.

Regionalism, realism and hegemony

Such a focus on alliances against common enemies draws attention to the importance of conceptions of hegemony in explaining the motivation for regional interaction. In his analysis of different theories of regionalism, Hurrell (1995) distilled four main 'hegemonic' discourses. First, the above-mentioned common defence against a common enemy – the basic idea that the power of the many is greater than the power of one. The second involves incorporating and socialising potentially dangerous hegemons into a favoured regional order – for example, enmeshing West Germany into the European project or shaping the nature of China's rise through engagement in regional projects and processes. Here, there is sometimes a blurring of realist and liberal positions as the enmeshment idea has commonalities with liberal institutional understandings of how states can be 'socialised' into preferred ways of doing things through participation in liberal regional integration projects.

Third, weaker states 'band-wagon' in regional projects with stronger hegemons – to gain special preferential treatment either by being seen to support the hegemon's preferences, or by trying to ensure access to the hegemon's lucrative economy (or both). In short, it is seen as in the national interest to link the state in an asymmetric relationship with the hegemon. This approach has been used to explain the regional strategies of a number of Latin American states towards the US – although not always with successful outcomes (Mera 2005).

The fourth sees regionalism as a function of hegemonic preferences. Thus, American support for European regionalism and ASEAN can be explained in terms of meeting Washington's security and, to a lesser extent, economic objectives. But those regional projects in Latin America that might obstruct the aims of the US were not exactly encouraged. Similarly, we might suggest that the changing stance towards regionalism in China from scepticism to active engagement provided a new stimulus towards integration in Asia – and fears about a China-dominated Asian region has at least something to do with the differing visions of region promoted by the US and Japan (Breslin 2009).

Actors and processes: towards 'new regionalism'

When it comes to considering the relationship between hegemony and regionalism, the focus on regional actors is very clearly on the state. In the other understandings of regionalism that we have briefly surveyed, the role of the state is less absolute. For example, some see a role for supranational agencies and actors in higher authorities 'above' the state. Furthermore, to varying degrees neofunctional, intergovernmental and institutional approaches all see a role for non-state actors in moving the regional project forwards, be this in economic elites seeking new regional sites of governance, or regionalism as a result of states coming together to deal with common governance issues caused by the transnational activities of economic actors. Nevertheless, while the state is not the only actor, it is the state that ultimately signs treaties and international agreements that bring into force formal regional organisations. And in this respect the study of regionalism has been dominated by what we might call broadly 'statist' approaches.

But from the mid-1990s, this twin focus on states as actors and formal institution building as the end point of regional integration appeared out of step with what was happening in many parts of the world. As such, there was a turn towards what has become known as a 'new regionalism'. 'New' because they emerged from the dissatisfaction with the early and thus 'older' waves of theorising about regionalism and also because they drew from a range of contemporary regional experiences beyond just the European case (Gamble and Payne 1996).

In order to have a more holistic study of regions that allowed for a more comprehensive understanding of what a full range of regional integration processes mean for international politics, the analysis was divided into form and process. On one side, there is what might be called the 'idea' or 'ideology' of region or the conscious and deliberate attempts to create formal regional institutions – regionalism. On the other side, there are those real interactions that bind not just states, but people, economic activity, ecosystems and so on – processes of 'regionalization that fills the region with substance such as economic interdependence, institutional ties, political trust, and cultural belonging' (Vayrynen 2003: 39).

In many respects, the study of how regionalisation resulted in regionalism is exactly what earlier studies had been all about – and this remains a focus of new approaches. But for new regional theorists, there is no reason to expect that regionalisation will necessarily lead to institutional forms of regionalism – and certainly no reason why these processes will result in anything that resembles European style regionalism. Rather, the study of the processes themselves is important and interesting in its own right irrespective of where these processes lead to (or don't lead). Furthermore, as Bull's (1999) analysis of various regionalism initiatives in Central America found, even where there are formal regional bodies, this is no guarantee that actual regionalisation will take place if market actors prefer to seek economic interactions with extra-regional economies.

So it is the regional 'space' that is important in new studies rather than the institutions of regionalism – the creation of regional spaces of activity that don't replace the nation-state as a site of governance and action, but typically coexist alongside territorial/statist spaces. Indeed, rather than just seeing regional integration as being something that occurs 'above' the nation-state, integration can also occur 'below' the national scale. For example, the way in which the economies of San Diego and Tijuana have become economically interlinked across the

US–Mexico border is a form of microregional integration that exists at a different level of integration to US–Mexican integration through NAFTA and indeed, alongside the very real continued importance of both nation-states (Grimes 2002).

Because there is no expectation of an inevitable end form of integration, and through the use of a wider variety of cases, new regionalism has, in many ways, become a search for the causes of diversity. Nevertheless, within this diversity, we can identify a number of common strands. For example, the role of non-state actors takes on a greater significance than in earlier studies of regionalism. Moreover, it is not just a case of non-state actors as sources of integration – for example, through transnational economic activity – but also as providing regional responses to regionalisation. NGOs and grass-roots movements have particularly important roles to play when it comes to coordinating regional responses to shared environmental and developmental challenges – a relatively common focus in the study of regionalisation in Latin America for example (Grugel 2006). Regionalisation is also driven by the relationship between migrant workers and diasporas – a form of financial regionalisation that emerges from the remittance of salaries and/or investments in the 'homeland' (Read 2004).

Why regionalism matters: still all about the economy?

While the environment and broadly defined development issues are clearly important, economic concerns have not lost their place as the primary point of interest for students of regionalism. And in terms of identifying non-state actors, this means concentrating on those who move money and goods across national boundaries creating new regional spaces. For Kenichi Ohmae (1995), the power of these economic actors means that states have become irrelevant. Economic activity will occur where it is most conducive and profitable, crossing national borders and jurisdictions at will creating new loci of economic activity based on what the market wants. This extreme position is perhaps a deliberate exaggeration to try and prove a point. Governments continue to be key actors not just in bringing formal regions into existence, but in facilitating regionalisation as well. It is governments that change fiscal, financial and currency regimes that allow others to move goods and money across borders. It is also governments that typically create the hard infrastructure of regional integration – building roads, railways and ports that allow for the transfer of goods and commodities. Thus, states are seen as paving the way for real economic integration that is driven by the actions and interests of non-state economic actors.

So the key question is why would governments act in this way? The answer partly lies in conceptions of the state – not the state as rational actor pursuing the 'national' interest in IR, but the state as representative of the interests of those who favour free markets and globalisation. Moreover, by the mid-1990s, engagement with the global economy was increasingly seen as the best – perhaps even the only – way of promoting economic growth and development. Key elites in developing countries that had previously sought to establish defences against the global economy and to avoid dependence on core economies now thought that linking to those core economies through participation in regional forums and domestic liberalisation was essential (Bowles 1997). This context is a crucial component in understanding this new turn in regional integration (and the study of this integration) – liberalisation that was occurring through the end of communist party rule in Europe, through the decline in communist ideology as China engaged in the capitalist global economy and through the retreat from dependency perspectives in Latin America.

The regional and the global

Regional Free Trade Agreements (FTAs): building blocks or stumbling blocks

Although the phrase 'fortress Europe' might have gone out of fashion somewhat, it was once a powerful metaphor for the concept of the European project as a means of protecting Europe from outside intruders – whether would be migrants, or producers from other parts of the world. This Europe was one where domestic producers (particularly famers) received massive subsidies to keep them afloat. And this Europe had removed internal barriers to international contacts that made it much easier and more profitable for those within the fortress to trade with each other than it was to pierce the fortress from without.

The idea of region as fortress has also been deployed to explain the creation of NAFTA. This was a region that could thus compete internationally in terms of the production of goods itself and for other markets, and protect key groups from potentially damaging competition from a truly global (and truly) free market. The NAFTA treaty was signed in 1992, the same year as the Maastricht Treaty moved Europe from a Community to a Union, and the then six members of ASEAN agreed to set up a Free Trade Area (FTA). The emergence of a world of competing regional blocs might not have been imminent, but nor was it wholly impossible (Frankel 1997).

The establishment of FTAs remains an important part of contemporary region building, and they have become central pillars of common regional governance in most of the world. But the extent to which this shows that regionalism is in opposition to globalisation is open to question for three main reasons. First, while FTAs are indeed often built around wider understandings of regional integration, there is more to preferential trade agreements than geographic regions. The Israel–Mexico Free Trade Agreement (2000), for example, would pretty much defy any definition of what constitutes a region. So perhaps the real issue is not so much the benefits of regionalism, but instead the failings of multilateralism at the global level that have created the need to seek alternatives at both bilateral and regional levels.

Second, in making the reforms required to meet the criteria required to join regional organisations like the EU or to reach agreement over FTAs, states engage in processes of economic liberalisation. To be sure, they might become more open and liberal to each other than to non-partners in the first instance, but the end result is both greater economic liberalisation across the world and, perhaps more important, the increasing predominance of the 'idea' of liberalisation. Global liberalisation can thus proceed through overlapping and intertwined regional processes (Mansfield and Milner 1999).

Finally, we should consider the extent to which regional processes are driven by and perhaps even dependent on wider global processes. Take, for example, economic integration in East Asia. Here we see investment from the rest of the region into China resulting in increased trade flows as the rest of Asia provides Chinese factories with resources and components. The creation of an ASEAN–China FTA not only facilitates these flows, but also makes it easier for Chinese interests to access the region – a relatively new and fast-growing element of regional integration in Asia. But this very real regional integration has, in no small part, been driven by the production of goods that are sold in other parts of the world, often with money that has its origins outside the region as well. Thus regional integration in Asia and indeed also in other parts of the world is essentially the local manifestation of wider global processes, often driven by the production decisions of major global corporations, and based on demand in key markets in the West.

Region as 'filter'

But the need for regional arrangements to maintain a level of openness to the global economy does not mean that they will be totally open. Indeed, the financial crises of 1997 in East Asia, Russia and Argentina revealed for many the dangers of unregulated global capitalism and the problem of trying to impose solutions at the global level. Within the crisis-hit countries themselves, over-rapid liberalisation and the lack of regulation were blamed for allowing rapid and excessive capital flight. Yet the international financial institutions imposed solutions that entailed even greater liberalisation in some places, and policy adjustments that were widely perceived in these economies to represent the interests of the most powerful (Western) states in the global political economy. With global multilateralism found wanting and reflecting the neoliberal preferences of the west, and most individual states seen as lacking the power and resources to do things on their own, regional solutions became increasingly attractive. National-level legislation alone was not able to deal with transnational problems, and global-level solutions were simply inappropriate. As such, for Katzenstein (2002), regionalism was attractive because it was neither too local nor too global, but 'just right'.

While the year 1997 might have shocked some parts of the world into rethinking the benefits of the region as regulator, in truth Europe had long since played this role. Not so much Europe as a 'fortress' but as a 'filter' that kept out the worst excesses of uncontrolled neoliberal globalisation and protected the European social welfare systems from liberalisation and privatisation (Wallace 2002: 149).

And in thinking about the move towards other forms of regulatory regionalism (Jayasuriya 2004) – for example, the creation of regional currency swap deals to protect currencies from speculative attacks in East Asia – the divisions between 'old' and 'new' thinking on regionalism have been eroded. Regional-level regulation is once again seen as a way in which states seek collective responses to shared economic problems, often based on demands from key domestic groups.

Conclusions: the future of regionalism

The study of regionalism seems to be dominated by attempts to replace previous approaches with new theories – theories that are developed in response to actual changes and waves of region building. Some of these innovations do indeed represent clear breaks with what went before and perhaps four of them stand out as being particularly important: the expectation of regions replacing states to the study of how states interact within regions; from a preoccupation with regional organisations to a focus on processes and regional spaces; the move beyond economic considerations towards developmental issues and actors; and perhaps most important of all, from a Eurocentric focus to a more holistic comparative study of regions using examples from across the world.

But despite these important changes, and bearing in mind the almost unique focus on the consequences and mechanisms of formal integration in the European case, there are a number of common strands that run through the different approaches and provide some form of continuity (and some blurring of the divisions between different approaches). And these continuities reveal the reason why regionalism remains such an important issue in world politics today.

The single most important consideration is the region as a site for the collective governance of shared transnational economic problems. This in turn generates a number of subsidiary questions: how do we identify what the region is in the first place? How important is identity in bringing a region together – and whose identity matters? How do great powers/hegemons influence the emergence (or not) of regional projects? And what is the relationship between regional and global forms of governance?

This final question perhaps provides the starting point for how we might think about regions in the future. If the crises of 1997 generated a rethink of the function of regions as sites of regulation, it is reasonable to assume that the global crisis that started in 2008 will also leave its mark. It will clearly take some time for the implications of the financial crisis to play out, but given the history of regionalism and regionalisation in the post-War period that this chapter has briefly covered, then we can make some predictions with a degree of certainty.

First, despite the observations of early theorists, and the aspirations of some practitioners, the state seems destined to survive and coexist alongside regional (and other) sites of governance and authority. Second, tensions between global and regional levels of regulation and governance will continue – and the balance between the two will be formed and reformed in response to key changes in the global political economy; not just economic crisis, but more 'normal' changes such as the increasing global significance of countries like China and India and those Gulf states that have financial power that far outweighs their formal power in organisations like the International Monetary Fund (IMF).

Third, regions themselves will also continue to be formed and reformed. In Europe and North America, the focus is on expansion of existing bodies to include (potentially) new members. But in many parts of the world, the question of what the region is or should be is still fluid and contested. Great power politics and strategic considerations are clearly important here as states seek to engage, enmesh, resist, block or sideline other regional powers. So too are new patterns of transnational interactions which create and re-create new regional spaces and actual processes of integration through regionalisation. Finally, we can expect the study of Europe to remain so exceptional in the study of regionalism that it more or less remains a separate field of enquiry in its own right.

To these four confident predictions, we can add two more speculations – perhaps areas to watch out for potential change. The first relates to regions as actors in IR. Not surprisingly, the EU has been the major regional actor in this way, acting with a single voice in establishing common external tariffs and in trade negotiations – both bilaterally and in international forums such as the World Trade Organization (WTO). The EU has also established policy positions on relations with different 'strategic partners' and engages with 'bilateral' partners in formal diplomatic arenas. The EU is also doing much to promote the idea of itself as an actor through the provision of funding for research on its own 'actorness' (Hill 1994) in IR.

More importantly, there has been the emergence of 'inter-regionalism' where regions come together in various forms to primarily discuss issues of common interest and to explore ways of working together (as opposed to signing treaties). Again, the EU is the key actor here, establishing formal arrangements with regional groups in Africa, South Asia and East Asia, Latin America, South Asia and Oceania (Söderbaum and Van Langenhove 2005). But there are also cases of inter-regional meetings between non-European regions – for example, between ASEAN and the GCC and between MERCOSUR and the Australia-New Zealand Closer Economic Relations (CER). The expansion and consolidation of such inter-regional dialogues (indeed, to become more than just dialogue) – particularly between non-European regions – would mark a significant new turn in the significance of regions for the modern world order in the future.

Finally, much of the focus on regionalism remains on economic flows, economic non-state actors and statist responses to shared regional economic issues. Of course, other issues and actors do have a role to play. Fighting piracy is a key concern in Southeast Asia and elsewhere and migration, development and environmental issues are growing in importance throughout the world; but by and large this is an economics-dominated issue and an economics-dominated sub-discipline. Economics is not going to go away – far from it. But the growing societal concern with human security issues suggests that 'people-centred' issues and actors could become ever more significant for regions in the future.

Guide to further reading

Early post-Second World War theorising about European integration continues to play a role in thinking about regional integration today. In addition to reading the texts cited in the body of this chapter, Ruggie et al. (2005), and for a similar appreciation of Mitrany's contribution including a full list of publications, see Anderson (1998). Rosamond (2000) provides a succinct introduction to various theories of European Integration. For a classic discussion of the relationship between realism and neoliberal institutionalism, see Jervis (1999). On realism and regionalism, Grieco (1999) is a good introduction to realism while a combination of Keohane and Nye (1977) and Moravcsik (1993), though now somewhat dated, remains essential starting points for understanding varieties of institutionalist positions.

There have been a number of attempts to provide overviews of interpretations of understandings of regionalism. Hurrell (1995), Mansfield and Milner (1999) and Panagiriya (1999) remain influential attempts to interpret what was at the time considered a radical 'new' wave of regional projects. Edited collections not only provide more space to explore different approaches, but also allow detailed analysis of particular dimensions of regional cooperation. For good examples of this see Jayasuriya (2004), Cooper et al. (2007) and Breslin et al. (2002).

Chapter 3

Climate Change and the Politics of the Global Environment

NEIL CARTER

The environment is commonly regarded as a matter of 'low politics', a second-order problem compared to the substantive concerns of 'high politics' (Mearsheimer 2001). The environment has steadily risen up the international political agenda since it burst on the scene at the 1972 Stockholm United Nations Conference on the Human Environment. There have been numerous cycles of interest in the environment when various issues, including acid rain, deforestation, ozone depletion and biodiversity loss, have experienced brief moments in the limelight. However, over the last decade one issue – climate change – has risen far above all the others to become the dominant concern of global environmental politics. Climate change diplomacy has become increasingly intense, with the negotiation of the Kyoto Protocol resulting in major political ructions that caused a genuine rift between the USA and the European Union (EU). The international effort to agree a post-Kyoto deal has made climate change a major item at the G8 summits at Gleneagles in 2005, Hokkaido in 2008 and L'Aquila in 2009. It would appear therefore that climate change has ascended to the realm of high politics.

This chapter will examine climate change as an issue in global politics. It will focus on the efforts to negotiate an effective climate change regime, focusing on the role of the USA and the EU, tensions between developed and developing countries and the ongoing challenges of overcoming territorial conceptions of sovereignty (see Mansbach, this volume). This discussion will demonstrate the extraordinary complexity that characterises climate change: it is a transboundary issue that needs international solutions but is beset by major collective action problems. It requires governments (and businesses and citizens) to set aside national interests and short-term political horizons to support policies that may have high short-term costs but deliver indefinable long-term benefits.

Climate change: what is the issue and why is it increasingly salient?

There is overwhelming agreement among the world's leading scientists that human-induced climate change is happening and that a lack of urgent action to reduce greenhouse gas (GHG) emissions will have catastrophic consequences for the planet and life as we know it (IPCC 2007). Global warming will result in rising sea-levels, melting glaciers, increased desertification, the destructions of coral reefs and the extinction of hundreds of species. Hundreds of millions of people will face food shortages, flooding and reduced access to drinking water; many will become environmental refugees.

There is a natural 'greenhouse effect' whereby various atmospheric gases keep the Earth's temperature high enough to sustain life. These gases allow radiation from the Sun to pass through but then absorb radiation reflected back from the Earth's surface, trapping heat in the atmosphere. Without the natural greenhouse effect it is estimated that the average global temperature would be about 33°C lower. However, there is now consensus among the world's leading scientists that human activities have strengthened the greenhouse effect by increasing the concentration of these GHGs in the atmosphere, notably by burning fossil fuels, deforestation, raising livestock and growing rice. Since the industrial revolution, carbon dioxide (CO_2) concentrations have increased by over a third, from 285 parts per million (ppm) to around 430 ppm CO_2e in 2005. (Total GHGs are measured in CO_2 equivalent, or CO_2e, which is the aggregation of non-CO_2 GHGs with CO_2, weighted to reflect their respective contributions to the change in net radiation at the upper troposphere.) The concentration of GHGs is now rising rapidly by 2.5 ppm annually. On current trends, a doubling of pre-industrial GHG concentrations to at least 580 ppm is expected by the middle of this century, rising to 800–900 ppm by 2100 (Stern 2009: 25).

The Earth's average temperature has risen by 0.7°C since 1900 and is predicted to rise by anything between 1.1°C and 6.4°C by 2100 (IPCC 2007: 13). It is widely agreed that any temperature increase in excess of 2.0°C is potentially very dangerous, yet even at 500 ppm CO_2e there is a 95 per cent chance of exceeding 2.0°C. Consequently, many scientists and environmentalists call for a target of 400 ppm CO_2e maximum or, at worst, 450 ppm CO_2e (Stern 2009: 27). As we are already at 430 ppm, with emissions still rising steadily, such a target will require global emissions to be stabilised first and then reduced. Clearly, this is a huge global challenge.

Climate change has become an increasingly salient issue in international politics for several reasons. First, the dramatic scientific message has finally been accepted by the ruling elites in most countries, strengthened by growing evidence that the effects of climate change are already observable. Second, the publication of the Stern Review (Stern 2007) demonstrated that climate change will have serious economic consequences: if the world does not act, the overall costs and risks of climate change will be equivalent to losing at least 5 per cent of global gross domestic production (GDP) each year, forever (Stern 2007: xv). Thus Stern provided a powerful economic case in terms immediately understandable to political and business elites. In particular, he communicated the need for radical measures in the short term – the next 10 to 15 years – by identifying how the economic costs of inaction will increase rapidly the longer the mitigation efforts are delayed. Third, public concern about climate change has escalated, with growing pressure on governments to act. Lastly, efforts are currently underway to negotiate a treaty to replace the Kyoto Protocol, which runs its course in 2012. The election of President Obama has also raised expectations that the USA, after a decade as an international pariah on this issue, will push climate change high up the US foreign policy agenda.

Climate change: a distinctive issue in world politics?

Climate change, like other global environmental issues, has several distinctive features that make it a very complex and challenging problem. In particular, it is an example of Hardin's (1968) parable of the 'tragedy of the commons', whereby individuals and communities over-exploit common environmental resources and continue to do so even when they know it is damaging their long-term interests. The global atmospheric commons is a 'sink' into which the waste pollutants generated by the consumption of fossil fuels are dumped. Individual actors have an interest in exploiting the commons to the maximum, because they gain the full benefits from their actions (e.g., someone driving to work or an electricity supplier burning coal to generate electricity), while the costs – climate change – are shared by everyone else on the planet. That is the 'tragedy': rational individual actions produce collectively irrational outcomes. The challenge is to intervene to stop that seemingly inexorable process. Yet there is no incentive for individuals to change their behaviour because they lose the benefits of exploiting the common sink while others simply free-ride on their altruistic efforts.

Climate change is a global problem both because every country has contributed to it and because everyone will suffer the consequences. Crucially, however, some countries have contributed more than others, and some will suffer more. In particular, the rich developed countries have generated far more GHG emissions – both historically and currently – than the developing world (with some exceptions). But it is quite clear that the worst effects of climate change will fall on the latter, partly because most are located in tropical and sub-tropical zones where the impact will be greatest, but also because their weak infrastructures limit their capability to adapt to these changes. Climate change also brings new divisions: for example, countries with extensive low-lying coastal areas and small island states will be particularly threatened by rising sea-levels and storm damage, although again some richer countries (e.g., The Netherlands) are better equipped to deal with these threats than poorer countries (e.g., Bangladesh).

Climate change poses some serious threats to traditional territorial notions of state sovereignty and to the state-centric focus of academic international relations. Climate change is a transboundary problem that does not respect national borders; it can only be effectively addressed through concerted action by national governments, businesses and citizens across the world to reduce their GHG emissions. If one country takes action to reduce its carbon emissions, it cannot exclude others from benefiting, so how can it persuade other countries to make reductions when they could just free-ride on the efforts of others? The doctrine of national sovereignty means that there is no international authority equivalent to a national government – no global government – with the power to force every country to conform. Moreover, the growth in GHGs is not the result of individual states pursuing particular policies or deliberate aggressive acts; rather it is an unintended by-product of the everyday social and economic activities of organisations and individuals. One implication is that solutions cannot be delivered by state actors alone: they also require a host of non-state actors – non-governmental organisations (NGOs), businesses, individual citizens – to change their everyday behaviour.

Yet, in other respects, climate change has reinforced the importance of the state because international efforts to mitigate it have involved cooperation between states. It is states that sign up to international treaties and national governments that have the responsibility to ensure that their emission reduction targets are met. While those targets cannot be delivered without the active involvement of non-state actors, ironically, the extent of the emission reductions required will increasingly force national governments to intervene extensively and creatively in the activities of businesses and the lifestyles of citizens (Giddens 2009).

Another important feature of climate change is the centrality of scientific knowledge and the uncertainty that surrounds it. Without science we would not know about climate change and we obviously depend on scientists to tell us about the nature of the threat, the need for action, the viability of alternative solutions and the kind of adaptation measures required. One of the distinctive contributions characterising global environmental politics has been the emergence of transnational networks of scientists who are sufficiently moved about the urgency of a problem to act as an 'epistemic community' promoting international action to address climate change (Haas 1990). Their capacity to influence the political process rests on their ability to persuade others that their knowledge is valid and sufficiently important to require a policy response. However, science is contested and the development of climate change science has been characterised by many uncertainties. Despite the strong scientific consensus that temperatures are rising and that global warming is largely due to human activities, the persistence of a handful of dissenting voices – albeit rarely the leading scientific experts in the field – is still exploited by political sceptics to impede the progress of climate change policy. This sceptical discourse has been much more influential in the USA, where it was actively mobilised in support of President George W. Bush's repudiation of the Kyoto Protocol, than in Europe.

Lastly, traditional realist accounts usually dismiss climate change as a security threat. However, there is a serious possibility of conflict between states over access to water sources, especially in the Middle East, or from the mass migration of environmental refugees in search of food across an international border (Homer-Dixon 1999). Moreover, an alternative critical approach to security argues that climate change poses a different kind of security threat. The conventional militaristic language that defines security threats nationalistically as coming from other states must be replaced by a recognition that climate change is transboundary and requires international cooperative solutions that address its root causes, rather than the symptoms (Dalby 2009; Deudney 2006; Lacy 2005).

Developing a climate change regime

The scientific consensus on climate change emerged slowly during the 1980s and 1990s. A key role was played by the Intergovernmental Panel on Climate Change (IPCC) formed in 1988. Its first report, published in 1990, confirming the scientific consensus that human activities were contributing to climate change and calling for immediate policy action to reduce carbon emissions, contributed significantly to the political momentum that resulted in the United Nations Framework Convention on Climate Change (UNFCCC) agreed at the 1992 Rio Earth Summit. The main objective of the UNFCCC was to stabilise GHG concentrations at levels that should mitigate climate change. It identified a set of operating principles: precaution, co-operation, sustainability and equity. In particular, it established the principle of 'common but differentiated responsibilities' as the basis of equitable burden sharing. Thus developed countries were expected to take the lead in combating climate change and to transfer financial and technological resources to developing countries to help them address the problem. However, the UNFCCC set no firm targets; developed countries were simply given the 'voluntary goal' of returning GHG emissions to 1990 levels. Nevertheless, the Rio treaty represented an important achievement, especially given the opposition of the USA to any binding commitments, but it was clear that its worthy principles needed to be turned into something concrete as soon as possible.

A new institutional framework was established to continue negotiations aimed at strengthening the nascent climate change regime. The first Conference of the Parties to the UNFCCC (COP-1) in Berlin in 1995 agreed the 'Berlin mandate' which recognised the need to work towards a protocol that set targets and strengthened commitments to reduce GHG emissions. Eventually, the Kyoto Protocol, hammered out over 10 days of intense negotiations in December 1997 (COP-3), agreed legally binding targets for developed countries (Annex 1). Together these targets aimed at an overall reduction in the basket of the six main GHGs of 5.2 per cent of 1990 levels for the 5-year period 2008–12. However, subsequent efforts to firm up the details agreed at Kyoto floundered at The Hague (COP-6) in 2000, and the following year the newly elected President Bush repudiated the Kyoto Protocol. As the USA was then responsible for over 20 per cent of global GHG emissions, this decision prompted a major crisis because the Protocol could not enter force until it had been ratified by 55 countries and by countries which together were responsible for at least 55 per cent of the GHG emissions of the developed Annex 1 countries. Frenzied diplomatic activity to bring other prevaricating developed countries on board resulted in the Bonn agreement in July 2001, where Japan and Russia were persuaded to sign up to a binding agreement. But it was not until November 2004 that Russia, after winning additional concessions through hard bargaining, finally ratified the agreement, allowing the Kyoto Protocol to enter into force in 2005. The USA and Australia were the only major developed countries not to ratify it, although Australia subsequently did in 2008. By 2009, 184 countries had ratified the Kyoto Protocol.

Proponents of the Kyoto Protocol regarded it as a major breakthrough in international climate change politics. The primary achievement of the Protocol was to bind most of the developed countries to emissions reductions on business-as-usual levels. This agreement represented the practical application of the principle of 'common but differentiated responsibilities', which underpinned the recognition by developed nations that (1) they were responsible for the largest share of historical and current GHG emissions; (2) the per capita emissions of developing countries were far smaller; (3) emissions in developing countries needed to continue to grow to meet essential social and development needs.

This principle informed the decision to set emission reduction targets for the 31 Annex 1 countries that differed in recognition of the capacity of different countries to make cuts. Key targets included 8 per cent for the EU, 7 per cent for the USA, 6 per cent for Canada and Japan, 0 per cent for Russia, while Australian emissions could increase by 8 per cent. The overall EU 8 per cent target acted as a 'bubble' within which member states had targets that ranged from reductions of 21 per cent for Denmark and Germany, and 12.5 per cent for the UK, 0 per cent for France and Finland, to an increase of 27 per cent for Portugal. To secure the support of Russia and other East European states, these net emission targets could be achieved by offsetting carbon sinks, such as afforestation projects, against actual GHG emissions. The Protocol also introduced three measures – the so-called Kyoto mechanisms – to enable countries to implement their Kyoto targets:

1. An international emissions trading regime allowing industrialised countries to buy and sell emission credits among themselves.
2. A Joint Implementation procedure enabling industrialised countries to implement projects that reduce emissions or remove carbon in another Annex 1 country in exchange for emission reduction credits.
3. A 'Clean Development Mechanism' permitting developed countries to finance emissions reduction projects in developing countries and receive credit for doing so.

Finally, importantly, the Protocol established the institutional mechanisms for future negotiations and regime strengthening.

Critics point out that even if the overall Kyoto abatement target is achieved, it will do no more than scratch the surface of the problem (Victor 2004). In short, the inexorable rise of global GHG emissions will continue unchecked. The compromises needed to secure agreement at Kyoto meant that the targets were too timid, and option of sequestering CO_2 into carbon sinks weakened them further. The Protocol is also characterised by two key tensions: the refusal of the USA to ratify it and the absence of any requirement that developing countries, particularly large rapidly industrialising countries such as China and India, should reduce their emissions. While the absence of the USA was a clear failure of the regime-building process, the latter was a positive demonstration by developed countries of the 'common but differentiated responsibilities' principle. However, both issues represent unresolved – and interlinked – tensions that dogged the Kyoto negotiations and continue to hamper efforts to strengthen the climate change regime.

The reluctance of the USA to embrace the Kyoto process reflects wider divisions among developed countries regarding their willingness to make firm commitments. Resistance has coalesced around the USA, in coalition with others in the JUSCANZ (Japan, USA, Canada, Australia and New Zealand) 'Umbrella Group'. Clearly, as the world's largest producer of GHG emissions (until China recently overtook it), the inclusion of the USA in any regime is vital to its success. Yet, while the EU and some other industrialised nations pressed for quantified targets throughout the climate change negotiations, the US government has always dragged its feet. President George H. W. Bush was reluctant to sign the Framework Convention at Rio and the Clinton-Gore administration then blocked agreement on targets or timetables at Berlin. Before eventually accepting a 7 per cent reduction target at Kyoto, Gore won significant concessions, including the introduction of an emissions trading system, while the main sticking point at the unsuccessful Hague Conference in 2000 was the insistence of the US government that it be allowed to offset its emissions against its forest sinks.

The intransigence of the USA demonstrates the importance of the political economy of climate change politics. Disagreements between developed countries can be attributed in large part to differences in energy resources and the structure of the energy industry (Paterson 1996). Countries that rely on fossil fuels for export income, such as Middle Eastern oil-producing states, and those with large energy resources, including the USA, have been most resistant to cuts. The latter has an abundance of fossil fuel energy: it is a major oil, gas and coal producer. The American 'gas-guzzler' culture of cheap, available energy generates strong domestic resistance to any interference with oil prices. The economic and political costs of implementing emission cuts are therefore seen as higher in the USA than elsewhere, and because climate change has lower salience in America than across the Atlantic, the US government believes the costs of adapting to climate change (rather than mitigating it) are affordable. Furthermore, American politicians have been subjected to strong pressure from a powerful domestic industrial lobby, particularly motor and energy (which bankrolled President Bush's presidential campaigns) interests, to obstruct the regime-building process (Lisowski 2002). Consequently, the Bush administration played the role of veto state with some aplomb, doing its best to reframe the climate change debate on its terms. For example, in the face of growing scientific consensus about climate change, under Bush the US government exploited remaining uncertainties, and it tried to persuade Russian President Putin not to ratify the Kyoto Protocol. Later, as it became harder even for Bush to continue denying climate change was a problem, he shifted tack by launching the Asia-Pacific Partnership on Clean Development and Climate, a 2005 initiative with Australia, China, India, Japan and South Korea to find voluntary ways of reducing emissions by accelerating 'the development and deployment of clean energy technologies'. It was, transparently, an attempt to undermine the Kyoto Protocol.

However, there has been a shift in climate change politics within the USA in recent years as the public mood, which identified events such as Hurricane Katrina with climate change, became more sympathetic to environmental issues. Initially, this shift was a bottom-up process that gathered momentum in the face of federal intransigence from the Bush White House. Several regions have developed their own cap-and-trade systems, including California and the Regional Greenhouse Gas Initiative launched by several north-eastern states. The election of President Obama brought the possibility of a transformation in the US role in climate change diplomacy, with potentially significant implications for the negotiation of an effective post-Kyoto treaty. Obama made his difference from Bush on climate change a key feature of his election campaign and entered office declaring that 'We will make it clear to the world that America is ready to lead. To protect our climate and our collective security, we must call together a truly global coalition' (Obama 2009). He made some remarkably 'green' appointments to key environmental positions, including Stephen Chu, Nobel prize-winning physicist, as Energy Secretary. Obama quickly launched a tranche of initiatives including a green economic stimulus package, investment in renewable technologies and an Energy Bill that, for the first time, would introduce federal targets to reduce GHG emissions and a cap-and-trade scheme. Yet, significantly, the familiar oil and gas lobby mobilised its considerable resources in opposition to the Bill with the aim of defeating or watering down the Bill as it passed through Congress during 2009.

By contrast, the USA's abrogation of leadership on climate change has left a vacuum that the EU has been increasingly willing to fill. Throughout the 1990s, the EU pushed for stringent international emission reduction commitments. At Kyoto, although it failed to win the kind of tough cuts it wanted, the EU still accepted the highest reduction target, which may have helped persuade other countries to accept more ambitious cuts than initially intended. By playing hardball, the USA had a more profound impact than the EU on the architecture of the Protocol because it was able to win concessions on the flexibility mechanisms such as carbon sinks and the use of emission trading (Oberthur and Kelly 2008: 36). However, when subsequent negotiations at The Hague (COP-6) failed and Bush repudiated the treaty, the EU stepped up to the mark in impressive style. The EU's decision to 'go it alone' by pressing ahead without the USA, illustrated by its telling diplomatic interventions at the reconvened Bonn COP-6bis and Marrakech COP-7, and later its success in delivering Russian ratification, effectively saved the Protocol and demonstrated the EU's resolve as an actor in international politics (Vogler and Bretherton 2006: 3, 13–14).

Subsequently, the EU has sustained this leadership role. It set up the world's first international carbon emissions trading system (ETS) in 2005. In March 2007, the European Council reasserted the EU's long-standing commitment to hold mean global temperature increases to 2.0°C above pre-industrial levels and declared that the EU would cut its CO_2 emissions by 20 per cent of 1990 levels by 2020, increasing this to 30 per cent if other developed countries agree to a new post-Kyoto treaty. To give substance to its 20 per cent reduction commitment, the EU agreed a Climate Change package in 2008 consisting of six pieces of legislation aimed at delivering the required emission reductions across the energy, business and transport sectors in the 27 member states. Thus the EU has exercised a 'soft leadership' strategy in climate change politics (Oberthur and Kelly

2008). The EU has limited political and economic power to force other countries to cut emissions, so it adopted an approach that combines 'leadership by example', diplomacy, persuasion and argument.

Why has the EU accepted, with some alacrity, this leadership role, when it might have just let Kyoto wither and die, thereby avoiding the considerable compliance costs of reducing emissions? Several factors, relating both to the specific challenge of climate change and to the wider role of the EU as an international actor, explain this decision. Most European governments – at least those in the old EU15 – regard climate change as a grave threat. EU member states are heavily dependent on imported energy and there is no gas-guzzling culture as in the USA; so governments have a stronger balance-of-payments incentive to cut carbon emissions and reduce imports of fossil fuels. Growing concerns about the security of energy supplies, particularly after massive increases in oil and gas prices around 2005 and the increasing dependency on Russian gas, have brought a new focus on policies aimed at improving energy efficiency and developing renewable energy sources (Oberthur and Kelly 2008). In addition, Bush's repudiation of Kyoto gave European leaders an opportunity to enhance the nascent reputation of the EU as a serious, unified player in global politics, and to strengthen its position vis-a-vis the USA. A combination of environmental pioneer states (Austria, Denmark, Finland, Germany, Sweden and The Netherlands) plus the UK have consistently played a leading role (Schreurs and Tiberghien 2007). Ideology and personality have played their part. Between 1998 and 2005 Germany was governed by a red–green coalition in which Joschka Fischer was an influential Green Foreign Secretary, backed for some time by the presence of Green ministers in Belgium, Finland, France and Italy. Tony Blair embraced the cause of climate change mitigation with enthusiasm, personally convinced by the arguments but he also saw it as a way of distancing himself from Bush at a time when he was the subject of strong domestic criticism over the Iraq war. The European Commission, backed by the European Parliament, has played a crucial role because it has recognised the need for the new policy measures, such as the ETS and the 2008 Climate Change package, both to ensure that member states met their Kyoto commitments and to enable the EU to lead by example in the negotiation of a post-Kyoto treaty (Schreurs and Tiberghien 2007). The EU institutions saw that following the failure to establish a constitution in 2005, climate change offered a popular means of reinvigorating and legitimising European integration because it required genuinely 'European' solutions.

The continued willingness of the EU to assume a leadership role is crucial if the second major tension – the North–South divide – is to be resolved. The Kyoto Protocol demonstrated that most developed countries at least accepted the responsibility to take the initiative in making cuts. Clearly, at least in the medium term, they must continue to make the lion's share of reductions because they have been responsible for around 70 per cent of GHG emissions since 1950, even though developed countries contain only about 1 billion of the global population of 6.7 billion people alive today (Stern 2009: 23). Developed countries also have far higher per capita emissions. Moreover, they have the resources to invest in the necessary shift to a low-carbon economy.

But it is also clear that any effective climate change regime must, sooner rather than later, bring the rapid growth of emissions in developing countries under control. The developing world will soon be the source of most emissions. Global GHG emissions are currently split roughly 50/50 between developed (and transition) countries (Annex 1) and the rest of the world. Several of the largest developing countries – China, Indonesia, Brazil, India – now rank in the top ten for the *absolute* level of emissions in terms of CO_2e (Garnaut 2008: ch. 3), although they remain far below the developed world in terms of per capita emissions. China, for example, has seen its GHG emissions grow by around 70 per cent since 1990, due to its rapid economic growth and heavy dependency on coal for its energy supply, to become the largest emitting country in the world, with over 20 per cent of global GHG emissions. It is projected that China will contribute 33 per cent of global emissions by 2030 assuming it continues its development path of energy-intensive rapid economic expansion (Garnaut 2008: ch. 3). With population growth concentrated in the developing world and the per capita growth of emissions rapidly escalating as poorer countries industrialise, then on business-as-usual projections the developing world might be responsible for as much as 80 per cent of global emissions by 2050.

Clearly, the principles of 'common but differentiated responsibilities', equity and sustainability are open to many different interpretations. Thus a major stumbling block for the USA throughout the Kyoto negotiations was the absence of any firm commitment by developing countries to reduce their emissions. The US Government was mindful of the 1997 Byrd–Hagel resolution to the US Senate that opposed the Kyoto Protocol on the grounds that it excluded developing countries and would harm the competitiveness of US industry. That concern has been exacerbated by the continued, rapid growth of China, which is now a major competitor.

However, the major developing countries, such as China and India, demand that they should not have any targets imposed on them while they remain so far behind the developed world. In particular, they point out that their per capita emissions are much lower than in developed countries: for example, per capita emissions in the USA are around five times higher than in China. As long as this gross inequality within the international system remains, it will be very difficult to persuade developing countries to take significant action to control their emissions. As the Indian climate change envoy to COP-15 observed, 'Western countries are hypocritical and must sacrifice some luxuries before asking developing countries to cut greenhouse gas emissions' (*The Age*, 7 August 2009). It is important to recognise that China and India are not – as some in the North have suggested – irresponsibly ignoring the problem of climate change. China, for example, is very conscious of its dependency on coal-fired electricity generation, and has introduced several initiatives to improve energy efficiency and to develop renewable sources of energy. There is an increasingly strong lobby within the Chinese political elite pushing for China to move towards a low-carbon economy by setting emissions reduction targets and introduce ETS (Reuters 2009). India, too, has ambitious plans for a massive expansion of solar energy. But any serious efforts to reduce emissions will depend heavily upon the transfer of financial and technological resources from

North to South to fund the introduction of clean technologies, renewable sources of energy and so on. But, in practice, developed countries have been unwilling to put their hands in their pockets, and big private corporations are reluctant to relinquish control of technologies without economic or financial compensation (e.g., access to markets).

One widely touted solution to the equity problem is the notion of 'contraction and convergence', which aims for per capita parity at a 'safe level' of 2.0 tonnes of CO_2 by 2050. Most developing countries are currently well below that figure while high-income countries are far above it. So developed countries must cut rapidly and substantially to 2.0 tonnes CO_2 per capita, while the former should be allowed to expand until, say, 2030 or 2040, but then be required to cut back to reach parity by 2050 (Schreuder 2009: 60). But even this radical proposal ignores another feature of the globalised economy, which is that a large proportion of the goods manufactured in industrialising countries such as China, Mexico and South Korea are exported to and consumed in the developed world – yet these 'embedded emissions' are not accounted for in official UNFCCC data.

Other commentators see market-based mechanisms as the key both to the overall problem of emissions reductions and to the North–South divide (Stern 2009; Tickell 2008). One of the significant developments since the implementation of the Kyoto Protocol has been the development of 'carbon commodification', whereby carbon reductions have been turned into commodities that can be traded in the market. Global carbon markets were worth €47 billion in 2007, up from $31 billion in 2006. The market saw transactions for 2.9 billion tonnes of CO_2e, with the EU ETS accounted for 70 per cent of the volume and over 78 per cent of the value (World Bank 2008a: 1). By any measure, carbon trading has grown impressively to establish itself as a new commodity.

The EU was initially unenthusiastic about the American insistence on the inclusion of emissions trading in the Kyoto Protocol, but when it adopted the mantle of climate change leader at the turn of the century, the EU turned to emissions trading as a means ensuring that member states would be able to meet existing and future emission reduction targets. The ETS, launched in 2005, is a carbon-trading scheme based upon the principles of cap-and-trade that allocates energy-intensive installations a number of carbon permits that can then be traded. The scheme helps overcome the free rider problem by requiring all large European organisations – currently around 12,000 sites are included – to join the ETS. By guaranteeing the scheme will remain in place businesses have the long-term security to justify investing in cleaner technologies plus the financial incentive to cut emissions so that they can sell surplus emissions permits for a profit in the new carbon market. The ETS has had its teething problems. Phase 1 (2005–07) was criticised because most permits were issued free, which enabled some businesses to make a significant profit from them. Most member states also oversupplied permits, which resulted in the price of carbon falling to a level so low that it was an ineffective incentive to reduce emissions. Overall, Phase 1 had little, if any, impact on GHG emissions. Phase 2 (2008–12) saw the European Commission exercising tougher control over the volume of permits allocated, a small number of which were auctioned, so it is predicted that the ETS will now deliver significant emission reductions. Phase 3 (2013–20) has been approved as part of the EU's Climate Change package. It will centralise the allocation of permits, with a larger proportion to be auctioned, and it will be extended to include aviation.

Another important Kyoto innovation was the Clean Development Mechanism (CDM), which is the only part of the Protocol that provides an active role for developing countries to reduce their emissions. The CDM permits developed countries to finance emissions-reduction projects in developing countries and receive credits for doing so that count towards their Kyoto targets. An additional incentive for Annex 1 countries is that it may be cheaper to achieve emission reductions in developing countries than domestically. The attraction for developing countries is that CDM may facilitate technology transfer and attract new foreign investment to projects that deliver sustainable development.

The CDM took off at a rapid rate after the Protocol entered into force in 2005, boosted by the EU's decision to allow credits earned under CDM to be traded within the ETS. By August 2009, there were 1751 registered CDM projects, which were estimated to deliver over 2.7 billion tonnes of emissions reductions by 2012 (IGES 2009). The assumption underpinning CDM is that all reductions in GHGs are equally good for climate change mitigation, whether they occur in the USA or Mali. However, there are political costs if developed countries are perceived as using CDM as an easy option to avoid having to rein in the consumerist lifestyles of their own citizens. In short, it will fuel the familiar refrain from the South that developing countries cannot be expected to take actions that might harm them if the rich North is unwilling to accept some pain too.

The CDM has had its problems (Tickell 2008). For example, there is a concern about the extent to which a CDM investment generates 'additionality', or simply finances a project that would have happened anyway. Many CDM schemes are intended to produce short-term, low-cost GHG reductions, such as an end-of-pipe methane gas capture scheme, rather than a more capital-intensive renewable energy scheme that might have a longer lead-in time before it generates emission reduction benefits. Nevertheless, by most accounts CDM has been a success, but it needs to be reformed if it is to generate the volume of transfers of technology and financial investment from rich to poor countries that will be essential to resolve North–South tensions (Stern 2009).

The future of climate change politics

The international politics of climate change has seen the negotiation of a post-Kyoto treaty secure a place – at least temporarily – on the table of high politics, with efforts focused on achieving a deal at the Copenhagen COP-15 in December 2009. It seems that climate change is now established on the agenda of international politics. Moreover, while the literature on international environmental politics has focused on the factors that enable or inhibit regime formation, it is likely that several more traditional realist concerns will bolster the importance of climate change. Growing concerns about energy security, encouraged by global fluctuations in oil prices and the growing dependence of Europe on Russian gas, make the case for any country to shift to a low-carbon economy increasingly persuasive. The inclusion of significant climate change measures within the fiscal stimulus packages introduced during 2008–09 in China, France, South Korea, the USA and elsewhere indicates that this kind of thinking is slowly percolating through international policy elites. Indeed, Todd Stern, State Department Special Envoy for Climate Change Issues, has observed that under the Obama administration, climate change has 'risen up to the top of the U.S. national security set of priorities' (America.gov 2009). There are also a range of trade and economic issues associated that are likely to generate conflict among developed countries (such as the EU's decision – opposed by the USA – to include aviation emissions within the ETS) and between developed and developing countries (such as the expansion of biofuels), which seem likely to ensure that climate politics remains on the top table.

Whatever deal is thrashed out to supersede Kyoto, the challenge of persuading the major developing countries to embrace a development trajectory based on the low-carbon economy will remain paramount. At a time of global recession, when many developed countries will have to make public expenditure cuts for years ahead, it is difficult to persuade governments to come up with the kinds of income and technology transfers necessary to meet even the minimum targets. Moreover, as the damage we have already done becomes increasingly evident, humankind will have to deal with the impact of climate change. Consequently, the international agenda is turning to the challenge of adaptation, which raises both new and similar challenges. On the one hand, there is a fear in some circles that focusing on adaptation shifts the emphasis away from mitigation. On the other hand, the costs of adaptation will be unavoidable, high and, again, unevenly distributed with developing countries suffering first and being less able to deal with the challenges. Hence the ongoing tensions between the developed and developing nations are here to stay and are likely to intensify – possibly at the cost of a meaningful international regime.

The only way out of this quagmire is if the developed world shows effective and sustained leadership; but the prospects look bleak. Serious doubts remain about the capacity of the USA to assume a leadership role. The USA is playing 'catch-up' (Paterson 2009). While the EU is on schedule to meet its overall Kyoto reduction target, the USA has seen its emissions *increase* by around 15 per cent since 1990, a far cry from its 7 per cent Kyoto reduction target. Moreover, the underlying obstacles to US leadership on climate change have not disappeared, as illustrated by the difficulties Obama faced in getting his Energy Bill through Congress in 2009. The sentiment underpinning the Byrd–Hagel resolution persists in the energy bill clause imposing protectionist measures on those (developing) countries not implementing GHG cuts. Yet it is questionable how far the USA can act as a genuine leader that can persuade developing countries to make cuts when the USA has such a sorry record of emissions reductions to date.

The EU has established itself as *the* international climate change leader, building new institutions and making emissions trading and CDM work. It has benefited economically from the important links it has established with China and India through the implementation of CDM. Yet the EU too faces serious challenges if it is to maintain its leadership role. Although the EU will meet its overall Kyoto target, most member states will require the help of the ETS and CDM credits to meet their targets. The EU has continued to act by example with its 2020 reduction targets, but its Climate Change package is significantly less ambitious than originally intended, partly because it was thrashed out in the depths of global recession. Its capacity for progressive leadership has also been weakened by its enlargement to 27 states, which has brought in a bloc of East European states, such as Poland with its heavy dependence on coal, that are opposed to measures that might damage economic growth.

Whatever deal eventually replaces Kyoto, it is important not to assume that regime formation and implementation represent everything there is to say about global climate change politics. There are numerous multilateral and bilateral agreements that exist alongside – albeit often inspired by – the Kyoto process. Transnational climate change governance has taken off rapidly in recent years. The carbon market has grown exponentially, with the EU ETS likely to be supplemented (and linked) to planned emissions trading systems in the USA, Australia and New Zealand. Beyond that, a myriad of public–private partnerships, private, voluntary and individual initiatives are flourishing (Paterson 2009: 150–1). In short, climate change governance has a momentum of its own that might be hampered, but not undermined by a failure in the overarching international regime process.

Guide to further reading

Several books offer lively introductions to international climate change politics (Giddens 2009; Schreuder 2009; Stern 2009; Tickell 2008). It is important to grasp the stark reality of climate change science (IPCC 2007) and the complexity of the relationship between science and policy (Hulme 2009). The Stern Report is essential reading to grasp the economic case for global action on climate change (Stern 2007). The academic journals *Climate Policy, Environmental Politics* and *Global Environmental Politics* are a rich source of reading on all aspects of climate change politics and policy. Political philosophers have also engaged constructively with the ethical issues raised by North–South issues and equitable burden-sharing (*Environmental Politics* 2008; Garvey 2008). There is a growing literature on climate change and environmental security (Dalby 2009; Homer-Dixon 1999; Lacy 2005). It is also useful to locate climate change in the wider literature on international environmental politics and policy (Carter 2007; Clapp and Dauvergne 2005).

Chapter 4

Global Power Shift: The Decline of the West and the Rise of the Rest?

NICK BISLEY

On 15 February 2009, the Boeing 757 carrying Hilary Clinton on her first diplomatic mission as Secretary of State flew out of Washington D.C. While the trip was of importance for many reasons, most obviously, it was the first major foray into foreign policy by the newly minted Obama administration, it was something as mundane as the aircraft's flight direction which was particularly striking. For the first time, the aircraft carrying a new Secretary of State on an inaugural trip abroad flew west, taking Clinton first to Japan and then on to Indonesia, South Korea and China. Hitherto, it had been customary that the first visit was to Europe, usually to Great Britain, and occasionally, if circumstances were sufficiently grim, to the Middle East. The diplomatic message sent by this choice was unambiguous and, for many, the move was illustrative of an ongoing transformation of the international system.

For at least the last 150 years, world politics has been dominated by powers residing on either side of the North Atlantic. These countries have enjoyed substantially greater wealth, power and influence than all others. By 1999, not only did the Western powers retain their huge advantage over everyone else, the United States was in such a position that its government could plan for a grand strategy premised on a never-ending perpetuation of its global military predominance (White House 2002). But just as this prompted debate as to the vices and virtues of American empire (Ferguson 2004; Johnson 2004), others began to notice that there were important changes afoot. On the back of historically unprecedented economic growth, China and India were beginning to exert an international influence to match their demographic scale and historical legacies. China was already the world's factory and a top-ten economy. India's information technology and outsourcing was having a global impact and a newly renovated Russia commanded the world's largest reserves of fossil fuels. In a now famous report, the investment bank Goldman Sachs identified four countries, Brazil, Russia, India and China, as the keys to the future of the global economy. They predicted that by 2035 the four, collectively known as the 'BRICs', would overtake the combined GDP of the G7 (Goldman Sachs 2001). These powers have also begun to match their economic achievements with creative and pragmatic diplomacy. Where in the past each had been hamstrung by limited resources and an ideological strait-jacket, their much more pragmatic foreign policies can now afford to be run in an activist fashion. New wealth and confidence has also led to increased military spending, prompting, in turn, uncertainty among their neighbours and the world more generally.

Many read these developments as indicative of a change in the international distribution of power. Some feel that the new era will be one of an Asian ascendancy (e.g., Mahbubani 2008), while others feel that the system will have multiple centres of power and influence, in a manner not dissimilar to the nineteenth century (e.g., Bell 2007). This chapter provides an overview of these arguments and assesses the extent to which the twenty-first century will be shaped by a global power shift and the implications that such a restructuring of the system might have for the pattern and dynamics of world politics.

The North Atlantic era

On the back of a remarkable period of maritime exploration, from the mid-sixteenth century European powers, and their offshoots, began to dominate the globe. In the Americas, Africa, Asia and the Middle East, Europe's great powers expropriated lands from indigenous populations, subjected local populations to their often brutal and arbitrary rule and found new stages on which to play out their rivalries and conflicts. So wide-ranging was the reach of European imperialism that by the beginning of the First World War, Britain, France, Belgium and the Netherlands ruled around a third of the world's territory and just under 30 per cent of its population (Townsend 1941). During this period European states and their colonial offspring, such as Australia, America, Canada and New Zealand, systematically improved their place in the international system. By the middle of the twentieth century, in almost any measure these states had become substantially better off than all others. They were the most militarily powerful, had a decisive advantage in virtually all technologies and generated the vast bulk of global GDP. At the micro level, their populations enjoyed vastly better standards of living, with higher levels of education spread far more widely across their populations, long life expectancy, significantly reduced infant mortality and widespread control of many diseases such as cholera, typhoid and smallpox which had ravaged humanity for centuries.

The end of the Cold War seemed to confirm Western dominance as a liberal model of politics, and a capitalist vision of economics ended the century ideologically undefeated. Along with this victory in the intra-European struggle over how human societies should be organised was a predominance of Western ideas in the constitutional structure of the international system and the nascent edifice of global governance. Thus, the material dominance of Western states was matched by the apparent monopolisation of Western ideas as to how states and societies should be run and how relations between those entities ought to be organised. Even in the efforts to create international mechanisms to limit state power that accelerated after the end of the Cold War, such as the emerging human rights regime and the international criminal court, Western powers and ideas have predominated.

The structural form that Western ascendancy has taken has varied over time, subject as it has been to intra-Western contestation. Since the collapse of the USSR, the international system has enjoyed the historically unusual situation of being unipolar. There is one unambiguously great power and no one, alone or collectively, is in a position to challenge this situation (Brooks and Wohlforth 2002). Some have even argued that the United States is more than the most important power in the system: it is a global empire (Harvey 2003; Mann 2003). However viewed, the United States is unique in its domination of so many dimensions of power: it enjoys massive military advantages, has the world's largest economy, as well as being at the leading edge of technology and innovation, it has a virtual monopoly on the world's best universities as well as a culture that is consumed and enjoyed the world over. It stands at the centre of a global network of military alliances, has the world's largest and most influential diplomatic corps and conceives of its interests and strategy in properly global terms. Since 1945, the United States has sought to advance its interests and values through an active, and at times interventionist, global strategy. To some degree this was constrained by the Soviet Union and the Cold War, but since 1991 the West, more particularly the United States, has been unrivalled. Not only is the United States the system's most important player, but its underlying values and forms of social organisation – democracy and free markets – also seem to be the only real game in town.

The West, while by no means an orderly and homogeneous grouping, has over a long period of time developed a dominant position in the international system. So significant has its influence been that the changing configurations of power within the grouping – from multipolar to unipolar – have become the central organising principles of the system as a whole. During the period of colonialism Western attitudes to local populations and to other Western rivals were of paramount importance to local conditions all over the world. After the unravelling of Western empires, it was still the cleavages among Western powers that shaped the broader contours of world politics. In the years since the end of the Cold War, world politics has again been shaped by the distribution of power and influence among the Western powers. During this period, however, the United States has no equal and the international system has had to grapple with the peculiarities of unipolarity (Ikenberry et al. 2009). The pressing question for students of world politics, therefore, is the extent to which US primacy, itself a manifestation of longer-running Western dominance, is likely to last given the emergence of a number of large and dynamic powers.

The end of an era?

When viewed from a long historical perspective, the West's ascendancy is historically recent and relatively short-run. For the bulk of the past 2000 years of human history, Asia has accounted for nearly two-thirds of global wealth (Maddison 2001). Economists describe the massive gap that began to open up between the West and the rest from the eighteenth century as the beginning of an era of great divergence in global economic history. In recent years, the resurgence of India and China, following on from the earlier success of the Asian tigers, for some, marks the beginning of the end of that era. Indeed, some go so far as to argue that the economic forces working to level out the very uneven distribution of wealth across the world will be among the most important factors shaping the world in the coming century (Sachs 2008). It is this process of flattening out the economic discrepancies between the rich and at least some of the less well-off which lies at the heart of the arguments about the decline of the West and consequent changes in the global order which appear to mark a return to longer-run historical trends.

Economic dynamism

The primary reason that many perceive world politics to be changing is a shift in the relative capabilities of states. The argument is not that the West is on the precipice of historical irrelevance, rather that it is no longer going to be the monopoly supplier of influence and leadership in the international system. It is, as one leading commentator puts it, not so much a case of the absolute decline of the United States or the West, but of 'the rise of everyone else' (Zakaria 2008: 1). At the centre of this is a question about economic performance. While the West and the United States continue to dominate total economic output, they have for some time lagged the growth rates of the emerging economies, the most dynamic of which is China. The modernisation programme launched by the People's Republic of China (PRC) in 1978 has produced one of the greatest success stories in world economic history (Lardy 1998). Between 1975 and 1999, the average annual GDP growth rate was 8.1 per cent (UNDP 2001: 179) and since 1979, the economic output of the PRC has quadrupled. It is not only China's dynamism that is so captivating, it is its scale. Never in human history have so many people had their life chances changed so dramatically and so quickly. The renowned development economist Jeffrey Sachs claims that 'China is the most successful development story in world history' (quoted in Zakaria 2008: 89). China leads the world in manufacturing, creating around two-thirds of the world's electronic goods and is the world's largest producer of steel, cement and coal. From being a poor and isolated country in the mid-1970s with few prospects, China is the fifth largest economy in the world, is fundamental to global supply chains and trade networks in almost all industries and in the wash-out of the 2008 global financial crisis is clearly the key engine of growth for the world economy.

For some time, China's economic success put the almost as important modernisation of India into the shade. The contemporaneous economic acceleration of the two Asian giants has shown that China is not unique, and that big complex economies that many thought of as basket cases can very rapidly turn themselves around. Since initiating a series of liberalisation reforms in the early 1990s, the Indian economy has been radically transformed. Although economists point

out that growth rates began to pick up in the late 1980s, since the reform programme the Indian economy has grown at an average rate of just over 6 per cent
(Panagariya 2008: 6). Over that time, India has become linked into the global
economy through a vast IT industry, it is an increasingly attractive venue for
foreign investment and its productivity, especially in manufacturing, is growing dramatically. India has the potential to overtake most developed economies
in sheer size by 2025 and to become as large as the United States by 2050
(Goldman Sachs 2007). With the resurgence of India and China, alongside the
well-recognised success stories of Japan, South Korea, Taiwan, Singapore and,
to a lesser extent, Thailand and Malaysia, the idea that we are about to enter an
Asian century appears compelling. In typically ebullient form, Larry Summers is
reported to have said: 'At current growth rates in Asia, standards of living may rise
100 fold, 10,000 per cent within a human life span. The rise of Asia and all that
follows it will be the dominant story in history books written 300 years from now
with the Cold War and the rise of Islam as secondary stories' (cited in Mahbubani
2008: 10).

The rapid increase in oil and commodity prices, itself driven to a large degree
by the growth in demand caused by India and China, has allowed a number of
countries well endowed with these natural resources to move up the global influence chain. Until the recent collapse in oil prices, Russia was the most significant
beneficiary of this process, but others around the world have found their economic circumstances rapidly and, in some degrees, quite unexpectedly improved.
The oil-rich states of the Persian gulf, Iran, Bahrain, the UAE, Kuwait and Saudi
Arabia and even, to a lesser degree, Iraq, have all had national coffers hugely
inflated by the long-running high oil and gas prices. Elsewhere in the developing world, most notably in Venezuela, Sudan and Nigeria, vast primary resource
holdings is generating surprising levels of national wealth in countries that have
historically been at the margins of the global economy.

The reasons for the economic vitality of the emerging powers are widespread.
Some point to elite policy choices, others to cultural matters, while natural advantages are also clearly important. A central theme among some of the more
prominent writings is the role played by the application of Western ideas to
non-Western societies. Some writers point to things like the embrace of market systems of economic exchange, the adoption of the principle of meritocracy
and the rule of law (Mahbubani 2008: 51–99). Others point to clothing, food and
business principles as examples of Westernisation (Zakaria 2008). However, the
most important factor behind the economic success of all the emerging powers,
for the big players such as China and India, as well as smaller entities such as
the UAE or Venezuela, is globalisation. As Phil Cerny's chapter in this volume
explains, the linkages between states and societies facilitated by the growth in
networks of trade, investment and communication have provided many with economic, political and cultural opportunities that had hitherto not been available.
Without the ability to tap into global markets, whether for capital, finished goods,
raw inputs or commodity sales, the dramatic changes in economic fortunes in
Shanghai, Caracas and Mumbai would have been unimaginable. Equally, as many

point out, the technological dimensions of globalisation – the rapid reduction in the costs imposed by distance, and particularly the ability of ideas to overcome geographic limitations – have been instrumental in the rise of many powers. The time needed to make good the gap between rich and poor is not only narrower than it has ever been, it is also likely to narrow further still, at least for those countries able to take advantage of the evolving global economy (Pape 2009; Zakaria 2008). But as Ray Kiely makes clear in Chapter 16, there will still be many who will not be able to make good on these opportunities.

Western sclerosis?

The ongoing economic achievements of the emerging economies are a compelling story. But, the relative shift in power is also, to some degree, a function of the longer-run under-performance of many Western powers. The West's share of global output is declining and will continue to do so for so long as its growth rates are outstripped by the emerging economies. It is not only the annual shortcomings in measures of global output that are of significance, but it is the longer-term decline. Between 1990 and 2008 America's share of global output declined by about 12 per cent while China's rose by over 300 per cent (Pape 2009: 23). This rests on the longer-run drop in American growth rates which have declined by 30–40 per cent since the mid-1990s. These trends are evident across the Western world, with a number of minor exceptions. Some feel that one of the important consequences of the global financial crisis of 2008–09 will be to exacerbate these trends and as it allows emerging economies the opportunity to advance their interests through diplomacy and international institutions because of Western weakness (Altman 2009). A related problem for Western countries, and particularly for the United States, is their growing dependence on credit from emerging economies. America is badly in debt. Both the governmental accounts and the private sector are indebted to the rest of the world to unparalleled degrees – again a trend that is set to be exacerbated by the global financial crisis and the American government's remedies. In 2008, the American government recorded a budget deficit of $454.8 billion (US Treasury 2008), and its current account deficit is the largest in its history. This debt is largely financed by high domestic savings in Asia, particularly in China and Japan. America's situation may be extreme, but most other wealthy countries are in a similar position with Germany, France, Britain and Italy all running substantial deficits. The concern that many have is not only the traditional fears that arise because of their dependence on external credit, but that Western countries are not using debt especially productively and are, in essence, relying on external savings to fuel domestic consumption.

The West relies not only on the credit of the rest of the world to fund its standard of living, but it is also increasingly dependent on importing cheap manufactured goods and energy. The significant savings produced by shifting productive processes to very low labour cost countries, such as China or Vietnam, have helped Western countries maintain their economic well-being at relatively low cost. They have also been able to export pollution through the movement of many industries to developing economies. Effectively, the labour force of the emerging economies has acted as a global deflationary force lowering consumer good prices and freeing up considerable volumes of wealth in Western economies. To some degree, one consequence of this was to allow speculation in property markets that led to the bubbles in the United States and the United Kingdom. Lower prices are contingent on continually delaying the inflationary catch-up as wages rise with development; at some point there is going to be a reckoning. Another central component of Western success has been relatively low energy prices. The United States imports nearly two-thirds of its petroleum needs. Interestingly, China and Japan rely, to an even greater degree, on imported petroleum and natural gas than the United States or Western Europe. Not only is this a significant drain on importing countries' national coffers, but as prices have risen – and are likely to remain high over the longer run – it has undermined an important foundation of Western prosperity. Equally it has also clearly distributed wealth from the importers to those sitting on significant energy reserves. The most notable beneficiary of this process in recent years has been Russia.

War   The apparent vulnerability of America's place in the world, and more broadly that of the Western world, is also a function of some self-inflicted wounds (Mason 2008). It is perhaps one of the most intriguing questions of world politics: how it is that the most militarily and economically powerful country in human history got itself involved in two long, expensive and seemingly intractable conflicts in Iraq and Afghanistan? The difficulties which the United States and its allies are facing in Iraq and Afghanistan are entirely of their own making. They have spent considerable amounts of money, blood and political capital to no great apparent benefit to their interests. Moreover, they have stretched their defence forces very thinly and have provided many in the Islamic world and elsewhere with much fodder for anti-Western sentiment. It is striking just how complicit many feel that the West, particularly the United States, is in its own decline. No less a figure of the American foreign policy establishment than Richard Haass puts it succinctly: 'by both what it has done and what it has failed to do, the United States has accelerated the emergence of alternative power centers in the world and has weakened its own position relative to them' (Haass 2008).

But it is not only the costs of West Asian follies that make many feel that the West may be past its use-by date. There are a number of pressing problems which the institutional structures dominated by the West have, at best, failed to deal with and, at worst, positively contributed to. The two most commonly pointed to are the *1.* shortcomings of the nuclear non-proliferation regime and the potential devastation *2.* of climate change (Emmott 2008; Mahbubani 2008). Others cite the manifest fail- *3.* ings of the range of multilateral institutions as illustrative of the failure of Western *Example* leadership. From the inability of the UN Security Council to resolve long-running conflicts, such as the Israeli–Palestinian dispute, through the ways in which the mechanisms of the multilateral trading system cannot get the United States or Europe to give up their wasteful agricultural subsidy programmes and on to the unrepresentative nature of the World Bank's structure, one sees examples of dramatic shortcoming almost everywhere one cares to look. In essence, the argument goes, the West has been shaping the contours of the international system for well over 100 years and the legacy of that custodianship has some very significant black marks.

Ambition and attributes

One of the most striking elements of the key emerging powers, most particularly the BRICs, is their physicality. In the first instance, they are geographically substantial and are all located in strategically significant parts of the world. They also all have very substantial populations. India and China together account for a third of the world's total population. Brazil has just under 200 million inhabitants while Russia has 140 million. Moreover, all, with the exception of Russia, are projected to grow substantially over the next 50 years. While size, location and demographics are very much the stuff of old-fashioned geopolitics, they continue to have salience in a world of globalisation. While a large population will not guarantee success, as Pape puts it, China, with four times the population of the United States, has the opportunity to create four times the number of knowledge workers (2009: 26). Size provides not only the basic foundation of economic success, it allows opportunities for the benefits of economies of scale and also provides the possibility for national resilience through a greater scope for the domestic economy to withstand international crises. None of these are inevitable, but the benefits of scale continue to matter in world politics. Importantly, the advantage of size is almost entirely in the hands of the emerging economies.

The argument that a new global order is being forged rests not only on traditional power resources that derive from their physical and demographic size, location and the ability to link this with economic success, but also because of an often neglected dimension: will. The emerging powers in the twenty-first century want to be global leaders. They are actively seeking great power status and have the material ability to begin to make good on this ambition. Precisely how they will do this is not clear, but it is unlikely that they will look to the twentieth century for a model. They not only have the capacity to be of great influence, they want to wield this to shape the broader international environment in their favour. Perhaps most importantly, there is a growing confidence that many emerging powers have not just an ambition to guide events, but that they can do so rather better than their erstwhile masters. As Mahbubani puts it: 'any lingering Western assumption that the developed Western countries will naturally do a better job in managing global challenges than any of their Asian counterparts will have to be rethought. An objective assessment would show that Asians are proving to be capable of delivering a more stable world order' (2008: 234).

Implications of the changing distribution of power

So, what will the rise of the rest mean for world politics? On this question there is little consensus in the literature. One central line of thought has been bubbling away ever since the collapse of the Cold War order, but has never quite found the circumstances in the world entirely amenable. The emergence of a raft of new and substantial powers on the stage now makes the case for a multipolar future for the system far more compelling. From this perspective, one sees in the emergence of new members of world politics' top tier a return to the basic pattern of European international relations of the late nineteenth and early twentieth century. Then the interplay of five great powers in Europe was the system's defining feature. Now its unipolarity appears to be breaking down. Indeed, one of the leading advocates of this position argues that the 1999 Kosovo campaign was the high watermark of unipolarity (Bell 2007). The changing distribution of power is most likely to create a world in which the United States still predominates, but one in which it is joined at the top table by China, India, Russia, Japan and the EU (NIC 2008). The range of great powers is thought to provide a clear parallel between the pentarchy of great powers in Europe's nineteenth-century international order. As then the world will see a range of roughly equivalent powers, some are ambitious and rising, while some are declining, with much friction caused by an overlapping and intersecting sets of interests (Emmott 2008). But unlike that time, there will also be a large number of major powers who will be of sufficient heft to affect the character of relations among the top tier, such as Indonesia, Brazil, Nigeria and South Africa.

The coming era's similarity to Europe's Concert period can be comforting because it shows that a stable balance among a multiplicity of powers can be achieved if it is carefully managed. The key to this will lie in the extent to which the powers can restrain the use of force in their foreign policies and forge a consensus not only around their common interests and threats, but also as to the basic purpose of international order. If powers try to build an order based on values, such as democracy or human rights, then instability is more likely. On the pessimistic side, the risk of conflict and major war sparked by the clashes of interests of the great powers is not only real, but significantly greater than it has been in the past 60 years under this scenario. From this perspective, stability in the system will hinge on the ability of the statesmen and women to manage crises and ensure that all the major players have their interests firmly tied into system stability.

In contrast, some see the flux in train in world politics as leading to something new. It is not just that the United States is in relative decline and a range of sizeable new powers are emerging, but also the emergence of major concentrations of non-state power that will recast the system. Where in the nineteenth century the only important power-centres were states and empires, in the emerging world, states are not the only powers that matter. This leads some to argue that the twenty-first century will be the first period of non-polarity in the modern era (Haass 2008). The central premise of this view is that the possibilities opened up by globalisation dramatically reduce the effective power of large states and significantly increase the leverage of non-state actors, whether firm, criminal or activist. A non-polar international system makes the application of diplomacy and statecraft more complex, if not necessarily less effective. In practical terms, non-polarity means that states will have to forge networks or coalitions of other states, institutions and non-state actors to coordinate policy so as to advance their interests. Haass goes so far as to argue that this new world order will make alliances lose much of their salience and instead demand that states become much more nimble and pragmatic in their network building. Non-polarity may be complex, potentially more so than unipolarity, but it is not necessarily more dangerous. With careful diplomacy and a flexible policy attitude, the underlying forces harmonising states and people's interests provide a solid platform on which to build a more stable world order.

Both of these visions of the future assume that the rising powers have chosen both to accept the basic structures of the existing international order and avoid contesting leadership of the system with the United States and the West. A third alternative sees the emerging powers essentially turning their back on the Western-centric world order and moving to establish a new setting for world politics (Barma et al. 2007). As the rising powers have become more affluent, so this view goes, one can already observe them establish trade and investment patterns that do not work through the existing North Atlantic hubs. In diplomatic moves such as the 2006 China–Africa summit, the muscle flexing of the Shanghai Cooperation Organization or the G20 lobby at the World Trade Organization, one sees evidence of this new world in the offing. The non-Western world commands the majority of the world's resources, most particularly its energy deposits, dominates manufacturing, has abundant labour pools and has shown a capacity to compete in complex globalised business operations. While the new powers accept some of the basic principles of the international system, most notably a strict understanding of sovereignty and the centrality of the state, their rise will involve more than just a redistribution of power. There will also be a reconfiguration of influence within the institutional structures of world politics, such as the United Nations (UN) and the multilateral economic institutions. But perhaps more importantly, the values that will underpin a non-Western world order will be decidedly illiberal. In this emerging world, the place of human rights norms, the ability of international institutions to project liberal values beyond borders and the broader practice of sovereignty pooling will be badly stunted. In the new order, so it is argued, states will have their domestic autonomy reinforced and there will be no expectations that they have moral and strategic obligations beyond their borders, save for the fulfilment of contracts. The global financial crisis, from this perspective, will only hasten the arrival of the time when the Western order is essentially sidelined by the diplomatic, trade and cultural networks of the non-Western world.

Western decline in context

Before considering which of these interpretations is most compelling it is worth pausing to reflect upon the underlying claims of Western decline. In the 1970s, many predicted the end of Western dominance after Vietnam and the oil shocks, and again in the 1980s as Japan seemed about to overhaul the United States and many expressed doubts about America's competitiveness (e.g., Kennedy 1987; Rosecrance 1976; Schlosstein 1989). But debates about American decline rapidly became passé (Cox 2001) as a long boom began in 1992 which lasted nearly

15 years, with only a minor downturn in 2001. Its economic success was such that as the twentieth century came to an end, American policymakers and scholars began to debate the extent to which America could or should predicate its global strategy on the assumption of never-ending military supremacy. Indeed, some positively embraced the idea that America was an empire, and a beneficial one at that (see Cox 2003).

Yet, in barely 5 years the United States found itself entrenched in two long-running and expensive wars which revealed starkly the policy limitations of massive military power. Most importantly, the United States was squarely responsible for the worst economic crisis in 70 years. Is Western decline real this time around? Previous experiences with this kind of debate make clear that one should not discount America's capacity to rebound from economic malaise. Nor should one ignore America's retention of significant degrees of structural power. Most obviously, the United States maintains its position as the most important military power on the planet and the only state capable of projecting significant force over any great distance. Equally, its diplomatic networks, cultural appeal and advantages in innovation and research and development investment seem likely to last. No country even begins to approach America's ability to influence other states, nor does the United States appear at all interested in changing its broader place in the world (Lynch and Singh 2008). America's global appeal, as an idea, as a place to live, work and study, has been significantly strengthened by the election of President Obama. Moreover, as some point out, the challengers are considerably weaker than many realise, many have key structural problems in their economies and they appear far too dependent on servicing the needs of wealthy states and societies. Others also point out that while the size and scale of many emerging powers is remarkable, the nature of power is changing so as to negate many of the advantages of scale. Slaughter argues that it is the ability to harness informational networks that will be the key to success in the twenty-first century and because of this the United States is very well positioned to maintain its advantage in world politics (Slaughter 2009).One must also recognise that, to a great degree, economic success in the emerging economies was a function of American prosperity and consumption. Prior to the recent global recession, scholars debated the extent to which the emerging economies were becoming economically less reliant on linkages with the West (becoming 'decoupled' in the policy debate). In the light of recent events, this debate has cooled as it has become clear that the links are still very strong (Rossi 2008). While Western power may be reduced and US influence in world politics will decline to some degree, for the foreseeable future, argue some, the United States will continue to be the most important power in system (Halliday 2009).

There are, however, a number of reasons why one should take seriously the argument that, at the very least, the rest will become significantly more important than in the past. First, the emerging powers are not only gaining in material strength; they are also increasing their influence in the structures of the international system and forging new networks to advance their interests and leverage their strengths (see Beeson, this volume). The international response to the global financial crisis, the G20 grouping of industrial and emerging economics, has not only demonstrated that it is best placed to coordinate international responses to economic crises, it clearly shows the increased leverage that China, India and others have. All of the key emerging powers are conducting activist and multilaterally engaged diplomacy that is intended not only to maximise their domestic economic and modernisation ambitions but also to promote influence. On top of this, the powers are creating new bodies, such as the Shanghai Cooperation Organization, that will further this end. If working through networks and cooperation is the key to success in the coming century, then the adept diplomacy of many emerging powers means they can more than hold their own. To point out that China, India or Russia's economic growth may not be as significant as one thought, and hence their influence curtailed, is to miss a very substantial set of diplomatic efforts that will noticeably enhance their stature and contribute to a significant restructuring of the international system.

Second, the emerging powers want to have a global influence commensurate with their growing size. Where in the past prognostications of transformation of structural change in world politics have fallen short, in part this has been because the named emerging powers have lacked the requisite ambition. For example, during the 1980s, much was made of Japan's remarkable economic success, and that it was likely to compete with the United States for influence at the global level. Not only did Japan's economy slump, among Japanese elites there was little appetite to undertake a diplomatic or strategic leadership position. The contemporary circumstances could hardly be more different. China, India, Russia as well as a number of the smaller emerging powers such as Brazil aspire to be major players in world politics in the coming century. Precisely what they imagine this to involve varies, and there are different assumptions about what being a great power might actually mean in the twenty-first century, but the ambition of the emerging powers and their desire to reshape aspects of the international system to suit their interests and values mean that the current period of transformation will produce greater change than any seen since 1945.

The contemporary context of world politics, most particularly the processes of globalisation – that is, the reduction in the cost imposed by geography on the movement of people, goods, capital and, most importantly, ideas – makes the arguments for system change more convincing. It does so primarily because it works to increase the leverage of smaller scale actors in the international system (Bisley 2007). This will have several important consequences. First, it will help emerging powers accelerate their development and increase the speed with which they will be able to have global strategic heft. Second, it means both that transnational groups such as activists and terrorists can have an influence that belies their small scale but also that the emerging powers will be able to have global influence with fewer resources. This is due to ways in which globalisation enmeshes states interests, reduces the policy-efficacy of traditional forms of state power and promotes the need to collaborate and cooperate among states, peoples and groupings. In the terrorist attacks of 2001 as well as the manifest failings of American policy in Afghanistan, one sees clearly two aspects of this. On that autumn morning a small group, acting on the fringes of international society, caused an aston-ishing degree of psychological trauma to the world's most powerful country. In South West Asia, the application of massive and highly expensive military power is unlikely ever to produce the kind of policy outcomes that the United States desires. While America may maintain its military might, recent events have cast real doubts on the ability of such forms of power to protect national interests at home and advance policy goals abroad. Thus, it is not merely the size and scale of the emerging powers, nor a simple linear projection of their economic success thus far out into the future which means world politics is in for a significant shake-up. Rather it is the ambition of these states, combined with changes in the context of world politics, as well as their material prospects, that mean that over the next 15–20 years it is likely that cast of major players on the stage of world politics will be very different from the past half a century.

The changing landscape of world politics

The twentieth century is widely thought of as an American century. Notwithstand-ing the periodic doubts about American and Western decline, the international history of the past hundred years was in many ways the playing out of America's rise to global predominance, itself the culmination of a longer-running Western global hegemony. Yet, for the first half of that century, the United States remained largely aloof from global affairs. Since 1945 that has all changed, hence the claims about the national character of the century seem to have great purchase. Half a century on and the landscape of world politics is in a state of flux. While the basic features of the international system pertain, the distribution of power within the system, the number of states with influence, the way they advance their interests and, indeed, the content of the norms and principles underpinning the system are all set to change to some degree. American predominance of the kind which was the hallmark of the recent past will have come to an end over the next 30 years. America is likely to remain among, if not still, the most important power in the system; however, the gap between it and the other major powers will have narrowed substantially.

Alongside the United States, India, China, Russia and Japan will comprise the five most important power-centres in world politics. The geographic con-centration of these powers' interests in Asia mean that world politics in the coming years is going to become Asian-centric. Just below them will be a wide array of major powers of substantial size and influence who may lack the where-withal for global influence, but who will nonetheless be of great importance within their regions and will shape the preferences of the five top states. These include the EU, Britain, France, Germany, Brazil, Turkey, South Africa, Nigeria, Australia, Pakistan, South Korea, Egypt and Indonesia. The institutional setting of world politics will remain fraught as the emerging powers' preferences for a more traditional understanding of sovereignty sit uneasily with the growing need to cooperate and coordinate policies. Geopolitical instability will be a hallmark of this new order. In the first instance it will be due to the uncertainty that emerges in times of transitions, as previously damped down security dilemmas resurface. The increases in defence spending in Asia of the past decade or so, prompted by uncertainty about China and India's rise, are indicative of these trends. As this world order becomes more consolidated, instability will become the strategic norm. The world's major powers will all have significant nuclear arsenals, major militaries and, most importantly, overlapping and physically contiguous security and economic interests. In the sea lanes of the Indian Ocean, fossil fuel links from the Persian Gulf, Russia or Central Asia or the choke points of maritime Southeast Asia, the number of powers and the scope of their intersecting interests will make the management of disputes and conflicts more complex and thus less stable. On the economic front a number of trends are evident, although these are ~Economic~ somewhat harder to ascertain. First, increased uncertainty and economic matura- ~changes~ tion are going to produce lower levels of economic growth over the longer run. As India and China mature, they will not sustain their present effervescent rates of growth. How the world will cope with such a slow-down is not at all certain, and recent experiences of growth slow-downs in emerging markets are not at all good. Second, it is more than likely that the openness that has been the hallmark of globalisation – an openness to trade, investment and ideas – will be significantly clamped down. Regulations on investment, protectionism in trade and labour markets and restrictions on population flows are much more likely over the coming years. This means that economic growth is likely to be slower and prices higher than they have been for the past 20 years. It is also likely that inequality will increase and that environmental problems will remain largely unaddressed.

The world appears to be on the cusp of a qualitatively new phase. National interests across the world have never experienced the degrees of connectedness of the present. Yet, the geopolitical and geoeconomic consequences of this appear to be somewhat counter-intuitive as linkages are coupled with increasing uncertainty, rivalry and animosity. The shift from a world dominated by Western power and ideas seems set to be displaced by a broader distribution of power and a dilution of Western ideas. Precisely how this will play out is impossible to determine; however, it is clear that world politics is entering a much riskier and complex context than at any point since the Second World War.

Guide to further reading

Paul Kennedy's work on the rise and fall of great powers (1987) continues to have salience even as the debate over its accuracy now seems somewhat dated. The Goldman Sachs 'BRICs' report was one of the first to alert people to the magnitude of change that appeared to be in train (2001) and so successful it has been that the firm produces regular follow-up publications (Goldman Sachs 2007). The literature assessing change in the structures of the international system is rapidly expanding. Some of the better examples include: the Singaporean diplomat and academic Kishore Mahbubani's argument that the coming century will belong to Asia (2008); the former editor of the *Economist* Bill Emmott's nuanced argument that Asian rivalry will be the central concern for the coming quarter of a century (Emmott 2008); and the editor of *Newsweek International* Fareed Zakaria's *Post-American World* (2008). While Lynch and Singh (2008) argue that, on the contrary, things are unlikely to change a great deal, Bell (2007) argues that we must learn the lessons of the nineteenth century if we are to avoid the redistribution of power causing significant problems. A number of government reports and strategy documents have also contributed to this debate, most notably, National Intelligence Council global trends report (NIC 2008). The leading American policy journals are a main forum for this debate and are the likely venue for cutting-edge assessments in the coming years; these include: *Foreign Affairs*, *Foreign Policy*, *The National Interest* and *Orbis*.

Chapter 5

There *Are* Alternatives: The Washington Consensus Versus State Capitalism

MARK BEESON

Margaret Thatcher famously observed that when it came to organising political and economic activity in the modern world, 'there is no alternative'. By this the former British prime minister meant that economic policies should be market-oriented, and that governments should be small, not 'interfering' with things best left to the private sector. These basic ideas became synonymous with 'neoliberalism' and were hugely influential during the 1980s and 1990s. Indeed, it has taken the recent global financial crisis to undermine the dominance of a policy paradigm that swept across much of the world and was enthusiastically promoted by powerful international financial institutions (IFIs) like the World Bank and the International Monetary Fund (IMF). The core economic assumptions that informed neoliberal ideas were spelled out in the so-called Washington consensus, which became a template for developing economies keen to emulate the wealthy West and the dominant paradigm across much of the world (Harvey 2007).

Yet, even before the authority of neoliberal ideas and the Washington consensus was dealt such a blow by the global economic crisis, not everyone was convinced of their efficacy. Not only were some governments around the world unconvinced about the usefulness of neoliberal ideas for developing countries, but many governments actually preferred alternatives. The remarkable economic development achieved in much of the East Asian region convinced many policymakers and scholars alike that there were potentially different paths to development, ones that were not necessarily based on small governments and market forces. On the contrary, the historical record in East Asia strongly seemed to suggest that the state had a potentially important role to play in fostering and directing the course of development (Kohli 2004).

The possibility that individual countries or even regions might have distinctive ideas about the best ways of organising economic and political activity has led to an increasingly extensive and sophisticated study of different forms of capitalism. While Mrs Thatcher may have been right about capitalism being the dominant global system, and even about the fact that it shares certain key characteristics, there are important and enduring differences between national economies. True, any capitalist system must include certain essential features – a credit-creating financial system; profit-driven, market-oriented commodity production; private ownership of the means of production; the dominance of wage labour; and individualistic, acquisitive behaviour – but there are various ways of organising such activities, and very distinctive ideas about the possible role of the state. Such differing perspectives have been given new importance by both the crisis of what is sometimes called 'Anglo-American' capitalism and the rise of new powers such as China, which subscribe to a very different pattern of economic and political organisation, which some have described as 'state capitalism' (Bremmer 2008).

This chapter explores the ways economic and political life are organised in different parts of the world and examines the neoliberal and state capitalist models, which represent different ends of a spectrum of capitalist organisation. An examination of existing and developing forms of capitalism provides an important insight into the forces that are likely to shape future outcomes around the world. The first two sections of the chapter trace the emergence of various models, before considering their mutual interaction. Finally, it considers the impact of the recent economic crisis on different economic and political systems.

Capitalism in context

There is nothing 'natural' or inevitable about the way economic systems are organised. Indeed, the entire history of the twentieth century was profoundly shaped by a major ideological – and sometimes military – contest between the capitalist and socialist states about the best ways of organising economic activity (Arrighi 1994). As we all know, the capitalists under the leadership of the United States won the Cold War and the rest, as they say, is history. And yet, the legacy of this period lingers on, and the apparent triumph of capitalism, or at least of *liberal* capitalism, is not as complete as it might seem. Even before the recent crisis that shook the free market system to its foundations, one of the largest economies in the world – the People's Republic of China – was still notionally 'communist'. While genuine socialists may be something of an endangered species in China these days, the general point holds: there are fundamental and enduring institutionalised differences in the way economies are organised and these reflect specific historical circumstances and developmental experiences of the countries involved (Haggard 2004).

Clearly, however, ideological contestation is no longer such an important factor in determining how economic systems are organised, and this helps to explain why market-oriented economic systems seem so 'natural' and uncontested (Gamble 2009a). And yet, we cannot understand the continuing uniformity *or* diversity of economic systems unless we recognise the impact that long-running geopolitical confrontation has had on economic development and what we now think of as 'globalisation'. After the Second World War when the US assumed a 'hegemonic' or dominant position in the international system and effectively assumed the leadership of the Western world, American policymakers had the chance to create a new international economic order which broadly reflected their norms and interests (Latham 1997). Crucially, however, there were limits to how far they could impose their preferred economic vision. Not only were some countries outside the capitalist camp, but some of the US's closest allies, such as Japan, persisted with a very different form of capitalism which became something of a model for much of East Asia (Beeson 2007). Even in the US's 'backyard', many Latin American economies adopted policies of import substitution and self-reliance in an effort to promote economic development.

Western Europe also developed quite distinctive economic structures, styles of labour relations and social welfare systems, despite benefitting significantly from US aid and investment in the post-war period (Albert 1993; Epsing-Anderson 1990). Significantly, the degree of international economic integration was much less than it is now – partly because of the limited role played by money markets and cross-border finance, partly because of the underdeveloped nature of multi-national corporations and partly because that was the way national governments wanted it. In what Ruggie (1982) famously called the 'compromise of embedded liberalism', individual governments retained a good deal of policy autonomy, something that tended to entrench national differences. There was also a general enthusiasm for the sort of policy approach developed by the influential British economist, John Maynard Keynes, who advocated a significant role for the state to overcome the crises to which capitalism, by its very nature, is occasionally prone (Hall 1989).

For 20 years or so, what has been described as the 'golden age of capitalism' saw unprecedented levels of economic development, not just in Europe, but in East Asia too. The multilateral economic institutions established under American auspices (see Higgott, this volume) seemed to function well and offer the prospect of continuing growth and stability. However, a number of factors began to undermine the old regime and pave the way for the eventual turn to neoliberal ideas.

The rise of neoliberalism

By the end of the 1960s, Keynesian policies seemed unable to address an emerging series of problems. Economic growth began to decline and unemployment rose. Even more alarmingly, inflation continued to rise despite growing unemployment – an unexpected development that was dubbed 'stagflation'. This was bad enough in itself, but during the 1970s a series of economic 'shocks' further destabilised the global economy. Perhaps the most decisive blow to the old order, though, were the problems experienced by the US, the hegemonic power of the era and, according to one influential school of thought, a vital source of stability for the overall international economic system (Kindleberger 1973).

The US was increasingly unable – or unwilling – to play the role of system sta-
biliser that the old order established at Bretton Woods was based upon and needed
to survive. True, some of the institutions remained outwardly the same, but the
role played by organisations such as the IMF was radically transformed as the US
unilaterally decided to break with the old order of managed exchange rates. This
period ushered in the contemporary system of predominantly 'floating' exchange
rates and trigged an explosion in cross-border financial transactions and the rapid
growth of money markets as financial institutions sought to profit from the new
system. While it may ultimately have been states that oversaw and effectively
authorised this massive growth in the size and importance of private sector activities, the net effect was to sharply increase the power of market forces generally
and financial capital in particular (Helleiner 1994).

Important as these changes in the underlying structures of the global economy
were, of equal, if not greater, significance in the longer term were changes in the
dominant economic discourse or ideology. Two figures loom large in this transformation from Keynesian to monetarist ideas, as the emerging economic paradigm
came to be called. Former US president Ronald Reagan and the aforementioned
Margaret Thatcher did more than anyone to popularise economic ideas that had
hitherto been marginal. The apparent failure of Keynesianism may have provided
the crisis which many observers think is a prerequisite for major, paradigm-
shifting institutional change, but it is also important to recognise how actively
supporters of the free market and monetarism promoted the new order (Cockett
1994).

Monetarism was a radical economic position which argued that inflation – one
of the key problems of the 1970s – was ultimately caused by the money supply. Pioneered primarily by the prominent American economist Milton Friedman,
monetarism essentially claimed that governments were to blame for inflation
because they printed too much money. For a while, at least, monetarism gave a
veneer of intellectual credibility to a wider array of economic, political and social
initiatives that would ultimately be subsumed under the broad rubric of neoliberalism. The new economic ideas were reinforced by similar changes in the study and
practice of politics, as 'public choice theory' with its inherent suspicion of governments and political processes became increasingly influential (Blyth 2002).
The central precepts of the emerging neoliberal paradigm were in part a renewed
emphasis on an older tradition of liberal ideas dating back to Adam Smith which
emphasised the efficacy of market forces and individual self-interest. But, what
was distinctive and ultimately transformative about neoliberalism was not just
a faith in the rationality and entrepreneurial self-interest of individuals, but a
political agenda to bring such potential benefits to fruition.

Much of this policy paradigm is now so familiar that younger readers may find
it difficult to believe that things were not ever thus. But they were different, and
in many places still are. At the centre of the policy paradigm that became synonymous with Margaret Thatcher's reformist government (which was anything
but conservative) was a programme of privatisation and deregulation. Formerly
publically owned utilities like water, gas and the railways were sold off in line

with the idea that the market is the best allocator of resources and provider of services, and that the government's role is simply to act in cases of 'market failure', such as defence or the police – although even security has become increasingly privatised in ways that seemed inconceivable only a decade ago (Mandel 2001).

In reality, however, the 'retreat of the state' has been rather overstated as it still accounts for a good deal of economic activity and social provision. Even more fundamentally, the degree of deregulation is generally equally overstated as it is simply not possible for capitalism of any sort to survive without some form of legal system, regulatory regime and political order. For all the talks about globalisation, there are some things that – thus far, at least – only states can do (see Cerny, this volume).

Capitalism in practice

There are a number of levels at which we can look at different forms of political economy. We can, for example, look at the reactions of different states to the pressures of 'globalisation' as Philip Cerny does in Chapter 1. Alternatively, we can look at the historical development and internal constituent parts of different nationally based systems to try and understand how they differ and why such differences persist despite the apparently universal pressures associated with globalisation. One useful concept in this context is 'path dependency'. Simply put, path dependency suggests that the present and the future are shaped by the past, and, in the absence of powerful systemic shocks, are likely to continue reflecting institutionalised, routine modes of interaction (Pierson 2000). This is a potentially important idea if we want to explain the persistence of different patterns of development and organisation. At the very least, we need to recognise that contemporary states and societies begin from very different starting points and may have profoundly different levels of 'state capacity' and consequent abilities to implement policies – even where policymakers appear to subscribe to broadly similar ideas (see Polidano 2000). Indeed, on closer inspection, therefore, not only are there still significant variations in policy outcomes across nations, but so, too, are the economic visions that inform them.

Even if we accept that the state still plays an important role in determining economic outcomes, there are still very different ways of embedding states in the societies of which they are such an important part. Here the 'varieties of capitalism' literature provides both a comparative snapshot of the different ways capitalism has been institutionalised and a way of conceptualising its component parts. One very broad brush distinction made by many observers is between 'liberal market economies' like those found in places like Britain, the US and Australia (the Anglo-American economies), which are hierarchical and based on competitive markets, and 'coordinated market economies', which make more use of non-market relationships and socially embedded networks to organise economic activities (Hall and Soskice 2001). Coordinated market economies are associated with countries such as Germany and especially Japan, where some of the most basic and important institutions of a capitalist economy, like relations between the banking and business sectors, have been organised quite differently over long periods of time (Zysman 1983).

Despite Japan's current economic problems, for many years it attracted much attention for the astounding rapidity and depth of its industrial expansion, and the distinctiveness of its corporate structures, financial system and labour relations. And yet, it is clear that much has gone wrong in Japan. As a consequence of domestic political failures and sustained external pressure for reform, it finds itself in the worst of all possible world – neither an effective coordinated economy, nor a reformed liberal model (Vogel 2006). Nevertheless, we need to recognise that Japan and many other parts of East Asia retain very different institutional arrangements within their economies, and that these are unlikely to be easily swept away where they enjoy continuing support from politically powerful domestic actors (Lincoln 2001).

For some observers, the difference in the constituent parts of coordinated market economies, where firms may have had close relationships with banks, other firms and even affiliated trade unions for many years, meant that these collective forms of coordination and cooperation were simply incompatible with the neoliberal model (Hollingsworth and Boyer 1997: 24). But it is clear that some of the close links between corporate and financial capital that were such a distinctive feature of the Japanese and German models have begun to unravel and are not as decisive or distinctive as they once were (Katz 1998; Streeck 1997). There is consequently a good deal of debate about the prospects for 'convergence', or the possibility that the international diffusion of ideas about public policy 'best practice' will encourage countries to adopt increasingly similar strategies (Radice 2000; Simmons and Elkins 2004). However, it is also evident that, even in an era of greater transnational economic interaction and political cooperation, not all countries share the same ideational frameworks or assumptions about the way the world works, or about the best ways of responding to global pressures (Drezner 2001).

The possible existence of different economic perspectives becomes especially important at a time when some observers feel that 'the economic credibility of the West has been undermined by the crisis' that has so profoundly affected the US in particular (Altman 2009: 10); this will plainly have major implications for the convergence debate. But even before this most recent crisis, many felt that the model championed by the US and the IFIs was neither appropriate nor useful for countries in very different circumstances and phases of development. On the one hand, it was apparent that every country that had ever successfully industrialised had done so by employing precisely the sorts of 'interventionist' policies that have been actively discouraged by the IFIs (Chang 2002). Without state assistance – even protection – industries were unlikely to develop, much less thrive in a world dominated by the established Western economies. On the other hand, one of the big comparative lessons of the East Asian and Latin American experiences was that the latter had failed to adopt industry policies as effectively or fully as the

East Asians had (Rodrik 2007). In other words, there was, and perhaps still is, a role for government intervention in helping to promote development and the sort of institutional environment within which economic growth might occur. This was not, however, a view shared in much of the West or the IFIs.

The Washington consensus and its critics

Despite a growing recognition that their internal structures and subordinate positions in the global economy meant that many impoverished economies were simply unable to take advantage of the supposed opportunities offered by a liberal economic order (see Kiely, this volume), the IFIs have largely continued to advocate further economic liberalisation. A growing number of critics have drawn attention to the World Bank's and the IMF's failure to relieve poverty and their role in promoting policies closely associated with the interests of the developed rather than the developing world (Peet 2003). Despite this, the IFIs have demonstrated a continuing adherence to a set of policies that have come to be known as the 'Washington consensus'.

Originally coined by the American economist John Williamson (1994), the Washington consensus describes what Williamson called the 'common core of wisdom embraced by all serious economists'. The following were, Williamson and other 'serious', mainstream economists thought, self-evidently the best policies for both developed and developing economies:

- Fiscal discipline;
- Redirection of public expenditure towards basic education, primary health care and infrastructure;
- Tax reform;
- Interest rate liberalisation;
- Competitive exchange rate;
- Trade liberalisation;
- Liberalisation of Foreign Direct Investment flows;
- Privatisation;
- Secure property rights.

While it may be hard to disagree with spending on health and education, other issues are far more controversial, especially given their potential impact on developing economies. The dangers of premature capital account opening had been demonstrated graphically in the East Asian crisis of the late 1990s, while the benefits of free trade were even more moot – something that helps to explain the continuing resistance to their universal adoption in Asia to this day (Beeson and Islam 2005). As Reinert (2007: 119) points out, in a world characterised by radically different levels of economic development and power, 'asymmetric free trade will lead to the poor nation specializing in being poor, while the rich nation will specialize in being rich. To benefit from free trade, the poor nation must first rid itself of its international specialisation in being poor. For 500 years this has not happened anywhere without heavy market intervention.'

In the face of growing criticism, the World Bank in particular has attempted to modify the impact, if not always the underlying ideological thrust, of some of its policies. The so-called post-Washington consensus marks a significant concession on the World Bank's part that markets may not always be perfect and that states may actually have an important role to play in the developmental process (Fine 2003; World Bank 1997). But the IFIs have generally persisted in seeing development as an essentially technocratic project and failed to recognise the inherently political nature of economic activity and reform – something that a belated interest in social safety nets and the need for greater local 'ownership' of the entire process could not disguise (see Higgott, this volume; Higgott 2000).

The suspicion remained that the IFIs were either, at best, under the spell of an especially powerful economic discourse or, at worst, simply the obliging handmaidens of American foreign policy. As radical scholars have never been tired of pointing out, even if many nations have benefitted from the institutional order created at Bretton Woods, the principal beneficiaries have been American-based economic entities and consumers, and the geopolitical agenda of the US itself (Arrighi 1994; Harvey 2003; Panitch and Gindin 2004). That, after all, was the point of being the dominant power: the US, like Britain before it, was able to shape the international system to reflect and further what it took to be in its national interest (Agnew 2005).

Now, however, things are looking rather different. Not only are there renewed doubts about the durability of the Anglo-American model of capitalism, but other countries are beginning, explicitly or implicitly, to challenge the dominance of neoliberalism and American hegemony more generally.

Competing capitalisms

There have always been different types of capitalism. What has attracted attention most recently, however, is the rapid rise to economic prominence of a number of economies whose leaders are not especially enamoured of neoliberalism or the Washington consensus, and who are far from liberal in their political beliefs and practices. Indeed, it has become fashionable to talk about the emergence of 'illiberal' political regimes, which may be ostensibly democratic, but which do not promote political liberty (Zakaria 2003). Of course, there have also always been non-democratic regimes, even if the concept of illiberal democracies is rather new and distinctive. But the rise of illiberal political regimes has attracted increased attention for a number of reasons. First, only a few years ago, some were predicting the liberal democracy would become the dominant paradigm the world over, because it was thought to be most compatible with a global economy and modern political sensibilities (Fukuyama 1992). Although such views may seem wildly optimistic now, there was a good deal of apparently compelling evidence about the seemingly inexorable spread of democratic practices (Huntington 1991).

As we now know, of course, the end of the Cold War did not bring about a process of political convergence or the end of ideological contestation. On the contrary, some believe that globalisation has actually intensified cultural or even civilisational fault lines, making the development of common social, political and economic practices even less likely (Barber 2001; Huntington 1996). Although many of these claims are controversial and highly contested, it is clear that the world is characterised by enduring differences in some of its most basic organ-isational principles and even sources of identity, which some claim account for differential economic outcomes (Mahbubani 2008). In such circumstances, the possibility that the different forms of capitalism might also endure becomes more plausible. What has given this idea even more credibility, however, has been the problems afflicting neoliberal capitalism in the US, and the – until recently, at least – apparently inexorable rise of new centres of economic and political power outside the established 'core' economies.

As Nick Bisley explains in Chapter 4, the last few years has seen a remarkable transformation in the established international pecking order. Although some of the 'new' centres of power in China and Russia have, in fact, long been major players in international affairs, it is striking that countries such as Venezuela are enthusiastically championing values and economic models that are markedly at odds with what has until recently been the relatively unchallenged neoliberal orthodoxy. Even in the Middle East, where the US has some important notional allies, rapidly expanding oil revenues have meant that a number of countries that have been relatively minor players in international affairs have suddenly found themselves enjoying greater influence (Kimmit 2008). The reason for this is sim-ple: rapid industrialisation, rising living standards and all the associated benefits of globalisation have – paradoxically enough – caused a dramatic spike in the price of raw materials, energy and resources, and this has thrust the likes of Russia back into the centre of global power politics (Gat 2007).

Although the recent economic crisis has served as a painful reminder of just how volatile resource prices can be, it is reasonable to assume that they will rise again once recovery occurs. Indeed, competition for finite resources and espe-cially energy looks likely to be one of the defining issues of the twenty-first century. What makes the behaviour of a 'state capitalist' like China so signifi-cant is that it is responding to the challenge of energy provision, not by relying on the market, but by using its own expanding foreign exchange reserves to make strategic investments. The rise of so-called sovereign wealth funds is perhaps the most striking example of the changing economic order and the desire that some states have to take a much more direct role in how national wealth is invested (Gawdat 2008). Such 'neo-mercantilist' strategies are fundamentally at odds with the neoliberal orthodoxy that has become so influential over the last few decades.

And yet, the recent crisis that has done so much to undermine the US economy in particular, and the standing of neoliberal economic policies more generally, has also revealed the continuing importance of the US economy to rest of the world. Some observers had thought that East Asia might have become increasingly 'decoupled' from the US, and less dependent on American growth and consumers, as a consequence. However, much of East Asia was very badly affected by a crisis that rapidly became global, with exports and production levels in some of the former 'tiger' economies like Japan, Taiwan and Singapore being especially hard hit (Bradsher 2009c). However, the US proved no more resilient in the face of economic downturn, and its overall standing as an irreplaceable engine of growth was severely damaged. On the contrary, the US began to be seen as a source of potential threats to the stability of the international economic system. One of the most noteworthy features of the crisis was the Chinese government lecturing the Americans on the unsustainable and irresponsible nature of their economic policies (Edgecliffe-Johnson 2009). Despite the recent economic crisis, therefore, it would seem that – all other things being equal – China could eventually become an alternative economic growth engine for the world economy. Equally importantly, China could also provide an alternative, non-neoliberal vision of how the world could be organised.

The Beijing consensus

If China can continue its remarkable economic expansion – a big if given the impact of the recent crisis and the profound environmental constraints that are emerging as a consequence of breakneck industrialisation and population growth (see Beeson 2009) – then it will overtake the US as the world's largest economy within the next couple of decades. This would be important enough in itself as it marks an epochal shift in the prevailing balance of material power and influence in the international system. However, what makes this especially significant in the context of a discussion of competing forms of capitalist organisation is that China has achieved this historically unparalleled transformation via a very different form of state capitalism. The label that has come to be attached to this model of development is 'the Beijing consensus'. The term was coined by Joshua Cooper Ramo, a former editor of *Time* magazine, to describe the highly pragmatic approach to policymaking that developed in China.

As with the Washington consensus, the Beijing consensus is something of a caricature, but it does capture something essential about capitalism in China that is dramatically different from its counterparts in the West. It could hardly be otherwise. After all, China remains notionally a communist country, and its historical experience imparts a very different pattern of path dependency, one which makes radical change difficult. It was the initial embrace of capitalism inaugurated by Deng Xiao Ping and the effective repudiation of socialism it bought in its wake that marked the really big change. This was a profound transformation of world historical significance as it did, indeed, seem to mark the end of serious paradigmatic competition to capitalism as the primary global form of economic organisation. It is important to remember that until relatively recently, those who embarked upon what was derisively known as the 'capitalist road' were seen as dangerous counter-revolutionaries who had sold out to the West. Since the 1970s, however, there has been steady incremental change towards a market economy and away from the old model of central planning (Naughton 2007).

Deng's famous aphorism – it doesn't matter whether a cat is black or white as long as it catches mice – perfectly captures the spirit of pragmatism that infused his own thinking and which is central to the Beijing consensus. Ramo (2004: 4) suggests that the Beijing consensus is 'defined by a ruthless willingness to innovate and experiment, by a lively defense of national borders and interests, and by the increasingly thoughtful accumulation of tools of asymmetric power projection'. There is a pragmatic commitment to do whatever seems to work – as long as it does nothing to undermine the sovereignty of the nation or the preeminent position of the extant political elite. In other words, the Beijing consensus is about maintaining political control and authority, while simultaneously allowing a pragmatic, but still limited, expansion of the role of the private sector (Huang 2008). However, it is important to recognise that China's expanding capitalist class has shown little interest in pressing for the political reform of a system from which it benefits, and with which it is closely connected (Tsai 2007).

The failure of the capitalist class to push for political liberalism is quite at odds with the European experience and contrary to the expectations of much Western political theory. While this is plainly a challenge for Western scholars, there is a more immediate and practical consequence of China's distinctive pattern of development: China is serving as something of a role model for other countries, especially those that dislike the intrusive and politically difficult demands of the Washington consensus. For many extant political elites, China's experience suggests it is possible to have political development without political reform. China's own increasingly sophisticated diplomacy when combined with its growing importance as a trade partner and source of investment is giving a surprising degree of ideational influence to its model at the expense of the rather discredited Anglo-American alternative (Lampton 2008).

While we might expect a former communist country with high levels of state ownership and involvement in the economy to continue having very different, structurally embedded patterns of organisation, what is novel about China's position is that first, it may eclipse the US as the world's largest economic power, and second it offers an alternative developmental paradigm for those countries unimpressed by the Washington consensus. Given such an environment, we might expect to see the persistence, rather than the end, of differences between capitalist systems.

Concluding remarks

It is, perhaps, particularly foolhardy to try and guess what will happen to the global economy in the middle of what many regard as the greatest economic crisis since the Depression. It is, however, possible to identify some of the factors that will impinge on future outcomes. Most obviously, the status of both the Washington consensus and the US economy as source of inspiration and stability would seem to have been seriously damaged in the short term. It is, of course, possible that the US will bounce back, and it is important to remember that we have witnessed major debates about American decline before and they have proved to be premature, at the very least. Now, however, things really do look rather different. The scale of the crisis currently engulfing the US, its dependence on countries such as China and Japan to fund its deficits, the fact that the crisis is entirely home grown and the need for massive state intervention to bail out a venal and incompetent financial sector suggest that the neoliberal model will be far less influential when order is restored.

Can China, or any other country for that matter, offer a real alternative to neoliberalism that is both sustainable and widely attractive? Probably not, but that may not matter. While it is difficult to see how other countries could easily emulate the direct ideological pressure and moral suasion that the US and the IFIs have attempted to exert over the years, the reality is that many governments will find their policy choices profoundly constrained by the depth of the crisis: paradoxically, there may be no alternative other than some form of statist interventionism. Capitalism of any sort is, in the final analysis, wholly dependent on the state for its survival. In a remarkable historical irony, therefore, if there is convergence occurring in the contemporary international economy, it may be along statist rather than neoliberal lines. In such circumstances the imprint of national political, social and economic structures may become more visible and important, rather than less.

Guide to further reading

There is a large and growing body of literature that charts the different forms of capitalism and the structural sources of their difference. The most influential of these is Hall and Soskice (2001) and the introduction to which provides an excellent summary of the arguments. The recent success of China and India, especially in the face of the relative shortcomings of the US and the UK in 2007–09, has prompted a range of responses. For an overview of different approaches to development which puts an emphasis on historical context and perspective, see Chang (2002). Ramo (2004) coined the phrase 'The Beijing Consensus' and the work is an interesting assessment of the political implications of China's economic strategy. Bremmer (2008) makes the case that world politics is entering an era in which global growth will increasingly depend on economies that have a distinctly statist approach to economic organisation. For a piece that considers the nature of America and China's competition for hegemony in East Asia, see Beeson (2009).

Chapter 6

Democracy and Democratisation

WILLIAM CASE

Democracy, though traceable to the ancients, began to cohere in its modern representative form as a way to organise political life during the European Enlightenment. It has spread around the world, however, through what Samuel Huntington (1991) identified as 'waves'. A first wave, beginning during the nineteenth century and extending into the twentieth, enveloped much of Europe. But it lost ground during the 1920s–30s amid the rise of totalitarian ideologies. A second wave coincided with the break up of empires after the Second World War, bringing democracy to Africa and Asia. But during the 1950s–60s, it retreated before military coups and modernising bureaucracies. Beginning in the mid-1970s, though, democracy surged anew, cumulating in the third wave.

The third wave of democracy began in Portugal, Spain and Greece and then ranged swiftly into South America. During the late 1980s, 'people power' in the Philippines also encouraged democracy's 'snowballing' across South Korea and Taiwan. At the end of the decade, the fall of the Berlin wall and the end of the Cold War enabled Eastern Europe to democratise, followed by parts of sub-Saharan Africa and Asia. Thus, by the early 1990s, the number of democracies had so increased that for the first time, a majority of the world's countries and people lived under them. By 2006, nearly two-thirds of the world's countries could be classified as democratic (see Diamond 2008b: appendix). Only China and Russia, Central Asia and Arab societies seemed to pose major holdouts. In this context, Francis Fukuyama (1992) was moved to proclaim the 'end of history', arguing that with Communism having vanished, democracy was now widely recognised as the only legitimate type of regime. Accordingly, during the late twentieth and early twenty-first centuries, democratisation arose as a key issue in world politics.

The aim of this chapter is to survey some major aspects of this remarkable reorganisation of political life. Where once military governments, single-party systems and personal dictatorships had prevailed, democratic institutions now often stood. Analysis begins by briefly rehearsing two major ways of understanding democracy. It then outlines some of the preconditions for democracy that have been identified, as well as the motivations possessed by different social groups for seeking democratic change. Some obstacles will also be enumerated before turning finally to the transitional pathways along which democratic change takes place.

This chapter also evaluates the extent to which democracy makes any real difference in the lives of ordinary citizens. Do participation, representativeness, policy responsiveness and accountability grow stronger under democratic conditions? Or has globalisation shifted decisional power away from governments to such a degree that democracy organised at the national level loses relevance? And as power gravitates to multilateral institutions and transnational corporations, are there any prospects for democratising politics at the global level? Finally, the chapter examines the prospects for what Diamond (2008b: ch. 3) describes as a 'democratic recession', asking whether democratic advances may be undone by authoritarian reversals and upheavals.

What is democracy?

Modern democracy has principally been understood by theorists in two competing ways: substantive and procedural. Substantive democracy refers to conditions of equality between socio-economic classes, ethnic communities, genders and other forms of identity and affiliation, culminating in a literature that finds expression in social, economic and industrial democracy. In this view, policies and programmes that give rise to social equality take precedence over institutions and procedures. By contrast, the notion of procedural democracy puts greater emphasis on civil liberties and competitive elections. In considering which interpretation is more analytically fruitful, Burton et al. (1991: 2) remind us that social equality may be a precondition for democracy, or it may follow as a policy outcome, but equality and democracy are not the same thing. Indeed, they contend that the conflation of these two aspects can cause analytic confusion. As one example, they observe that the former German Democratic Republic, in its commitments to social justice, distributed wealth relatively equitably, yet could hardly be considered democratic. Accordingly, scholars of the study of transitions generally agree that democracy is best understood in procedural ways. Only in the more vexed analysis of democracy's consolidation has an insistence on equality in outcomes returned.

In conceptualising democracy in procedural ways, O'Donnell and Schmitter's (1986) classic text distinguished between political liberalisation (civil liberties) and democratisation (competitive elections). They thus drew upon Robert Dahl's (1971) earlier notion of the liberal and inclusionary elements of what in the real world he elaborated as 'polyarchal democracy'. Civil liberties include free speech, press and assembly, enabling citizens to communicate freely and then organise in pursuit of their interests and causes. Elections, meanwhile, must be free, fair, regularly held and meaningful, enabling governments to be held accountable. These contests are free in that the voting franchise is inclusive. They are fair in that incumbent government eschews any partisan use of state agencies, facilities and funding, ensuring competitiveness. They are held regularly within fixed time frames, recorded in a constitution. And they are meaningful in that elected chief executives and legislators control the state apparatus, not cabals of generals, bureaucrats and sundry economic elites nestling unaccountably in 'reserved positions' (Schedler 2002: 41).

Democratic preconditions and motivations

Democracy requires that participants strike a fine balance between competitiveness and restraint. In a vibrant democracy, political parties, civil society organisations and social movements compete over institutional positions and policy outcomes, though not at all costs. Winners must display tolerance, while losers prepare to compete another day. This 'restrained partisanship' led scholars to canvas the preconditions that might underpin democracy's complex sets of institutions and procedures. These included appropriate historical legacies, past experience with democracy, social structures, developmental levels, institutional designs and cultural outlooks. According to Myron Weiner (1987), specifically British colonial experience, in exposing indigenous elites to the rule of law through new bureaucratic structures and to restrained competitions through elections, amounted to a 'tutelary model' that greatly favoured democracy. But as Diamond (2008b: 155) recounts, this model was often countered by a vice-regal tradition, involving 'an ugly, racist system of exploitation and domination that was intrinsic to the very nature of colonial rule'. Thus, if India and Jamaica have internalised enough British common law values and electoral traditions to remain democracies, Pakistan, Burma, Malaysia, Singapore and many African countries once part of the empire have not.

In examining the social structures deemed necessary for democracy, theorists have primarily examined socio-economic classes and ethnicity. In Britain and the United States, where private capital took the lead in fomenting development, capital-owning classes, in seeking to defend their property rights against state predation, sought to strengthen their resistance through elected parliaments. This echoed Barrington Moore's (1966) stirring dictum, 'no bourgeoisie, no democracy'. According to modernisation theorists, however, urban middle classes were more crucial. Uplifted by general prosperity and made confident by their business and professional dealings, they sought to extend their independent decision making from their private pursuits to political life. This led them to support political parties and join civil society organisations in ways that enabled them to hold governments accountable. And yet, the historical record equally shows that where these have been dependent upon the state for economic benefits and protection from the lower classes that vastly outnumber them, they can oppose democratic change. This is particularly so in countries that came late to industrialisation. One observes the recent actions of middle-class demonstrators in the Philippines and Thailand, cohering respectively in 'People Power II' and the People's Alliance for Democracy (PAD) which, in criticising populism and poor governance, both succeeded in ousting elected governments, actions funded by business magnates, winked at by the military and sanctioned by the courts. Even students can be unreliable democrats, with Huntington (1991–92: 604) casting them as the 'universal opposition', stridently criticising any regime in place, whatever its tenor. Accordingly, Eva Bellin (2000), in charting the varying political preferences and behaviours of these classes, has labelled them at most as 'contingent democrats'.

In the view of Rueschemeyer et al. (1992), then, it is the industrial working class that is the most reliable democratising agent. Organised into powerful trade unions and seeking the representation in government that can improve labour welfare, workers drive democracy by achieving democratic concessions from the government and the capital-owning classes who often collude with one another. However, though the working class might sometimes operate along these lines, it seems just as easily drawn into patterns of top-down populism and corporatism, as well as protectionist strategies, that can as easily support authoritarian rule. Thus, if organised labour helped to advance democratisation in the nineteenth-century Europe, it has since been identified also with the authoritarian rule of Peron in Argentina and Ahmadinejad in Iran. Further, labour is today often disorganised, dispersed throughout global production networks, rather than concentrated in specific countries, greatly reducing its effectiveness.

Ethnicity too lacks any straightforward impact on democracy's prospects. In societies in which multiple ethnic communities reside, Huntington (1984) argued, democracy was stronger due to the dense mosaic of impenetrable ethnic redoubts and cultural baffles that resisted any systematic intrusiveness of state power. The surprising persistence of democracy in India, notwithstanding its low level of development, is often attributed in part to its extraordinary ethnic, linguistic and religious complexity (see, e.g., Kohli 2001). And yet, Rabushka and Shepsle (1972), in dispensing with more commonly received wisdom, argue that ethnic divisions and conflict can lead to the breakdown of democracy, citing the cases of Malaysia and Lebanon as evidence. Arend Lijphart (1969) and Benjamin Reilly (2001) have showed how communal peace can be preserved, by painstaking constitutional engineering, electoral innovations and power-sharing processes. But in so reducing competitiveness in order ethnically to apportion state power and positions, questions arise over how democratic the regime then is.

A more powerful thesis, then, first proposed by Seymour Martin Lipset (1959), focuses on developmental levels and democratic outcomes. Put simply, it contends that as societies grow richer and better educated, hierarchical statuses and patterns of deference begin to break down, encouraging social groups, especially the middle class, to become more participatory. Usually parsed as modernisation theory, this expectation, along with its more contemporary refinements, has been enormously influential. In some studies, even necessary average per capita income levels have been specified. And yet, even though most rich countries are indeed democracies, some, like Singapore and the Gulf states, are not. Rapid economic growth, generating a kind of performance legitimacy, and petroleum exports, generating revenues that sooner empower the state than social forces, can dampen pressures for democratic change, even in rich countries. At the same time, though in a much cited study, Przeworski et al. (1996) argued that democracy is more likely to persist in rich countries than poor ones, we note its lengthy practice in places like India, Botswana and Mali.

Accordingly, the debate over economic development and democracy has grown convoluted. If development's causality is frequently brittle, it may be, then, that directionality cuts the other way. With democracy freeing the participatory impulse of citizens, its liberal elements may carry over into private entrepreneurship and innovation, helping fuel economic development. But this argument stands in contrast to the post-war record of industrialising gains in Japan, Korea, Singapore and, in some measure, Taiwan, documented in an immense literature on state-led strategies and industrial policies (e.g., Wade 2004).

Given the ambiguities that haunt the search for democracy's preconditions, most theorists have abandoned it. To be sure, national wealth often helps. And hyper-nationalism, radical Islamism and state oil revenues usually do not. But there are so many exceptions. With democracy often failing to appear in settings where it might be predicted, and in other cases taking root where it would not be, during the third wave, much scrutiny shifted to elite-level preferences, bargaining and outright contingency.

How does democratic change take place?

With structures so indeterminate, democracy theorists like Dankwart Rustow (1970), O'Donnell and Schmitter (1986) and Burton and Higley (1987) shifted attention to national leaders and elites. They addressed the ways in which elites interacted with one another (whether in restrained or warlike ways), appealed to their followers (either galvanising or under-mobilising them), while giving shape to the directionality of structural forces. As O'Donnell and Schmitter (1986: 19) intoned, 'there is no transition whose beginning is not the consequence – direct or indirect – of important divisions within the authoritarian regime itself.'

As comparativists turned to the dynamics of democratisation, an immense literature appeared that came collectively to be labelled transitology (Schmitter 1995). And focusing intently on inter-elite relations, a new vocabulary emerged that included hardliners and softliners in the authoritarian coalition and minimalists and maximalists standing in opposition. Further, in tracing the ways in which the coalition unravelled, popular upsurge took place, and democratic change unfolded researchers-identified patterns of top-down 'transformation' (as in Spain and Brazil), bottom-up replacement (Portugal, the Philippines and Indonesia) and a more evenly negotiated process that Huntington termed 'transplacement' (Korea).

In emphasising contingency, this approach seemed to its detractors to offer no more than description. But some constraining conditions were gradually discovered. Most notably, the pathways by which democratic change took place were tracked back to the distinctive forms of authoritarian rule from which they had emerged. Using a simple typology of military governments, single-party systems and personal dictatorships, comparativists identified military governments as most likely to undertake top-down transformations (Geddes 1999). With generals abhorring the politicisation of their institution that so eroded professionalism and corporate élan, they were often keen to cede state power and return to the barracks. Thus, where they could claim some success while in power, deepening industrialisation while eliminating social 'cancers', they initiated processes of pre-emptive transformation, then negotiated from a position of strength, giving rise to extensive 'pacting' through which to gain amnesties while retaining control over selected state enterprises and budgets. On this count, Spain's transformation during the mid-1970s, mediated by the prime minister and encouraged by the king, was viewed as paradigmatic (Gunther 1991). But where their records were disastrous, as in Greece and Argentina, humiliated by defeat in war, militaries were pushed from power much more briskly. In these cases, contention arose over any amnesties that had been granted, leading in some cases to generals being jailed.

By contrast, under personal dictatorships, with strongmen having so personalised the state apparatus and most aspects of economic life, they had no counterpart to the barracks to which they might safely retreat. In the case of the Philippines, as Mark Thompson (1995) has shown, Marcos possessed no refuge outside the state, and hence refused to negotiate any withdrawal from power. Under personal dictatorships, then, it is only through replacement, made manifest in people power, that democratic change can take place.

Finally, single-party systems, while resilient, lack the coercive capacity of militaries. Yet where economic crisis or societal pressures loom large, they may be willing to cede state power. Further, their willingness to do this may be increased by the fact that in contrast to personal dictatorships, they possess party organisations that may find a stake in any democratic regime of multiparty elections that follows. Thus, for some Communist parties in Eastern Europe, as well as the Institutional Revolutionary Party in Mexico, the democratisation of politics did not amount to the end of world. It seemed, then, that single-party systems most often underwent democratic change through the process of transplacement described above.

But despite these constraining conditions and identified pathways, due to the continuing centrality of contingency the analytic focus on elites was increasingly criticised for the modest levels of explanatory power that it was able to generate. Accordingly, attention began finally to shift from elites to the institutions and structures in which their statuses were anchored, encouraging new and deeper study of militaries and dominant parties. Moreover, as democracy's third wave began to weaken, comparativists observed that in some cases, military officers had been socialised in ways that enabled them to perpetuate their regimes, once understood as transient, over long periods of time, as in Burma (Kyaw 2009). Single parties too could maintain their dominance for long periods if they effectively controlled patronage, as the United Malays National Organization (UMNO) has done in Malaysia. Transitology, then, while once having been expected to flow logically and seamlessly into the study of democracy's consolidation ('consolidology'), shifted instead into new enquiry over authoritarian durability.

But even where transitions to democracy took place and seemed likely to consolidate, scrutiny shifted from elites to the much more varied field of civil society. In O'Donnell and Schmitter's early formulation popular upsurge, a sudden spike in mass-level activism and street protest only took place in the wake of the breakup of the authoritarian coalition. As Diamond (2008b: 102) has noted, civil society organisations had, in this view, to be 'resurrected'. But this begged the question of why elites, where processes of transformation had taken place, would feel so pressured as to consent to democratic change. Further, who were the minimalists with whom softliner elites would negotiate in a process of transplacement? And where elites were swept clean away through a process of replacement, from whence did these pressures arise? Thus, as recognition grew that the dynamics by which transitions to democracy took place were far wider and more complex than had been believed, new attention was given to civil society organisations. In particular, scholars focused on the ways in which they coordinated direct action, increased political education and levels of mobilisation, and then, in turning to political society, filled the interstices between opposition parties and politicians in ways that enabled them to form more effective front organisations (Weiss 2006).

In addition, while the study of democratic transitions had long been conducted in domestic arenas, new attention was now given to external factors. During democracy's second wave, perhaps the most enduring transitions took place in Germany, Italy and Japan through a process of conquest and imposition by Allied countries. But in the third wave, the democratisation of Grenada and Panama through US military action remained vastly overshadowed by the far more numerous and momentous cases in which internal dynamics were weightiest. In almost all cases of democratic transition, then, most attention was given to patterns of inter-elite and elite–mass relations.

But if cases of democratisation by imposition were rare during the third wave, other forms of exogenous pressure grew in importance. In particular, during the late 1970s, the United States began to scale back its support for dictators with whom it had allied in waging the Cold War. This new turn in foreign policy aims was taken first during the presidency of Jimmy Carter, then accelerated under Ronald Reagan. Across the developing world, where governments demonstrated greater respect for civil liberties, human rights and electoral contestation, the United States began to dispense developmental aid, principally through its agency, USAID. Governments that resisted were confronted by various economic sanctions, usually involving trade and investment restrictions. Further, while the German government had long supported party-building programmes in developing countries, it was joined now by some other Western countries in undertaking broader programmes of explicit democracy promotion. As its mainstay agency, the US Congress formed the National Endowment for Democracy (NED) in 1983 which, together with its various subsidiaries, provided financial support and training for NGOs, political parties, newspaper publications, judiciaries and teams of election monitors. British, Dutch, Scandinavian and Taiwanese organisations have provided much the same. Thus, as elections began to take place in ever more national settings, large numbers of monitors were recruited by these democracy promoting agencies in order to evaluate freeness and fairness.

In addition, as more countries democratised, they seemed to encourage democratic change in other places, helping give impetus to the third wave identified by Huntington. Through what were variously characterised as demonstration effects, snowballing and neighbourhood effects, politics were democratised with surprising speed across South America. By the 1990s, only Paraguay lagged behind. One notes also the ways in which democracy activists in Korea had learned from the strategies adopted by their counterparts in the Philippines, bringing pressures to bear that finally disposed the government to bargain. Even more dramatically than in South America, then, the Korea and Philippine cases showed that political learning could drive democratic change more rapidly than structural forces such as developmental levels and global economic positioning.

However, just as doubts had accumulated over the importance of preconditions and elite-level preferences for democratisation, so too have they begun to mount over the potency of external factors. If war-time imposition succeeded in several important country cases after the Second World War, the recent effort led by the United States in Iraq, in generating what most observers would regard as unacceptable costs, appears to have grievously retarded democracy's advance. Even the US government, in the last years of the Bush presidency, retreated from its democratising mission to a more realist posture in its conduct of foreign policy.

The impact of less-coercive forms of democracy promotion has also been disappointing, with efforts to reform institutions and procedures often being either distorted or repulsed by many governments, especially in Russia under Vladimir Putin and in Central Asia under a variety of autocrats (see Carothers 2006). Indeed, election monitoring agencies have grown so fearful of raising the ire of the governments at whose pleasure they operate that they routinely overlook many polling transgressions, announcing blandly that despite any cheating, the government would have anyway been returned to office. Further, governments in countries like Burma and Sudan, in seeking the international investments and markets that generate the patronage required for their survival, have turned their backs on Western countries that threaten sanctions over undemocratic behaviour, forging ties instead with an uncritical China. What is more, even the neighbourhood effects that seemed to weigh so heavily across South America have had little lasting effect in regions like Southeast Asia. With Association of Southeast Asian Nations (ASEAN) bound together by its operating principle of non-interference, people power in the Philippines affected South Korea than it did in the neighbouring Southeast Asian countries. And if the *reformasi* movement that brought democratic change to Indonesia during the late 1990s was emulated by some civil society organisations in Malaysia, it ultimately amounted to little, with Mahathir warding off pressures on his authoritarian rule. In this context, Thomas Carothers (2002), a leading analyst and practitioner of democracy promotion, pronounced the 'end of the transition paradigm'. Larry Diamond (2008b: 106), in evaluating the impact of international forces more generally, has remained more optimistic, but contends that they can only contribute to democratic change when other internal factors are strongly in its favour.

Does democracy make a difference?

Even where democratic change has taken place, questions are regularly raised over whether it makes any difference in ordinary people's lives. On one level, democracy's worth seems clear. In respecting the civil liberties of individuals and social groups, while registering the choices of citizens through elections, democracy allows for what is commonly cast as popular sovereignty, therein raising human dignity in ways that authoritarian regimes cannot. Further, in its respect for due process and human rights, democracy spares citizens the arbitrary detention and extrajudicial killings that so frequently characterise coercive authoritarian rule. And democracy may, in concrete ways, advance 'human security' too. On this score, Amartya Sen has argued that under democracy, famine is less likely to occur, owing to the feedback loops that readily communicate to governments information about shortages and mass-level discontent (see Diamond 2008b: 28). Finally, at the global level, democracy may contribute to more ordinary security. Although the relationship is hardly ironclad, the record suggests strongly that countries that are democratic, in their liberal commitments and belief systems, are less likely to wage war against one another than are those that are not. In this context, an academic subfield of democratic peace theory has flourished. Accordingly, there appear to be good reasons for large majorities of citizens, when responding to surveys administered in many dozens of societies, regularly declaring their preference for democracy over authoritarian rule.

And yet, in the real world, democracy too often lags behind these ideals. As one example, during the prime ministership of Thaksin Shinawatra in Thailand, though the government was popularly elected, press freedoms were truncated through harassment of journalists and ever more concentrated patterns of media ownership. Human rights were also seriously violated through the killings of alleged drug traffickers and Muslim separatists, actions taken by security forces that were welcomed by large numbers of Thai citizens. Further afield, the democratisation of politics has done less to moderate corrupt practices than to decentralise them, with payments and vote-buying fanning out now from the national leader, his or her family members and cronies, top bureaucrats and generals to the political party leaders, legislators on multiple tiers and the ordinary voters that democracy has empowered. Indeed, Ross McLeod, in writing about the dispersion of corrupt practices across Indonesia today, refers to Suharto's period of authoritarian rule as a 'better class of corruption'. Thus, even as democratisation takes place, little may be achieved in terms of advancing social equality.

Democracy theorists responded, then, with a new research agenda on consolidation, trying to weave notions of regime longevity and policy performance into their conceptualisation. Lengthy investigation was thus conducted into requisite elite-level attitudes, supportive mass-level outlooks and appropriate institutional design, generating prolonged debate over the merits of presidential and parliamentary systems (see, e.g., Linz 1990; Stepan and Skach 1993). But with theorists unable to reach consensus over what consolidation involved, much less over which sets of factors would most favour it, these debates were gradually abandoned. In their wake, a more focused agenda has set in addressing democracy's quality. In recognising that the records of democracies vary greatly, theorists now examine a variety of aspects, including rule of law, popular participation, representativeness, policy responsiveness and accountability (e.g., *Journal of Democracy* 2004). They even began to rank different democracies through 'audits', identifying abuses that have, in some cases, grown so great that they have been reclassified as undemocratic. For example, politics in the Philippines, the incubus of people power, as well as in Thailand, re-democratised in 2007, have been assessed by Freedom House (2009) as 'partly free'. And yet, though an evaluative framework has been taking shape, doubts persist over whether it will be able to show how these categories affect each other, whether in mutually reinforcing or negating ways, or even specify the clear thresholds necessary for measurement.

Can democracy be globalised?

Debates over democracy and democratisation, though feverishly conducted by theorists and practitioners, appear in the view of some analysts to be quite misplaced. Put simply, even if democracy has made gains across many countries, it has at this level also grown more irrelevant. To be sure, democratic ideas have spread round the world. But so too have investment capital, production chains, trading networks and regulatory norms. And the price for most countries, particularly in the developing world, that participate in these activities – attracting investors, entering export markets and finding assistance amid economic shocks – is to cede much of their policy autonomy to far-off decision makers, in particular, transnational corporations and multilateral institutions. But even in the Western countries in which the organisations are usually headquartered and to which they might seem beholden, governments have lost much autonomy to globalised entities. Thus, as citizens exercise their civil liberties and vote in elections at the national level, the value of their participation and seeking accountability in this way is diminished in tandem with the capacity of governments to demonstrate responsiveness.

Moreover, in combating the cross-national problems that more globalised activities create, many more international or regional organisations must probably be formed. Many observers have thus noted the need for regulatory agencies whose authority effectively supersedes that of particular governments in order to deal with environmental ills, diseases, international crime and the contagion of financial crises (see, e.g., Drezner 2007). But as multilateral institutions like the International Monetary Fund, the World Bank and the World Trade Organization (WTO) are joined by an array of new regulatory agencies, questions mount over how to maintain popular sovereignty in this new and complex setting.

Organisations and movements of what is sometimes called global civil society have taken up this call, sometimes through direct action, mounting mass protests at the venues where multilateral institutions have met. And in organising their activities, these elements have been greatly aided by communications technologies that have bolstered civil society at the national level, in particular, the Internet and mobile telephony. In an effort to foster transparency, the WTO has responded by uploading copious amounts of information about its internal workings onto its websites. Its officials argue too that they are responsive to the national governments that have selected or vetted them – and that these governments are in turn accountable to their citizens. But plainly, this chain of democratic accountability is too extended and disarticulated to foster any meaningful sense of mass-level participation.

Mechanisms for increasing responsiveness and accountability among multilateral institutions and regional agencies have been recently canvassed. David Held (1999: 106–7), perhaps the leading scholar on this front, envisions the nation-state withering away, for 'states can no longer be ... the sole centers of legitimate power within their own borders.' To be sure, in this vision, states are diminished, but do not disappear. Rather, they are 'relocated' within an overarching transnational framework of democratic law in which people possess 'multiple citizenships'. Under what Held has called 'cosmopolitan democracy', people retain or even enhance their political participation at the local and national levels on relevant issues. But in responding to today's transnational challenges and institutions, they participate increasingly also in global politics, primarily through global civil society. Held (ibid.: 108) thus lauds the 'new voices' that were heard at the Rio Conference on the Environment, the Beijing Conference on Women and the Cairo Conference on Population Control. He is less clear on how accountability might be obtained through voting and elections, though cites the representativeness of the United Nations as a 'normative resource' and 'innovative structure which can be built upon'.

But such schemas still strike many as quite utopian. That democracy's viability should wither at the level of nation-states offers no assurance that it will be recovered among international financial institutions and regional agencies. Indeed, for Robert Dahl (1999: 21–3), the size and complexity of even the EU, let alone global institutions, increase the need for delegation so much that mechanisms for participation, representativeness and accountability grow unacceptably stretched. He thus sketches a dilemma in which, while 'a world government might be created in order to deal with problems of universal scope ... the opportunities available to the ordinary citizen to participate effectively ... would diminish to the vanishing point.' On this count, Dahl notes too that even in established democracies, citizens are rarely able to influence their government's conduct of foreign affairs. And so, he asks, 'What grounds have we for thinking ... that citizens in different countries engaged in international systems can ever attain the degree of influence and control over decisions that they now exercise within their own countries?' And how might even the 'general good' be determined when democracy is extended across countries and regions, vastly increasing the 'diversity of interest, goals, and values among the people in the unit'? Accordingly, though democracy has made important advances in the world for the past quarter-century, it may now have reached a plateau. It may even be falling into reverse, unable to cope at the global level, while quietly being undermined from within.

Democratic recession?

In its analysis, as well as its real-world practice, the headiest days of the third wave appear to have passed. Indeed, some of the most insightful work being conducted today addresses the question of authoritarian durability. To be sure, where democratisation has taken place, it has seldom broken down. And even where reversals have occurred, as in Turkey in 1980, Fiji towards the end of the decade, Peru in 1992, several African countries during the 1980s–90s, Thailand in 1991 and 2006 and Pakistan in 1999, re-democratisation has usually followed. Even so, Larry Diamond (2008b: ch. 3) argues that during the first decade of the twenty-first century, the world slipped deeply into democratic recession. It is not just that the pace with which new democracies have been appearing has slowed. More gravely, in many cases where democratic change had been unfolding, it has stalled or even been rolled back, yielding cases of low-quality democracy, or, where it has dropped below critical thresholds, has become what has been described as electoral authoritarianism (Schedler 2006).

Under this latter regime type, governments regularly hold elections, offering a snapshot of propriety on election day. But they have truncated civil liberties beforehand, thereby hindering opposition parties from contesting effectively. Opposition parties are permitted to organise, set up headquarters, raise funds, select their own leaders and candidates and then recruit cadres and at least modest constituencies. But they are also prevented from reaching wider audiences by the government's control over most media outlets; they are restricted in circulating their own party publications; and they are barred from organising mass rallies, even during campaign periods. Opposition members who persist are often targeted with crippling defamation suits, the rescinding of government contracts and bank loans or even arrest. Further, on the electoral dimension, outcomes may be skewed through delineation exercises that involve extreme malapportionment, gerrymandering and distorted forms of multimember districting. Meanwhile, government candidates may make partisan use of state resources in campaigning, practices winked at by a weak election commission. In these circumstances, opposition parties are able to articulate the grievances of their followings, though only in muted ways. And they are able to win enough legislative seats that they gain a toehold in parliament, though never so many that they can replace the government.

Thus, many governments have borrowed some of the elements of democracy in order substantially to avoid it. Recognising the legitimacy that democracy has come to attain, they have mostly abandoned the crude military rule, single-party systems and personal dictatorships that once proliferated. They have turned instead to strategies of electoral authoritarianism, gracing their multiparty elections, however distorted, with some legitimating cover. As the long-time prime minister of Malaysia, Mahathir Mohamad, used to say to his critics, 'If you don't like me, defeat me in my district' (quoted in Case 2002: 7). The offer, of course, was disingenuous, for there was little prospect of turning Mahathir's constituents, coddled with patronage, against him. Mexico under the Institutional Revolutionary Party, Russia under Putin, Singapore under the People's Action Party and Cambodia under Hun Sen offer other prominent examples of this regime type, one which is probably the most subtle, yet serious challenge to democracy's deepening.

To be sure, even under conditions of electoral authoritarianism, governments have, in underestimating the intensity of societal discontents, sometimes been 'stunned' by the results of the elections they have held. Diamond (2008b) records that one in seven of the governments organising elections along these lines have eventually lost. Moreover, these defeats sometimes set democratic change in motion, amounting to yet another pathway of transition that theorists have labelled democratisation-by-election. Perhaps the best-known example involves the Philippines, where Marcos's attempt to steal the election triggered popular upsurge and replacement.

But even after democratisation takes place in this way, some social groups, especially those based in new urban middle classes, sometimes grow alienated with the democracies that follow. Associating democratic politics with poor governance, stagnant economies, unfunded populist distributions and diminished personal security, these groups may resort to upsurge again, though this time to oust elected governments. Through street actions that have been variously designated as 'rally democracy', 'muscular democracy' and the 'People Power II' noted above, citizens have forced governments from power in the Philippines, Thailand and at the local level in South America. Moreover, in doing this, they have sometimes won the sanction of disaffected elites in the legislature, the courts and, most crucially, the military. This has done little, however, to bolster democracy's quality or policy performance.

Thus, as 'reform fatigue' sets in, increasing numbers of citizens may grow more attuned to the 'rationalized' authoritarianism that China, in having perpetuated several decades of rapid industrial expansion, and Russia, more recently revitalised by commodities exports, are sometimes understood to practice. Fired with economic prowess and nationalist pride, these countries appear to have rediscovered the fact that performance legitimacy, so long as it lasts, can trump the political legitimacy of low-quality democracies.

The standing of democracy has also declined in tandem with that of the United States, its foremost advocate on the international scene. It is deeply ironic that during the presidency of George Bush, a tenure marked by a sharp increase in democratising commitments, the valuation of democracy around the world was eroded by the ineptitude with which these ambitions were pursued. Most signally, in response to Middle East's pervasive authoritarianism and the rise of religious terrorism, US policymakers came to define democratisation in national security terms. But with the invasion of Iraq marking an escalation from strategies of benign democracy promotion to democracy-by-imposition, the United States elicited quite unintended consequences. Put simply, as the mayhem in Iraq worsened, the United States found its political and military prestige diminished, while the very authoritarianism and terrorism that it had hoped to roll back gained strength. In this context, the United States returned to an earlier realist posture, seeking allies in its 'war against terror' among the region's autocracies, most notably, Saudi Arabia and Egypt. It also became more authoritarian itself, weakening civil liberties at home, while engaging overseas in detention without trial, 'extraordinary rendition' and interrogation techniques amounting to torture. And its change in attitude seemed hastened too by the fact that where democratic change had taken place in the Middle East, the elections then held in settings like Lebanon and Gaza were often won by Islamist parties and hardline movements. Hence, the fillip given to democracy given at the end of the Cold War seems now to have vanished amid new kinds of international conflict.

In late 2008, US prestige took another blow, with a global financial crisis traceable to dealings on Wall Street calling the sustainability of unbridled capitalism into question. Thus, even as President Bush left office and the war in Iraq subsided, US commitments to democratic change were now overshadowed by concerns over economic recovery. To be sure, the well-being of industrial workers everywhere, from the factories of the United States and Europe to the exporting countries of Asia, was put at risk by the crisis. But it was the threat to the livelihoods of America's corporate chieftains and its middle class in the United States that finally brought much higher priorities to the fore than the promotion of democracy. For many observers, it has become difficult to imagine how in these circumstances democratisation might resume. One possibility, however, would involve the fragmentation of the global economy and the rediscovery of local communities, enabling states to regain their autonomy and citizens again to participate in their decision making and hold them accountable.

Guide to further reading

The literature on how democracy is best understood is voluminous. The classic text is Joseph Schumpeter's (1994) *Capitalism, Socialism and Democracy*; but see also 'What Democracy is ... And is Not' by Philippe Schmitter and Terry Lynn Karl (1991) and the introductory text by Jean Grugel (2002). The debate over democracy's preconditions, once vibrant, has long since waned. But a concise cataloguing of factors is provided in *Politics in Developing Countries: Comparing Experiences with Democracy* edited by Diamond et al. (1990). With analysis moving next to the dynamics of democratic transitions, attention shifted initially from structural forces to voluntarist calculations. Strong expressions in this genre include Dankwart Rustow (1970), O'Donnell and Schmitter (1986) and Burton et al. (1991). But probably the key overview of transitional processes is given in Samuel Huntington's (1991) *The Third Wave*. See also the fine collection of essays by Guillermo O'Donnell (1999). For an early analysis of civil society and democracy, see John Keane's (1988) *Democracy and Civil Society*. The literature on democratic consolidation, whether understood in terms of institutions, elite and mass-level attitudes, or the emergence of civil society, has also grown vast, even as the term lost currency precisely because of its multiple meanings and unclear causal directions. But Larry Diamond (1999) offers a comprehensive overview. And his (2008) more recent *Spirit of Democracy* addresses the new uncertainties over democracy's prospects. See also Thomas Carothers (2002), whose groundbreaking 'The End of the Transition Paradigm' addresses the limits on quality that bedevil so many new democracies. By contrast, David Held's (1995) work, in particular, *Democracy and the Global Order: From Modern State to Cosmopolitan Governance*, assesses the possibilities for internationalising democracy, strengthening its relevance in a more globalised polity and economy.

Chapter 7

Nationalism and Ethnicity in World Politics

RICHARD W. MANSBACH

Observers of world politics regard ours as the epoch of globalisation in which peoples organised in territorial states become ever more interconnected by and enmeshed in global political, economic, cultural and knowledge networks that reduce local autonomy and link the fates of people geographically remote from one another. Globalisation deterritorialises and denationalises state activities. Its advocates believe that as globalisation thickens, it will be accompanied by cosmopolitan identities in which individuals view themselves as members of a single global community. A key question is, of course, whether globalisation is reversible.

In terms of identities, globalisation is antithetical to localisation in which individuals identify with disparate and exclusive communities that evaluate their well-being *relative* to 'outsiders'. A basic fact of global politics is that the world remains divided into groups that mistrust one another. Among the most significant 'local' communities are nations and ethnic communities, and 'nationalism' is the ideology that places nations and ethnicities at the acme of human loyalties. Globalisation advocates believe that nationalism is waning, but, as we shall see, nationalism remains a powerful though changing force and an ideology that appeals to innumerable people in the developing and developed worlds. Its persistence reveals an intensification of identity politics in which individuals and groups assess goals and policies on the basis of 'who they are' (Ferguson and Mansbach 2004).

To some extent, the revival of nationalism is a reaction to the homogenising impact of globalisation and the end of the Cold War's ideological bifurcation of global politics. A dramatic resurgence in identity theory is apparent in scholarship as diverse as Huntington's civilisational thesis and the several strands of constructivist thought. National movements reflect the unleashing and manipulation of old (or forged) identities and memories. Thus, the passionate separatist yearnings that gripped Bosnian Muslims, Croatians, Albanians, Armenians, Tibetans and others reminded Daniel Moynihan (1993: 174) of Milton's 'Pandaemonium', that 'was inhabited by creatures quite convinced that the great Satan had their best interests at heart'.

In recent years nationalist fervour has been encouraged and manipulated by political leaders, for example, Russia's Vladimir Putin who has used symbols ranging from the canonisation of the murdered Tsar Nicholas II and his family as part of linking the Russian Orthodox Church to the regime and the restoration of the Soviet national anthem to citing the threat posed by Russia's 'enemies' such as Chechen rebels, American hegemony and Georgian adventurers. 'An ugly nationalism', declared *The Economist* (2008: 34), 'is abroad in Russia'. For their part, leaders of former Soviet republics like Georgia, Moldova, Latvia, and Ukraine and former Soviet bloc countries like Poland have pointed to resurgent Russian power to mobilise nationalist sentiments at home. Indeed, on every continent '[n]ational movements are regaining popularity, and nations that had once assimilated and "vanished" have now reappeared' (Tamir 1993: 3). Today, as in past centuries, nationalism is a companion of change; it was and remains 'a subversive and revolutionary force' (Szporluk 1998: 27).

What are nations, nationalism and ethnicity?

'Nation' is a contested concept that refers to a self-conscious community of people who differentiate themselves from others on the basis of one or several more shared and exclusive traits such as language, common history, culture, religion and/or ancestry. Like 'tribes', 'ethnicities' often refer to peoples united by common ancestry. Although Weber conceded that 'the whole conception of ethnic groups is so complex and so vague that it might be good to abandon it altogether', he defined ethnicities as 'human groups that entertain a subjective belief in their common descent because of similarities of physical type or of custom or both' (Weber, cited in Verkuyten 2005: 74, 75). Ethnicity, then, 'is based on a myth of collective ancestry, which usually carries with it traits that are believed to be innate' (Horowitz 2000: 52). However, as Weber argued, a genuine blood tie is not necessary for a sense of shared ethnicity, and the formation of a political community might itself foster ethnic solidarity. Definitions may also encompass '[p]hysical similarities, cultural characteristics, language, religion, historical events and myths' (Verkuyten 2005: 75) that justify a common origin. Indeed, the only consensual attribute of a nation is that 'nationals' share an intangible sense of ownership of the nation as a whole. 'The essence', argues Connor (1996: 70), 'is a psychological bond that joins a people and differentiates it, in the subconscious convictions of its members, from all nonmembers in a most vital way.' A nation, then, is a self-conscious ethnic group.

Equally controversial is the question of how nations arise. Some scholars argue that nations are primordial, that is, they are rooted in the mists of antiquity, often in a shared ancestry. China's emperors, for example, depicted themselves as heirs to mythical sage kings who were divinely mandated by Heaven. In the case of Japan, Shinto proclaimed emperors to be divine and depicted an unbroken dynastic line of over two millennia from the founding sun goddess. Ancient Romans believed that their city had been founded by the twins Romulus and Remus, sons of the god Mars and the priestess Rhea Silvia who, according to legend, were suckled by a she-wolf. This myth was altered when the Roman Republic was transformed into an empire by Augustus who commissioned the poet Virgil to write the *Aeneid* to legitimise imperial Rome and, by inventing Trojan ancestry, to differentiate Romans from Greeks (Balsdon 1979: 30).

In contrast to the primordial perspective is the view that nations are constructed by those who see themselves as having a common fate. Although this view is associated with contemporary constructivists, it dates back to Ernest Renan (1994: 17) who in the nineteenth century answered his question 'what is a nation?' by adding a voluntary aspect to the primordial conception: 'Only two things, actually, constitute this [a nation's] soul . . . One is in the past, the other is in the present. One is possession in common of a rich legacy of remembrances; the other is the actual consent, the desire to live together . . . The existence of a nation is . . . an everyday plebiscite.' Alluding to Renan, Benedict Anderson (1991: 6–7, emphasis in original) described a nation as an 'imagined community'. 'It is *imagined* because the members of even the smallest nation will never know most of their fellow-members, meet them, or even hear of them', and 'it is imagined as a *community*, because, regardless of the actual inequality and exploitation that may prevail in each, the nation is always conceived as a deep, horizontal comradeship. Ultimately it is this fraternity that makes it possible, over the past two centuries, for so many millions of people, not so much to kill, as willingly die for such limited imaginings.' Thus, Gellner (1983: 7, emphasis in original) emphasises the subjective basis of nations, arguing that individuals 'are of the same nation if and only if they *recognize* each other as belonging to the same nation' and that such recognition 'turns them into a nation, and not the other shared attributes, whatever they might be, which separate that category from non-members'. For Anderson, nationalism is a historically embedded phenomenon that, as Hobsbawm (1990: 14) argues, is linked to social and economic modernity. Hobsbawm (1983: 1) also observes that traditions 'which appear or claim to be old are often quite recent in origin and sometimes invented'.

The debate between constructivists and primodialists misses the fact that 'identity and memory are virtually the same concept' and that both view as critical 'the role of memory and rhetorics of collective identity in constructing and maintaining the nation-state' (Boyarin 1994: 23, viii). As Smith (1986: 2, 3) contends, 'there can be no identity without memory (albeit selective), no collective purpose without myth' and 'the constituents of these identities and cultures – the myths, memories, symbols and values – can often be adapted to new circumstances by being accorded new meanings and new functions'. Myths, memories and symbols 'represent and reinforce the boundary definition of a nation' (Smith 2001: 8). The debate also reflects a misunderstanding of how history works *with* novelty to produce identities. In the course of their lives, people recognise only a few of their shared traits as worthy of self-definition, and the behaviour of other communities towards them may promote new traits or the rediscovery of old ones. Which common features will animate individuals is by no means predetermined, since identities are more a state of mind than anything else. Political actors and the entrepreneurs seeking additional legitimacy may produce new categories of 'others' to provide mirror images for identity groups they seek to lead. To cement in-group unity and attract support, such entrepreneurs may emphasise the psychological distance – the degree of dissimilarity between cognitive frameworks or ways of looking at, assigning meaning to and coping with the world – between followers and 'others'. Thus, 'the emotional attachment to lineage, ancestry and continuity is shared by both those who have power and those who are deprived of it' (Conversi 2004: 2).

For such reasons, it is difficult to overestimate the importance of acts of remembering. Such rituals reinforce and renew collective myths and memories. Whether memorialising an idealised Battle of the Boyne by Irish Protestants or the Battle of Kosovo by Serb nationalists, almost any (even fictionalised) historical event can be resurrected to challenge authority. Acts of remembering, such as national pageants, recollections of ancient wrongs, tribal ceremonies, religious pageants, ethnic parades and even monuments, are part of the contest over the meaning of history. Historical memories sustain old identities and loyalties so that they may flicker for generations. Religion, literature, dialect, poetry, painting, music and ritual are only a few of the ways in which ancient identities are nourished. Any may be factors in the 'rediscovery' of 'nation' and demands for autonomy or 'national self-determination'.

'Nations' should be distinguished from 'states'. If nations are 'imagined communities' of people, the existence of which is the produce of an earlier and continuing process of identity formation, states are juridical entities that enjoy territoriality and internationally recognised boundaries. Such recognition entails sovereignty that affirms that the state enjoys legal control over its territory and all those people who reside within its boundaries and is the legal equal of all other recognised states, implying that states have no right to intervene in one another's domestic affairs. Finally, a state is said to have a government that enjoys the authority to act on behalf of the state. Sovereignty, as Held et al. (1999: 29) argue, 'lodges a distinctive claim to the rightful exercise of political power over a circumscribed realm' and 'seeks to specific the political authority within a community which has the right to determine the framework of rules, regulations and policies within a given territory and to govern accordingly'. Thus, as a *legal* concept, state sovereignty is *not* the same as state autonomy (the capacity to act independently) or state power (the actual ability to accomplish its objectives and realise its ends), both of which are *empirical* attributes. In fact, states frequently fail to measure up to the ideal of sovereignty. Many cannot exercise control over their borders, do not enjoy authority over much of their territory or segments of their population and do not even have a functioning government (Krasner 1999). In extreme cases, these are known as 'failed states'.

Some nations are stateless, for example, the Kurds and Palestinians, whereas some states are multinational. For his part, Gellner (1983: 1) argues that nationalism is 'a political principle which holds that the political and the national unit should be congruent'. This was the premise of historical nationalism as it accelerated in the eighteenth and nineteenth centuries which saw the union of the passions and energy of 'nation' with the bureaucratic, fiscal and territorial resources of 'state', thereby producing a polity of unprecedented political, military and economic power. Finally, a 'nation-state' is a territorial state whose boundaries are congruent with a single, dominant nation.

The evolution of nationalism: theory and practice

The French Revolution played a major role in the emergence of nation-states by shifting the basis for rulers' legitimacy from what Hall (1999: 133–72) calls 'territorial-sovereign' to 'national-sovereign' identity. However, Bobbitt suggests that this polity was a *transition* to the modern nation-state. Instead, he (2002: 146, 196, 178, emphasis in original) argues that the French revolutionary and Napoléonic wars ushered in the 'state-nation', defined as 'a state that mobilizes a nation – a national ethnocultural group – to act on behalf of the State' that 'can thus call on the revenues of all society and on the human talent of all persons'. The state-nation 'was not responsible *to* the nation; rather it was responsible *for* the nation', a relationship that the nation-state, according to Bobbit, would reverse. The state-nation was energised by mass conscription, citizen soldiers and standing armies. And, as Sheehan (2008: 14) contends, 'the more universal military service became... the more tightly the strands of identity and obligation, welfare and duty, were knitted in a single category of citizenship.' One consequence was the emergence of enormous armies driven by aggressive expansionism in the nation's name.

Bobbitt suggests that the transition from state-nations to nation-states accelerated during the mid-nineteenth century and featured the 1848 revolutions, the Crimean War and broader suffrage in much of Europe, climaxing in Italian and German unification. Nation-states were legitimised by the principle of national self-determination by which the 'nation' was the repository of sovereignty, and 'nation' linked 'state' to 'society' to an unprecedented degree. The doctrine of self-determination, spread globally by Europe's colonisers, would later boomerang and bring an end to the overseas empires of Europe's state-nations (Jackson 1993: 119–26). As Klaebel (2007: 225) observes, 'With the emergence of the idea of national self-determination and later the process of decolonization, "nationalism" entered many communal narratives, suggesting a link between three "objects" of desire: a specific parcel of land, a specific "people" (the community *as* nation) and the apparatus of the sovereign state.' Europe's colonial wars were brutal affairs, and wars among Europeans themselves became total, identity-based conflicts made possible by industrialisation. It was during the transition from state-nations to nation-states that subjects became genuine citizens and assumed exclusive allegiance to 'their' states.

At least, two forms of nationalism are evident in this sequence – liberal (or benevolent) and historicist (or malignant). According to Mayall (1990: 30; also Lind 1994), 'liberal' nationalists regarded self-determination as 'a liberal principle' and 'objected to the idea that the cause of freedom and self-determination could be served by the deliberate use of force'. Like the French Jacobins and Napoléon, liberals like Mazzini and Kossuth believed that national identities were crucial to bring about a republican order in Europe based on popular sovereignty. This version of nationalism reached its apogee in Europe with the 1848 revolutions, but, after their failure, European nationalism was infected by racial myths and worship of violence.

By contrast, 'historicist nationalists' took a different view of force and the role of nationalism in global politics. Early in the nineteenth century, Hegel had already elaborated an organic model of the individual's relation to the nation-state. Napoléon's conquest of Prussia had created mistrust of democracy among the country's elites, and the destruction of feudal institutions in that country had driven its leaders towards authoritarian solutions built on national loyalty. Eulogising the Prussian state, Hegel (1969: 619) argued that reason found expression in the collectivity and that '[m]an must therefore venerate the state as a secular deity'. War, he argued, was a healthy purgative for a nation, allowing citizens to appreciate the triviality of daily existence. Historicist nationalism dominated German unification, especially after 1848. In Bismarck's Prussia, the historian Heinrich von Treitschke argued that nations were competitors in a world from which only the strong could emerge whole. Strong nations were, he declared, obliged to extirpate inferior races, as 'the Redskins in America withered before the Basilisk eye of the Palefaces' (cited in Bowle 1964: 359). Like Social Darwinists, Treitshcke, with his organic view of nationalities, considered other nations inferior to his own and believed that the greatness of human history 'lies in the perpetual conflict of nations' (cited in Bowle 1964: 353).

Thus, as Mayall (1990: 31) argues, 'the line can be traced from Hegel's insistence that the conquests of the historical nations contribute to human progress through the frenzied enthusiasm of the belligerents during the early stages of the First World War, to the contemporary scene of freedom fighters engaged in real and imaginary wars of national liberation.' After 1848, nationalism gradually became synonymous with exclusion and otherness. No longer were the boundaries between nation-states softened by the cohesion of aristocratic elites. In the cases of liberal and historicist nationalism, elites manipulated similar identities for different ends. Those like Bismarck and Louis Napoléon who manipulated nationalism to reinforce state power in an authoritarian context hijacked the ideology for their ends, and their example has been emulated by modern demagogues from Mussolini to Milosevic. Thus, Etzioni (1992–93: 21) argues that national self-determination and democracy are adversaries: 'While they long served to destroy empires and force governments to be more responsive to the governed, with rare exceptions self-determination movements now undermine the potential for democratic development in nondemocratic countries and threaten the foundations of democracy in the democratic ones.'

National self-determination and the nation-state

The idea of 'national self-determination' provided the nation-state with legitimacy. National self-determination, which can mean either autonomy for a 'people' within an existing state or a 'people's' ownership of its own state, was very much in the air in the second half of the nineteenth century, especially as it applied to multinational empires such as Austria-Hungary. Referring to the Versailles Conference, American President Woodrow Wilson (2006: 415) declared on 25 September 1919 that 'There was not a man at the table who did not admit the sacredness of the right to self-determination, the sacredness of the right of any body of people to say that they would not continue to live under the Government that they were then living under.' Wilson's Secretary of State Robert Lansing was aghast at the prospect. 'Will it not breed discontent, disorder and rebellion?' he asked. 'The phrase', he continued, 'is simply loaded with dynamite. It will raise hopes which can never be realized. It will, I fear, cost thousands of lives' (cited in Binder 1993).

In recent decades, nationalism and national self-determination have become critical sources of localisation, eroding collective identities of states and challenging globalised political authority. In the 1950s and 1960s, nationalism and national self-determination – enshrined in the UN Charter, Article 1(2) – were the ideological bases of decolonisation. Today, nationalism is, as Rosenau (2003: 107) argues, 'a form of exclusionary localism' because 'it emphasizes boundaries and the distinction between us and them, with the result that even in the United States the idea of a melting pot has tended to give way to what some regard as a multicultural regime in which different minorities stress their ethnic and racial ties even as they downplay the relevance of an inclusive identity that links them to the varied groups that reside in their country'. In other words, nationalism and ethnicity are identities that are associated with closure and with the thickening of vertical barriers across space. 'Wherever nationalism is highly salient in states today, or wherever nations aspire to become states, exclusionary localism can be readily discerned, with the ethnic cleansing policies of Serbia in the 1990s the most notorious recent example that can be cited in this regard' (Rosenau 2003: 107).

Nationalism no longer automatically reinforces state power. If nineteenth- and twentieth-century statesmen invoked nationalism to unify citizens against a foreign foe or attract public attention from domestic woes, contemporary nationalism increasingly divides states and escapes leaders' control. And, if the eighteenth and nineteenth centuries witnessed the wedding of 'nation' and 'state', the trend towards their divorce has accelerated since the First World War. There is a growing queue of groups in global politics that want their own state, even if this means the collapse of existing states like the Soviet Union and Yugoslavia or state failure. In much of the developing world, ethnic and tribal loyalties threaten the integrity of existing states. Bloody examples in Rwanda, Sri Lanka, Sudan and elsewhere illustrate how politicians manipulate ethnic divisions. Not only did the USSR split into quarrelling nationalities, but several remain at each other's throats – Armenians and Azeris, Georgians and Ossetians, Russians and Georgians and Russians and Moldovans. According to one analysis, there were over 200 politically active ethnic movements by the mid-1990s (Gurr 1996). After all, as Connor (1993: 16) notes, 'seldom do political and ethnic borders coincide' and, when faced with demands for nation self-determination, there is a 'universal tendency of governments to render decisions upon the implicit assumption of the need to preserve the entire political unit' and 'proclaim the right to stamp out rebellion and the duty to prevent secession'.

'If we don't find some way that the different ethnic groups can live together in a country', asked former US Secretary of State Warren Christopher, 'how many countries will we have?' His answer: 'We'll have 5,000 countries rather than the hundred plus we now have' (cited in Binder 1993). Since almost any group can claim to be a distinctive 'people', there is a risk of fragmentation of political authority into ever smaller and less viable polities. Far from ending history, the end of the Cold War saw an upsurge in civil conflict and tribal violence. Even on the marchlands of Europe and Canada, there are 'ethno-national' groups that contend that their culture has been swallowed up by majorities within nation-states – Spanish Basques, French Bretons and Corsicans, Canadian Inuits and Native Americans, Philippine Muslims, Celtic Scots and Welsh and others. In Québec's case, efforts by the Francophone advocates of secession have had to confront the opposition of non-Francophone English and other minorities (allophones), as well as the threat of the Cree and other indigenous groups who claim large areas of Québec to secede on the basis of the same right to national self-determination claimed by Francophone Québéçois.

Nationalism and ethnicity need *not* imperil globalisation. People, after all, have multiple identities and are simultaneously members of many polities which may overlap. There is no reason, for example, that one cannot identify oneself as both a Basque or a Scot and a European. The former identity may be relevant on some issues, and the latter on others. 'Europe' provides economies of scale that would be unavailable for a tiny island of psychological security. In this sense, it is rational for individuals who are members of extensive polities to advocate ethno-national secession from existing states. Thus, ethno-national movements such as those of the Basques and Catalans in Spain, the Flemish and Walloons in Belgium or the Bretons in France may reduce the cohesion of 'their' state but are unlikely to impede globalisation. Indeed, they may benefit from it.

Nevertheless, nationalism can be invoked to resist or dilute cultural homogenisation associated with globalisation. Thus, in Asia, as elsewhere, globalised culture has been mixed with and modified by efforts to update and assert traditional values and norms. Global culture is, in effect, filtered through local languages and meaning systems that help preserve local cultures, producing a 'typical pattern of hybridization: selective absorption, rejection, and assertion of national identity constructs' (Blum 2007: 74). The result has been a combination of acceptance and resistance on the part of local elites bent on anchoring nationalism, preserving power and reinforcing traditional normative structures linked to religion, language and/or ethnicity.

A second problem arises if nationalism and ethnicity prove to be Hobbesian categories based on passion rather than reason. Thus, Horowitz (2000: 186, 17) suggests that ethnic conflicts are frequently intractable and that the 'contest for worth and place is the common denominator of ethnic conflict among unranked groups' that are divided 'by a vertical cleavage'. To some extent, whether such conflicts are zero sum depend on the degree to which national or ethnic cleavages crosscut or reinforce other social cleavages such as economic status. If the latter, conflicts may prove irreconcilable and produce state collapse.

Negative localism: state failure, national diasporas and national assimilation

Although national and ethnic pride can prove to be healthy individual and collective identities, they can also produce negative localism and, as we have observed, seriously impede globalisation. The negative localism associated with nationalism and ethnicity afflicts both the developing and developed worlds and may assume several forms.

State failure

The failure to build viable and stable states after the retreat of colonialism and the post-Cold War upsurge in violence within and across states in much of Africa and parts of Asia are partly associated with national, tribal and ethnic rivalries, revived and manipulated by ambitious politicians seeking political power and loot. In Africa, Europeans imposed states and political boundaries that inhabitants never fully accepted and that divided ethnic groups or enclosed ethnic rivals within the same states. The governments of such states may represent or be in the hands of one of the ethnic contenders, may be deemed illegitimate by members of other ethnic groups, may be unable to exercise authority over the state's territory, may be unable to provide security or essential services to citizens and frequently confront armed opponents. Such states 'can no longer reproduce the conditions for their own existence' (Di John 2008: 10).

State failure is multi-causal (Carment 2003; King and Zheng 2001). However, although the relationship is complex, ethnic heterogeneity and ethnic animosities often play a role in state failure. 'The civil wars that characterize failed states', concludes Robert Rothberg (2003: 5), 'usually stem from or have roots in ethnic, religious, linguistic, or other intercommunal enmity.' When combined with poverty and uneven economic development, overpopulation, refugee communities and environmental stress, state institutions in countries from Sudan and Ivory Coast to Guinea and Somalia and from Haiti and Burma to Lebanon and Iraq collapsed, resulting in failed states. According to *Foreign Policy*'s (2008: 67) Failed States Index, of the 20 states 'most at risk of failure' 11 are in Africa (Somalia, Sudan, Zimbabwe, Chad, Democratic Republic of Congo, Ivory Coast, Central African Republic, Guinea, Ethiopia, Uganda and Nigeria), six are in Asia (Afghanistan, Pakistan, Bangladesh, Burma, North Korea and Sri Lanka), two are in the Middle East (Iraq and Lebanon) and one (Haiti) is in the Caribbean. Six of the ten weakest states are in Africa – Sudan, the Democratic Republic of the Congo, Ivory Coast, Zimbabwe, Chad and Somalia – and the others are Iraq, Haiti, Pakistan and Afghanistan. Virtually all are multiethnic societies.

Ethnic and national assimilation

A second form of negative localism is partly a result of globalisation and the reaction to it. Ethnic xenophobia of resident national groups is one consequence of the large-scale movement of persons as refugees and as migrants across state frontiers combined with the spread of terrorism. Residents argue that such migrants cannot assimilate into dominant cultures and that they create economic and social problems for their adopted societies including lower wages, human smuggling, street crime and spiralling welfare costs. The issue of economic migration from poor to rich countries has become a focus of political contention both within and among states. Migration is partly a product of demographic forces. Population growth has ended and in some cases populations are decreasing in wealthy countries owing to factors such as urbanisation and greater opportunities for women. Simultaneously, populations are 'graying' owing to better health care. Especially in Europe and Japan the consequences include spiralling costs for health care and social security and a declining tax base with fewer young people to fill jobs, especially lower-paying jobs. By contrast, burgeoning populations in Africa, the Middle East and parts of Asia are producing a surplus of young workers in search of employment and higher wages. 'These movements of people, often from former colonies', writes Modood (1997: 1), 'whether welcome or not, have created a multiculturalism that is qualitatively different from the diversity of personal difference or lifestyles of historic, territorially based that already characterize some Western European countries.'

Until recent decades, Europe was dominantly Christian and Caucasian, but large numbers of Muslims of different nationalities arrived after the Second World War as a result of guest-worker programmes, filling poorly paid jobs that Europeans avoided. Although initially guest workers, notably Turks, were only supposed to be temporary residents, many remained and were joined by family members. By 2005, Europe's Muslim population reached between 15 and 20 million or four to five per cent of Europe's total population and will double by 2025 (Leiken 2005: 122). Excepting Germany, most Muslim immigrants in Europe originated in the country's former colonial territories. In Germany, most Muslims are of Turkish descent; in France of North African origin; in Britain from Pakistan; and in the Netherlands from Indonesia.

Following the terrorist attacks of 9/11, Europeans grew uneasy about the increasing numbers of Muslims in their midst, even as many of the children and grandchildren of the first generation of Muslim migrants were alienated from Western culture. 'Jihadist networks', writes Robert S. Leiken (2005: 120), 'span Europe from Poland to Portugal, thanks to the spread of radical Islam among the descendants of guest workers . . . In smoky coffeehouses in Rotterdam and Copenhagen, makeshift prayer halls in Hamburg and Brussels, Islamic bookstalls in Birmingham and "Londonistan," (Phillips 2006) and the prisons of Madrid,

Milan, and Marseilles, immigrants or their descendants are volunteering for jihad against the West.'

Polls reveal that almost 60 per cent of Germans think that Muslim immigration from the Middle East and North Africa is a 'bad thing', although majorities elsewhere continue to regard such immigration as positive (Pew 2006) and 'the vast majority of Europe's 15–20 million Muslims have nothing to do with radical Islamism and are struggling hard to fit in, not opt out' (Giry 2006: 87). Among European and North Americans, fear of Muslim extremism is highest in Russia, Spain and Germany and lowest in Canada, the United States and Poland (Pew 2005). For their part, many Muslim residents in Europe – 51 per cent in Germany, 42 per cent in Britain, 39 per cent in France and 31 per cent in Spain – believe that Europeans are hostile towards them (Pew 2006). In addition, large majorities of European Muslims – 81 per cent in Britain, 69 per cent in Spain, 61 per cent in Germany and 46 per cent in France – identify themselves as Muslims first and only secondarily as citizens of their country (Pew 2006). Among Europeans, fear has fuelled xenophobic nationalism and has increased support for right-wing, anti-immigrant politicians.

France, long regarded as epitomising a nation-state with a single, distinctive secular and national culture, now has the largest proportion of Muslims in its population of any European country and is confronting challenges to its ethnic homogeneity. More than Americans or British, the French believe that immigrants should assimilate, speaking the local language and adopting local mores. This belief has been challenged by growing communities of North Africans concentrated in the impoverished outskirts of French cities that erupt in violence from time to time. Controversy surrounds French efforts to foster a secular national culture by banning the wearing of 'conspicuous' religious symbols such as headscarves in French schools, a position that enjoys overwhelming public support.

Unlike France, America's multicultural tradition allows immigrants greater latitude to express their identities, but even in the United States, there is growing nationalist concern about the assimilation of the country's Mexican immigrant community. This sentiment is controversially represented by Harvard's Samuel Huntington who argues that Hispanic immigrants are not assimilating into American society. Americans, Huntington argues (2005: xvi), define their national identity to include 'the English language; Christianity; religious commitment; English concepts of the rule of law, the responsibility of rulers, and the rights of individuals; and dissenting Protestant values of individualism, the work ethic, and the belief that humans have the ability and the duty to create a heaven on earth, "a city on the hill" '. In his view, Hispanics are establishing insulated cultural islands, and the sheer number of Hispanics in the United States – up from almost 9 per cent of the population in 1990 to over 13 per cent in 2003, of whom as many as a quarter are illegal – threaten to undermine America's culture. Huntington's provocative claim rests on the assertion that Hispanics do not assimilate into American society as did earlier waves of immigrants from Europe. The result, he contends (2005: 221; also Hanson 2003: 20), will be 'a culturally bifurcated Anglo-Hispanic society with two national languages'.

In addition to sheer numbers, a number of factors, Huntington argues, make Mexican immigration unique, including the fact that Mexico is America's neighbour, thereby permitting continuous movement back and forth across the border, the high concentration of Mexicans in particular localities like Los Angeles, the high proportion who enter the country illegally, the persistence of the immigration northwards and Mexico's historical claim to American territory. Huntington argues that the barriers to Hispanic assimilation include failure to learn English, poor education levels, low income and low naturalisation and intermarriage rates. The density of links across the US–Mexican border, Huntington (2005: 247) contends, 'could produce a consolidation of the Mexican-dominant areas into an autonomous, culturally and linguistically distinct, economically self-reliant bloc within the United States'.

Huntington's analysis is an extension of his view that we are entering an era of clashing civilisations. He is a nationalist whose views are those of one who fears that relentless globalisation will undermine existing national cultures and perhaps even national integrity and independence. To his critics, Huntington is a xenophobic nationalist, whose belief that American culture is rooted in Anglo-Protestant tradition is false and whose fears are overheated. To his supporters, he summarises the resentment towards a global tidal wave that threatens national identities, boundaries and traditional values. Some of Huntington's critics contend that Hispanics do, in fact, assimilate in the same way that their predecessors did. Others argue that his version of American culture has been made obsolete by generations of immigrants and that he does not understand how the United States has repeatedly integrated waves of immigrants into a culture that reflects them all.

Neomercantilism

Globalisation is generally seen to have gone farthest and be least subject to reversal in the economic realm. Cerny (1996: 124–5) writes of the 'competition state'. 'The key to the new role of the state', he argues, 'lies in the way that economic competition is changing in the world.'

> [S]tate structures today are being transformed into more and more market-oriented and even market-based organizations themselves, fundamentally altering the way that public and private goods are provided ... [W]e may be witnessing the transmutation of the state from a civil association into a more limited form of enterprise association ... operating within a wider market and institutional environment. This is not merely a change in degree, but a change in kind.

'The functions of the state', Cerny (2003: 65) maintains, 'although central in structural terms, are becoming increasingly fragmented, privatized and devolved.' Thus, the 'ongoing division of labor ("globalisation")' places states 'under ever-increasing pressure, and with it sovereignty-based IR theory' (Osiander

2001: 283). Cerny's competition state is echoed by Bobbitt's (2002: 211) 'market-state'. 'Whereas the nation-state, with its mass free public education, universal franchise, and social security policies promised to guarantee the welfare of the nation, the market-state promises instead to maximize the opportunity of the people and thus tends to privatize many state activities and to make voting and representative government less influential and more responsive to the market.'

However, economic nationalism or neomercantilism has not disappeared. Mercantilism's normative assumption is that economic policy should advance *state* power, especially its military power, rather than benefit individuals or the world economy as whole. Like nationalists of all stripes, mercantilists evaluate policy in terms of the *relative* rather than *absolute* benefit it affords the nation in comparison to other nations, seek to strengthen the nation's boundaries and encourage its independence from outsiders. To this end, mercantilists, as Buzan (2008: 252) argues, 'seek to make the international economy fit with the patterns of fragmentation in the political system by reducing the scope of the global market. They emphasize the integrity of the national economy and the primacy of state goals (military welfare, societal). They advocate protection as a way of preserving integrity, but may be attracted to the construction of their own economy dominating at the centre.' In encouraging economic independence and discouraging economic interdependence and transnational links, protecting 'domestic' industries from foreign competition and assisting 'national champions', even at the expense of foreign rivals, mercantilists and neomercantilists undermine the basic premise of those who support globalisation – that the free movement of goods and services globally without being hindered by political boundaries benefits everyone. Furthermore, economic nationalism has merged with anti-globalisation sentiments. 'There are', as Rupert (2000:17) observes, 'sectors of the anti-liberalization movement which explicitly rejected free trade in favor of a more assertive nationalism, and which continue to organize against globalisation in any form.'

Currently, all major trading states have developed sophisticated non-tariff barriers to free trade such as America's 'antidumping' policies that ostensibly aim to 'ensure competition by punishing foreign firms that sell their products at "unfair" prices in U.S. markets' but that has become 'little more than an excuse for special interests to shield themselves from competition' (Mankiw and Swagel 2005: 107). Moreover, the Democrats' 2008 electoral triumph bodes for neoliberal policies as Democratic congressional support for free trade has fallen steadily (Bhagwati 2005: 3).

Although indications of a revival of economic nationalism abound, the most striking evidence is the failure of Doha Round of global trade talks that were initiated in 2001. In Doha, it was agreed that negotiations would focus on freeing trade in agriculture and services, both contentious issues in global trade, with an eye towards reaching agreement by 2005. Unfortunately, none of the three impediments identified by Bergsten (2005: 1; also Tonelson 2006) as preventing agreement, which requires WTO consensus, has been overcome: 'massive current account imbalances and currency misalignments pushing policy in dangerously protectionist directions in both the United States and Europe; the strong and growing anti-globalisation sentiments that stalemate virtually every trade debate on both sides of the Atlantic and elsewhere; and the absence of a compelling reason for the political leaders of the chief holdout countries to make the necessary concessions to reach an agreement'. The 'most contentious issue' at Doha involved agricultural subsidies in the developed world that prevent developing countries from selling their products overseas (Panagariya 2005: 4). Efforts to reach agreement collapsed in July 2006 as the United States and the European Union failed to agree over agricultural subsidies and, in response, developing countries like Brazil refused to open their markets to developed countries' manufactured goods and services. This outcome threatens 'long-term damage to the notion of multilateralism' (Sutherland 2005: 1).

Additional evidence of economic nationalism emerged with dramatic increases in grain and commodity prices in 2008. Confronted with domestic unrest, countries as varied as Ukraine, Argentina, Pakistan, India and China reacted by imposing export taxes and export bans on grains and fertilisers thereby intensifying food shortages elsewhere, especially in East Africa.

Finally, in the United States opposition to concluding bilateral trade agreements with countries such as Colombia and South Korea, along with unwillingness to make the hard decisions that would have rescued the Doha Round, suggests that Washington may no longer be prepared to exercise leadership in maintaining a liberal economic system. Without the hegemon to lead, economic liberalism will surely slow and perhaps even be reversed in some respects.

Conclusion: nationalism in the near future

State failure, demands that migrant communities assimilate and neomercantilist policies are only some of the manifestations of surging national and ethnic sentiments. Whatever one's view of Huntington, his nationalist impulse is widely shared in the United States and Europe, especially since 9/11. It is reflected in the fence being constructed along America's border with Mexico, the tightening of immigration controls in the European Union and public scepticism towards Doha, NAFTA and other trade agreements in the United States.

A more important factor in accelerating and reinforcing nationalism is the dramatic financial and economic crises that began with America's toxic sub-prime mortgage market and that have been spread around the world by the transnational links among banks, corporations and states. Globalisation, it seems, spreads not only wealth but also impoverishment. Globally, the response to these crises has been massive state intervention in the form of aid to banks and corporations, greater regulation of capital flows and financial enterprises and deficit spending. 'The ideology of the dictatorship of the market', declared French President Nicholas Sarkozy (cited in *BusinessDay* 2008) in October 2008, 'is dead.' 'Historians will one day see that this crisis marks the real start of the 21st century', a century which will see the 'return of politics' in managing national economies that will prove to be 'an intellectual and moral revolution'.

We cannot say yet whether President Sarkozy is correct. However, previous eras of intense interdependence have ended when confronted with political and economic turmoil. Indeed, as Ferguson (2005: 66) reminds us, the 'last age of globalisation' with its 'relatively free trade, limited restrictions on migrations, and hardly any regulation of capital flows' that characterised the late nineteenth and early twentieth centuries abruptly ended in the First World War in 'economic warfare' and 'postwar protectionism' and collapsed during the Great Depression. As in the 1930s, the near future is likely to see national and regional efforts to curb the effects of globalised financial and economic distress at the expense of international and transnational cooperation or to assuage resulting discontent by brandishing nationalist symbols and threatening political and economic adventurism overseas. In the face of rising unemployment, domestic resentment against immigrants who would compete with citizens for jobs is likely to intensify and to strengthen xenophobic and nationalist political parties that seek to 'regain control' of national borders already seen to be threatened by terrorism and transnational crime. Finally, notwithstanding globalisation, the profound geopolitical cleavages that threaten violence in the Middle East, South Asia and Africa are likely to persist, along with the identity conflicts – ethnic, tribal and religious – that accompany them. Although globalisation will persist and, in some respects, may deepen, national and ethnic identities and loyalties retain a powerful and widespread ideological appeal and will repeatedly emerge to counteract globalising tendencies.

Guide to further reading

Several analyses provide an understanding of the historical origins and conceptual variants of nationalism and ethnicity (Connor 1993, 1996; Gellner 1983; Hobsbawm 1990; Mayall 1990; Smith 2001). There are also excellent works concerning the evolution of nationalism in relation to the state (Bobbitt 2002) and the specific attributes of ethnicity (Verkuyten 2005). These can be extended to analyses of contemporary nationalism and ethnicity and their relationship to globalisation (Blum 2007; Horowitz 2000; Rosenau 2003) and their role as one among various competing identities (Ferguson and Mansbach 2004). There are also recent works dealing with nationalism and ethnicity and 'failed states' (Di John 2008; Rothberg 2003), and the problem of assimilating national and ethnic minorities who have migrated for economic and political reasons, often to the developed world (Huntington 2004; Leiken 2005; Modood 1997; Phillips 2006). Valuable analyses are also available on economic nationalism (Bergsten 2005; Mankiw and Swagel 2005, Tonelson 2006).

Part II

Conflict, Crises and Authority

Chapter 8

Old and New Wars

MATT KILLINGSWORTH

In the period between the signing of the Peace of Westphalia and the end of the Cold War, wars were generally thought to have shared a set of characteristics. They were fought by agents of the state, usually a professional standing army and, as such, were centrally coordinated and funded. They also had clear beginning and end points; they started when war was officially declared and ended with a cessation of hostilities, an armistice and eventually a peace treaty. Linked to this, wars were fought with clear priorities and motives. Finally, wars were fought with a shared understanding regarding conduct during war; despite its violence, there were commonly accepted rules which governed what ought to occur with regard to things such as the targeting of civilians and the treatment of prisoners of war.

In recent years, however, many scholars have argued that war has changed. Due to a range of factors, including globalisation, the rise of identity politics and technological transformation, war no longer resembles the traditional understanding of its form and function. As such, these scholars aver modern warfare demonstrates inherently new characteristics that demand new methods of analysis.

The aim of this chapter is to assess these claims made about the transformation of war brought about by globalisation, new technologies, the rise of intra-state conflict and economic- and identity-based war. The chapter is presented in three parts. The first part presents an overview of the 'traditional' understanding of war, sometimes referred to as 'old war'. The second part of the chapter will look more closely at the 'new war' literature, with a particular focus on Mary Kaldor's arguments and the literature concerned with the Revolution in Military Affairs (RMA), concluding with an overview of some of the critiques of this literature. The third part examines the wars in Iraq and Afghanistan and assesses the degree to which they represent 'old wars' or 'new wars'. The chapter concludes with a brief reflection on the extent to which the experience of war in the first part of the twenty-first century is likely to be continued over the short to medium term.

Defining war

'War' has assumed a degree of omnipresence in world politics. Not only does it seem that there is always a war being fought somewhere in the world, but the term has also been appropriated by political elites to describe their latest policy initiative such as the war on poverty, the war on drugs and the war on terror. In this respect, 'war' has become somewhat of a general term that has lost much of its definitional value. Considering this, it is helpful to first offer a definition.

A typical definition is that offered by Quincy Wright, who argues that war 'was a violent contact of distinct but similar entities' (cited in Freedman 1994: 69). This definition is insufficient because it does not adequately distinguish war from any other acts of violence, such as crime or gang warfare, for example. Also this definition makes unreasonable assumptions about the nature of combatants; war is more often than not fought by *dissimilar* entities. A number of authors have suggested that the best way to distinguish between war and other forms of violence is through determining the number of battle deaths. The Correlates of War Project established a threshold of 1000 battle deaths per year as a defining requirement, a number that Jack Levy notes has been widely accepted (1998: 141). But this is also problematic. As a number of authors point out, under the 1000 deaths per year threshold, the 1982 Falklands War and the civil war in the Solomon Islands, citing just two examples, would not qualify as wars (Ayson 2007: 177; Sheehan 2008: 214).

While the above definitions all capture some important aspects of war, they are not especially helpful in this context. In what is arguably the most influential book on the subject, Carl von Clausewitz's *On War* (1832) famously defined war as 'an act of force to compel our enemy to do our will' which is 'nothing but the continuation of policy with other means' (von Clausewitz et al. 1984: 75, 87). Leaning heavily on this classical understanding, Hedley Bull presents a definition that is of particular use to students of world politics. Bull defines war as 'organised violence carried on by political units against each other' (Bull 1977: 184). He qualifies this definition by noting that it can only be considered war when the violence is carried out by a political unit against another political unit. As will be elaborated below, while a number of characteristics of war have changed, it is war's inherently political character which remains largely unchanged.

Old war

Prior to the advent of the modern state, a variety of actors fought wars, including the Church, barbarian tribes and city-states, each relying on a variety of different military formations, such as citizen militias and mercenaries. Even in the state-system's formative years, sovereigns continued to rely on a combination of feudal and mercenary forces. But this arrangement became increasingly untenable, as wealthy landowners often refused to fight for the sovereign. Mercenary forces often supplemented feudal forces, but only when the sovereign could raise the necessary funds to pay them. However, mercenary forces proved to be increasingly unreliable; they were known to switch allegiances for increased payment or, worse still, if funds ran out, 'unpaid mercenaries became a scourge, sometimes as greatly feared as the intruders who had inaugurated the militarisation and castellation of Europe in the first place' (Keegan 1994: 13).

As European sovereigns were increasingly able to stabilise borders and centralise economic and political authority during the seventeenth and eighteenth centuries, they were able to establish professional, standing armies. As John Keegan argues (1994: 12), the establishment of permanent, standing armies, via the regiment, became the devise 'for securing armed forces to the state'. During the same period, the state successfully, in many small steps, disarmed the civilian population, while simultaneously the scale of its own armed forces overwhelmed the force open to others under its jurisdiction (Tilly 1990: 69). In this view, the evolution of the modern state is closely tied to the phenomenon of war, leading American sociologist Charles Tilly (1975: 42) to conclude that 'War made the state and the state made war.' Central to this process was the fact that only the territorialised state was in a position to bear the dramatically increased costs associated with sustaining a professional, standing army. Through regulating tax revenue and centralising and consolidating the political aspects of war, the state was able to further enhance its war-fighting capacity and capability (Münkler 2005).

As the modern state assumed control over the means for fighting war, there also developed, at first tacitly, then through formal international agreements, understandings about how war was to be fought. Martin van Creveld (1991: 40–1) notes that:

> To distinguish war from mere crime, it was defined as something waged by sovereign states and by them alone. Soldiers were defined as personnel licensed to engage in armed violence on behalf of the state ... They were supposed to fight while only in uniform, carrying their arms 'openly' ... They were not supposed to resort to 'dastardly' methods such as violating truces, taking up arms again after they had been wounded or taken prisoner ... The civilian population was supposed to be left alone, 'military necessity' permitting.

The modern state was also able to successfully claim to represent the collective interest. In this respect, the state came to define the 'public', and the 'public arena' became that in which force was legitimate (see Weber et al. 1991: 71). As Patricia Owens (2008: 983) put it, 'War was for the political end of states and was justified as the legitimate means for the pursuit of state interest. It could be distinguished from less organised violence because it was defined as an activity carried out by a newly fashioned "public" entity which established the law and exceptions to the law.'

It is within this environment that Clausewitz understood war. The 'old wars' that Clausewitz describes in *On War* share a number of important characteristics. The first, and perhaps most important of these characteristics, is that old wars were fought by the representatives of states; through an organised and centrally controlled armed force, states pursued their political will through the use of violence.

The second characteristic of old wars was the nature in which they are fought. Clausewitz (1984: 142–3) is very specific about means and ends: 'in tactics, the means are fighting forces trained for combat; the end is victory.' But key to victory is politics, as Howard (1983: 37) notes, 'the most splendid of victories was nothing in itself unless it was the means to the attainment of a political end.' Clausewitz (1984: 95) further regards the most important aspect of war to be the battle. He writes that warring parties need to be prepared and willing to engage in overwhelming force: 'the whole of military activity must relate directly or indirectly to the engagement'. He elaborates on this later, when he writes that 'if the enemy is thrown off balance, he must not be given time to recover. Blow after blow must be struck in the same direction; the victor, in other words, must strike with all of his strength and not just against a fraction of the enemy's.' As old wars were fought for primarily political purposes, they should be thought of as a temporally bound episode with a clear beginning and end. They were expected to last only until the desired political purpose has been achieved. War started when it was formally declared and ended when armistices were signed, victors celebrated and 'the losers' punished.

Understanding war as an act of a force that compelled your enemy to do your will led Clausewitz to conclude that wars will tend to escalate to extremes. Elaborating on this point, Howard (1983: 49) notes that you cannot compel your enemy without destroying their power to resist: 'so long as he has any capacity for resistance left . . . you are logically bound to destroy it . . . there is no stopping place short of the extreme.'

Two points regarding absolute war need to be made. First, although not explicit in Clausewitz's work, this idea of 'absolute war' is assumed to be undertaken by great powers. Thus, old war should be understood as symmetrical in that it is undertaken by parties of roughly equivalent standing and stature. Second, the two world wars fought in the first half of the twentieth century came as close as could be possible to fulfiling Clausewitz's idea of 'absolute war'. The unprecedented and massive mobilisation of state resources represents a logical endpoint to Clausewitz's ideas.

Finally, although not discussed in *On War*, notions of conduct, or how wars should be fought, are an important characteristic of old wars. Finding the origins in the idea of Just War Theory, the mid-nineteenth century witnessed the emergence of a set of codified laws of war. The most important of these are the 1864 Geneva Convention, the 1868 St Petersburg Declaration, the 1899 and 1907 Hague Conferences and the 1908 London Conference, all of which contributed to the developing body of international law with regard to conduct during war, including the treatment of prisoners, the sick and the wounded and the banning of certain weapons and methods used during war. As with any laws, they were not always necessarily followed. However, the importance of these laws lies not in the fact that they were necessarily obeyed, but rather that they established codified norms that delineated legitimate warfare from other forms of organised violence.

In summary, old wars are those fought and funded by the state for clear political ends. When these ends are met, the war should end. They are also fought with a similar understanding from all parties regarding conduct during war. While this was arguably the predominant mode of warfare up until the end of the Second World War, a great deal of literature has since devoted itself to arguing that it has been all but discontinued, and that enough changes have occurred in the nature of violent conflict to prompt arguments suggesting that contemporary wars are distinct in significant ways from previous forms of conflict.

New wars

The revolution in military affairs

The 1991 Gulf War can be identified as the beginning for much of the discussion on the so-called RMA. As Colin McInnes (2002: 119) notes, 'the Gulf War saw the widespread and deliberate exploitation of leading edge technologies ... [that] provided the first hard evidence of a technological revolution.' In particular, the use of precision-guided weapons, and the ability, via mounted cameras on the planes from whence they were dispatched, for the viewer to watch those weapons 'sail unerringly into hapless vehicles [or buildings] singled out for destruction' only served to reinforce the idea that we were witnessing something very 'new' in the way that wars could be fought (Beier 2006: 268). That the RMA has been embraced by those responsible for military strategy is borne out in the following comparison: of the total munitions used in the 1991 Gulf War, 9 per cent of them were precision guided, while in 2003, the Coalition of the Willing had used 68 per cent precision-guided munitions (cited in Angstrom 2005: 16).

According to advocates of the RMA, the ability to conduct 'clean wars' via the use of 'smart' weapons represents something distinctly different in the way that wars are fought. According to Lawrence Freedman (1998: 44), advocates of the RMA believe that 'the technologies of the information age should allow military power to be employed to its maximum efficiency with speed, precision, and minimum human cost. There is no need to target civilians nor even to hit them inadvertently ... ' The new technologies that form the centrepiece of the RMA will not only change the way that war is fought but also fundamentally alter the way that victory is attained. Following the logic of the RMA, the increased reliance on 'smart' weapons would ideally lead to quick, clean victories with minimal collateral damage. Similarly, the heavy reliance on technology would not only limit the theatre of war but also lead to the use of fewer ground troops.

While it is undeniable that technological advances have changed aspects of war-fighting, the 'revolution' that RMA literature alludes to is thus far limited to wealthy states and more specifically the United States. Yet, as we know, most contemporary conflict takes place in the developing world. Thus, in this respect, the RMA sheds little light on possible changes in the way that these wars are fought. Furthermore, while the RMA represents the type of war that powerful states are best suited to winning, McInnes (2002: 139) points out that this 'creates an incentive for enemies to fight precisely the sort of war that the West does *not* want to become engaged in'. Finally, the idea that war can be 'clean' appears naïve. War remains a bloody enterprise where combatants still seek to win through inflicting the most amount of damage possible on their enemy.

'New wars' literature

Pointing to wars in Bosnia–Herzegovina (Kaldor 2006), Rwanda, Somalia and Liberia (Allen 1999; Shawcross 2000) and Chechnya and Sierra Leone (Münkler 2005), the 'new war' literature argues that the prevalence of old, state-based war has decreased, while the number of civil wars, as well as wars between non-state entities, has increased. Indeed, according to Herfried Münkler (2005: 1), 'states have given up their de facto monopoly of war, and what appears ever more frequently in their stead are para-state or even partly private actors . . . for whom war is a permanent field of activity.'

The advent of new wars is both a function of and facilitated by globalisation, whereby 'the intensification of global interconnectedness – political, economic, military and cultural – and the changing character of political authority' is transforming the nature of war (Kaldor 2006: 4). One of the most prominent of the new war analysts, Kaldor argues that new wars can be contrasted with old wars in terms of ends, means and the way in which they are financed. Whereas old wars were fought for primarily geo-political or ideological gains, Kaldor argues that it is identity politics, and particularly 'an idealised nostalgic representation of the past' (Kaldor 2006: 7), over which new wars are fought. This notion of identity politics is also closely associated with globalisation, and is affected first by a growing inability to distinguish between the domestic and international, the internal and external, and second by the effect that new media technologies have on notions of identity.

A second distinction that the new war literature makes relates to the organisation of war. Whereas in the past war had been centrally organised, controlled and fought on behalf of the state, new wars are fought by highly decentralised groups, 'such as paramilitary units, local warlords, criminal gangs, police forces, mercenary groups and also regular armies, including breakaway units from regular armies' (Kaldor 2006: 7). Third, the method of war fighting is also thought to be 'new'. New wars are distinguished by the avoidance of large-scale Clausewitzian battles. Instead, war is progressed through contests over control of territory through control of the population, population displacement and violence directed against civilian populations. Fourth, whereas old wars were fought with an appreciation of codified laws of war, new wars are notable for their barbarism, violence and total disregard for the established norms and laws of war.

The new war literature emphasises that 'force is mainly directed not against the enemy's armed force but against the civilian population, the aim being either to drive it from it a certain area . . . or to force it to supply and support certain armed groups on a permanent basis' (Münkler 2005: 14). Statistics are held up to support this claim, with many writers citing the much-discussed transformations in the ratios of soldier to civilian deaths in war across the twentieth century. At the end of the nineteenth century, this ratio was 9:1; by 1945, it had become 1:1; and by century's end, it had completely reversed to 1:9 (e.g., Kaldor 2006: 107).

One of the most dramatic and visible results of this new form of conflict has been an increase in refugees or permanently displaced persons (see Hammerstad, this volume). Drawing a connection between new types of conflict and permanently displaced peoples, Albrecht Schnabel (2001: 109) notes that the 'global dynamics of flight and refuge are changing,' much of it resulting 'from the changing nature of conflict'. Again, statistics support this point: the number of internally displaced people increased from 327,000 per conflict in 1969 to 1,093,300 per conflict in 2004 (cited in Kaldor 2006: 107).

Finally, the new war literature argues that the economy of war making has also changed. While old wars were financed by states out of traditional revenue streams, new wars are financed in entirely different manner. They draw on more unorthodox and often ad hoc measures such as looting, robbery, pillage, extortion, hostage taking as well as more complex and better organised revenue-raising means such as arms and drug trafficking, oil smuggling and money laundering. Duffield (2000: 73–4) argues that the end of the Cold War meant that 'warring parties have been forced to develop their own means of economic sustainability. Reflecting the logic of globalization, this has often meant moving beyond the state in pursuit of wider alternative economic networks.' Adamson (2005: 32) similarly argues that 'globalization is transforming the international security environment by stimulating shifts in the resources, infrastructure and capacities available to non-state political entrepreneurs to engage in political mobilisation transnationally and globally.' Some have gone so far as to claim that whereas in the past, wars were fought for primarily political motives, war is now fought for economic ends (e.g., Berdal and Malone 2000).

In summary, 'new wars' need to be understood within the context of globalisation, and in particular the fragmentation of state authority and all that this encompasses. Globalisation has facilitated the decline in incidence of inter-state conflict while simultaneously creating a fertile environment for the increase of intra-state conflict. New wars are fought by a combination of state and sub-state actors; in this respect, it is said to have become privatised. The targeting of civilians and the deliberate displacement or systematic murdering of peoples (including such methods as genocide, ethnic cleansing or rendering an area uninhabitable) are all central features of new wars.

Despite the apparent prevalence of new wars, a number of authors have questioned the relevancy of the distinction made between old and new wars, with many of them questioning the novelty of new wars. As Newman (2004: 179) observes, '[m]uch of this is not new: all of the factors that characterise new wars have been present, to varying degrees, throughout the last 100 years. The actors, objectives, spatial context, human impact, political economy, and social structure of conflict have not changed to the extent argued in the new wars literature.'

Critics of the new war literature also make more specific arguments. Regarding civil wars, Newman (2004: 180) points out that rather than increasing, as claimed in the new war literature, the quantitative incidence of civil war has in fact declined since 1992. Stathis Kalyvas (2001: 99) goes further when he suggests that the distinction between 'old' civil wars and 'new' civil wars is invalid due to the shortcomings of data in contemporary war and ignorance of historical detail on earlier wars.

Newman (2004: 181–2) is also critical of the claim that patterns of victimisation and human impact are peculiar to the late twentieth century. He argues that there is little evidence to substantiate this and points out that atrocities and forced human displacement have been endemic features of war.

According to Owens (2008), the emphasis that the new war literature places on the breakdown between public and private, and the subsequent ramifications this has for understanding conflict, is also flawed. She argues that 'public-private distinctions shift and change as an effect of political power' and that 'there is clear historical and sociological evidence to support the conceptual claim that a variety of public-private distinctions are made and remade during war' (Owens 2008: 988). Reflecting a theme that is present in most of the critiques of the new war thesis, Owens (2008: 988) suggests that debates about political violence 'should be understood historically as the transnational constitution and circulation of military and economic power'.

The strongest critiques of the new war literature are those that question the underpinning idea of the new war thesis: that new wars should be understood within the context of globalisation. Mats Berdal (2003) argues that 'globalisation' as a term suffers from definitional impreciseness. The 'totalising' pretensions of the term limit its use as an analytical tool. When used in such a way, efforts to understand individual cases and specific mechanisms are invariably flawed. Not only is the term itself problematic, Berdal (2003) questions the extent to which economic aspects of globalisation are inherently conflict-generating. For Berdal, an emphasis on economic motivations does not adequately explain why people resort to violence; greater attention should be paid to historical and cultural roots. Many also argue that the economic motives of 'new' wars are vastly overstated. Newman (2004: 183–4), adopting an argument popular with globalisation sceptics such as Paul Hirst and Grahame Thompson (2003), points out that 'the processes associated with globalization that affect conflicts – a hallmark of the new war thesis – existed throughout the twentieth century.'

In sum, critics point out that in many respects the claims made about the structural transformation of warfare from an 'old' to a 'new' model are, at best, open to theoretical and empirical criticism. At worst, the distinction is utterly invalid, resting as it does on dubious claims and often more than a little ignorance.

The war on terror: a new war?

In 2002, the Bush administration put forward the idea that the war against Al Qaeda represented a new form of conflict:

The war against terrorism ushers in a new paradigm, one in which groups with broad international reach commit horrific acts against innocent civilians, sometimes with the direct support of States. Our Nation recognises that this new paradigm – ushered in not by us, but by terrorists – requires new thinking in the law of war, but thinking that nevertheless should be consistent with Geneva. (cited in McDonald 2008: 233)

Indeed, for a number of reasons, the 'war on terror' appears to be the perfect example of a new war.

First, it is being fought by a variety of state and sub-state actors (the Taliban in Afghanistan and various insurgents in Iraq) which in turn has led to a blurring of the distinction between combatants and non-combatants. But it is not only the insurgent movements that can be characterised as 'non-state'. In Iraq, work that had traditionally been undertaken by national armies has instead been delegated to private American security contractors, the most infamous of which was the Blackwater group. Second, both the wars in Afghanistan and Iraq are characterised by their lack of definitive, even traditional, battles. Rather, these wars are characterised by the Coalition's reliance on the use of technologically superior weapons, including precision-guided munitions and 'unmanned aerial vehicles' (UAVs) or 'drones' and ongoing ground skirmishes, from which it is difficult to ascertain 'winners' or 'losers'.

Third, while it is not always clear whether civilians have been targeted, it is clear that civilian deaths far outweigh military deaths. With specific reference to Iraq, Kaldor (2006: 169) argues that 'because it is difficult to distinguish insurgents from the civilian population, it is civilians who appear to be the main victims of attacks and of detentions.' Continuing her argument that the war in Iraq is best understood as a 'new war', Kaldor also points to the resultant large numbers of permanent refugees and displaced persons. In Afghanistan, Human Rights Watch (see 'Troops in Contact') reports that 'as a result of Operation Enduring Freedom (OEF) and NATO-led International Security Assistance Force (ISAF) airstrikes in 2006, 116 Afghan civilians were killed in 13 bombings. In 2007, Afghan civilian deaths were nearly three times higher: 321 Afghan civilians were killed in 22 bombings, while hundreds more were injured.'

Fourth, traditional understandings of the justification for going to war and of conduct during war have been challenged or even entirely ignored, especially in Iraq. While there is a general consensus among policymakers and academics alike that the ongoing military actions in Afghanistan constitute what Adam Roberts (2005: 116) calls a 'justifiable use of force', no such consensus exists with regard to the invasion of Iraq. The first problematic aspect of the most recent war in Iraq regards the basis for going to war in the first place and more particularly the problem associated with so-called pre-emptive war. The oft-quoted 2002 United States National Security Strategy (NSS) advocated pre-emption to address new threats to US national security. Pre-emption is 'based on the idea of preventing an attack by disabling a threatening enemy' (Roberts 2003: 45). But, as Roberts (2003: 45) notes, 'general acceptance of any doctrine of pre-emption would involve a major conceptual shift in international relations.' Equally, the conduct of Iraqi and Afghan insurgents – the violence and barbarism of their assaults on civilians as well as soldiers – seems to further link this broader conflict with the attributes of the 'new' wars.

Concluding remarks

But what does all this mean? Is the war on terror representative of a 'new war' and does the type of conflict that we have witnessed in Iraq and Afghanistan represent a new norm? Indeed, does the new war thesis provide us with insights into the way that conflict will play out in the future? It is clear that organised conflict no longer entirely reflects that described by Clausewitz. Wars are no longer primarily fought between powerful states. Nor are they primarily fought by well-organised, centrally funded and commanded professional military apparatuses. However, the degree to which this is caused or facilitated by globalisation or rapid advances in military technology is debatable.

While the reasons for going to war might have become slightly more complex than those explained by Clausewitz, Colin Gray (1999: 169) makes a valid point when he notes that the *nature* of warfare has not changed (and furthermore, is unlikely to change): its 'nature as organised violence for political goals survives untouched by radical shifts in political forms, motives for conflict or technology.' Essentially, new wars represent a continuation of modern conflict. Likewise, the new war literature's focus on the decreasing capacity of states is perhaps exaggerated. As the wars in Iraq and Afghanistan demonstrate, the ability of powerful states such as the United States to involve themselves in large, ongoing conflicts seems undiminished. While the advent of nuclear weapons means that we are unlikely to see so-called great power wars in the foreseeable future, this certainly does not mean that states will stop using force to achieve their policy goals. In many countries foreign policy has gained a distinctly military edge in recent years. As such, Clausewitz's insights into war continue to remain remarkably valuable.

Whether or not the conflicts that we have witnessed in the first part of the twentieth century serve as a likely pointer to future conflict is difficult to assess. Technological advances in war fighting will certainly continue to affect the way that war is fought. We may also have seen the end of symmetrical warfare: Western European countries in particular are increasingly reluctant to risk the lives of their soldiers in remote wars and norms against the use of force are of growing salience. What is unlikely to change is the violent and destructive nature of warfare. The primary actors in war are also unlikely to change: the state retains an important position in the international system, and ultimately its fundamental linkage to a policy purpose remains undiminished.

Guide to further reading

Heavily influenced by Clausewitz's experiences fighting on the losing side against Napoleon's armies, *On War* (1984) remains the most influential text on the subject. Michael Howard's *Clausewitz* (1983) provides a clear and approachable synopsis of Clausewitz's *magnum opus*. Van Creveld (1991), an Israeli war historian, sets out an early argument about the changing character of war in a book which traces the evolution of warfare from the birth of the modern nation-state to present times. Berdal and Malone's (2000) collection of exceptional essays investigate the degree to which modern wars are fought for economic rather than political ends. An interesting collection of essays that explore the changing nature of warfare in the post-Cold War era can be found in Duyvesteyn and Angstrom (2005). Kaldor's (2006) influential book argues that changes in the international system caused by globalisation have resulted in changes to the key features of conflict, hence the advent of 'new wars'. Record (2003) provides insight from a former professional staff member of the Senate Armed Services Committee on the problems associated with attempts by the United States to fight the war on terror as a traditional war.

Chapter 9

Transnational Terrorism

ANDREW PHILLIPS

On September 11, 2001, history resumed. A mere 12 years earlier, the rubble of the Berlin wall had seemed to symbolise a grand historical terminus. With communism following fascism into oblivion, political theorist Francis Fukuyama was prompted to speculate about the possible 'end of history' (Fukuyama 1989), with the defeat of America's last remaining totalitarian adversary supposedly heralding the irrevocable global triumph of open societies constituted around the twin pillars of parliamentary democracy and market capitalism. By the second year of the new millennium, the ruins of the World Trade Centre conversely invited a far more sober assessment of history's course. On 9/11, nineteen middle class hijackers from Saudi Arabia and Egypt exploited the very openness and technological sophistication of liberal societies to inflict more death and destruction on the US mainland than had any of America's totalitarian enemies in the twentieth century. The 'Manhattan raid' and the contemporaneous attack on the Pentagon dramatised to a global audience the vulnerability of the world's only superpower, and catalysed an immediate and profound transformation in the foreign policies of the United States and its closest allies. Dismissed by many as a second-order strategic concern in the 1990s, transnational terrorism is now widely regarded as one of the most potent threats to international peace and security. The nature of this threat, its historical evolution, contemporary import and prospective significance form the subjects of this chapter.

Transnational terrorism defined

Terrorism is understood here to refer to acts of violence (or the threat of violence) that are intentionally directed at non-combatants for the purpose of securing political objectives. Terrorism is essentially a form of compellence, whereby terrorists seek to leverage the distress evoked by acts of indiscriminate violence targeted at non-combatants in order to extort tangible changes in their adversaries' behaviour. Terrorism can refer to the activities of both state and non-state actors, as demonstrated, for example, in the 'terror bombing' of civilian population centres undertaken by both sides in the Second World War to compel opposing governments to sue for peace. In its contemporary usage, however, terrorism most often refers to actions undertaken by non-state actors, for example,

136

the Provisional Irish Republican Army's (PIRA's) selective use of terrorism in the British Isles as part of its campaign to compel the British government to acquiesce to the six counties' integration into the Republic of Ireland.

Terrorism is a form of violence that is intentionally provocative in its transgression of moral and legal norms preserving non-combatant immunity, but it is nevertheless driven in almost all instances by actors pursuing coherent political objectives. As such, terrorism comprises a form of violent political contention that must be distinguished from other forms of private international violence, such as piracy, privateering, mercenarism and transnational organised crime, which are driven by predominantly economic motives. Terrorism is additionally distinguishable from both state-based conventional warfare and guerrilla warfare. Terrorism's frequent characterisation as a 'weapon of the weak' captures the truth that terrorism is most often embraced by those who have no realistic possibility of prevailing against their opponents in a conventional armed contest (Crenshaw 1981: 387). From the Napoleonic revolution in warfare onwards, state actors have traditionally sought victory either through a decisive battle of annihilation (Bond 1996: 43) or through a steady, relentless process of attrition (Gray 2007: 81). Both strategies favour protagonists endowed with great material strength. Conversely, terrorism relies on strategies of provocation, polarisation and exhaustion. The selective use of atrocity is thus deployed to goad governments into disproportionate responses to terrorist violence, to polarise populations into pro- and anti-government factions, and eventually to exhaust governments into capitulating to the terrorists' demands (Crenshaw 1981: 387; Harmon 2001: 44).

In its emphasis on corroding the enemy's will to resist through recourse to a protracted armed struggle, terrorism shares strong affinities with guerrilla warfare. Nevertheless, as a mode of warfare, terrorism may be distinguishable from guerrilla warfare by the disproportionate weight it accords to highly publicised atrocities as a mechanism for shaping the consciousness and behaviour of target audiences. Guerrilla warfare routinely involves the painstaking cultivation of a mass base of popular support in 'liberated' rural base areas and the incremental expansion of guerrillas' geographic reach and popular appeal over time, with victory expected to materialise once the guerrillas secure sufficient mass support and military wherewithal to prevail over government forces in conventional combat (Hoffman 2002: 22). Conversely, terrorists typically seek to exploit both the anonymity of urban environments and the opportunities for publicity afforded by mass media outlets to perpetrate shocking acts of 'propaganda by the deed'; in undertaking high-visibility and conscience-shocking acts of violence such as hijacking airliners, bombing public places or assassinating public officials and community leaders, terrorists hope to dramatise governmental impotence, intimidate rival ethnic or religious communities and, perhaps most importantly, energise spontaneous popular support behind their cause (Hoffman 2002: 20). The urban terrorist and the rural-based guerrilla thus embody different styles of asymmetric warfare, employing different strategies to mobilise popular support and laying different relative emphases on the significance of highly publicised atrocities as a mechanism for communicating grievances and catalysing transformations in the consciousness of allies and adversaries. In practice, however, these forms have historically overlapped to a strong degree, a trend that has continued and intensified with the wars in Afghanistan and Iraq.

Finally, any definitional overview of terrorism would be incomplete without acknowledging its increasingly transnational character under conditions of globalisation (Cronin 2002/03). As improvements in transportation and communication technologies have facilitated growing transnational flows of money, *materiel*, people and ideas, an ever-greater proportion of terrorist activities have acquired a transnational dimension. Thus, for example, separatists with geographically limited agendas such as the Liberation Tigers of Tamil Eelam (LTTE) made extensive use of diaspora financing in the 1990s to advance their political goals, all while prosecuting military campaigns which remained predominantly confined to their respective homelands (Gunaratna 2003: 208). The increasing ease with which locally oriented terrorists have been able to tap into transnational support networks in a rapidly globalising world has considerably increased their resilience in the face of government repression (Adamson 2005: 33). Nevertheless, it has been terrorists such as Al Qaeda, who are transnational not only in their mobilisation of resources, but also in their choice of targets and in the scope of their political ambitions, who have aroused the greatest international consternation. It is this form of terrorism, equally transnational in its means, goals and targets, with which we will be preoccupied for the remainder of this chapter.

The historical evolution of transnational terrorism

Far from emerging *ex nihlio* following the end of the Cold War, transnational terrorism has existed in some form from at least the last quarter of the nineteenth century. A consideration of the successive waves of 'rebel terror' (Rapoport 2001) that have punctuated the last 130 years illustrates this point. Transnational terrorism's origins can be traced to the anarchist terrorism that convulsed Western Europe, North America and Tsarist Russia from 1880 to 1914 (Rapoport 2001: 419). Facilitated by factors as diverse as the invention of dynamite, the rise of mass circulation newspapers and the wrenching social changes accompanying rapid urbanisation and industrialisation, the anarchists' campaign of violence constituted the Western public's first sustained exposure to modern terrorism. While insignificant by contemporary standards, the casualties inflicted by anarchist terrorists in venues as diverse as cafes, parliaments, theatres and stock exchanges nevertheless terrified the middle classes (Jensen 2004: 135). The resulting scapegoating of immigrant communities by the popular press and government authorities on the basis of largely imagined international anarchist conspiracies provided a foretaste of the polarising effects of terrorism that would frequently recur in subsequent decades (Jensen 2004: 143). Equally, anarchists' narcissistic pursuit of martyrdom and their uncritical faith in the catalysing effects of the 'propaganda of the deed' have also found their echoes in succeeding waves of terrorism, as we will shortly see.

The anarchist wave of terrorism sputtered into history with the onset of the First World War, but was succeeded by a wave of anti-colonial terrorism that spanned the twentieth-century's middle decades. Unlike anarchist terrorists, who were uncompromisingly revolutionary in their desire to overturn all formal systems of government, anti-colonial terrorists sought the more modest objective of securing national self-determination in territories then subject to foreign rule. While terrorism featured conspicuously in various wars of decolonisation in Africa and Asia, it was in the Middle East that terrorism featured most prominently, playing a critical role in the National Liberation Front's (NLF) successful campaign for Algerian independence, and in the Palestinians' so far unsuccessful quest for an independent state. Of all the exponents of anti-colonial terrorism, the Palestinians were by far the most active transnationally, taking advantage of the enhanced mobility provided by international air travel and the vastly increased propaganda opportunities provided by television to prosecute their struggle against Israel on a global stage (Hoffman 1998: 67). The brutal murder of 11 Israeli athletes by Black September at the Munich Olympics in 1972 provided the most notorious testament to the effectiveness of this new form of warfare. Global revulsion at the terrorists' atrocities notwithstanding, the massacre at Munich catapulted the Palestinian cause to worldwide prominence, and shortly thereafter yielded Yasser Arafat's Palestinian Liberation Organization (PLO) the prize of widespread diplomatic recognition as the legitimate voice of the Palestinian people (Hoffman 1998: 75).

Reflecting the global strength of anti-colonial sentiment generally and the contentious nature of the Israeli–Palestinian conflict specifically, anti-colonial terrorism failed to generate a coordinated response from the international community. Contrarily, the third wave of terror, which struck Western Europe in the 1960s and 1970s, conversely stimulated the development of wide-ranging counter-terrorism measures that bear comparison with analogous initiatives that have developed globally since 9/11. Drawing tactical inspiration from the Palestinians and ideological inspiration from Mao and Lenin, extreme Leftist terrorist groups such as the Baader-Meinhof Group, the Italian Red Brigades and Direct Action perpetrated a series of hijackings, kidnappings, bombings and assassinations from the late 1960s onwards (Rapoport 2001: 421). Hoping both to expel the American military presence in Western Europe and to overturn the capitalist system, the chief legacy of these terrorists was rather to inadvertently help to consolidate international policing and counter-terrorism cooperation between their would-be targets. Like their anarchist predecessors, the radicals of the 1960s and 1970s underestimated the resilience of the established order while also overestimating the transformative potential of 'propaganda by the deed', with the enhanced state repression they elicited accelerating their own demise (Hoffman 1998: 83).

The fourth wave of terror dates from the late 1970s onwards, and differs from the first three primarily by dint of its religious–ideological colouration. The origins of transnational jihadist terrorism lie largely in an ongoing internal crisis of governmental legitimacy that began to engulf large swathes of the Islamic world in the 1970s and 1980s (Doran 2002: 27). During this period, popular frustration mounted towards autocratic governments such as that of Anwar Sadat in Egypt and Zia ul Haq in Pakistan. These and other corrupt and repressive regimes had failed to meet their citizens' economic and political aspirations, and had also become increasingly reliant on the United States for their internal and external security (Bronson 2006: 125–8; Clarke 2004: 36–9). This crisis of governmental legitimacy coincided with the waxing of United States' involvement in the Greater Middle East to fill the power vacuum created by Britain's post-1968 withdrawal from all bases east of the Suez Canal. It also coincided with the growth of politically engaged forms of religious fundamentalism in the Islamic world, a trend that was radically accelerated in 1979 with the Islamic revolution in Iran and the onset of the anti-Soviet jihad following the Red Army's invasion of Afghanistan (Kepel 2003: 93–5).

Transnational jihadist terrorism thus emerged out of the intersection of localised crises of legitimacy, increasing superpower involvement in the Muslim world and the coterminous rise of intensely politicised forms of Islamic identity. Their world-views forged in the Afghan jihad of the 1980s, jihadists such as Osama bin Laden and Ayman al-Zawahiri beheld a global Islamic community (or *ummah*) being victimised by a combination of apostate local tyrants (the 'near' enemy) ruling at the behest of their infidel Western sponsors (the 'far' enemy). For bin Laden and others, the emancipation of the *ummah* could only come once the apostate tyrants had been overthrown and their Western sponsors ejected from Muslim lands (Doran 2002: 31–3). This would in turn permit the destruction of the 'Zionist entity' of Israel, the erasure of artificial national boundaries dividing the world's Muslims and the unification of the *ummah* under the banner of a global Caliphate ruled according to *sharia* law (al-Zawahiri 2005). To this end, Al Qaeda operatives from the 1990s launched a series of audacious terrorist attacks aimed at goading the West into embarking upon an unwinnable war in the Muslim world that would end with its humiliation, thereby precipitating the ensuing collapse of its 'apostate' client regimes throughout the Middle East and beyond. These provocations eventually succeeded in catalysing the US invasions of Afghanistan and Iraq since 9/11, but Al Qaeda's subsequent efforts to commandeer local insurgencies have met with only very limited success, and the jihadists' prospects of long-term victory remain doubtful. This observation notwithstanding, impact of jihadist terrorism on Western states' foreign policies since 9/11 has nevertheless been both dramatic and profoundly destabilising, with its impact on global politics defying any comparison with earlier manifestations of transnational terrorism.

The contemporary significance of transnational terrorism

While transnational terrorism has long been recognised as a significant problem internationally, the 9/11 attacks imbued the threat with a historically unprecedented level of importance. In the years following the attacks, the struggle against

importance of 9/11 attacks

jihadist terrorism has been a dominant feature of world politics, and has been characterised by a contradictory mixture of international cooperation and confrontation. On the one hand, the immediate post-9/11 period saw a flurry of ① initiatives aimed at suppressing the threats posed by the entwined challenges of transnational terrorism and the proliferation of weapons of mass destruction (WMD) (Heupel 2008: 8). In contrast to its earlier lackadaisical efforts to curb transnational terrorism, the United Nations Security Council swiftly passed res- A olutions imposing universally binding obligations on member states to refrain from providing material sponsorship to terrorists (Rosand 2003: 334). In parallel to this prohibition, the Security Council also imposed positive duties to prevent non-state actors from either acquiring WMD or using member states' territory B for sanctuary or transit (Heupel 2008: 14). With the codification of these universal norms and the establishment of standing organisations within the UN (e.g., the Counter-Terrorism Executive Directorate, the 1540 Committee) to monitor compliance and assist member states in meeting their obligations, the interna- C tional community's capacity to resist transnational terrorism was significantly strengthened.

The system-strengthening initiatives sketched above were spearheaded by the United States, but its role in bolstering the international counter-terrorism architecture was overshadowed by the more confrontational and revolutionary strand ② of American foreign policy that also emerged after 9/11. Seized by the urgency of the terrorist challenge and exasperated by the perceived inadequacy of existing collective security institutions, the Bush Administration embraced a strongly unilateralist foreign policy agenda after 9/11, most notoriously proclaiming the need for pre-emptive strikes and 'regime change' as necessary expedients to prevent the uncontrolled spread of WMD to both 'rogue' states and terrorists (National Security Strategy 2002: 15). The endorsement of preventive war in particular (misleadingly couched as 'pre-emptive' and thus legal within the terms of international law) aroused significant alarm internationally, given that it dovetailed with pre-existing neo-conservative aspirations to indefinitely preserve America's status as the world's only superpower. More controversial still were attempts to 'drain the swamp' of sentiment for jihadist terrorism through the promotion of a 'forward strategy of freedom' in the Middle East. This strategy of armed democracy promotion reached its apogee with the March 2003 invasion of Iraq, a gambit *(trap)* that perversely reinvigorated the global jihadist movement (National Intelligence Estimate 2006: 2), while simultaneously absorbing American attention for the remainder of the Bush Administration. *change in foreign relations*

In the short term, the invasion of Iraq significantly increased strains between ③ the United States and many of its traditional allies in Western Europe and the Middle East. Europeans fretted about the dangerous precedent for the UN's collective security system that they saw being established with the invasion of Iraq, an invasion that had proceeded without the express consent of the UN Security Council (Gordon and Shapiro 2004: 170). Middle Eastern allies such as Saudi Arabia meanwhile opposed the invasion, both because of an understandable wariness regarding the Administration's democracy promotion agenda for

(willingness)

the region and also, at least in part, because of prescient fears of the war's potential to both destabilise the Middle East and further radicalise domestic Islamist dissidents (Record 2004: 94). By contrast, China made no concerted effort to thwart American plans in Iraq, rather capitalising on the post-9/11 rapprochement between the two countries to continue its economic and geopolitical ascent (Gries 2005: 402). Its vocal opposition to the Iraq war notwithstanding, Russia's relations with the United States also improved momentarily after 9/11 (Herd and Akerman 2002: 358), with mass casualty attacks by Chechen separatists in Moscow (2002) and Beslan (2004) reinforcing perceptions of a common US–Russian interest in suppressing Islamist terrorism in all its forms.

Transnational terrorism emerged as an issue of incalculable international significance after 9/11, but its impact on world politics was decisively influenced by the reactions that Al Qaeda's provocation yielded from the United States, and by the responses that these reactions in turn elicited from other countries. In the short term, the revolutionary turn in the US foreign policy strained alliances with traditional security partners, while common counter-terrorist concerns provided a focal point for cooperation with countries such as Russia and China that had formerly been regarded as strategic competitors by the Bush Administration. However, while counter-terrorism concerns lost none of their urgency during the Administration's second term, by then older patterns of cooperation and rivalry had begun to re-assert themselves. While most of America's NATO allies remained aloof from the war in Iraq, mass casualty attacks in Madrid (2004) and London (2005) as well as numerous foiled terror plots in Germany (2001, 2007), Britain (2006 and 2007) and elsewhere highlighted the continuing danger posed to Western societies by transnational jihadist terrorism. NATO's assumption of a lead role in prosecuting the counter-insurgency struggle against the Taliban and Al Qaeda remnants in Afghanistan served to further bolster Western unity in the face of the jihadist threat, while also demonstrating the alliance's capacity to adapt to the challenges of the radically changed security environment of the post-Cold War period. At the same time, the expansion of Western influence in Central and South Asia from 2001 onwards as part of the 'war on terror' aroused both Russian and Chinese suspicions, with the Shanghai Cooperation Organization (SCO) strenuously backing Uzbekistan's demands for the closure of recently established American bases in that country in 2005 (Olcott 2005: 331).

Debating the 'war on terror' – the contemporary intellectual impact of transnational terrorism

Aside from its profound real world impact on the course of global politics, the 'war on terror' provided a sharp intellectual jolt to the discipline of international relations. Given the state-centrism of most International Relations (IR) thinking, the 9/11 attacks exposed IR scholarship as offering an interpretive framework that was at best incomplete and at worst anachronistic in its reading of world affairs.

Subsequently, many of the most stimulating debates surrounding transnational terrorism have focused less on its implications for international relations theory, and more on practical questions relating to the nature of the struggle against jihadist terrorism and the most appropriate means for managing the jihadist terrorist threat.

Clausewitz's injunction that victory in any war presupposes that one first properly understands the nature of the conflict in which one is involved (Clausewitz 1976: 88) provides a useful entrée into debates over both the nature of the anti-jihadist struggle and the means by which it might most successfully be prosecuted. Drawing inspiration from the works of Samuel Huntington, some academic and journalistic commentators have characterised the struggle against jihadist terrorism as constituting merely the most conspicuous manifestation of a larger 'clash of civilizations' between Islam and the West deriving from a combination of innate cultural differences and enduring historical rivalries (Blankley 2005; Hanson 2002; Sullivan 2001). Seen through this lens, the confrontation with jihadist terrorism expresses broader tensions between the Western and Islamic worlds that are largely insoluble. A civilisational interpretation of the 'war on terror' thus implicitly appears to recommend a policy of both defence and disengagement. Given the jihadists' implacable opposition to Western values, intensified international cooperation in the areas of policing and intelligence sharing is essential to secure citizens' safety from jihadist assaults. Equally, however, given that the jihadists are assumed to embody a broader dissonance in values between Islam and the West, a civilisational approach *a la* Huntington would counsel that this values gap be openly acknowledged and interaction between the two blocs minimised if inter-civilisational friction is to be contained (Huntington 1996: 211).

Civilisational accounts of the 'war on terror' can be criticised on multiple grounds, ranging from their reliance on essentialist characterisations of Western and Islamic 'civilizations' to the manifest impracticality of a policy of civilisational disengagement given the increasingly cosmopolitan nature of open societies under conditions of globalisation. Civilisational accounts have also been condemned for their tendency to downplay the more proximate political imperatives underpinning the conflict (Abrahamian 2003: 537–8; Barkawi 2004: 25–6; Tuastad 2003). Critical accounts of the 'war on terror' have thus conversely foregrounded the catalysing role of Western foreign policy both in contributing to Al Qaeda's genesis (through its sponsorship of the anti-Soviet jihad in Afghanistan in the 1980s) and in sustaining its subsequent expansion (see, e.g., Johnson 2002: xiv). Particular emphasis is given to the role played by Western governments in sponsoring brutal and corrupt secular dictatorships in the Middle East to ensure continued access to the region's vital energy supplies (Ali 2002: 265; Chomsky 2003: 214–16; Scheuer 2007: 258). While critical accounts acknowledge the brutal and indiscriminate nature of jihadist terrorism, they identify its root causes in the 'blowback' deriving from self-interested Western foreign policies. The West has sustained repressive autocracies and in so doing inflamed the popular anti-Western sentiments upon which jihadist terrorists have relied in seeking to cast themselves as the legitimate defenders of a global Islamic community (the *ummah*). Despite their hostility towards civilisational portrayals of the 'war on terror', critical accounts thus nevertheless frequently implicitly enjoin changes in Western foreign policy (e.g., decreased reliance on Middle Eastern oil and thus on regional autocrats) that bear some resemblance to the former's calls for disengagement, and can be similarly critiqued on pragmatic grounds.

Opposing both civilisational and critical accounts, a third set of approaches has emphasised the ideational and the political roots of the 'war on terror'. Having identified intellectual affinities between jihadist ideology and earlier twentieth-century expressions of totalitarianism, some commentators have cast jihadism as a pathological counter-reaction to the global spread of market civilisation and the accompanying crisis of traditional values and institutions this has engendered in rapidly modernising Muslim-majority countries (Berman 2003; Mousseau 2003; Podhoretz 2007). Seen through a neo-conservative lens, this characterisation has been invoked to justify policies aimed at eradicating jihadism through the coercive transformation of these countries into market democracies, effectively replicating in Iraq and Afghanistan the grand strategy that purged Germany and Japan of their totalitarian tendencies in the Second World War (Podhoretz 2007: 213).

The disappointing results of the neo-conservative strategy in both countries have nevertheless produced more nuanced accounts that have retained an awareness of jihadism's totalitarian complexion, but that have also acknowledged the role played by local grievances in enabling transnational jihadists to extend their geographical reach into strife-torn states and thereby mobilise a global constituency in support of their cause. Casting the jihadists' campaign as a global insurgency, some analysts have advocated a global counter-insurgency campaign based around the concept of 'disaggregation', in which military power would be employed in conjunction with selective political concessions and improvements in local governance to prise transnational jihadists from host communities in countries such as Iraq and Afghanistan (see, e.g., Kilcullen 2005: 608). While constituting a less ambitious strategy than the neo-conservatives' advocacy of armed democracy promotion, this strategy nevertheless also acknowledges the need for a counter-terrorism strategy that moves beyond a posture of passive defence, and instead explicitly addresses the role played by failures of governance in contributing to the conditions under which jihadist terrorism has thrived.

The future significance of transnational terrorism for international order

Disagreements concerning both the nature of the struggle against jihadist terrorism and the best means of prosecuting it are likely to persist for some time, if only because preliminary indications suggest that the 'war on terror' will endure into the foreseeable future. This is so for several reasons. First, increasing Great

Power demand for the Middle East's scarce energy reserves is likely to see growing rather than diminishing foreign interference in the region in the next few
decades, further inflaming the grievances that sustain the jihadist movement.
Revived regional interest in civil nuclear energy programmes will furthermore
increase proliferation concerns throughout the region and will also increase the
likelihood of nuclear knowledge and technologies diffusing to jihadist terrorists
and their sympathisers. A combination of surging demographic growth, limited
economic opportunities and unresponsive government in relatively oil-poor states
such as Egypt and Yemen will meanwhile nurture the conditions of political instability and popular despair within which extremism can thrive, providing further
recruitment opportunities for the jihadists.

For these reasons, the 'Long War' against jihadist extremism will continue for
some time to come. Its effects are likely to be felt in three areas. First, at the level
of state–society relations, counter-terrorism concerns will license the continuing
expansion of states' powers of policing and surveillance. Concerns over the trade-
off between civil liberties and national security will remain a source of contention *disagreement*
within democratic societies, while in authoritarian states, the spectre of terrorism will continue to be invoked to stave off calls for political liberalisation. State *fear*
powers to regulate and supervise religious beliefs and practices will also continue
to expand, as will more concerted efforts to codify the nature of the relationship
between faith and state identity. In secular societies, where religion has long been
regarded as a matter of private conviction and where there has also existed an
institutionalised separation between church and state, this encroachment of state
power into the 'private' domain will prove to be particularly controversial. The
French 'headscarves affair' provides merely one instance of this development,
but it is illustrative of a divisive cultural politics that will increasingly attend the
efforts of traditionally 'post-religious' societies to reconcile respect for cultural
diversity with their commitment to maintaining a predominantly secular public
sphere (Roy 2007: 26–8).

Second, counter-terrorism concerns will continue to exert a strong but ambigu-
ous effect on Great Power relations, sustaining a trend that has been manifested
since 9/11. Multilateral cooperation in areas such as the suppression of terrorist financing and the prevention of nuclear terrorism will continue, but states'
common interests in suppressing jihadist terrorism will be refracted through
the prism of their varying and partially antagonistic national security agendas.
Given its status as the primary security partner of both Israel and the conservative Gulf monarchies, the United States will remain the preferred target of
jihadist terrorists, and will continue to lead the struggle against jihadist terrorism. America's Western European allies will meanwhile continue to cooperate
intensively with the Americans in areas such as intelligence sharing, but their
support for American military activity in the Greater Middle East will be constrained by both widespread public pacifism and governments' largely unspoken
desire not to antagonise their own restive Muslim communities through sustained
military involvement in the Islamic world. Rather than relying on military power,
the countries of the European Union are likely to attempt to stabilise their Islamic

periphery through recourse to similar strategies (i.e., economic integration and political cooperation) as those that rehabilitated transitional societies in Southern Europe in the 1970s and 1980s and in Eastern Europe in the 1990s.

The embryonic US–Indian strategic partnership is also likely to be heavily conditioned by counter-terrorism concerns. Given the presence of a strong domestic jihadist threat in India, New Delhi will find much scope for counter-terrorism cooperation with the United States, but the government will nevertheless need to take the sensitivities of India's substantial Muslim minority into account, particularly if Muslims' highly negative perception of America's role in world affairs endures beyond the Bush Administration. Equally, America's strategic partnership with India will also be constrained for the foreseeable future by America's continued reliance on Pakistan, India's greatest rival, as an essential partner in the 'war on terror'. Meanwhile, concerns about Muslim separatism in parts of China and the Russian Federation will also provide at least the appearance of a common interest between these countries and the United States. Both countries are likely to continue to exaggerate the linkages between the global jihadist movement and separatists in places like Xinjiang and Chechnya in order to legitimise their heavy-handed rule in these territories. At the same time, America, Russia and China are each likely to disingenuously invoke the common threat of terrorism in order to preserve or extend their influence in the strategically vital and energy-rich region of Central Asia, potentially reprising the 'Great Game' that punctuated Anglo-Russian imperial rivalry in the region during the nineteenth century.

Finally, the impact of transnational terrorism will be most strongly felt in growing North/South tensions, which will derive from the North's increasingly permissive attitude towards the pre-emptive and preventive use of force as a means of neutralising terrorist threats emanating from the world's weak and failing states. Historically, material constraints on Western military power prevented the sustained projection of force into the African and Asian interior until the mid-nineteenth century (Black 2005: 131). From the mid-twentieth century onwards, the UN system of collective security institutionalised norms of sovereign equality and non-intervention at a global level, providing small and weak states with a robust, if admittedly imperfect, guard against armed encroachments on their territory by the Great Powers (Cohen 2006: 492). In the twenty-first century, military innovations such as pilotless drones and precision-guided munitions (PGMs) have again conferred upon strong and wealthy powers the ability to project force swiftly and easily into weaker states, while anxieties about the threats posed by terrorism and WMD proliferation have also provided the strong with compelling grounds for unilaterally abridging norms of non-intervention in the name of assuring their citizens' safety from terrorist attack (Nichols 2005: 8–12). In a world where many states lack the capacity and sometimes the political will necessary to suppress terrorist activity within their borders, strong states are more and more likely to resort to armed self-help to compensate for such local shortfalls in capacity and resolve. In exceptional circumstances, such expedients may prove to be unavoidable, but their prospective institutionalisation threatens to inflame North/South tensions and undermine established conventions designed to assure the security of strong and weak alike. Were this to occur, the international community's collective capacity to confront the threat of transnational terrorism would be significantly weakened, making for a less predictable and less secure world.

The preceding observations illustrate transnational jihadist terrorism's pivotal significance as a threat to international order. Nevertheless, what they also illustrate is that jihadism's most profound impact on international order is likely to be indirect, and powerfully determined by the character of states' responses to jihadist violence. The spectacular nature of jihadist violence notwithstanding, it is worth remembering that terrorism remains a weapon of the weak, and that the jihadists' turn to transnational terrorism represents an acknowledgement of both their inability to prevail against their enemies on the battlefield and a recognition of their past failures in fomenting popular revolution in their home states. Jihadists lack the material power resources that rendered totalitarian empires such as Nazi Germany and the Soviet Union such potent threats to international peace and security in the twentieth century. Additionally, the jihadists' ideological appeal to a mass audience is limited by their inflexible dogmatism and their penchant for inflicting indiscriminate violence against Muslims and non-Muslims alike (Phillips 2009). Lastly, while jihadist violence has exposed the fragility of international order, the swift construction of a comprehensive global counter-terrorism architecture after 9/11 conversely also demonstrates that order's powerful regenerative capabilities in the face of armed challenges to its integrity (Mendelsohn 2009). While it has left an indelible mark on the global security environment, it is for these reasons that this most recent wave of 'rebel terror' is likely to eventually follow its predecessors into oblivion.

Guide to further reading

Excellent general introductions to the study of terrorism as a phenomenon in world politics include Hoffman (2002) and Crenshaw (1981). Rapoport (2001) provides a succinct synoptic overview of the history of modern terrorism, while Jensen (2004) is also helpful for understanding the often neglected 'first wave' of anarchist terrorism. Hoffman (1998) provides an indispensible overview of the renewed internationalisation of terrorism from the late 1960s onwards, while Adamson (2005), Mousseau (2003) and Cronin (2002/03) also provide cogent analyses of the complex and evolving relationship between transnational terrorism and globalisation.

The 'war on terror' continues to provoke intense partisan passions, which are reflected in the polemical tone of works by commentators writing from both critical perspectives, such as Ali (2002) and Chomsky (2003), and those writing from a neo-conservative position, such as Podhoretz (2007). A more balanced overview of the struggle against jihadist terrorism and its likely future course can be found in Scheuer (2007), while Berman (2003) is also useful in illuminating the ideological contours of the struggle between liberalism and jihadist extremism.

The ongoing wars in Afghanistan and Iraq have seen transnational jihadist terrorism feature ever more conspicuously in insurgent conflicts in these countries, a theme that is explored in both Kilcullen (2005) and Phillips (2009). Finally, Nichols (2005) provides an interesting perspective on the systemic implications of transnational terrorism, according particular emphasis to its contemporary and prospective impact on the rules governing the use of force in world politics.

Chapter 10

Peace Operations and Humanitarian Intervention

ALEX J. BELLAMY

Since the nineteenth century 'atrocitarians' lobbied for the great powers to intervene in the Balkans to put an end to Ottoman massacres (Bass 2008), the commission of genocide and mass atrocities has tended to provoke calls for international society to act. In the 1990s, genocide in Rwanda (1994) killed at least 800,000, war in the former Yugoslavia (1992–95) left at least 250,000 dead and forced thousands more to flee. Protracted conflicts in Sierra Leone, Sudan, Haiti, Somalia, Liberia, East Timor, the Democratic Republic of Congo (DRC) and elsewhere killed millions more. Today, conflict in the Darfur region of Sudan has cost the lives of around 250,000 people and has forced more than 3 million people to flee from their homes. Historically, genocides have ended in one of two ways: either the *genocidaires* succeed in destroying their target group or they are defeated in battle. This cold fact is borne out by recent cases. The Rwandan genocide ended with the defeat of the Rwandan government and *interehamwe* militia at the hands of the Rwandan Patriotic Front (RPF); the carnage in Bosnia came to an end when the military balance turned in favour of a Croat–Muslim coalition backed by NATO airpower; and the bloodshed in Darfur has declined primarily because the *janjaweed* militia and their government backers have succeeded in forcing the black population into exile.

Facts like this pose a major challenge to world politics. Contemporary international order is based on a society of states that enjoy exclusive jurisdiction over a particular piece of territory and rights to non-interference and non-intervention that are enshrined in the Charter of the United Nations. Article 2(4) of the UN Charter forbids the use of force as an instrument of state policy with only two exceptions – each state's inherent right to self-defence (Article 51) and enforcement measures authorised by the UN Security Council. This system is in turn prefaced on the assumption that states exist primarily to protect the security of their citizens. In other words, the security of the state is considered important, and worth protecting, because states provide security to individuals. Moreover, the principles of non-intervention and non-interference have helped international society dramatically reduce the number of inter-state conflicts. Although inter-state war is not yet obsolete, it is very rare thanks in part to this normative order. However, it should be clear from the proceeding paragraph that although

149

the norms of non-intervention and non-interference have helped reduce inter-state war, the assumption that states are always the best providers of security to individuals is often found wanting. In the past century, threats to individual security have tended to come more from an individual's own state than from other states. While states are often the main perpetrators of genocide and mass atrocities, there are also cases where states are simply incapable of protecting their populations – either because the state has collapsed entirely as in Somalia in the early 1990s or because it lacks the capacity to defeat or make peace with rebel groups.

All this raises questions about the role of international society in mitigating the worst effects of armed conflict and protecting populations from genocide and mass atrocities. In the 1950s, the UN began to develop 'peacekeeping' operations aimed at providing impartial monitoring of ceasefires, political transitions and assistance to states to maintain order. In the decades since, the fate of peace operations has ebbed and flowed and different types have emerged ranging from small monitoring missions (e.g., UNTSO in the Middle East) through to large and complex multidimensional operations with a range of different military, policing, civilian and humanitarian tasks (e.g., Mission de l'Organisation des Nations Unies en RD Congo (MONUC) in the Democratic Republic of Congo) and transitional administrations where the UN assumes temporary sovereign control over a territory (e.g., Kosovo). In the main, these peace operations are conducted with the consent – albeit sometimes coerced consent – of the host state. This leaves the thorny question of what should happen when the host state is the main perpetrator of genocide and mass atrocities and refuses to consent to the deployment of multinational forces. In those circumstances, should the security of individuals be privileged over the security of states? Should a state's right to be secure and free from armed attack be dependent on its fulfilment of certain responsibilities to its citizens, not least a responsibility to protect them from mass killing? Or, should the imperative of maintaining international order override concerns about human security? It is these questions that animate the contemporary debate about humanitarian intervention.

This chapter provides an overview of the military tools that international society uses to manage and mitigate armed conflict. It begins by briefly surveying the development of peace operations conducted largely with the consent of the host authorities. The second part of the chapter turns to the question of what should happen when the state refuses to grant its consent or is the main perpetrator of mass atrocities. The third and final part of the chapter focuses on the emergence of a new international principle which seeks to reframe the way that international society protects populations from genocide and mass atrocities. This new principle, called the 'responsibility to protect' (R2P), holds that states have a responsibility to protect populations from genocide and mass atrocities, that international society has a duty to assist them and that when the host state manifestly fails to do so, the international community has a responsibility to take timely and decisive action. The challenge now, I argue, is to clarify the R2P principle and develop practical measures for translating it from words to deeds.

Peace operations

Historical evolution

Although the term 'peacekeeping' was invented in the 1950s, the international management of armed conflict has a far longer history. In the nineteenth century, the Concert of Europe managed political violence by intervening against revolutionaries and to protect Christians in the Ottoman Empire. Between 1919 and 1939, the League of Nations oversaw plebiscites in contested territories and deployed peacekeepers to the Ruhr and Danzig (see Schmidl 2000). The development of peace operations conducted by the UN after the Second World War needs to be seen against the backdrop of the Cold War. It was initially conceived that the UN would be a collective security institution. However, Cold War politics stymied the UN's efforts to adopt this role forcing it to develop alternative ways of contributing to international peace and security. Peacekeeping – a term not envisaged by the UN Charter – was one of the principal means of doing this. In 1947, the General Assembly despatched an observation mission (United Nations Special Committee in the Balkans (UNSCOB)) to report on cross-border movements during the Greek Civil War. The following year, the Security Council also began to be engaged in two of the world's most pressing crises, the Palestinian conflict and the struggle over Kashmir (Luck 2006: 32), leading to the deployment of two further observation missions. These ad hoc missions began to be conceptualised into a coherent role for the UN. The terms of reference for what was widely regarded as the UN's first self-styled peace operation, UNEF I – deployed to the Sinai to help defuse the Suez Crisis of 1956 – contributed to the establishment of core principles of consent, impartiality and minimum use of force.

In total, the UN conducted 14 missions during the Cold War. All were intimately connected with decolonisation. UN peace operations during the Cold War were therefore a tool for managing one of the most significant structural shifts in world politics – the globalisation of the sovereign state. Closer attention also reveals that almost half of all the UN operations deployed in this period were in the Middle East. This supports the view that peace operations were an important part of the UN's 'preventive diplomacy' role, seeking to prevent local conflicts escalating into a global imbroglio. In the Middle East case, both the superpowers recognised the potential for escalation but neither was prepared to wage war in order to defend their claims and allies in the region. This created an opening for consensus in the Security Council and helps explain the strong regional bias in the deployment of peace operations towards the Middle East. It is worth noting that, by contrast, the same period saw only one UN operation (UN Operation in the Congo (ONUC)) deployed to sub-Saharan Africa and this too came in relation to a crisis that divided the superpowers (Bellamy and Williams 2009).

As the Cold War came to an end between 1988 and 1993, peace operations underwent a triple transformation (Bellamy and Williams 2009). First, there was a *quantitative transformation*. During this period, the UN conducted more peace operations than it had undertaken in its previous 40 years. Moreover, traditional

transition of peace-keeping 1988-1993

peacekeeping contributors were augmented by a flood of new countries, including great powers such as the US, France and the UK, prepared to deploy their troops as UN peacekeepers. Second, there was a *normative transformation* catalysed by a growing belief among some member states that the remit for peace operations should be broadened to include the promotion of humanitarian values and human rights. Finally – and as a result of the normative transformation – there was a *qualitative transformation*. The UN was asked to carry out complex missions reminiscent of ONUC in the 1960s but on a far more regular basis. In places such as Cambodia, Bosnia and Somalia, the UN launched operations that were qualitatively different from earlier missions, marrying peacekeeping with the delivery of humanitarian aid, state-building programmes, local peacemaking and elements of peace enforcement. These missions were also much larger and more expensive than anything the UN had attempted before, with the exception of ONUC.

Still operating on the basis of Cold War ideas about peacekeeping, these new missions lacked the resources, doctrine and institutional capacity they needed to succeed, and led to a series of high-profile failure. In Angola, peacekeepers were forced to stand aside as a peace deal collapsed and bloody war recommenced. In Somalia, American peacekeepers became the targets of militia violence and the mission there collapsed after the US sustained casualties in the infamous 'Black Hawk down' incident. In Bosnia, four years of dithering was capped off with the collapse of a UN 'safe area' in Srebrenica and the massacre of 7600 men and boys. Worst of all, however, in Rwanda an ill-equipped UN force was instructed to stand aside during the genocide. By 1995, the catastrophes in Angola, Somalia, Bosnia and Rwanda had prompted many states to re-evaluate the value of peace operations and the nature of their contribution to it. The number of UN peacekeepers deployed around the world fell dramatically as member states expressed a preference for working through regional organisations and alliances, such as Economic Community of West African States (ECOWAS) and NATO, and the Security Council became reluctant to create new missions. This ushered in a period of hesitant introspection at the UN, during which the organisation produced reports detailing its failings in Rwanda and Bosnia. These reports identified serious problems with the way that the UN mandated, organised and conducted its peace operations and exposed gaps between the tasks peacekeepers were expected to fulfil in the post-Cold War era and the conceptual and material resources made available to them (Bellamy and Williams 2009).

Attitudes began to change in 1999 with high-profile and largely successful interventions in Kosovo and East Timor. In the months that followed, the Security Council authorised new missions to Sierra Leone and the DRC. This renewed demand for peace operations helped prompt the UN Secretary-General to commission a major report into the conduct and management of peace operations. Commonly referred to as the Brahimi Report after its chairman Lakhdar Brahimi, this panel of experts made a series of recommendations which laid the groundwork for a new approach to UN peace operations (UN 2000). The panel called for improved decision making at UN headquarters, a better fit between mandate and means to ensure that operations have the resources they need to succeed, measures to improve the rapidity and effectiveness of deployment as well as the professionalism of the mission itself. The panel also argued that the UN should reconfigure its understanding of consent and impartiality so that it be presumed that UN forces have a mandate to protect civilians from harm. UN operations, the panel argued, should be capable of protecting themselves, their mandate and civilians under their care, using force if necessary.

Although not all of the recommendations have been put into practice, the Brahimi Report helped transform UN operations. Typically, twenty-first century operations are larger and more robust than their predecessors. For example, in the DRC and Haiti the UN has used force against rebel militia groups that refused to disarm and engaged in hostage taking. Moreover, today's operations are more complex and multidimensional, incorporating a wider range of civilian personnel – including larger numbers of police – in order to close the 'public security gap' in the aftermath of war. As we will see below, all of this has improved the effectiveness of UN forces. It has also stimulated fresh demands for new and larger missions that the UN will struggle to satisfy unless member states are more forthcoming with troops and material resources. This brings us to the question of whether peace operations are an effective tool of conflict management.

Does peacekeeping work?

According to data gathered by the Uppsala Conflict Data Program (UCDP), since the early 1990s, the number and intensity of state-based armed conflicts involving the world's governments has reduced by as much as 40 per cent. Some analysts have argued that a significant part of the credit for this should be given to peace operations (Mack 2007). Peace operations significantly reduce the likelihood of wars reigniting after such agreements have been concluded (Fortna 2003, 2004, 2008). Where peacekeepers are deployed, the likelihood of war reigniting falls by at least 75–85 per cent compared to those cases where no peacekeepers are deployed (Fortna 2008: 171).

In the post-Cold War era, traditional peacekeeping operations deployed with the consent of the belligerents reduced the likelihood of war reigniting by as much as 86 per cent. For large and complex multidimensional operations – often deployed in regions with unstable consent and lingering violence – the figure remained above 50 per cent (Fortna 2004: 283). In addition, since 1990, peace operations have become more proficient in reducing the likelihood of war reigniting (Fortna 2004: 283). This is all the more important if we consider that the single most important factor in determining a country's risk of descending into war is whether it has endured war in the past 5 years (Collier et al. 2003). By dramatically reducing the risk of war reignition, peace operations make a vital contribution to reducing the frequency and lethality of war in our world.

But the contribution of peace operations does not end there. Statistical analyses also support Samantha Power's claim that 'for all the talk of the futility of foreign involvement' in cases of genocide and mass killing, the evidence categorically points to the fact that even small steps by concerned outsiders save lives (Power 2002: 73). Big steps, properly coordinated and executed, save lots of lives. In only a third of cases has outside intervention either had no effect in terms of saving lives or made matters worse (Seybolt 2007: 270). In these cases, there is a correlation between the size, composition and legitimacy of an operation and its ability to save lives. Well-equipped operations despatched with the broad-ranging support of international society are much more likely to save lives than contentious, ill-equipped and ill-conceived operations.

None of this is meant to obscure the myriad problems that are clearly part of the history of peace operations but it is clear that, overall, peace operations are an effective tool of crisis management. The problem, however, is that in many cases it is the host state itself that is perpetrating grave crimes. In such cases, the state is unlikely to give its consent to the deployment of UN peacekeepers and, guided by the principle of non-interference, the UN Security Council has been reluctant to authorise operations without the consent of the host state. This brings us to the difficult question of when, if ever, states should intervene to put an end to genocide and mass atrocities without the consent of the host state and sometimes without the authorisation of the UN Security Council.

Humanitarian intervention

When states kill large numbers of their own population or prove incapable of protecting them from other groups intent on doing them harm, the question of humanitarian intervention arises. Because states very rarely consent in such cases to the deployment of peacekeepers, and because the UN Security Council remains reluctant to authorise armed intervention into fully functioning states without the consent of the government, the protection of populations from mass killing may sometimes require intervention without either host state consent or Security Council authority. This section surveys the debate about whether, and in what circumstances, such humanitarian intervention might be legitimate.

The case for intervention

The case for intervention is typically premised on the idea that external actors have a *duty* as well as a *right* to intervene to halt genocide and mass atrocities. For advocates of this position, sovereignty should be understood as an instrumental value because it derives from a state's responsibility to protect the welfare of its citizens. As such, when states fail in their duty, they lose their sovereign right to non-interference and non-intervention (Tesón 2003: 93). There are a variety of ways of arriving at this conclusion. Some liberal cosmopolitans draw on Kant to insist that all individuals have certain pre-political rights that deserve protection (Caney 1997: 34). Many advocates of the Just War tradition writers arrive at a broadly similar position but ground their arguments in theology. Paul Ramsey (2002: 20), for instance, used Augustine's insistence that force be used to defend or uphold justice to argue that intervention to end injustice was 'among the rights and duties of states until and unless supplanted by superior government'.

(3) Political leaders who adopt this position tend to maintain that today's globalised world is so integrated that massive human rights violations in one part of the world have an effect on every other part and that social interconnectedness itself creates moral obligations. The most prominent proponent of this view was former British Prime Minister, Tony Blair. Shortly after NATO began its 1999 intervention in Kosovo, Blair gave a landmark speech setting out his 'doctrine of the international community' and endorsing the concept of sovereignty as responsibility (Blair 1999). Blair maintained that sovereignty should be reconceptualised because globalisation was changing the world in ways that rendered traditional views of sovereignty anachronistic. Enlightened self-interest created international responsibilities for dealing with egregious human suffering and sovereigns had responsibilities to the society of states because problems caused by massive human rights abuse in one place tended to spread across borders.

(4) A further line of argument is to point to the fact that states have already agreed to certain minimum standards of behaviour and that humanitarian intervention is not about imposing the will of a few upon the many, but about protecting and enforcing the collective will of international society. Advocates of this position argue that there is a customary right (but not duty) of intervention in supreme humanitarian emergencies (Wheeler 2000: 14). They argue that there is agreement in international society that cases of genocide, mass killing and ethnic cleansing constitute grave humanitarian crises warranting intervention (see Arend and Beck 1993). They point to state practice since the nineteenth century to suggest that there is a customary right of humanitarian intervention (Finnemore 2003). In particular, they point to the justifications offered to defend the American- and British-led intervention in Northern Iraq in 1991 to support their case (see Roberts 1993: 436–7).

This movement towards acceptance of a customary right of humanitarian intervention was reinforced by state practice after Northern Iraq. Throughout the Security Council's deliberations about how to respond to the Rwandan genocide in 1994, no state argued that either the ban on force (Article 2(4)) or the non-intervention rule (Article 2(7)) prohibited armed action to halt the bloodshed, suggesting tacit recognition that armed intervention would have been legitimate in that case. Throughout the 1990s, the Security Council expanded its interpretation of 'international peace and security' and authorised interventions to protect civilians in safe areas (Bosnia), maintain law and order and protect aid supplies (Somalia) and restore an elected government toppled by a coup (Haiti). These instances prompted Richard Falk (2003) to describe the 1990s as 'undoubtedly the golden age of humanitarian diplomacy', while Thomas Weiss (2004) argued that 'the notion that human beings matter more than sovereignty radiated brightly, albeit briefly, across the international political horizon of the 1990s.' Progress did not stop, however, at the turn of the century. Since 2000 the Security Council has on several occasions mandated peacekeepers to protect civilians under threat in the DRC, Burundi, Cote D'Ivoire, Liberia and Darfur. Furthermore, since 2002 the UN's standard rules of engagement have permitted peacekeepers to use force for this purpose.

Problems & Against Intervention

Although appealing, several aspects of this defence of humanitarian intervention are problematic. First, it is not self-evident that individuals *do* have pre-political rights. Parekh (1997: 54–5), for example, argues that liberal rights cannot provide the basis for a theory of humanitarian intervention because liberalism itself is rejected in many parts of the world. Second, critics argue that any norm endorsing the use of force to protect individual rights would be abused by powerful states, making armed conflict more frequent by relaxing the rules prohibiting it but without making humanitarian intervention any more likely (Chesterman 2001; Thakur 2004).

Failures in operations

Above all, however, is the charge that advocates of humanitarian intervention exaggerate the extent of consensus about the use of force to protect human rights. There is a gap between what advocates would like to be the norm and what the norm actually is. We should remember that the putative 'golden era' of humanitarianism included the world's failure to halt the Rwandan genocide, the UN's failure to protect civilians sheltering in its 'safe areas' in Bosnia and the failure to prevent the widely predicted mass murder that followed East Timor's referendum on independence in 1999. The world stood aside as Congo destroyed itself, taking 4 million lives, and – more recently – failed to halt the mass killing in Darfur. Moreover, closer inspection of the relevant cases from the 1990s suggests that the advances were more hesitant than implied by advocates of intervention. Most notably, the Security Council has still yet to authorise intervention against the wishes of a fully functioning sovereign state. Finally, with a few partial exceptions, interveners themselves have typically chosen not to justify their actions by reference to a new norm of humanitarian intervention, lest they encourage others to do likewise (see Wheeler 2000).

The case against intervention

Nowadays, only a handful of marginal states (e.g., Cuba, Iran, Venezuela, Zimbabwe) are prepared to argue that humanitarian intervention is *never* warranted. Even China (2005), the state most closely associated with the principle of non-interference, publicly acknowledges that massive humanitarian crises are a 'legitimate concern' for international society and that the Security Council is entitled to take action in such cases. By and large, therefore, contemporary opposition to humanitarian intervention focuses not on this, but on the questions of who can *legitimately authorise* intervention and *in what circumstances.*

While advocates of intervention are prepared to acknowledge its legitimacy in certain cases even when it is not authorised by the Security Council, opponents maintain that international order requires something approximating an absolute ban on the use of force outside the two exceptions set out by the UN Charter. The starting point for this position is the assumption that international society comprises a plurality of diverse communities each with different ideas about the best way to live. According to this view, international society is based on rules – the

UN Charter's rules on the use of force first among them – that permit coexistence (see Jackson 2002). In a world characterised by radical disagreements about how societies should govern themselves, proponents of this view hold that unfettered humanitarian intervention would create disorder as states waged wars to protect and violently export their own cultural preferences.

What is more, a right of unauthorised humanitarian intervention would open the door to potential abuse. Historically, states have shown a distinct predilection towards 'abusing' humanitarian justifications to legitimise wars that were anything but humanitarian. Most notoriously, Hitler insisted that the 1939 invasion of Czechoslovakia was inspired by a desire to protect Czechoslovak citizens whose 'life and liberty' were threatened by their own government (in Brownlie 1974: 217–21). More recently, some commentators have argued that the US and the UK abused humanitarian justifications in an ill-fated attempt to legitimise the 2003 invasion of Iraq, emphasising the humanitarian case for war as it became clear that the legal reasons given (the existence of Iraqi weapons of mass destruction (WMD)) were ill-founded. It was precisely because of the fear that states would exploit any loophole in the ban on the use of force that the delegates who wrote the UN Charter issued a comprehensive ban with only two limited exceptions – force used in self-defence and under the authority of the Security Council. According to Chesterman, without this general ban there would be *more war* in international society but not necessarily more genuine humanitarian interventions. Chesterman argues that states do not refrain from intervening in humanitarian emergencies because they are constrained by law, but 'because states do not want them to take place' (2002: 231). Creating a humanitarian exception to the ban on force would not enable more humanitarian interventions, but it would make it easier for states to justify self-interested invasions through spurious humanitarian arguments.

Finally, it is important to note that a majority of states continue to oppose humanitarian intervention – seeing it as a dangerous affront to another core principle, self-determination, which underpinned post-war decolonisation. This position was clearly in the ascendancy during the Cold War. In 1977, when Vietnam invaded Cambodia and ousted the murderous Pol Pot regime, responsible for the death of some 2 million Cambodians, it was condemned for violating Cambodian sovereignty (Wheeler 2000: 90–1). These sentiments persist today. Nearly 30 years after the Vietnamese experiences, Pakistan argued against collective action to halt the Sudanese government-sponsored mass killing and expulsion of civilians in Darfur on the grounds that 'the Sudan has all the rights and privileges incumbent under the United Nations Charter, including to sovereignty, political independence, unity and territorial integrity' (UNSC, S/PV.4988, 11 June 2004).

Unsurprisingly, there are also a number of problems with these positions. First, its overriding assumption that states protect their citizens does not hold in every case, as the examples offered at the beginning of this chapter attest. Second, critics argue that this perspective overlooks the wealth of customary practice suggesting that sovereignty carries responsibilities as well as rights (see Tesón 1997). Third, although there are a number of notorious historical cases, the fear of abuse is exaggerated (Weiss 2004: 135). It is fanciful to argue that denying a state recourse to humanitarian justifications for war would make them less war-prone – it is unlikely that either Hitler in 1939 or Bush and Blair in 2003 would have been deterred from waging war by the absence of a plausible humanitarian justification. Fourth, this position overlooks the wide body of international law relating to basic human rights and the consensus on grave crimes such as genocide.

Summary: the irresolvable debate?

Almost all governments recognise that crimes such as genocide and mass killing are a legitimate concern for international society. Some governments, international officials, activists and analysts argue that sovereigns have a responsibility to protect their citizens from mass killing and other abuses and when they fail to do so, others acquire a right to intervene. A majority of the world's governments, however, argue that this responsibility does not translate into a right of humanitarian intervention without the authority of the UN Security Council because that would contradict other cherished principles of international order, including the rule of non-aggression and the right to self-determination. Since the end of the Cold War, the UN Security Council has authorised collective intervention to protect populations from mass killing. In this sense, there is a norm of UN-sanctioned humanitarian intervention (Wheeler 2000), but it is heavily circumscribed in practice to cases where the host state has collapsed or where the recognised government is not the target of intervention and lends its support. This presents a dilemma about what to do in cases where some governments believe that intervention is warranted to save people from genocide and mass atrocities but where there is no consensus in the Security Council. This dilemma was exposed by NATO's decision to intervene in Kosovo in 1999. The debate sparked by this provided a catalyst for a fundamental rethink of the way that international society conceptualises the problem of sovereignty and the protection of citizens.

Towards responsibility to protect

The humanitarian crises of the 1990s prompted new thinking about the nature of sovereignty which developed some old ideas about the sovereign's responsibility to protect its citizens. The first person to begin thinking along these lines was Francis Deng, a former Sudanese diplomat who was appointed the UN Secretary-General's special representative on internally displaced people in 1992. In a book published in 1996, Deng and his co-authors argued that 'sovereignty carries with it certain responsibilities for which governments must be held accountable. And they are accountable not only to their own national constituencies but ultimately to the international community' (Deng et al. 1996: 1). According to Deng, legitimate sovereignty required a demonstration of responsibility. Conceptualising sovereignty as responsibility removed the validity of objections to international assistance and mediation based on the principle of non-interference.

NATO's intervention in Kosovo prompted UN Secretary-General Kofi Annan to enter the debate and make a vital contribution. In 1999 he insisted that 'state sovereignty, in its most basic sense, is being redefined by the forces of globalization and international cooperation.' He continued, 'the state is now widely understood to be the servant of its people, and not vice versa. At the same time, individual sovereignty – and by this I mean the human rights and fundamental freedoms of each and every individual as enshrined in our Charter – has been enhanced by a renewed consciousness of the right of every individual to control his or her own destiny' (Annan 1999).

Together, Deng and Annan pointed towards a new way of thinking about sovereignty as responsibility. The Canadian government then created the International Commission on Intervention and State Sovereignty (ICISS) to develop a way of reconciling sovereignty and human rights (see Evans 2008). The Commission's report was premised on the notion that when states are unwilling or unable to protect their citizens from grave harm, the principle of non-interference 'yields to the responsibility to protect' (ICISS 2001: xi). The concept of R2P that it put forward was intended as a way of escaping the logic of 'intervention versus sovereignty' by focusing not on what interveners were entitled to do ('a right of intervention') but on what was necessary to protect civilians threatened by genocide and mass atrocities. Influenced by Annan and Deng, the ICISS argued that the R2P was about much more than just military intervention. Appropriate responses to humanitarian emergencies included non-violent measures such as diplomacy, sanctions and embargoes, and legal measures such as referring crimes to the International Criminal Court. Furthermore, in addition to the 'responsibility to react' to massive human suffering, the ICISS insisted that international society also had responsibilities to rebuild polities and societies afterwards. Of the three responsibilities, the Commission identified the 'responsibility to prevent' was the single most important (ICISS 2001: xi). The Commission also proposed the adoption of criteria to guide decision making about when to intervene.

At the 2005 World Summit, over 150 world leaders adopted a declaration affirming the R2P which was itself subsequently reaffirmed by the UN Security Council in 2006. According to the UN Secretary-General, Ban Ki-moon, who succeeded Kofi Annan in 2007, the R2P principle adopted by states in 2005 rests on three pillars. First, the responsibility of the state to protect its own populations from genocide, war crimes, ethnic cleansing and crimes against humanity. Second, the international community's duty to assist states to fulfil their responsibilities. Third, the international community's responsibility to respond in a timely and decisive manner when a state is manifestly failing to protect its population, using Chapters VI (peaceful means), VII (coercive means authorised by the UN Security Council) and VIII (regional arrangements) of the UN Charter (Ban Ki-moon 2009).

The approach adopted by the UN Secretary-General has been described as 'narrow but deep' (Luck 2008: 1) in that it applies only to a narrow category of cases but requires a deep commitment from states. International society is expected to shoulder the responsibility of preventing genocide and mass atrocities by helping states to build the necessary capacities, developing early warning systems and being prepared to act 'up-stream' of an outbreak of violence with a range of diplomatic, humanitarian, legal and other peaceful measures. Heeding the concerns of states such as Russia and China, the R2P insists that military intervention be authorised by the UN Security Council and rules out unilateral force.

The World Summit's declaration on the R2P received a mixed reception. Todd Lindberg (2005) described it as nothing less than a 'revolution in consciousness in international affairs'. Prominent international lawyer Simon Chesterman agreed, arguing that 'what we're seeing is a progressive redefinition of sovereignty in a way that would have been outrageous sixty years ago' (in Turner 2005). Others were more equivocal. John Bolton, the American Ambassador to the UN and a well-known realist and UN-sceptic, described the R2P as 'a moveable feast of an idea that was the High Minded *cause du jour*' and said of the World Summit Outcome Document: 'I plan never to read it again. I doubt many others will either' (Bolton 2007: 213–14).

To what extent has the R2P advanced and replaced debates about humanitarian intervention? One group of critics complain that the principle amounts to little more than an assault on state sovereignty. They argue that it is little different from the interventionist doctrines put forward by liberals in the 1990s and has all the negative connotations associated with humanitarian intervention (e.g., Chandler 2005). A second group of critics make the opposite point. Michael Byers (2005), for example, argued that the 2005 World Summit Outcome Document watered down the original R2P concept to such an extent that the new principle would not advance the humanitarian intervention debate or protect threatened populations.

While the first group of critics ignores the fact that the R2P has been adopted by world leaders of all stripes and carefully limits the scope for armed intervention, the second group focuses too heavily on the question of armed intervention and underestimates the potential impact of R2P. Thus, while we need to be mindful of the principle's limitations, as the UN Secretary-General's special adviser, Edward Luck, has pointed out, there are several good reasons for thinking that the R2P is likely to make a lasting impact on international peace and security. First, R2P is a politically potent concept based on a consensus produced by one of the largest gatherings of heads of state ever seen. Second, the Outcome Document specifically pointed to the prevention of genocide, war crimes, ethnic cleansing and crimes against humanity, creating a mandate for renewed attention to prevention. Third, the Outcome Document points to the kinds of tools, actors and procedures that could form the basis for operationalising the R2P. As such, it provides a blueprint for future policy initiatives. Finally, the process of negotiating the Document and forging consensus required compromise by both sides of the intervention debate and produced a shared conception of sovereignty as responsibility that bridges the divide (Luck 2008: 3).

Ultimately, however, the R2P will be judged not according to its ability to help finesse difficult judgements about humanitarian intervention but by the extent to which it reduces the frequency with which the world is confronted with an apparent choice between 'sending in the Marines' or standing aside (Feinstein 2007) in the face of unconscionable inhumanity.

Conclusion

The challenge now, as the current UN Secretary-General Ban Ki-moon has argued, is to translate R2P from words into deeds and to change the practice of how the world responds to genocide and mass atrocities. This will necessarily involve measures to enhance the effectiveness of peace operations conducted with the consent of the host state but must also involve fresh thinking and new practice in relation to non-consensual intervention. If the principle continues to develop and gain momentum, chapters about humanitarian intervention might become obsolete as global institutions, regional organisations and individual states develop the capacities to better prevent and respond to such crimes. It is not yet clear, however, whether changing the terms of debate has altered its fundamental logic. The test will come partly in how the world responds to new and emerging crises – and the slow, inadequate and half-hearted response to Darfur does not bode well in this regard – and partly in how successful UN reform is in building the necessary capacities and decision-making capabilities.

Guide to further reading

Several works offer a comprehensive introduction to peacekeeping, including its history, theory, key challenges and specific cases (Bellamy and Williams 2009). This could be augmented with specific studies on contemporary peace operations (Durch 2006) and detailed study of what makes peace operations more – and less – effective (Fortna 2008). There are a number of very good books tracing the norm of humanitarian intervention since the Cold War (Wheeler 2000), the place of intervention in international law (Chesterman 2001) and the more recent politics of humanitarian intervention (Weiss 2007; Welsh 2004). Although the R2P principle is relatively new, there is a very good insider's account of the principle's development and application (Evans 2008) and a study of the principle itself and efforts to operationalise it (Bellamy 2009).

Chapter 11

The New World of Security: Implications for Human Security and International Security Cooperation

MELY CABALLERO-ANTHONY

The global security environment has changed dramatically. While the risks of major armed conflict and interstate wars are now on the decline (Human Security Centre 2005), the global community is increasingly confronted with new security challenges emerging from a host of transnational threats which are non-military in nature. Of late, there is growing recognition that these new security challenges, now referred to as non-traditional security (NTS), are proving to be more severe and likely to inflict more harm to a greater number of people than conventional threats of interstate wars and conflicts. As a consequence, policymakers around the world have had to re-think their security agendas and find new and innovative ways to address these new security challenges.

At least within the context of Asia, one can see clearly how these emerging security challenges are transforming the nature of inter-state relations. Examples of non-military security challenges to Asia include the spread of infectious diseases like H5N1 (the 'bird flu') or Severe Acute Respiratory Syndrome ('SARS'), managing the aftermath of natural disasters like the 2004 tsunami, transborder pollution which has caused 'the haze' over Southeast Asia as well as problems of irregular migration and transnational crime. These NTS challenges pose dangers to the region irrespective of national boundaries and in return, they demand transnational solutions.

Since many of these new security challenges present states and societies with common risks and threats, states have, therefore, tended to draw closer and establish institutional arrangements to respond to what are often complex security challenges. As a consequence, there is a noticeable trend among state actors to turn to regional modalities as a preferred framework to respond to growing list of transborder problems. These, in turn, have had profound implications for regional security cooperation among states in Asia.

These trends point to two very salient points about the so-called new world of security in Asia. The first is the nature of security cooperation in Asia, and the second is the evolving nature of varying conceptions of security which arguably has become not only more comprehensive, but also multi-level.

On the first point, it must be noted that cooperation between states in the context of the international system is not new. In international relations theory, liberal and neoliberal institutionalists posit that states will engage in cooperation where and when there are actual or potential mutual interests and gains to be derived. Institutions are one mechanism with which cooperative security can occur. With the rising interdependence of states regarding security issues, institutions can assist in defining states' interests. Further, cooperative security as a 'security system' among states has been developed further to the building of 'security communities' wherein states, through a sustained process of close interaction and learning, forge and consolidate shared norms and values (see Acharya 2001; Adler and Barnett 1998).

More importantly, the trend towards closer security cooperation leading to the goal of establishing security communities has also been largely defined by the changing nature of security challenges which are no longer confined to threats to the territoriality and sovereignty of states. Events have shown that contemporary challenges such as environmental degradation, infectious diseases, poverty and extremism cannot be addressed by military means alone, though they might constitute threats to national and regional security. The capacity of state to respond to a number of security challenges had also been rendered inadequate. Rather, the nature of transnational challenges highlight the need for cooperation among states in order to find effective coping mechanisms through alternative agencies, such as those focused on health, police, labour migration and the environment.

In seeking responses to these evolving NTS challenges, analysts have, therefore, gone beyond the more traditional understanding of security threats to look beyond the nation-state which alone cannot address many of these issues that do not respect national borders. Analysts focusing on NTS have instead called for the replacement of state-centrism with a framework that encompasses the security of individuals, societies and groups.

In brief, these developments have once again brought to the fore the debates about re-thinking and re-conceptualising security. Thus, in discussing the dynamics of NTS threats and the nature of security cooperation in Asia, this chapter will focus on two points. First, it will look at how NTS work has evolved in the Asia and become part of security lexicon in the region. It will then proceed to highlight some of the critical NTS challenges confronting Asia and discuss the implications of these threats on institution building and regional security cooperation.

Non-traditional security: old wine in new bottles?

A common trend that has been observed by a number of security scholars in Asia is the growing tendency to highlight and designate any security concern that is non-military in nature as non-traditional security or NTS (see Caballero-Anthony et al. 2006). The appropriation of the security label attached to risks/threats from, for example, environmental degradation, pandemics and so on has, therefore, been a significant development. It is significant in that 'security-framing' is deemed to be an effective way to bring attention to these NTS challenges, convey urgency and command governmental resources to address them. The question, however, is how NTS has fitted into the evolving concept of security in the wider Asian region.

At a global level, the end of the Cold War has drawn attention to a variety of non-military security concerns. Among certain Asian countries, a broad view of security encompassing these dimensions was common, and has since gained greater acceptance in the West as well. Issues such as the character and scale of economic change, population explosions, climate change, globalisation and its perceived negative effects in some countries on their state autonomy and national values all became more salient to both peoples and governments. For instance, including environmental concerns and problems stressed 'the threat to the physical survival of humankind that supposedly arises from environmental degradation' which could threaten 'not only the quality of life but life itself'. These were initially called 'nonconventional dimensions' of security and also termed 'a comprehensive view of security' (Alagappa 1998).

Within the Southeast Asian sub-region of Asia, comprehensive security has, for a long time, been considered as the dominant concept and had structured the understanding among the political elites about what security meant for the region. As noted by an Asian security scholar, Muthiah Alagappa, regardless of the labels and the varied interpretations that came with the term, comprehensive security implied that security 'goes beyond (but does not exclude) the military to embrace the political, economic and socio-cultural dimensions' (Alagappa 1988).

However, the concept of comprehensive security came under strong criticism, particularly in the aftermath of the Asian financial crisis that hit the region in 1997–98. During that period, the emphasis on state security as the main security referent was challenged as increasingly the plight of vulnerable groups and societies that had suffered as a consequence of the economic crisis were exposed. The debates on the reconceptualisation of security have, therefore, gone beyond the general expansion of security to promoting 'human security' as a possible framework in order to replace the conventional state-centric approach (see Hampson et al. 2001). Essentially, advocates of the human security framework have called for a re-thinking of security by expanding the security referent beyond the state to include the chronic and complex insecurities commonly faced by individuals and societies (see JIIA 2001). Human security, at least in the Southeast Asian context, has provided an important avenue to raise the developing world's (in)security experience to broaden/deepen the discourse on security and for re-thinking the requirements of the international order.

The concept of human security has been criticised by various scholars. The 1994 United Nations Development Programme's Human Development Report on human security has been said to lack precision. Roland Paris has pointed out that its definition of human security is too broad and covers 'virtually any kind of unexpected or irregular discomfort' which could constitute a threat to a person's security. The list of seven specific elements comprising human security in the report was also considered too broad and 'difficult to determine what, if anything, might be excluded' (Paris 2001: 80–90). After examining various statements and assertions from proponents of human security, Paris concludes that 'if human security means almost anything, then it effectively means nothing' (Paris 2001: 93).

Further, in the selection of values that are protected, it was argued that scholars needed to provide a compelling rationale for highlighting certain values over others. Nevertheless, 'human security' may be labelled as a broad category of research in the field of security studies, one that is 'primarily concerned with nonmilitary threats to the safety of societies, groups and individuals', and that security studies have benefited from both a 'broadening' and a 'deepening' of the field due to the addition of non-conventional or 'non-traditional' security studies (Paris 2001: 96–7).

Against this background, where would one then fit in the concept of NTS? One could suggest that if comprehensive security is the expanded notion of security beyond military security, then NTS can be viewed as a subset of comprehensive security that characteristically requires non-military responses to address a number of emerging security 'threats'. NTS could also be considered as the broader umbrella that brings in issues of human security since its security referent extends beyond the state to include individuals and societies.

The second point has to do with the question of the kinds of issues/threats that would fall under NTS. One would note that despite the emerging trend towards security framing, there is yet to be a consensus definition on what it really means since the issues that would fall under NTS are often contextually defined. For example, what may be NTS issues in one country like economic security, food security or energy security could already be part of the traditional concept of security in the other. As some have pointed out, energy security which is now included in the rubric of NTS in Asia had long been a part of Japan's traditional security issues. I have highlighted these two points to emphasise the fact that NTS issues are not only contested but also complex.

To help in the conceptualisation of NTS, the newly established Consortium on Non-Traditional Security Studies in Asia (NTS-Asia) has defined NTS issues as those challenges that affect the survival and well-being of peoples and states that arise primarily out of non-military sources, such as climate change, resource scarcity, infectious diseases, natural disasters, irregular migration, famine, people smuggling, drug trafficking and transnational crime. Aside from these issues being non-military in nature, they also share common characteristics, namely, transnational in scope (neither purely domestic, nor purely inter-state); come at very short notice and are transmitted rapidly due to globalisation, communication revolution and so on; cannot entirely be prevented, but coping mechanisms can be devised; national solutions are often inadequate and would thus essentially require regional and multilateral cooperation; and finally, the object of security is no longer just the state (state sovereignty or territorial integrity), but also the peoples (survival, well-being, dignity), both at individual and at societal levels (Caballero-Anthony et al. 2006).

In brief, while efforts are being made to bring more attention to NTS issues, the main argument here is to examine not just the emerging threats or risks to peoples' lives and security, but more importantly, to identify/explore new approaches that can allow for more 'sustainable security' that addresses the security concerns of both states and societies and tackles both old and new threats (Oxford Research Group 2006). In fact, a recent study undertaken for the SIPRI Yearbook 2007 had similarly argued that '[i]f the ultimate objective of security is to save human beings from preventable premature death and disability, then the appropriate security policy [should] focus on prevention instruments and risk reduction strategies for their causes' (Skons 2007: 243).

Thus, in re-thinking security and addressing a wide range of security challenges, it is further argued that it might be more useful and less problematic conceptually to look at non-traditional formulations of security rather than NTS per se. In this way, we overcome what could be artificial conceptual binaries in a highly contested concept like security, and thus allow for non-traditional approaches to even conventionally framed security issues (Gopinath 2007).

NTS threats to human and state security

Although it was noted earlier that identifying NTS issues are context-relevant, it is nevertheless important to take stock of what these new challenges are and, more importantly, to investigate their implications for human security before we could argue for the need to incorporate these issues into the new security agenda in Asia. To start with, we begin by mapping what is/are the threat(s); who is/are threatened? by whom? And, whether this is a potential or an actual threat (i.e., threats in future of already felt?). Following these – we need to examine what has been the response, by whom? – to whom? And whether these responses are effective, and if not, what are the gaps, obstacles and other related factors?

For the purpose of a more manageable discussion, I shall choose five NTS challenges which are most critical to Asia:

Infectious diseases and pandemics

Health has not traditionally been regarded as a security concern until the UN Security Council resolution on HIV/AIDS in 2000 and recent warnings about the threat of the next global pandemic, reflected in the World Economic Forums Global Risks 2006 report, suggest that threats to health are now gaining traction in policy circles (WEF 2006: 4, 10–11). With regard to the threat of a global pandemic, the World Health Organization (WHO) had estimated that a possible full-fledged bird flu pandemic could result in 2–8 million deaths, up to 20–40 million in a worst case scenario (WEF 2006). Consequently, the lexicon of health security is increasingly appearing at the forefront of the global agenda (Kruk 2007). Adding to this threat is the re-emergence of new strains of older diseases like tuberculosis and cholera that are increasingly resistant to medical treatment.

The unprecedented scale of movement of people and goods, along with other 'disease multipliers' – such as the misuse or over-use of antibiotics, accelerating urbanisation in 'mega-cities' with poor sanitation and weak healthcare infrastructures – exacerbates the possibility of a global pandemic and threatens to overwhelm the healthcare capacities of many of Asia's states. The recent reappearance of the avian influenza (i.e., bird flu) in Hong Kong, India and Indonesia underscores the looming pandemic the world, especially countries in Asia, is facing in the future. While the bird flu virus remains a threat primarily to poultry, there is still a possibility that the virulent strain could potentially mutate into a human disease which could kill tens of millions. To highlight the vulnerability of Asia in particular to lethal diseases such as the bird flu, Indonesia and Vietnam already have had the highest number of fatalities from H5N1, totalling 165 deaths (WHO 2008) and behind these numbers are hundreds more who suffer economic hardship, thus the ability to afford vaccines or other countermeasures. On a regional scale, H5N1 is already responsible for $10 billion of direct economic costs to Asia (Kruk 2007: 10) and, with an estimated forecasted cost of $99–$283 billion for a bird flu pandemic in East Asia alone, this challenge is as much one confronting healthcare agencies as it is a possible economic crisis (Caballero-Anthony 2006). To illuminate the gaps in world readiness against pandemics, an analysis in the Fourth Global Progress Report on Responses to Avian Influenza and State of Pandemic Readiness published by the UN and the World Bank stated that the world is only about 40 per cent prepared to grapple with the social, economic and political impacts of an influenza pandemic (*All Africa* 2008b).

These scenarios raise a number of salient questions about the implications on regional security cooperation. Among these are: whether health and human security can be or is already mainstreamed in the security agenda of states in Asia? If so, are there enough regional mechanisms in place, such as a regional diseases surveillance system to monitor the outbreak and spread of infectious diseases?

Equally important are questions about the role that sub-national entities and civil society play in the construction and maintenance of regional health regimes. If civil society actors are part of the 'securitising actors' that highlight the importance of health and human security, can a multi-level lateral approach deal with this complex of public health emergencies?

Pandemics such as bird flu aside, otherwise common diseases – such as malaria, diarrhoea and asthma – which afflict global health, especially in the developing countries, have seen a phenomenal rise as a result of climate change and had been causing millions of deaths a year (Inter-Press News Service 2008). The trend of increasing incidence of such diseases with a rise in global temperature highlighted the inherent health risks associated to climate change, which would necessitate collective effort by the world community. However, as the discussion below shows, measures against environment-induced infectious diseases would largely depend on concrete steps, yet to materialise, in dealing with climate change and other forms of environmental degradation.

Climate change, environmental security and natural disasters

The urgency of dealing with climate change, identified to aggravate hunger and illness worldwide, has been highlighted by a number of scientists, research institutions, international bodies and even policymakers such as European Commission President Jose Barroso who warned that the risks posed by climate change are greater than those posed by the ongoing global financial crisis (*EU Energy* 2008; Indo-Asian News Service 2008). However, the global consensus on the grave security challenges posed by climate change is not matched by a consensus on how best to address this problem. The differing political responses and contentious negotiations taking place in the international community is reflected in the remarks by the US Secretary of State, Condoleeza Rice, who argued that the 'one-size-fits-all approach would not work...' (*Straits Times* 28 September 2007). The most recent UN climate talks held in Poland, whereby developed nations took the brunt of the blame for failing to do more to address carbon emissions, is a case in point that could signal an arduous process prior to a decisive collective effort by the world to mitigate the effects of climate change (Reuters News 2008b).

Given the lack of a general consensus on the appropriate measures that the international society should take to mitigate the effects of climate change, it would be difficult to see this issue becoming a top priority for developing countries in Asia. Yet ironically, it is these countries that have often been the most deeply affected by the effects of climate change – coastal flooding, loss of biodiversity and colossal damage to the environment. As the largest and most populous continent, Asia is expected to bear the brunt of climate change effects, including a worsening of food and water security situation, which shall be discussed later. As highlighted earlier, climate change also contributed to the rise in incidence of pandemic outbreak. Just when climate change urgently needs to be addressed, the Asian competition for oil and gas reserves is becoming sharper, driven by rapid economic growth. Asia is also a water-stressed region and averting climate change-induced water conflicts will become a major challenge for the region.

Against the sharpening contours of Asian geopolitics, some of the questions we need to examine in relation to climate change are: the likelihood of developing a multilateral approach on energy, environment and climate security and how to create greater institutional and state capacity to identify and build adaptive capacities and mitigation strategies to protect communities against the risk-multiplier effect of climate change?

In fact, it is important to highlight that most, if not all, countries in Asia in particular are not well prepared against natural disasters induced by climate change. The floods which struck Jakarta in February 2007 exposed the inadequacy of the Indonesian authorities in dealing with such contingencies despite warnings to intensify preparations (*South China Morning Post* 12 March 2007). Natural disasters, as a result of climate change, entail wide-ranging security risks with respect to population dislocation, disrupted public services as well as the rise in incidence of infectious diseases. Non-climate change-induced natural disasters have also been a bane to human security in Asia. Such occurrences, for instance, earthquakes, often put governmental capacities to test and for many times, preparations against such contingencies had been sorely wanting. The lack of preparedness against natural disasters carries effects beyond just the direct damage to people's lives and properties – the breakdown of local infrastructure as well as outbreak of infectious diseases and economic livelihood problems could have wider-ranging human security consequences.

Food and water resources scarcity

The natural resources-rich countries in Southeast and the wider Asia face the risk of rapidly diminishing resources given the rapid extraction of natural resources for economic development. The decimation of forests and destruction of wetlands not only increase the incidence of natural disasters such as floods but also increase environmental degradation which has wider implication on the availability of resources for exploitation. A good instance is the availability of usable water sources, which had borne the impact of rapid industrialisation. As a result of inadequately managed resource exploitation and economic development, Asia could face the potential threat of biodiversity disaster and consequently, severe water and food security woes in particular unless immediate and definitive measures are taken.

Water security issues

Indeed, water security has been identified as a looming security issue in Asia. According to a 2006 UN report, Asia possesses less fresh water – only 3920 cubic meters per person – than any other continents notwithstanding the region's rapid economic development which would put increasing demand for potable water especially in the growth of agricultural activities, water-intensive industries and the middle class (*Jakarta Post* 30 September 2008). According to Dr Tony Tan of the Singapore National Research Foundation, the stress put into water availability would especially be felt in developing countries – Asia in particular – which is experiencing the bulk of the world's urban growth (AFP 2008c). Climate change and environmental degradation have exacted a toll on water scarcity through chronic flooding and droughts, as a result of changing rainfall and storm patterns as well as the depletion of natural water repositories such as forests and swamps. Water scarcity could also have wider implications, such as in the area of food safety. A study conducted by the Sri Lanka-based International Water Management Institute found that about 80 per cent of the 53 cities surveyed have been using untreated or partially treated wastewater for agriculture as a result of water scarcity, against the backdrop of rising food prices (Inter-Press Service 2008). Such practice, though improper due to the ensuing health hazards associated with the consumption of such agricultural products, was most prevalent in Asia, including China, India and Vietnam. Water scarcity, as a result of channelling natural fresh water supplies to non-food production, would contribute further to food shortages (Molden et al. 2007).

Food security issues

Food shortages, combined with multiple crises involving climate change, energy and water scarcity as well as shortage of arable land, are tipped to intensify in the foreseeable future. Overall, the world's population would increase towards 9 billion by 2050, with a corresponding 110 per cent increase in demand for food (Reuters News 2008c). This surge in demand would no doubt place immense strain on the already dire food situation. In fact, due to the skyrocketing food prices, the number of hungry people had increased by nearly 50 million in 2007 according to Food and Agriculture Organisation (FAO) Director-General Jacques Diouf in July 2008 (*All Africa* 2008a). According to a recent report by the FAO, another 40 million people had been forced into starvation in 2008, with the number of undernourished people in the world now standing at 923 million in total (Reuters News 2008a). Asia bears a significant brunt of the food shortage crisis, with an estimated 1.2 billion in the region affected by the food price surges. According to the Global Hunger Index 2008, the developing world – Asia, in particular the Philippines, India and Timor Leste – food security and malnutrition have been pressing issues which require attention (IFPRI 2008).

Food security in Asia would not merely be restricted to food price woes and the shortage of arable land and usable water for land agriculture, but also the issue of declining fish stocks. Fish, the major source of protein for the population in developing regions such as Asia, faces attendant risks of being over-exploited and subjected to negative impact of socioeconomic development, especially in the inland area where freshwater fishing has been dominant in Southeast Asian countries notably in the Mekong River basin, as well as climate change effects. Ever since the bird flu had begun to afflict Asian regions, consumers had shied away from fowl and turning increasingly to fish. Yet, the rising consumption and the complexity of a multitude of factors stood poised to threaten this very aspect of food security, especially as far as Asia is concerned. Beyond starvation, food security also straddles into epidemics. For instance, poor households affected by HIV are generally characterised by food insecurity, among other socioeconomic factors.

Other than the potential outbreak of socio-political strife as the result of food and water insecurity, there is also growing concern that the competition of scarce land and water resources as well as interstate fishing feuds could potentially lead to inter-state conflict. While some analysts consider such scenario as far-fetched, these emerging concerns nevertheless call for greater efforts towards fostering regional and international cooperation in natural resources management (Sachs 2008).

Global economic slowdown and human security

Asia is socioeconomically diverse and non-uniform, with some parts of the region remaining impoverished to this date. Yet, the ongoing global economic slowdown merely added an additional veil of uncertainty over socioeconomic development progress and existing NTS challenges in the region. Even though the economic slowdown would not resemble the Asian financial crisis back in 1997–98, the resultant impact is considerable and wide-ranging. Notwithstanding financial prudence after 1997–98, Asia – both developed and developing nations – would not be able to escape the current crisis unscathed by any standard. Despite a stellar performance which stood in contrast with many developed economies which are struggling with recession, the economic slowdown experienced by Asia's emerging economies such as India amply highlighted the wide-ranging impact this crisis has on the world – Asia not exempted.

Within Asia, different countries and segments within the societies would experience varying consequences the economic slowdown had brought about. The more developed countries in Asia, with their more affluent populations, are among the first affected by the initial credit crunch. Some of the most vulnerable – primarily the retirees and less educated – saw their investment funds vaporise virtually overnight as notable financial institutions such as Lehman Brothers collapsed. However, on the broader scope, the most pressing concern among the people remains the issue of job security. Under the yoke of the economic slowdown and consequent decline in industrial outputs, many of the export-dependent Asian states such as Singapore are facing prospects of reduced job growth and liquidation of the financially more vulnerable small and medium enterprises. Even within the developed Asian societies, those at the lower end of the income strata would be potentially affected, especially when charitable organisations targeting these less endowed groups in the societies had begun to encounter shrinking donations.

To be sure, the global economic slowdown would seriously affect the developing nations in Asia. News of investors' woes and bankers being laid off aside, the impact this ongoing crisis would bring to the less endowed peoples in Asia could not be overlooked, especially when more than 900 million in the region continue to live in poverty. According to an official from the Asian Development Bank, under the present global economic conditions 400 million new poor would join the ranks of 620 million who already subsist on less than $1 per day as well as the hundreds of millions in Asia who have no access to clean water and proper sanitation (*Straits Times* 24 November 2008). For some of these countries, food security has become a more pressing concern as a result of the economic slowdown, which is not only inhibiting the ability of these governments to adequately feed their peoples but also constraining the ability of external food aid for them. Donor governments, due to tightening budgets, would potentially face the problem of sustaining contributions to the UN World Food Program which helps feed 923 million hungry and undernourished people worldwide (Associated Press 2008).

While job security in the more developed countries in Asia has been highlighted as a growing concern, a worse situation may possibly face their less developed counterparts, in particular with respect to the well-being and prospects of migrant workers, who began to feel the impact as employers in their host countries tightened their pockets under the strain of the present crisis which shrinks industrial outputs, rendering excess migrant workforce redundant to current needs. At present more than 53 million migrant workers – mostly low- and medium-skilled labourers – from Asia are employed worldwide (AFP 2008a). The drastic decline in demand for migrant workforce reduces the amount of remittances sent back to the sending countries, impacting not just the livelihood of these workers' families, but also the overall socioeconomic development of these states. For instance, the Philippines would see 50,000 to 100,000 of its citizens working in the agricultural and service sectors in the United States returning home, resulting in a reduction of remittances which constitute 12 per cent of the country's gross domestic product (Canwest News Service 2008).

In fact, only recently the chief of the Organization of Economic Cooperation and Development (OECD) Angel Gurria added to the gloomy future when he forecasted an additional 25 million unemployed as a result of the global economic slowdown by 2010 (AFP 2008b). The present crisis would not just afflict the developed economies, but also Asia in general, especially the less endowed segments in the region. This problem aggravates the already existing NTS challenges such as resource scarcity in Asia, while also possibly serves as a harbinger of socio-political strife as a result of growing groundswell of discontent. Many of China's estimated 200 million rural migrant workers are projected to lose their jobs and the potential long-enduring effects of the economic slowdown could hold considerable socio-political risks for a government which bases its legitimacy of rule on continued socioeconomic development. Indeed, the Chinese government already has been grappling with thousands of violent public outbursts each year by the socially marginalised, especially in the interior.

With respect to the global economic slowdown which is tipped to afflict wider segments of societies in Asia in particular, the following issues are extremely pertinent. One of these is examining ways to sustaining aid to the poor, through the collaborative efforts of governments, business groupings, civil societies as well as regional/international institutions such as the World Bank and Asian Development Bank. In light of efforts in the Asian region to enhance economic cooperation, one would also examine the prospects for economic and financial integration in Asia, such as the development of a regional monetary fund and/or regional trade financing facility. An important element is also the issue of on governance in Asia, especially by eradicating institutional malpractices such as corruption, in order to promote investor confidence.

Energy and security

As the world grapples with the credit crunch and the ensuing economic meltdown, the focus has been shifted away from energy security. However, an increasing world energy demand is expected although a multitude of factors, such as the global economic crisis, added a veil of uncertainty over future supply security and could contribute to an expected continuation in the volatility of oil supply and prices, the bulk of which would be borne by the average citizen on the street. The plunge in oil prices may have been good news for consumers for the short term, especially in current times of economic gloom, but could nonetheless herald potential risks in the longer term. Recently, the chief economist of the International Energy Agency, Fatih Birol, remarked that global oil production would peak much earlier than expected – by 2020 – due to a collapse in energy-related investment as a result of the financial crisis (Dow Jones International News 2008). To add to the complexity of energy security issues, the Organization of Petroleum Exporting Countries (OPEC) lately moved to reduce output in order to address the falling energy prices, sparking future supply security concerns. More importantly, the fall in energy prices would also stifle research and development (R&D) of cleaner alternative fuels. Most crucially, the ongoing global financial crisis would take its toll on present and future energy production programmes, which require an annual investment of US$360 billion to meet demands (*Financial Times* 3 November 2008).

The socioeconomic and environmental impact of energy use is multifaceted. Carbon emissions due to the burning of fossil fuels lead to ozone layer depletion, increased global warming and result in the melting of ice glaciers, consequently the rise in sea levels and coastal flooding. An estimated 1 million people in South and Southeast Asia have been placed at risk from flooding along the coastal regions, with negative impact on the infrastructure as well as the aquaculture (Caballero-Anthony and Koh 2008). Besides climate change, another environment-related concern stems from the construction of energy infrastructure which could potentially lead to environmental and biodiversity degradation, taking the negative environmental impact of the Laos–Thailand Nam Theun 2 (NT2) hydroelectric power project funded by the World Bank in 2000 (see Barton et al. 2004).

Energy has been central to international economic development since the industrialised era, in particular for the developing nations in Asia. Governments in some of these countries are prone to be adversely affected, socio-politically, by fluctuating energy prices. With the fall of oil prices, several countries in the region had contemplated reinstating fuel subsidies for political expediency, taking the case of Indonesia for example. However, this would encourage excessive energy consumption and wastage as well as reduce the incentives for industries to introduce energy efficiency measures or alternative fuels. For some governments in the region, fuel subsidies remain a politically sensitive issue; yet they might risk straining their financial resources in the long term as energy prices continue to fluctuate, thus impeding their ability to sustain or extend the subsidies and diverting scarce resources from more tangible socioeconomic development programmes. From the perspective of inadequate governance during energy production that results in dire socioeconomic consequences, China's implementation of local energy projects, in order to feed the rising domestic demand, had been fraught with problems of socioeconomic marginalisation, for instance, discrimination against migrants displaced by the dam construction projects, reported enslavement of workers as well as deaths in unsafe coal mines (Andrews-Speed and Ma 2008).

Towards a nuclear future?

The endeavour to find clean and renewable sources of energy in order to reduce reliance on traditional fuel sources and also address the issues of climate change, which entails a multitude of consequences relating to resources and health, has led to a 'nuclear renaissance' with the growing interest in nuclear power. But while the traditional framing of nuclear threat had emphasised comprehensive disarmament and elimination of nuclear weapons, the impetus for civilian use of nuclear energy in the region has raised the risks and vulnerabilities that nuclear power plants pose to societal and environmental security. In particular, some Southeast Asian states have been keen towards the idea of nuclear power even though inherent risks exist (BBC Monitoring Asia-Pacific 2008). Concerns have been raised in the region over the feasibility of harnessing nuclear energy due to the poor public safety and institutional records of some of these countries, not to mention the attendant dangers of locating nuclear power plants in places where natural disasters such as volcano eruption and earthquakes are common, taking Indonesia for instance. Such fears are not unwarranted if one could recall the radioactive leakage from the Japanese Kashiwazaki-Kariwa nuclear power plant in 2007 as a result of an earthquake (*Risk Management* 2007).

Unless safety issues are properly addressed, the proliferation of nuclear energy in Southeast Asia could carry adverse consequences. Indeed, the geographical proximity of countries in the region, linked by vast water bodies, would imply that radioactive leakage in one country's nuclear power plant could have transnational impact on neighbouring states. Already, the Indonesian haze problem is not simply a domestic environmental issue, but also a problem for neighbouring Southeast Asian countries such as Malaysia and Singapore. Safety concerns aside, there are also the equally salient issues of high costs involved, in particular for less developed countries, and the grave implications for regional security against concerns about proliferation of nuclear weapons (see Mohan 2007; Sukma 2007). The institutional malaise in some Southeast Asian nuclear power aspirants would put not only the prospects of safe reactor operation, but also the viability of any nuclear accident contingency measures into question. The ongoing global financial crisis and the declining oil prices (at least for the moment) could put paid to nuclear energy endeavours even though the potential consequences of utilising nuclear power have already generated divisive debates within states and the broader region.

Against these concerns, some of the important issues that should be examined are as follows: First is the prospect for collective regional approach to nuclear power in order to foster greater regional cooperation on nuclear energy (e.g., ASIAATOM, the Asian equivalent of Europe's EURATOM). Closely related to this is the need to developing nuclear transparency in the region through confidence building measures (CBMs) and involving a wider regional/international constituency beyond officials to include civil society organisations, private sector and the scientific community.

Second are the possibilities of developing a common energy grid network which could help to enhance energy security of Asia as a whole. Third is the dissemination of clean energy technological know-how throughout the broader Asian region. Fourth is the important issue of governance at the state and regional level, with attention paid to the emerging role of civil societies which champion environmental and socioeconomic causes. The last are the possibilities of exploring NTS formulations to develop new areas for more people-centred security cooperation in the region.

Non-traditional security and the future

The security landscape of the world has undergone a metamorphosis since the end of the Cold War. Prospects for major inter-state war in the future have become dimmer while emerging NTS issues have become paramount concerns in the eyes of states and non-state organisations across the world. This chapter has shown, through a consideration of experiences in Asia, the salience of these issues for all states and societies regardless of wealth and power. Among these issues included the outbreak of infectious diseases like SARS, Nipah virus and avian influenza, and more recently, the so-called Swine-flu virus that has had a global reach since it first broke out in March of 2009. There is also the Indian Ocean tsunami tragedy in 2004, the recent tainted milk scandal in China, the ongoing resource scarcity and poverty in the less endowed countries in the region as well as the most recent global financial crisis.

As highlighted in the discussions above, these NTS concerns could also have ramifications on national security, such as heightening the potential of inter-state armed conflicts in a region already troubled by long-standing historical animosities and territorial disputes. Emerging NTS issues may have created potential risks and certainly warrant greater concerns. Nevertheless, it could also herald a new era for unprecedented levels of inter-state cooperation essential to mitigate the transnational impact of above-mentioned NTS challenges at the present and in the future.

Guide to further reading

For good overviews of the changing nature of security and their different dimensions, see Snyder (2008) and Collins (2007). To get a sense of the diversity of views about security challenges, particularly in Asia, see Caballero-Anthony et al. (2006). An early articulation of this argument is Dupont (2001). Brown et al. (2004) provides an interesting series of articles exploring a range of new security challenges drawn from the influential academic journal *International Security*. For a discussion of human security, see the regular publications of the Human Security Report Project at Simon Fraser University in Canada (most easily accessed via the Web at http://www.sfu.ca/internationalstudies/human_security.html). An influential critical view of human security is Paris (2001), while a more sympathetic assessment, particularly in the context of Asia, can be found in Tow et al. (2000). The report of the UN's High Level Panel on Threats, Challenges and Change is an excellent illustration of this thinking and the policy implications as viewed from the UN (2004).

Chapter 12

Gender Matters: Problematising Masculinity and Femininity in Contemporary Global Politics

LAURA J. SHEPHERD

Imagine you're in a restaurant. You've ordered your meal, but you'd like to wash your hands before you eat. You ask a member of staff the way to the bathrooms (or restrooms, toilets, cloakrooms – whatever is the culturally acceptable term) and you are directed through a single outer door, to be confronted by a pair of doors. On each door there is a sign, bearing an image rather than a word. Which door do you go through? Can you make sense of those signs? If so, then you have a theory of gender. You have a theory, or an understanding, of what the signs signify and of their social importance, because in order to make sense of the signs you have to accept that there are two types of people and that each type of person is represented by one or the other figure in the sign. The chances are good that you know automatically which door you'd go through. But think for a moment about your silhouette today: do you most closely resemble the figure on the left or the figure on the right? We don't go through whichever door we go through because we look like the figures on the signs; we go through the doors because we understand what the signs mean. They may bear no relevance to the way we look, today or ever, but they order the way we behave in the world. If you recognise yourself as part of the group signified by the picture on the right, you would certainly not (apart from in exceptional circumstances) go through the door on the left, and vice versa.

This is not, however, a chapter about how to avoid embarrassment when dining out. So what has the issue of where you wash your hands got to do with world politics? This chapter examines the issue of gender in global politics and argues that the political salience (i.e., importance) of identity, particularly gender identity, should not be underestimated in the study and practice of I/international R/relations.* Through accounting for the ways in which gender matters to a variety of other 'IR' issues, I argue that paying analytical attention to the issue of gender ensures a more comprehensive understanding of global politics. In doing

Summary to Essay.

---

* Usually, 'international relations' refers to the practices of politics between states and 'International Relations' (or 'IR') refers to the academic discipline devoted to the study of these practices.

so the chapter not only draws attention to the wide variety *of* gender matters in global politics, but also highlights the single analytical commitment that unifies the vastly disparate feminist approaches to International Relations: the claim *that* gender matters in the study and practices of global politics.

Some scholars claim that there are gendered social behaviours that issue directly from biological sex – for example, women are inherently more peaceful than men, mothering comes naturally to women, men are usually more aggressive than women and so on. This is known as an *essentialist* account of gender as it rests on the assumption that there is an 'essence' of man/woman that determines behaviour in spite of socialisation. In contrast, many theorists argue that sex is biological (i.e., 'natural') and gender is social (or 'cultural'). Such theories accept that gendered behaviours are largely a product of socialisation, that is, they are constructed through interaction with society and vary according to social and historical context. This is an alternative way to think about gender, and is generally known as a *constructivist* account. A third way of understanding gender derives from political and cultural theories of discourse and understands gender as performative. On this view, the sexed body is as much a product of discourses about gender as discourses about gender are a product of the sexed body. This can be seen as a *performative* or *poststructural* account.

Typically, feminist IR scholars based in each of these three categories ask different questions about different aspects of gender and global politics and use different methods to go about answering the questions they pose. However, the theories of gender do not map neatly onto the conventional analytical frameworks used to describe the study of IR, as I will discuss further below. This makes it difficult to provide an overview of gender and global politics in one short chapter. However, ideas about appropriate and inappropriate gendered behaviours are wide-ranging, influential and sometimes unconscious, but because they affect (and effect) how we behave in the world, they are of interest to the scholar of global politics, as global politics is practised and studied by gendered individuals. Below, I discuss three issues of interest to scholars of global politics (security, globalisation and development) and I discuss each through the lens of a different type of feminist IR (empiricist, constructivist and poststructuralist). It is of course vital to remember that working alongside the feminists mentioned in each field below are many other feminist scholars using other ideas about gender to inform their work, just as there are a range of non-feminist theories about each issue I mention. But if these insights are taken seriously, then we are encouraged to look at the discipline of IR in its entirety as if gender matters.

Statecraft and security: how does gender matter in foreign policy decision making?

Empiricist feminist IR takes as unproblematic the existence of stable gender identities: there are women, who we can easily identify as women and who are likely to behave as other women do, and there are men, who are also easy to identify and who most frequently behave like other men. While the stability attributed to sex does not necessarily map onto an essentialist understanding of gender (as there are empiricists who believe that gendered differences in behaviour are not hard-wired into the human brain but are instead socially constructed), the dichotomy between 'M' and 'F' is assumed to be a constant and, crucially, assumed to play an important role in determining behaviour. In IR, these assumptions translate into research that seeks to investigate how these differences manifest in various political and institutional contexts and with what effects. Are there significant differences between how men and women behave in leadership positions? Are men more likely to support policies that are in keeping with 'masculine' values than women? Is there a 'gender gap' in beliefs about war or military intervention?

There are increasingly nuanced and sophisticated studies being undertaken by empiricist scholars using gender as a variable in their research. Most of these projects fall into one of two broad categories: first, there is work that investigates whether gender is a significant influence on attitudes towards policy (the 'gender gap' literature) and, second, there is related but distinctive work that explores the relationship between gender equality at the domestic level and gender-sensitive policies at the international level. The 'gender gap' literature has a long intellectual heritage (see Caprioli 2000, who mentions relevant work dating back as far as the early 1970s) and, often using large-scale public opinion survey data, has demonstrated that 'women generally are less favourable to [military] escalation than men, but only slightly more opposed to it; and women are less opposed to [troop] withdrawal than men, but only slightly more in favour of it' (Mueller 1973 cited in Caprioli 2000: 54).

Although there are ongoing methodological and theoretical debates about the validity and utility of such findings, across a range of empirical contexts (different wars, different national polities and different generations), it is generally held to be true that women are less likely to support the use of force as a means to resolving international disputes. For example, in her study of the 1991 Gulf War, Karen Gallagher 'identified a large gap, with women in support of attacking Iraqi forces at 22% versus men's 48%, and with women opposed to attacking Iraqi forces at 73% versus men's 48%' (cited in Caprioli 2000: 54). (Interestingly, recent studies have suggested that the events of 11 September 2001 in the USA have led to a quantitative and qualitative realignment, such that women's 'views of defense spending and missile defense (among other issues) now closely resemble those of men', as discussed in Eichenberg 2003: 111).

This research has served as the foundation for a range of recent related studies extending the parameters of the debate. Urbatsch (2009), for example, investigates whether those responsible for parenting girls are more or less militaristic than those parenting boys (on the grounds that it is overwhelmingly more likely to be boys affected by militaristic policies) and concludes that 'those in households with boys have more dovish or isolationist foreign policy preferences, while those in households with girls have more hawkish preferences' (Urbatsch 2009: 19). There have also been behavioural surveys that suggest that 'the addition of girls and women into decision-making settings may well have an impact on the process [of negotiation], even if we cannot conclude yet that it will make a difference regarding the *outcomes* of that process' (Boyer et al. 2009: 43, emphasis in original). These latter surveys link to the other strand of research in this field, which explores the influence of gender on political leadership, asking whether the participation of women in formal political institutions is likely to 'feminise' the policies of those institutions and, relatedly, whether empowering women at the domestic level leads to a more peaceful international outlook.

While mainstream IR scholarship has theorised the link between domestic politics and international relations (most notably in the literature on 'democratic peace'), feminist empiricists have taken this agenda further and sought to explore a number of related issues. Mary Caprioli and Mark Boyer acknowledge that the data available regarding the militarism of women in political power are too limited to extrapolate general findings (2001: 505), but they do offer an interesting statistical analysis that integrates this variable into a broader study of whether higher levels of domestic gender equality correlate with more aggressive policy decisions made by 'crisis actors' (state leaders). Crucially, 'the presence of a female leader increases the severity of violence in a crisis' in the data analysed (Caprioli and Boyer 2001: 514), but the authors are careful to note that this should not be taken as evidence of a general tendency (516). They do conclude, rather more robustly, that 'a domestic norm of tolerance and equality . . . seems to be mirrored in states' international behaviour at least with respect to the level of violence used during international crisis' (Caprioli and Boyer 2001: 516; see also True and Mintrom 2001: 44–6, 49).

Without taking seriously the issue of gender in these fields of enquiry, it would not be possible to understand how and why gender matters in political negotiation and decision making. If it is indeed the case, as the above research suggests, that women are more likely to be circumspect in their support at the ballot-box for violent resolution of disputes but less likely to be restrained when in positions of political power themselves, we need to understand why this is so, and what the implications are of these findings. Ultimately, IR scholars have been concerned for decades with the issue of war and how best to prevent it: if there is robust empirical evidence that empowering women at the domestic level translates into peaceful international politics, then '[f]oreign policy goals to ensure peace . . . should concentrate more on supporting organizations aimed at improving the status of women' (Caprioli 2000: 64). We also need to investigate the social processes that condition or construct female leaders as 'hyper-masculine' and therefore cause a disjuncture between the ideal of gender-equal political participation and the reality of such equality having only very limited effects. However, large-scale quantitative studies such as those described above are not suitable for such investigations, so in the section below I discuss constructivist feminist IR, which offers many insights into these and other issues.

Political economy: how does gender matter in processes of economic reform and neo-liberal globalisation?

In her response to Francis Fukuyama's opinion piece on 'women and the evolution of world politics' (1998), Ann Tickner suggests that arguing about 'who can be more aggressive than whom' (1999: 11) is not as useful to the discipline of IR as careful consideration of conflict, inequality and oppression. Tickner is explicit in her espousal of a constructivist theory of gender, as she dismisses Fukuyama's 'biologically rooted theories' as a 'deterministic' and unpromising analytical starting point (Tickner 1999: 11). The assumption that all women are like *this* (peaceful, nurturing, passive, emotional) and all men are like *that* (aggressive, competitive, active, rational) as a result of biology rather than social construction precludes not only the possibility of variety in gendered behaviour but also the possibility of change. Constructivist feminism, therefore, investigates gender matters in global politics without assuming that gendered characteristics are determined by biological sex. The behaviours associated with men, according to essentialist theories of gender, are better understood as being associated with masculinity and, likewise, the characteristics that describe women are better understood as being descriptive of femininity. This opens the space for us to recognise women behaving in masculine ways and vice versa and also allows us to understand the study and practices of international relations in new and interesting ways.

As I mentioned at the beginning of this chapter, the study of neo-liberal globalisation offers a useful lens on constructivist feminist IR. This is because ideas about gender are thoroughly bound up in the processes of integration, fragmentation, economic restructuring and im/migration that characterise globalisation. (While there is of course no agreed definition or even analytical acceptance of 'globalisation', here I draw on the feminist literature that interrogates globalisation from a constructivist perspective and which therefore minimally agrees that there are a set of processes that can be thus characterised and, further, that are intrinsically gendered.) There are four inter-related concepts that help to structure globalisation, and all four are gendered in very specific ways.

'The global'

Gender is represented in 'the global' through the continual association of women with the private sphere, as determined by an understanding of gender that maps the duality of men and women onto the dichotomy of public and private. In IR, this is mirrored in the association of 'low/soft' politics (e.g., domestic matters, welfare, social security and so on), even the description of which is gendered, with femininity and the rendering of the international as a domain of 'high/hard' politics to which only masculine/ised subjects have access (i.e., only subjects that are masculine by birth or behaviour or both).

'The economic'

The economic realm is constructed as an abstract, apolitical and even asocial domain in conventional analysis (Wichterich 2000: 30). However, on further investigation through gendered lenses, men are the subjects of formal economic enterprise, 'adventurous, risk-taking, fast-paced, globe-trotting young men' (Marchand 2000: 223) or their corollary, dignified and mature corporate shareholders and executives (see Hooper 2001). Either way, the notion of the economic that informs processes of globalisation is gendered, and gendered masculine.

Mobility and dynamism

In keeping with the public man/private woman assumption described above, there is a secondary core assumption about the mobility of masculinity versus the fixity of femininity that influences globalisation. This aspect of conceptual organisation draws heavily on gendered and sexualised understandings of colonialism, imperialism and conquest, where the split between the developed (colonial) and developing (colonised) world is constructed in gendered terms as conforming to conventional binary opposition.

> [P]ortraying the state as a feminized spinster/siren and the market as a masculinised roving bachelor on the make ... justifies erosions in regulation of global capital' and normalises 'a kind of "love 'em and leave 'em" production, trade and finance that enriches only a few at the expense of far too many.
> (Runyan 2003: 139)

In order to carve out a space for agency in an era of globalisation, vast populations of women have been forced into relocating to find employment, for example, in the infamous export-processing zones in Mexico and China (see Wright 2006). However, just proving the ability for mobility does not grant feminine subjects access to power, as the value accorded to the employment they can find is limited.

Info-technology

The devaluation of women's labour has been enabled by the articulation of certain skills as 'natural' to women and therefore not to be rewarded. Women are hired to work on assembly lines and in domestic services 'because of their famous "dexterity", "docility", "patience", "attentiveness" and "cheapness"' (Elson and Pearson 1989; Salzinger 2003, cited in Wright 2006: 25). These attributes are feminised, but also assumed to be found in women. As they are found in all women, they are neither rare nor special, thus the women themselves are rendered disposable, as any one woman could be replaced by any other. In contrast, the rarefied realm of info-technology is masculinised and therefore comfortable with and accepting of masculine/ised subjects, as info-technology is constructed as high-risk, complex, detached and rational in the extreme.

What are the implications of a set of beliefs about globalisation that implic- itly or explicitly rely on these gendered concepts? As Cynthia Enloe explains, globalisation

> has a futuristic ring: traditional national boundaries will mean less as data and capital goods are transferred electronically around the globe; teenagers in their Benetton sweaters will grow up with a global consciousness. But to turn this vision into reality government officials are relying on old-fashioned ideas about women.
>
> (2000: 174)

At every level, from individual employers of domestic help through small businesses to multi-national corporations, hiring, firing, financing and restructuring are inseparable from gendered imaginings of whose work is valued in which ways and under what circumstances (see also Peterson and Runyan 1999: 130–46). It is quite unlikely that deeply entrenched beliefs about appropriate roles for men and women will change overnight. Thus, constructivist feminists who interrogate globalisation seek not only to make explicit the implicit assumptions about gender that inform neo-liberal policies (in the hope that exposing the unstable and unsustainable foundations of the ideas will expedite the erosion of those foundations) but also to explore ways in which processes as they are can be made more equitable.

This research agenda has included the thorough critique of international financial institutions such as the World Bank and international organisations such as the United Nations. Both of these institutions have been involved in 'gender mainstreaming', in efforts to ensure that processes of economic restructuring (and, indeed, state-building and post-conflict reconstruction, as I discuss in the following section) pay due attention to (how) gender matters. Jacqui True and Michael Mintrom explain gender mainstreaming as 'a concept that, on the one hand, suggests a shift away from a focus on "women's issues," and on the other hand, politicizes traditional male and female roles' (2001: 31). Ultimately, gender mainstreaming programmes intend to ensure that 'gender issues are incorporated into the planning of policies, and not simply added on as an afterthought' (Hafner-Burton and Pollack 2002: 353).

At a minimum, effective gender mainstreaming can ensure that all policy formulation and implementation do not have negative effects on stakeholders (those affected by the policies) according to their gender. For example, a gender-sensitive micro-finance programme funded by the World Bank would look at how women frequently do not have access to formal economic enterprise, due to social or political constraints, and might seek to include informal economic activity such as craftwork or small-scale agriculture as a viable means of securing funding. The implications of this are wide-ranging: women become eligible for Bank funding, they can build social networks through Bank-funded education programmes, they can achieve a degree of economic independence and so on. Similarly, a gender mainstreaming in the United Nations Department of Peace-Keeping Operations means that peace support operatives (those tasked with overseeing refugee camps, for example) must enact all policy decisions in a gender-sensitive manner, questioning whether women have different security needs to men, or whether traditional gender roles within a conflict society make demilitarisation of male child soldiers qualitatively different to the demilitarisation of female child soldiers.

The very existence of departments within such powerful institutions that are tasked with paying attention to gender is quite an achievement. However, as I have commented elsewhere, I am sceptical about the radically transformative potential of gender mainstreaming policies (see Shepherd 2008: 168–70). Too often, there are financial and conceptual impediments to effective gender main-streaming, where gender is seen as a 'soft' issue to take second place to more immediate 'hard' issues such as resource provision and security. 'Gender' is also frequently used as a synonym for women (see Carver 1996), which both repre-sents gender mainstreaming programmes as partisan 'special pleading' on behalf of an inherently vulnerable group (and thus circumscribes women's agency) and ignores the fact that there are multiple ways in which gender can be understood to affect and effect subjectivity. Although critiques of gender mainstreaming are by no means only advanced by those working from a poststructural perspec-tive, in the following section I discuss these critiques further and outline a third way in which IR feminists are seeking to illustrate how gender matters in global politics.

Development: how does gender matter in processes of state-building/post-conflict reconstruction?

The body of feminist work I discuss in this section is possibly more theoretically complex, but that doesn't mean that there is not a strong practical application to the work. Indeed, as poststructural feminisms share with poststructuralism more broadly a focus on representation, meaning and identity, in some ways this liter-ature asks the most directly political question: how is it that the reality we take for granted, which includes gendered disparities of power and multiple forms of (sometimes violent) oppression along gender lines, comes to be accepted as such? There are many answers to this question, but those working with this approach all endeavour to 'show that things are not as self-evident as one believed, to see what is accepted as self-evidence will no longer be accepted as such' (Foucault cited in Campbell 1998: 191). Representations of political activity in media coverage (who is seen as authoritative? who is included at the negotiating table? whose presence – or absence – is accepted as 'normal'?), representations of gender in policy documents and representations of global politics more broadly, in pop-ular culture and arts, are all constitutive of how we understand global political processes and our place within them. Representations 'are never merely descriptive, but always normative, and, as such, exclusionary' (Butler 1994: 166), as they prescribe our acceptance of the way things are and thus delimit the boundaries of common sense, which Stuart Hall called 'the moment of extreme ideological closure' (1985: 105).

With regard to gender matters, then, poststructural feminism engages in a range of critiques, but in this section I will map out the literature's engagement with development and state-building, as this field of study represents a particularly interesting interjection into conventional ideas about how we should 'integrate' gender into these political processes. First of all, poststructural feminism suggests that gender is not there to be integrated, but rather is always already present, in the organising logics of the disciplines and institutions involved. While constructivist feminists working on globalisation, as discussed above, offer many of the same insights, alternative theories of development draw on queer theory (discussed below) to advance an explanation of how discursive logics, which are implicitly and explicitly gendered and sexualised, prescribe and proscribe the subject matter with which disciplines and institutions are concerned. In the 1960s and 1970s, early feminist interventions in development (which have been labelled as a 'women in development' [WID] approach) largely sought to 'add women and stir', with the modest aim of 'wanting to improve women's lot within the existing system' (Waylen 1996: 39). By contrast, the second wave of interventions (known as a 'women and development' [WAD] approach) took a more holistic view, arguing that women have specific knowledges and skills that should be fully valued and incorporated into the development process, which would ultimately challenge the very nature of development. The formulation of a 'gender and development' (GAD) approach in the early 1990s was founded on an acknowledgement of the need both to understand gender relations on the ground and to investigate the specific ways gender ideology and relations contribute to women's subordination and the sexual division of labour and power (Parpart 1995: 235).

Beyond GAD, we can identify a feminist critique of development that seeks a new definition of development, one that does not depend on the imperialism of Northern concepts, 'one that is grounded in the experience(s) and knowledge(s) of women in the South' (Parpart 1995: 236–7). The existing development paradigms that inform academic and policy work, it is argued, are conventionally based on nationalist and colonialist discourses, as well as discourses of modernity and liberal triumphalism, all of which rely on logics of gender and sexuality in order to make sense. 'Interventions in the post-structuralist mode have opened up new spaces within development studies which allow us to examine the discursive power of nationalism in the economic agenda-setting of the nation-state' (Rai 2008: 12) and of colonialism in the economic agenda-setting of the international development institution (see, e.g., Bergeron 2004; Kabeer 1994; Kothari 2005). '[D]evelopment policies and programs are largely predicated on the assumption that developmental problems can be reduced to . . . "solvable" problems which involve the transfer of Western technical expertise to the developing world'

(Parpart 1995: 225); thus dominant development paradigms perpetuate a masculinised, even paternalistic approach to knowledge transfer, conforming to the gendered oppositions of developed/rational/advanced/expert (read: masculine) versus developing/emotional/backward/student (read: feminine). Even gender mainstreaming programmes in place in key development institutions have done little to challenge this logic (see Griffin 2007, 2009).

'Queer theory', most closely associated with the work of Judith Butler (1993, 1999, among others), posits that we understand bodies, culturally, socially and politically, through the prism of ideas we have about sex and gender. Much poststructural feminist work on development draws on queer theory to challenge the ideas that we have about bodies, about the status of biology and about the things to do with sex and sexuality that are generally considered to be 'natural'.

> Our experiences have implications for the appearance, condition, and performance of our bodies. For example, women may have hysterectomies, bear children or not, remove or grow body or facial hair. Both men and women may or may not exercise until they are muscular, or suffer from war or sport injuries . . . Similarities between bodies of one 'biological' sex are exaggerated, and [similarities] between bodies of different sexes are played down . . . Thus, although the categories of sex *appear* natural and absolute, they are 'cleaned up' by human intervention.
>
> (Jolly 2000: 85–6, emphasis in original)

This literature proposes, therefore, that representations of gender, sex and sexuality in development policy and state-building legislative apparatus do not simply describe bodily realities, but rather are constitutive: of domestic units, sexual relations, parental care and a host of other social arrangements as well as of the physicality of the gendered body. With regard to development policies formulated and implemented by the World Bank, for example, Penny Griffin argues that Bank discourse functions to reproduce 'a heteronormative discourse of economic viability through policy interventions that are intrinsically sexualised, that is, predicated on a politics of normative heterosexuality' (2007: 221). According to World Bank discourse (which is evidenced in a multitude of policy documents and strategic plans), all women are heterosexual and all homosexuals are men (and most frequently only mentioned in medicalised discourse about the management of HIV/AIDS) (Griffin 2007: 234–5, 236 fn. 6).

The implications of such heteronormative practices are profound. 'These norms are all-pervasive, and not only determine the sexual aspect of our lives, but also shape our access to economic resources, and our ability to participate in social and political activities' (Jolly 2000: 79). The marginalisation of queer sexualities in development and state-building, whether by omission or by design, both affects and effects whose participation is considered legitimate, whose interests are represented and, ultimately, whose modes of being in the world are deemed to be of value. Relationships that have conventionally been considered 'private' are increasingly being publically addressed. Even if relationships between individuals are assumed to be heterosexual and are most frequently heterosexual in 'fact' (i.e., in the specific case in which the relevant policy is enacted), the beliefs about marriage, monogamy and power that are intrinsic to the model of heterosexuality propagated by influential development institutions may still have negative consequences (see Bedford 2007: 303). If intimate relationships are not conceptually bounded within a heteronormative model, development practitioners still need to ensure that due consideration is given to how sexual behaviours are thought of in the specific social and political context. '[P]articular labels and models may indeed be welcomed by many ... but they may also be combined with, or rejected in favour of, other indigenous ways of understanding same-sex sexualities' (Corrêa and Jolly 2008: 33), which may or may not be premised on the notion that sexuality defines identity (see Sharma 2008: 68–9). Ultimately, this literature seeks to challenge the mostly silent norm of heterosexuality that pervades development planning, in an effort to ensure that the types of social and political spaces that are produced through development practices and built through state-building processes are inclusive rather than exclusive and that no mode of being in the world is marginalised or devalued because of particularly powerful notions of 'common sense'.

Third and finally, tracing connections between state-building processes and the images we hold of global politics, this body of work draws attention to the ways in which state-building (re)produces the spatial norms of domestic and international and how these norms are themselves gendered. Drawing on insights from critical geopolitics (see, e.g., Agnew and Corbridge 1995; O'Tuathail and Agnew 1992; Peck and Tickell 2002), poststructural feminists working on development and state-building have emphasised the need to '[think] about neoliberalism as involving processes that *produce* spaces, states and subjects in complex and multiple forms' (Larner 2003: 511). In my own work, I have investigated how, for example, UN state-building suggestions reproduce the idea that the only appropriate form of political authority is the state, and, further, how the meaning of 'state' is differentiated through the various spatial tropes deployed by the institution. That is, 'states' in which conflict occurs (and therefore 'states' to which the many UN documents speak) are frequently articulated in association with predicates such as 'local' and 'indigenous', whereas 'Member States' of the Security Council are called upon for 'financial, technical and logistical support' and the development of sensitive training programmes (see Shepherd 2008). The state is constituted as the legitimate form of political authority, but the 'international' is the repository of knowledge concerning the procedures and practices necessary to achieve and consolidate this authority. The inhabitants of the proto-states/states-in-development (in contrast to developed states) must conform to gendered understandings of appropriate behaviours (both public and private, as discussed above), for without adherence to these gendered norms, the proto-state can never be recognised *as* a state. Sovereignty is the regulatory ideal: sovereign, stable individuals contained within a sovereign, stable state.

Conclusion

In order to provide an overview of gender issues in twenty-first century world politics, I have described three distinct bodies of work within feminist IR, all of which start from the premise that gender matters. To summarise, empiricist feminism asks how men and women exhibit different behaviours and perhaps see the world differently. Constructivist feminism asks how the beliefs and ideas we have about gender inform – or construct – our engagement with the world. Post-structural feminism asks how the very world we live in is produced through and productive of certain understandings of gender. Analysis of gendered identities is an integral part of understanding IR because, while we may lapse into using the analytical abstractions of 'the state' and 'the United Nations', political practices are performed by gendered bodies. Moreover, *analyses* of such political practices are also performed by gendered bodies. Although there is clearly no such thing as 'the feminist perspective' on international relations, all of the scholars referenced above seek to investigate how gendered assumptions, gendered logics and gendered human subjects are intrinsic to the study and practice of politics. Conventional IR is characteristically silent about the existence of human subjects and about the relevance of experiential subjectivity to matters of security. '[I]f all experience is gendered, analysis of gendered identities is an imperative starting point in the study of political identities and practice' (Peterson 1999: 37). 'Messy bodies' are absent, as are many of the socio-political relations that fall outside of those relations designated international. Power may be central to the conceptual armoury of International Relations, but orthodox studies consistently marginalise the different forms of gender and power relations that are both produced by and productive of practices of international relations.

Guide to further reading

Most introductory IR texts include a chapter on gender and/or feminism (see, e.g., Sylvester 1996; Tickner and Sjoberg 2007; True 2009) and anyone seeking an overview of feminist IR would be well advised to read these. There are also a number of classic works exploring the development and innovations of feminist IR that continue to influence and inspire scholars: Enloe's ([1989] 2000) *Bananas, Beaches and Bases: Making Feminist Sense of International Politics*; Sylvester's (1994) *Feminist Theory and International Relations in a Postmodern Era*; and Zalewski's (1992) article that uses the Bosnian war as a vehicle for the analysis of feminism's place in the discipline. With regard to subject-specific texts, Cohn's (1987) article is one of the earliest and most fascinating feminist discourse analyses, in which she describes her encounters with 'defense intellectuals' and maps the masculinisation of nuclear weapons technologies. Hooper (2001) explores the gendered politics of *The Economist*, and two volumes of works edited by Zalewski and Parpart (1998, 2008) consider 'the "Man" question' in International Relations. There is a range of texts that engage with issues of gender, violence and security (see, e.g., Shepherd 2008; Sjoberg and Gentry 2007; Whitworth 2004) and many that explore the violences of development (see, e.g., Griffin 2009; Rai 2008; Wright 2006). Finally, a recent volume edited by Ackerly et al. (2006) gives an excellent introduction to debates over feminist methodologies in IR.

Chapter 13

Inequality and Underdevelopment in World Politics

RAY KIELY

Global inequality and underdevelopment are particularly contentious issues in contemporary world politics. In essence, they are issues which ask the following questions: What is the (global) North–South divide? How has it emerged, how is it reproduced and what can be done about it? Has the recent era of 'globalisation' eroded a North–South divide and promoted some forms of convergence, or at least poverty reduction, in the global order?

This chapter examines each, but especially the last of these, questions. Debate over the relationship between globalisation, inequality and underdevelopment has been particularly contentious. On the one hand, there are relatively upbeat assessments concerning a shift towards convergence between rich and poor countries in the global economy. A variant on this argument suggests that while inequality in some forms may not have been reduced in recent years, what matters is the fact that global poverty *has* been reduced, and this has occurred because of the opportunities that globalisation presents to developing countries. Not all states have necessarily taken advantage of these opportunities, but it is precisely in these states where rapid economic growth and poverty reduction have not occurred. Related to these upbeat assessments are various arguments concerning the dispersal of capital flows throughout the world, the rise of manufacturing in the developing world, the rise of China and India and the increase in primary commodity prices in recent years, which in turn have facilitated high growth rates in Latin America and much of Africa.

On the other hand, more sceptical assessments question the extent to which poverty has been reduced, point to the increase in inequality within countries and (at the extremes) between them, the continued concentration of capital and high value production in the developed countries, the limits of the kinds of manufacturing that has taken place in much of the developing world, including in India and China, the continued limits of development based on excessive reliance on primary commodity exports, and thus of growth rates in the so-called periphery. These problems have all been exacerbated, so the sceptics argue, by the financial crisis of 2007–08, and the consequent shift towards a global recession. Though this is likely to have adverse effects everywhere, these will be most acute in the developing world. The upbeat assessments thus exaggerated the positives that occurred in the boom years, and anyway now look woefully inadequate as the world moves into a very serious recession.

This chapter assesses the claims made by both the 'optimists' and the 'sceptics' concerning inequality and underdevelopment. It does so by first briefly outlining the ways in which inequality and underdevelopment were theorised in the post-war era, as part of the great development debate. This section will suggest that notwithstanding the over-generalisations employed by both sides, this debate retains considerable relevance in the era of globalisation. The next section examines the position of the optimists, pointing to some of the evidence used to back up this case. It then moves on to examine the more sceptical side, again examining some of the evidence used to back up this case. The chapter then provides a more in-depth analysis of various trends in the global economy, and suggests that these, on the whole, tend to support the more sceptical arguments. Finally, the chapter concludes by summarising the arguments made in the chapter, and using these to reflect on why inequality and underdevelopment are such serious issues of concern.

The great development debate: inequality and underdevelopment 1945–82

The post-1945 era was one in which development became a particular area of concern. While the idea certainly pre-dated 1945, it became more prominent in the context of the Cold War and the beginning of the end of formal empires. Both superpowers supported political independence for the colonies, though both of course were concerned that they exercise considerable influence over the political trajectory of the newly independent sovereign states.

It was in this context that the debate over the causes of global inequality and underdevelopment emerged. Though there were considerable variations and nuances in the debate, we can identify two basic positions: modernisation and dependency theories. The former was the mainstream theory of development, which essentially argued that developing societies – the 'third world' – were backward and undeveloped, and therefore in need of development. This position was developed most famously by Walt Rostow (1960), who suggested that all nation-states pass through similar stages of development. So, poorer societies in the 1960s were at a similar stage of development to say, Britain in the 1780s. The task of development was to hasten the transition to development in the poorer societies. Rostow argued that this was good not only for developing societies, as they would become richer, but also for the security of the West, as richer societies were less likely to be attracted by the communist alternative. Modernisation theory suggested that the task of development could be facilitated by poorer countries embracing Western investment, technology and values such as entrepreneurship and meritocracy. Whether or not this was an accurate portrayal of Western societies (and the diversity among such countries), in terms of both the transition to development and the reality of modernity in the 1950s, is a moot point. Certainly, civil rights movements in the 1950s would not have recognised this characterisation of the United States.

The crucial argument of modernisation theory, then, was that contact with the West was on the whole favourable to the development of the third world. On the other hand, some structuralist economists had argued that the situation of poorer countries could not be explained in isolation from the richer world, and that contact with the latter was in some respects part of the problem. Thus, one of the legacies of colonialism was that third world countries specialised in producing primary products, and this led to an excessive dependence on the world price movements of the one or two goods that accounted for most of their foreign exchange earnings. This was in contrast to the developed countries, which were far more industrialised and diversified, and so were not excessively reliant on the price movements of a handful of products. Moreover, Raul Prebisch (1959) and Hans Singer (1950) argued that primary producers faced certain disadvantages which meant that there was a tendency for the terms of trade to decline for primary goods as against industrial goods. What this meant in barter terms is that in, say, a 10-year period, primary producers would have to exchange more tonnes of cocoa in order to buy a similar amount of tractors. Prebisch and Singer suggested that this tendency occurred because there was a low income elasticity of demand for primary products; in other words, as average incomes rise, so consumers spend a disproportionate amount of their income on primary products. Furthermore, while the prices of manufactured goods may fall, they are less likely to fall as quickly as those of primary goods as there were many primary goods producers but comparatively few producers of industrial goods. Clearly then, this account of inequality focused on hierarchies in the world economy and how colonial powers had enforced specialisation in lower value primary production in the colonies. Even in independent Latin America, this practice had occurred as powerful land-owners accrued huge wealth from land-ownership and used this to import manufactured goods rather than promote domestic manufacturing production. This account thus suggested that the Western-dominated world economy was not the solution to underdevelopment, as modernisation theory contended, but, in some respects at least, was part of the problem.

At the same time, this account suggested that development in the third world could be achieved through pro-industrialisation policies designed to overcome the colonial legacy. In this way, poorer countries could reduce their dependence on the import of expensive manufactures and the export of cheap primary goods. This policy of import substitution industrialisation (ISI) was the main development strategy employed in the third world from the 1950s (or earlier) until the late 1970s and early 1980s. Ironically, though the rationale for such a strategy was very different from that associated with modernisation theory, in practice on policy the two theories effectively converged around the idea that development and modernisation could occur through industrialisation.

Dependency theory challenged this view, suggesting that industrialisation remained dependent on the West. The mechanisms that sustained dependence included reliance on foreign capital, foreign technology and foreign markets.

Furthermore, the industrialisation that was said to be occurring in the developing world was highly exploitative and reliant on cheap labour. None of this was leading to convergence with the developed world; instead it was simply promoting new forms of subordination, hierarchy and dependence in the world economy. Some theories of dependency related this to a crude zero-sum game which suggested that the rich world was rich only because it had underdeveloped the poor world, implying that protectionist ISI policies did not go far enough, and that de-linking from the Western-dominated world economy was the only effective way forward for the third world (Frank 1969). In this account, poorer societies were not so much undeveloped as *under*developed.

This was essentially what was at stake in the debate over inequality and under-development in the period from the 1940s into the 1970s. On the one side, modernisation theory: poorer countries should embrace the opportunities provided by the Western-dominated world economy, and in the process hasten the transition to development. On the other side, dependency theory: poorer countries are poor in part because they are in a structurally subordinate and dependent position in the world economy, and thus need to find ways to protect themselves from the constraints that these hierarchies generate. By the 1970s and into the 1980s, it was clear that for all their differences, both sides suffered from some similar weaknesses. In particular they tended to over-generalise and homogenise a diverse set of countries. In the process they tended to make sweeping predictions concerning the inevitability of development (modernisation theory) or stagnation (dependency theory). For instance, the rise of East Asian newly industrialising countries such as South Korea and Taiwan undermined crude versions of dependency theory, as these countries grew rapidly and exported to the Western economies. On the other hand, these countries did not simply embrace 'the West', and protected certain sectors from foreign competition in order to develop their own national industries. Moreover, the success of these countries may have been contingent on certain specific factors that could not easily be replicated elsewhere. It was precisely this focus on contingency and specificity that was missing in the modernisation versus dependency theory debate. It was also in this context that some argued that the study of development had reached an impasse, and that from now on we could only focus on specific cases of development without employing the generalisations associated with the modernisation and dependency theory (Booth 1985).

Moreover, changes in the global economy led to important changes in the development strategy in the third world. In particular, the debt crisis of 1982 saw a shift from the developmentalist strategies associated with ISI, towards neo-liberal policies that encouraged trade and investment liberalisation, privatisation and the rollback of state intervention in the economy (or at least a shift to intervention that extended the market rather than restricted its role). This was justified on the grounds that ISI encouraged the promotion and protection of inefficient industries, rather than facilitating specialisation in those sectors where countries were (relatively) most competitive; in other words, it meant the promotion of the principle of comparative advantage. While in the short term, the results of neo-liberal policies were disastrous, and living standards for many fell in the lost decade of development (the 1980s), the 1990s saw a new period of optimism concerning the relationship between development and globalisation.

These shifts – from grand theory to local and national development trajectories, from ISI to neo-liberalism – appeared to undermine the foundations of the 'great development debate' of the 1940s to the early 1980s. However, while it is certainly true that these theories were guilty of over-generalisation, I will suggest below that the optimistic and sceptical accounts concerning question of growth, poverty and inequality replicate these older debates, albeit in the new context of (neo-liberal) 'globalization'.

Global inequality and underdevelopment: the optimistic position

This section outlines the optimistic position, which argues that underdevelopment has been reduced in recent years, and this either has reduced global inequality or has at least reduced absolute poverty. The main evidence used by the optimists is that the number or proportion of people living in absolute poverty has declined since the 1980s. The World Bank (2002: 30) has, for instance, claimed that there has been a decline in the number of people living in absolute poverty, from 1.4 to 1.2 billion. At other times, the Bank and others have suggested slightly different figures, but on the whole the news is upbeat – the number of people living in absolute poverty is falling (Bhagwati 2004; Wolf 2004). Such good news suggests that the Millennium Development Goals (MDGs) are likely to be fulfiled, or at least they will be in those states that have carried out appropriate policies. These MDGs were adopted by the United Nations General Assembly in September 2000, and they specified eight goals to be achieved by 2015. These included the eradication of extreme hunger and poverty (though in practice this was linked to the target of halving the number of people living on less than a dollar a day), achieving universal primary education, promoting gender equality and various health and environmental indicators (www.un.org/millennium/declaration/ares552e.pdf). While these are desirable goals, the main issue is about whether and how these can be achieved, how the goals can be measured and whether or not power relations hinder the success of achieving such goals.

The key point for the optimists though is the question of adopting the correct policies, which involves the promotion of a 'globalization friendly' strategy (World Bank 2002). As other chapters in this book have shown (see Higgott and Cerny, this volume), 'globalisation' is a difficult term to define and is used in a variety of ways by both academics and politicians. In this case, being globalisation friendly means adopting policies that allow countries to embrace the opportunities generated by the world economy, and this in practice means liberalisation. At the very least, it means policies of trade and investment liberalisation. In practice this means policies that encourage competition and specialisation, rather than protection, and so means that tariffs and subsidies are reduced, import controls are removed and restrictions on foreign investment are loosened. It may also mean financial liberalisation, the freer movement of money into (and out of) countries, but there is some disagreement over the extent to which this should occur. The basic argument is that trade liberalisation will encourage specialisation in those sectors in which countries have a comparative advantage, and thus stop producing high-cost, inefficient goods. Investment (and possibly financial) liberalisation will encourage investment by transnational companies, and thus leads to a shift of investment from capital-rich to capital-poor areas.

This argument would appear to be reinforced by the surge in foreign capital investment, including into the so-called periphery since the early 1990s. The total global amount of direct foreign investment increased from $59 billion in 1982 to $202 billion in 1990, $1.2 trillion in 2000, down to $946 billion in 2005 and back up to $1.3 trillion in 2006 (UNCTAD 2002b: 3–5; 2007: 9). Developing countries generally accounted for around one-third of this total. This increase in direct foreign investment (DFI) has also led to the growth of manufacturing in the developing world. In 1970, 18.5 per cent of the total exports from the developing world were manufactured goods; by the end of the 1990s it was over 80 per cent (UNCTAD 2002a: 5). Optimists thus contend that industrialisation can occur through open investment policies which allow foreign (or national) companies to take advantage of low labour costs, and this promotes properly competitive industrialisation rather than the high-cost, white elephant approach associated with ISI. Critics that point to the cheap labour associated with industrialisation do not offer a viable alternative, and anyway this should be seen as a necessary stage that developing societies must pass through. In the long run, competitive industrialisation will lead to full employment, which in turn will lead to upgrading to more a more developed kind of manufacturing, as occurred in the case of the earlier developers. Though this argument does not follow the rigid stages associated with modernisation theory, the broad contentions certainly replicate this approach.

Moreover, with the growth of the likes of China, this has a favourable impact for the rest of the developing world, even if they have not industrialised at comparable levels. China has increasingly relied on the rising import of inputs, and the global export value of iron and steel, ores and minerals and non-ferrous metals increased by between 30 and 45 per cent in 2004, which (in part) reflected rising demand from China, which is now the leading importer of many commodities (WTO 2005: 1–2). In 2004 Latin American exports expanded by 37 per cent, much of which was accounted for by rising demand in East Asia, especially China (WTO 2005: 11). Some African countries, particularly Sudan and Congo, have similarly boosted their sales in the Chinese market, as have some East Asian countries.

Global inequality and underdevelopment: the sceptical position

The sceptical position challenges this upbeat assessment on both empirical and theoretical grounds. This section concentrates on the former. The first issue is that of poverty reduction, where there are some grounds for questioning the view that absolute poverty has fallen. Absolute poverty is defined as living on less than 1 dollar a day, adjusted to take account of local purchasing power. Crucial here is the way in which purchasing power parity (PPP) is measured, and this is done through a system of international price comparisons, which were made in 1985 and 1993, and have then been adjusted to take account of annual changes to particular economies. The alleged decline in poverty cited above partly reflects a shift away from poverty counts made on the basis of international price comparisons in two different periods – 1985 in the case of the first figure, and 1993 in the case of the second, lower figure (Reddy and Pogge 2003; Wade 2003). The shift from the 1985 count to the 1993 count had the effect of lowering the poverty line in 77 out of 92 countries for which data were available, and these countries contained 82 per cent of the total population of the 92 countries (Reddy and Pogge 2004: 42). The World Bank's *World Development Report* on 1999/2000 was actually far more pessimistic than the optimistic assertions cited above, as it used the 1985 base year calculations to argue that absolute poverty had increased from 1.2 billion in 1987 to 1.5 billion in 1999 (World Bank 1999: 25).

The measure of absolute poverty is also questionable because of the method of calculation, based on PPP. This method attempts to factor in local variations in the purchasing power of particular goods, a laudable aim, but one that is particularly difficult when measuring poverty (Reddy and Pogge 2003). This is because the basket of goods that is used to make the comparison includes goods that are unlikely to be consumed by the poor, and which measure average income. This underestimates the numbers of people living in poverty, as consumers with rising income (above poverty level) spend a decreasing proportion of their income on food, and an average rise in income over time will therefore translate into smaller comparisons of those goods which the poor actually consume, and whose price differentials may be far more significant (Reddy and Pogge 2003).

Moreover, the data on growth rates and poverty reduction for China are questionable, and yet these alone account for any poverty reduction that has occurred in the world (Milanovic 2007). Indeed, in 2007, the Asian Development Bank presented the first official results based on PPP measures for China, and suggested that China's economy is 40 per cent smaller than that was previously suggested, and that the number of people living below the poverty line is 300 million, which is 200 million more than the previous estimates. For India, revised estimates suggest that the official poverty line is closer to 800 million rather than the previously suggested 400 million (Keidel 2007).

Furthermore, if the poverty headcount is switched from $1 to $2 a day, which is more realistic a measure of poverty for the United States, then the PPP adjusted poverty figure, then even the Bank's own problematic figures look less promising, for the number in this category *increased* from 1981 to 2001, from 2.45 to 2.74 billion, a 12 per cent increase. This has enormous implications for assessing the MDGs, because it may be that it is not the case that poverty has actually been reduced, merely *the way in which poverty is calculated*.

What then of the relationship between poverty reduction and globalisation? The World Bank report *Globalization, Growth and Poverty* argues that poverty reduction has taken place because of globalisation friendly policies. However, the central contentions of this work are seriously flawed (Wade 2003; Kiely 2007a) for at least five reasons: (i) it uses trade/GDP ratios as a proxy for openness, but this measures trade outcomes and not trade policy; (ii) in any case the trade/GDP ratios of many of the poorest countries are not low – the average in 1997–98 for the poorest 39 countries was 43 per cent, about the same as the world average (UNCTAD 2002: part 2, chapter 3); (iii) the Bank attempts to overcome this problem by measuring changes in trade/GDP ratios (from 1977 to 1997), rather than actual amounts, but this has the effect of excluding those with high but unchanging ratios from the list of high globalisers, and this would include many poor countries with little or no growth in this period; (iv) following on from this point, China and India have seen shifts in these ratios, as well as trade policy such as tariff rates, but they are not more open than some of the poorest developing countries that have experienced little growth. Average tariff rates in India did decline from 80 per cent at the start of the 1990s to 40 per cent at the end of the decade, while China's declined from 42.4 per cent to 31.2 per cent in the same period, but the latter figures remain higher than the average for developing countries (Rodrik 2001); (v) if we measure trade policy indicators such as average tariff rates, then the Bank's own data suggest that if we measure openness not by trade/GDP ratios or changes in these ratios since 1975, and instead focus on trade and investment policies in 1997, allegedly high globalisers had higher average tariffs (35 per cent) than low globalisers (20 per cent) (Sumner 2004: 1174). The IMF index of trade restrictiveness measures trade policy through quantifying average tariff rates and non-tariff barriers, and there is no evidence of greater trade restrictiveness on the part of the poorest countries. Thus even if there has been poverty reduction, it is unclear that this is because of globalisation friendly policies.

The boom in foreign investment should also be treated with considerable scepticism. Although foreign investment levels had increased, this had often reflected a shift in ownership from the state to private sector, rather than genuinely new, 'greenfield' investment. Indeed, investment/GDP ratios were lower across the board since the reform process started in the early 1980s. Thus, investment/GDP ratios for sub-Saharan Africa fell from a peak of around 23 per cent in the early 1980s to around 15 per cent in 1985, but by 2000 were only up to around 17 per cent. For the big Latin America five (Argentina, Brazil, Chile, Colombia and Mexico), the investment/GDP ratio peaked at close to 25 per cent in 1981, and fell to 16 per cent by 1984. By 1989, just before the FDI boom, it stood at 19 per cent, and by 2000, it had only increased to 20 per cent (Kozul-Wright and Rayment 2004: 30). Similarly, while it is true that there has been an increase in manufacturing in the developing world, sceptics suggest that this alone does not constitute 'development'. The issue of Chinese development is also relevant to this point, and both will be discussed in the next section.

Finally, the sceptical position suggests that recent events in the world economy confirm their rather more cautious account concerning inequality and underdevelopment in the global order. The move to a global recession in 2008 has led to a significant reduction of capital flows to developing economies, much of which was used to finance debt-led consumer booms rather than genuine industrial development. Coupled with a decline in demand for developing country exports – both primary products and manufacturing goods – many developing economies, including in Eastern Europe, face severe economic crisis. Indeed, they may even be facing the prospect of another lost decade of development, like that of the 1980s. While certain policies do affect particular development trajectories, so too do the structured inequalities of the world economy. Some places are in a structurally subordinate and dependent position in the world economy. Just how they are dependent and subordinate is discussed in the next section.

Explaining inequality and underdevelopment in the world economy

While there is strong evidence to back up the claims of both the optimists and the sceptics, the last section suggested that the latter is on the whole more convincing. The implication that follows, and which in some respects replicates the claims of (some versions of) dependency theory, is that there are structured inequalities that constrain late developers, and thus make it difficult to overcome inequality and underdevelopment. Unlike the claims of cruder versions of dependency theory, however, these are not insurmountable, but (unlike the claims of neo-liberalism or modernisation theory) they are real obstacles.

The first point to note is that while foreign investment has increased, it remains concentrated in the developed world. As was stated above, about two-thirds of foreign capital goes to the developed and one-third to the developing world, and this itself is highly concentrated. While foreign investment figures do not tell the whole story, as there may be subcontracting agreements by foreign firms to local firms, it is also the case that on a per capita basis, foreign direct investment is even more concentrated, as developing countries make up a large proportion of the population. But perhaps most important, *the type* of manufacturing that is generally occurring in the developing world is not necessarily overcoming underdevelopment. Since the reform period started in the 1980s, while the developed countries' share of manufacturing exports fell (from 82.3 per cent in 1980 to 70.9 per cent by 1997), its share of manufacturing value added actually *increased* over the same period, from 64.5 per cent to 73.3 per cent. Over the same period, Latin America's share of world manufacturing exports increased from 1.5 per cent to 3.5 per cent, but its share of manufacturing value added fell from 7.1 per cent to 6.7 per cent (Kozul Wright and Rayment 2004: 14). For developing countries as a whole, manufacturing output's contribution to GDP has barely changed since 1960: it stood at 21.5 per cent in 1960, and increased to just 22.7 per cent in 2000. There is significant regional variation, with East

Asia particularly expanding, but these figures hardly tell a story of increasing convergence or even the end of inequality. By the end of the 1990s, developing countries as a whole accounted for only 10 per cent of total world exports of goods with a high Research and Development, technological complexity and/or scale component (UNCTAD 2002a: 56).

What these figures suggest is that developed countries still tend to dominate in high value sectors, based on high barriers to entry, high start-up and running costs and significant skill levels. In the developing world, there are large amounts of surplus labour and barriers to entry, skills and wages are low. While this gives such countries considerable competitive advantage in terms of low start-up and labour costs, at the same time the fact that those barriers to entry are low means that competition is particularly intense and largely determined by cost price, which also means low wages. Thus, the clothing industry, where developing countries have achieved considerable increases in world export shares in recent years, has a very low degree of market concentration. In contrast, more capital-intensive or high-tech sectors have very high degrees of market concentration and are mainly located in the developed world (UNCTAD 2002a: 120–3).

The optimist, neo-liberal, response is that these labour-intensive sectors are only a starting point, allowing countries to upgrade as more developed countries shift to higher value production. But actually in practice upgrading has occurred by states deliberately protecting themselves from import competition from established producers, via a process of import substitution industrialisation. In the context of a tendency towards free trade, upgrading is far from inevitable and indeed, faced with competition from established overseas producers, is unlikely to occur.

We thus return to the claims of the Prebsich–Singer thesis. However, rather than focusing on trade between primary goods and industrial goods, we now need to examine *different kinds of industrial goods*. A number of studies have suggested that the price of manufacturing exports from developing countries have tended to fall against more complex manufacturing and services from developed countries, including Chinese exports (Maizels et al. 1998; Zheng 2002). Intense competition within sectors where barriers to entry are low leads to competition between developing countries all trying to increase their exports in low value manufacturing. Seen in this way, China's growth is less an opportunity for other developing countries, and more one that resembles a zero-sum game. On the other hand, as we have seen, China's growth has facilitated a primary commodities boom, which optimists claim could lay the basis for development. But over-dependence on one or two primary commodities is always precarious, as countries are adversely affected when demand falls. The boom came to an end in 2008, and many countries faced a new development crisis. For development to occur, there needs to be far more diversity in production, and a shift towards scale economies, technological sophistication, skills and infrastructure – neither low value manufacturing nor primary commodity production can provide this, and neither are they likely to in the future. There are thus indeed structured inequalities in the global economy, and these are particularly acute for would-be late developers.

Conclusion

This chapter has outlined debates on inequality and underdevelopment and has shown how earlier debates over modernisation and underdevelopment continue to influence current debates over the relationship between globalisation and development. In reviewing both optimistic and sceptical accounts concerning a positive relationship between the two, the chapter has suggested that the latter position is more convincing. But there are two further questions that need to be addressed, at least briefly. First, why does inequality matter? And second, what are the alternatives?

In terms of the importance of inequality, the argument is often made that it is an inevitable feature of all societies, and it is better to have a richer but unequal society, than a more egalitarian but poorer society. Related to this point, an additional argument made is that inequality does not matter so long as people are lifted out of poverty. There are three responses to this. First, while it may be the case that inequality is an unintended outcome of the social interaction of millions of individuals, the fact that it is unintended does not mean that efforts should not be made to alleviate it. If we are to take the claims made for democracy and equal opportunity seriously, then there is a need for collective action both nationally and within the international order to alleviate inequality. Just because no single individual intended certain unequal outcomes, it does not follow that no one is responsible for it. Second, inequality may be social and even economically dysfunctional. This is because it can be linked to crime and anti-social behaviour, and it can undermine sound economic principles. It is clear that the financial crisis of 2007 onwards must in part be linked to attempts to sustain financial expansion through the granting of credit to people (and countries) that could ill afford to pay it back. When this became clear – in the sub-prime mortgage crash in the United States and a new debt crisis in parts of the developing world and especially in Eastern Europe – the economic results were devastating. Third, the generation of inequality is cumulative, as capital tends to concentrate in certain areas and bypass or marginalise other parts of the globe. It is therefore wrong to suggest that poverty and inequality can be entirely separated – it is true that the wealth of a specific, rich individual is not caused by the poverty of a specific individual in the developing world. But both are part of a social order which encourages the concentration of capital in some areas and marginalisation in others.

These points lead to the final issue, which is that of alternatives to neo-liberalism. The current economic crisis may lead to a new international order, where a more 'managed' capitalism, perhaps along the lines of the Bretton Woods order, re-emerges. However, increased state intervention per se does not mean the end of neo-liberalism – contrary to neo-liberal ideology, neo-liberal policy has always included a great deal of state intervention, not least to expand market regulations. Moreover, a new debt crisis in Eastern Europe has so far been managed along classically neo-liberal lines of spending cuts, liberalisation and higher interest rates. What then of national alternatives, based on the revival of ISI policies? WTO rules are far less conducive to such policies than was the case in the era of ISI. Moreover, the domestic social alliances that encouraged ISI policies after 1945 have broken down. It is therefore likely that national capitals, happy with access to global circuits of capital and uninterested in developmentalist policies that would encourage productive investment, would oppose a return to ISI. Recent events in Latin America bear this out, where the likes of Chavez in Venezuela have experienced considerable opposition from the wealthy elites.

But perhaps most fundamentally, like neo-liberalism, ISI is premised on the belief that upgrading to a 'developed capitalism' can occur so long as the correct policies are carried out. The disagreement is over what policies are deemed to be 'correct'. In a context where 'value added', upgrading and thus development is increasingly derived from increasingly monopolised information (embedded in WTO rules), it is unclear that technical policies of upgrading will lead to sustained 'modernization' and the eradication of 'underdevelopment'. While policies matter, so do power relations, at both the national and international level. Only a radical transformation of these relations is likely to seriously challenge inequality and underdevelopment.

Guide to further reading

A.G. Frank (1969) is the major statement of underdevelopment theory. D. Held and A. Kaya (2007) is a useful reader on the debates over the relationship between globalisation and inequality while R. Kiely (2007b) challenges the optimistic account and relates the debates back to older theories of development. W. Rostow (1960) is the major book associated with modernisation theory. UNCTAD (2002a) usefully outlines a sceptical account of the relationship between globalisation and inequality, with lots of very useful, if now dated, empirical data. World Bank (2002) is the main official argument that proposes an optimistic account of the relationship between globalisation and poverty reduction.

Chapter 14

Energy Security and World Politics

FRANK UMBACH

A number of recent events have highlighted how important energy is to the global economy, and just how vulnerable individual states and consumers can be to changes in supply. At one level this is simply a function of the growing imbalance in the supply of, and demand for, energy worldwide. At another level, however, energy supply problems reflect the dependence of much of the industrialised world on potentially unreliable suppliers. Nothing illustrated this more dramatically than the dispute between Russia and the Ukraine in the winter of 2008/09, when the Ukraine and 17 EU member states suddenly found its supplies of gas cut-off. Securing realisable energy supplies has consequently become a major goal of governments everywhere as they attempt to make themselves less dependent on potentially unreliable suppliers. Energy security is consequently no longer simply a 'technical' question of providing energy efficiently, but a deeply geopolitical issue that highlights growing interdependencies and inequalities across the world.

This chapter provides an overview of the worldwide energy environment and its impact on security issues by focusing on the European Union (EU) and China in particular. The EU provides the quintessential example of a wealthy, industrialised region that is highly dependent for its energy on regimes and regions that frequently have very different domestic political structures and approaches to international relations. The rise of China as an economic superpower has created an enormous new source of demand for energy, highlighting the conflicting interests and approaches that are found in different parts of the world, and the potentially zero-sum nature of energy competition. In a world of finite resources, governments everywhere are keen to make sure they are not going to lose out in the event that energy becomes unavailable or prohibitively expensive.

The rise of energy security

A number of factors – especially concerns about the possibility of oil running out and the unreliability of key producers – have helped to tighten energy supplies and led to new energy price shocks (Elhefnawy 2008: 42; Umbach 2009). Fears of a new 'axis of oil', or a loose coalition of states among energy producers and energy importers including Russia, China, Iran and Venezuela, have heightened fears about a potential authoritarian alliance against the West in general and American hegemony in particular (Leverett and Noel 2006). The growing power of national oil (and gas) companies (NOCs) and the energy-exporting states (Hoyos 2007; John Baker III Institute 2007) has created a global 'sellers' market' of energy sources and raw materials, shifting the strategic calculations of the energy-importing states (Burrows and Teverton 2007). The growth of 'resource nationalism' is not only threatening to undermine the market-based supply of energy, but is also jeopardising future global investments, energy efficiency and planned production levels. Saudi Arabia, Russia, Iraq and Iran, which together hold 50 per cent of the world's conventional oil reserves, are all reluctant to accept the foreign direct investment (FDI) that is necessary to develop oil and gas production in line with the international projections of global energy consumption. As a result, the supply–demand gap is likely to widen as political factors increasingly determine access to oil fields in Africa, the Caspian Basin and the Middle East.

At the same time, China's investments in Africa's extractive industries are seen in Europe and the United States as undermining efforts to foster economic diversification, and creating new 'rentier economies' with unstable social and political institutions (Downs 2007; International Crisis Group 2008; Jakobson 2008; Raine 2009). Countries with large oil resources often have weak governance structures and neglect the development of other, non-resource-based economic sectors (Ross 2004 a, b). Thomas L. Friedman argues that there is a direct correlation between crude oil prices and political freedom. According to his 'First Law of Petropolitics', the higher the average oil and gas prices on the international market, the lower the internal political and economic enthusiasm about reform, leading to 'petro-authoritarianism' (Friedman 2006). This helps explain the present policies of those 'petro-ist'-states such as Russia, Iran, Venezuela, Nigeria, Sudan and others, which are highly dependent on oil and gas and have either weak institutions or authoritarian systems.

A third factor that has contributed to anxiety about energy are the attacks of September 2001 and other new forms of terrorism. Since 2001, terrorist attacks on oil and gas pipelines or thefts of crude oil have increased worldwide (Blanche 2002). Terrorist attacks on oil and other energy infrastructure are part of what some have called an 'economic jihad' (Stracke 2007). While the impact of such attacks has thus far generally been localised and small scale, at the very least they add to the overall level of uncertainty in volatile energy markets. Western security experts and governments also fear coordinated terrorist attacks on their electricity infrastructure, Thus, the safety and security of energy sources and energy infrastructure have become another important security challenge with which to cope – for both industry and governments (European Commission 2005; German Ministry of Interior 2008; Ness 2006).

Climate change has become another prominent security concern and is closely linked with energy policies and security (see also Carter, this volume). Energy supply disruptions can result from extreme weather conditions or accidents. In August and September 2005, the hurricanes Katrina and Rita shut down 27 per cent of US oil production and 21 per cent of US refining capacity in the Gulf of Mexico (Yergin 2006) with worldwide implications for global oil prices and energy policies. More generally, there is a close interrelationship between energy security and climate change that results from burning fossil fuels (IEA 2007b). And yet, energy security and mitigating climate change may be incompatible goals: the expanded use of domestic coal, for instance, can strengthen energy supply security, but will increase CO_2 emissions. Achieving only a 5 per cent reduction in emissions through a switch from coal to gas (in particular pipe-based), on the other hand, may have a negative impact on energy supply security and affect the economic competitiveness of individual economies and businesses (IEA 2007b: 18, 102 ff.).

As far as the wealthy, energy-intensive economies of Europe and North America are concerned, therefore, the evolving international energy order presents some profound, unpalatable and deeply troubling challenges. The reality is that oil and gas have become strategic goods, the value of which may not be determined by the market alone – a possibility that presents a major practical and philosophical challenge for the liberal-market economies of the Western world. In short, energy security may be too important to be left to the private sector in a world where market forces may be shaped by geopolitical pressures. Significantly, disruptions in regional or global energy supplies can no longer be easily offset by alternative oil and gas imports, a possibility that has been highlighted by the aggressive and highly politicised energy policies of Russia. Simply put, Russia can no longer be assumed to be a reliable supplier and has already used energy as a strategic or political weapon for geopolitical objectives, despite an assumed mutual interdependency between the EU and Russia (Larsson 2006; Umbach 2006). The following analysis expands on these underlying themes by initially providing an overview of projected worldwide energy trends until 2030. This analysis provides the backdrop for a discussion of the EU's common energy policies and an assessment of their capacity to cope with the manifold challenges of the energy security–climate change nexus in the twenty-first century.

Global energy security

Since the 'oil shocks' of the 1970s and 1980s, international concern has increasingly focused on the potential costs of supply disruption associated with an over-dependence on oil imports. The rise of new consumers, such as China and India, has increased these concerns and highlighted the scarcity of conventional oil and gas reserves. In addition, rising exploration, production, refinery and transportation costs, combined with growing concerns about the high concentration of the remaining oil and gas resources in the Persian Gulf, have all transformed the traditional global energy security structures (Barnes and Myers Jaffe 2006; Simmons 2005). Recently, concerns about energy security have extended to natural gas, which is increasingly used to produce electricity and increasingly traded internationally (i.e., Liquefied Natural Gas/LNG; Victor et al. 2006). Its potential importance can be seen by the fact that nearly 32 per cent of the population (about

1.6 billion people) in the developing non-OECD countries outside of Europe and Eurasia still did not have access to electricity in 2005. There are also more fundamental concerns about the adequacy of investment in energy infrastructure generally.

According to the International Energy Agency (IEA), if the present worldwide energy trends continue until 2030, world primary energy demand will grow by 1.6 per cent per year on average between 2006 and 2030, from 11,730 million tonnes (Mtoe) to more than 17,010 Mtoe (IEA 2008: 37 ff.). In other words, the world needs up to 45 per cent more energy by 2030 than in 2006. China and India will account for more than 50 per cent of the increase in global energy demand in this timeframe. Collectively, non-OECD countries will account for 87 per cent of this increase. Consequently, their share of world energy demand will rise from 51 per cent to 62 per cent, whereas the percentage for OECD countries will decrease from 49 per cent to just 38 per cent. Global primary oil demand (excluding biofuels) will increase from 85 million barrels per day (mb/d) in 2007 to 106 mb/d in 2030, albeit their share of world energy use will be reduced from 34 to 30 per cent. The bulk of the increase in world oil production is expected to come from OPEC countries, in particular from the Persian Gulf, which all have to cope with conservative depletion policies, insufficient foreign investment and rising geopolitical challenges inside and outside their countries.

The collective OPEC share of worldwide production will rise from 44 per cent in 2007 to 51 per cent in 2030. Accordingly, 46 per cent of the projected growth in world gas production to 2030 will need to come from the Middle East, whereas more than 60 per cent of the region's incremental output will probably be consumed in the region itself (IEA 2008: 41 f.). Like oil, natural gas resources are highly concentrated in a small number of countries and gas fields: Russia, Iran and Qatar alone hold 56 per cent of the global reserves, and just 25 fields worldwide hold more than 50 per cent of natural gas reserves in the world.

Although global demand for environmentally cleaner natural gas is increasing by 1.8 per cent annually till 2030, its share in total energy demand will rise only marginally from 21 to 22 per cent of all energy resources. The Energy Information Administration (EIA) in the United States has recently forecast that these non-OECD countries will account for 74 per cent of the total global increase of natural gas consumption to 2030 and will increase their share of total world natural gas consumption from 50 per cent in 2006 to 58 per cent over this period (EIA 2009: 1 f.).

The IEA predicts an annual increase in global coal demand of 2 per cent (faster than other fossil fuels), which will increase the share of coal in the global energy mix from 26 per cent in 2006 to 29 per cent in 2030, making it the second most important energy source worldwide despite the global efforts to mitigate climate change. Non-hydro renewable energy sources (also by excluding biomass) – wind, solar, geothermal, tide and wave energy – are projected to grow faster than any other energy source worldwide, at an average rate of 7.2 per cent. But they will not be able to change fundamentally the overall global dependence on fossil fuels as the global primary energy sources until 2030. In the electricity sector, however, renewable energy sources could overtake gas as the second largest source of electricity (behind coal) soon after 2020 (IEA 2008: 39).

Another major challenge is the need for massive investment in energy infrastructure around the world in both the up and downstream sectors, which may rise to US$26 trillion between 2007 and 2030 (IEA 2008: 39 f.). While the financial crisis of 2008 is unlikely to affect long-term investments, it could delay many projects. As a result, insufficient investment may create even more bottlenecks for global energy supplies. As the IEA has warned, more than 50 per cent of projected global energy investment between 2007 and 2030 is needed just to maintain the current level of supply capacity that has to be replaced by 2030. Those investments need to be implemented in time due to the long-term nature of these projects.

While it is clear that new, large-scale investment is required urgently, geopolitical risks are rising: the high concentration of the world's remaining oil and gas reserves in an ever smaller number of potentially unstable producer states and regions makes the supply of energy increasingly uncertain. In such an environment, the foreign policies of regions such as the EU as the world's largest energy importer become critical – especially when there is increasing competition from the word's most rapidly expanding economy in China and the prospect of unreliable supplies from Russia, upon which it remains highly dependent. The key issue is whether the EU and other developed economies can accommodate such changes and the challenges which they present to their economies and styles of governance.

Energy security and the European Union

The EU faces some unique challenges, but also shares a number of points of commonality with the circumstances of other wealthy Western powers. Its particular challenges flow from the nature of the EU itself, and the fact that each EU member state has been sovereign in deciding its own national energy policies. Moreover, for historical, geographic and economic reasons, the 27 member states of the EU have a very different national mix of energy resources (oil, gas, coal, nuclear and renewables). As a consequence, they often perceive the challenges of energy imports and supply security in very different ways, and accordingly, have defined different strategies to cope with them. These historical circumstances explain the lack of a common and coherent energy policy within the EU.

At present, 54 per cent of Europe's energy is imported. The EU's own energy production is forecast to fall from 46 per cent today to 36 per cent by 2020. These imports have cost an estimated €350 billion and €700 for every EU citizen until the summer of 2008 (European Commission 2008). Future capacity will still be predominantly generated by fossil resources, albeit with a rising percentage of gas, while the number of oil and solid-fuel power stations will continue to decline (European Commission 2008). To strengthen its future energy security, the European Commission's energy demand management strategy has always emphasised the broadest possible energy mix, diversification of energy supply and imports, promotion of renewable energies and a neutral policy towards the nuclear option. For those member states that use nuclear power, its share in the fuel mix is already considerable: nuclear power accounts for 42 per cent of France's energy supply, 35 per cent in Sweden, 26 per cent in Lithuania, 24 per cent in Bulgaria and the Slovak Republic and 21 per cent in Belgium. Concerns about the EU's dependence on Russia and the challenge of climate change meant that nuclear power has once again become an attractive option for many EU countries, including Great Britain, France, Finland, Italy, Lithuania, Bulgaria, Romania and Poland.

The EU's dependence on the import of fossil fuels is widely seen as the 'Achilles heel' of Europe's energy security (IEA 2008; Keppler 2007; Nies 2008; Umbach 2008b). The great paradox of EU policy is that despite its growing reliance on more environmentally friendly imports of natural gas, this is creating a growing dependency on a few suppliers. Indeed, the gas import profile of the EU-27 is not very diversified. Eighty-four per cent of gas is imported from just three countries: Russia (42 per cent), Norway (24 per cent) and Algeria (18 per cent). Moreover, Sweden, Ireland, Finland and many of the new EU member states are dependent on just one monopoly supplier, Gazprom, the Russian energy giant, while Greece, Hungary and Austria are more than 80 per cent dependent on this same supplier.

The EU's future strategy is predicated on a liberalised internal market for gas and electricity, enhanced measures for security of supply and a common approach to an external energy policy with a global dimension (European Council 2007). However, the European Commission has identified major weaknesses and problems that need to be overcome if the EU is to achieve greater energy security (European Commission 2008). The key issues revolve around the need to diversify energy supplies and improve external energy relations; increasing oil and gas stocks and improving crisis response mechanisms; improving energy efficiency; and making the best use of the EU's indigenous energy resources.

Such a wish list may seem unremarkable and sensible, but even before the last Russian–Ukrainian gas conflict of 2009, the EU had identified structural and political weaknesses, most particularly the insufficient physical infrastructure preventing a more effective crisis supply management. Significantly, the EU acknowledged that infrastructure investments are 'not exclusively driven by market forces'; as a consequence, the European Council decided for the first time to try and address the lack of strategic infrastructure within the European internal energy market (European Council 2009b). These efforts are directed towards the interconnection and diversification of energy supplies, sources and supply routes, notably in the gas sector, to strengthen the EU's energy supply security in a geographically balanced way by enhancing connectivity for central and peripheral European energy markets (Umbach 2009). This new energy infrastructure is also intended to promote economic and political solidarity between the EU member states by equipping them to assist one another in case of new energy supply threats like the latest Russian–Ukrainian gas conflict of January 2009.

Most important is the EU's '20–20–20 initiative' of March 2007 to increase energy efficiency by 20 per cent, to reduce its emissions by 20 per cent by 2020 (compared to the levels in 1990) and to broaden its energy mix by a 20 per cent share of renewable energy sources (today 8.5 per cent). If the new energy policies are being implemented, the EU would be able (1) to keep its own production at around 44 per cent (instead of falling on 36 per cent) and (2) to maintain its net imports of fossil fuels by 2020 at roughly the same level as present. Even the EU gas import demand will drastically been reduced and might be no higher than today instead to rise from roughly 300 billion cubic metres (bcm) to almost 490 bcm in 2030 (European Commission 2008: 19 f.).

It now depends on the political will of the EU-27 whether the agreed policy decisions, instruments, strategies and infrastructure projects are being implemented. In general, however, the EU has achieved much more than most experts and observers might have expected and may offer grounds for cautious optimism on energy issues more generally. However, such innovative policy adjustments have occurred at the same time that China has experienced rapid economic development and growth in energy demand. The question is whether the EU's policies or those of the United States will be able to accommodate such a dramatic transformation in the international system.

Energy security and the rise of China

In a remarkably short period of time, China has replaced the United States as the centre of the world's raw materials market. At the very least, this is a telling indicator of the scale and impact of China's breakneck development and its re-emergence as a world power. This would have had long-term geopolitical consequences under any circumstances. In the context of a global scramble for finite supplies of energy and resources, it has the potential to become an explosive issue. The key questions in this context are whether the international system will be able to accommodate and adjust to the rise of China and its gargantuan appetites, and how the United States will respond to the challenge it inevitably presents (Hale 2004).

Historically, the United States has accorded enormous strategic significance to energy security. The so-called Carter doctrine, proclaimed in 1980, warned other countries that the Untied States would be prepared to use force to protect what it saw as its national interests in the Persian Gulf. It is not necessary to be a conspiracy theorist to recognise that the Persian Gulf generally and Iraq in particular have assumed a prominence in subsequent strategic thinking in the United States that helps to explain why successive administrations have been willing to commit massive amounts of blood and treasure in an attempt to shore up American interests and attempt to stabilise a critically important source of energy imports. Oil remains the United States' most important source of energy and more than 50 per cent of it is imported. Crucially, about 22–24 per cent (in comparison – EU: 31 per cent; East Asia: 60–70 per cent) of this is sourced from the Middle East, with other potentially problematic suppliers in Central Asia, Africa and Venezuela making up much of the rest. Consequently, energy security has come to preoccupy strategists in the United States, especially during the administration of George W. Bush (see National Energy Policy Development Group 2001). In such circumstances, the rise of China assumes great strategic importance.

Since 2000, China has accounted for 40 per cent of the world's crude oil demand. In 2003, it displaced Japan as the world's second largest energy consumer. Despite being the second largest energy producer and sixth largest oil producer in the world, China currently produces neither enough crude oil nor natural gas to meet its needs. China has only 2.43 per cent of global crude oil reserves and 1.2 per cent of the world's reserves of natural gas. Its crude oil production will decline from 3.67 mb/d in 2006 to just 2.7 mb/d by 2030. As a result of its limited oil reserves and its increasing oil demand, imports account for about half of China's total oil consumption, and that may rise to 84 per cent by 2030 (IEA 2007a: 122–3). Significantly, China is adopting the same sort of neo-mercantilist policies that Japan employed when its industrialisation process was intensifying in the 1970s and 1980s (Heginbotham and Samuels 1998). China is using its growing foreign exchange reserves to try and secure long-term energy and resource security through strategic investments in Africa, Australia and Latin America. It is an approach that is markedly at odds with the essentially market-driven approach of Europe and the United States, and the potential for conflict is consequently clear (Zweig and Jianhai 2005). The recent protectionist plan of China's government to prohibit or restrict export of rare earth metals, which are produced only or primarily in China and play a important role in green and other cutting-edge technologies (from hybrid cars to superconductors and precision-guided weapons) contradicts not just the global WTO order. It would also, for instance, boost its automobile industry, hinder the US, Japanese and European competitors to develop the next generation of electricity cars and realise its adopted plan to become the world's leader of electric cars (Bradsher 2009b; Evans-Pritchard 2009). Furthermore, China's blockade of harsher economic sanctions towards Iran because of its suspected nuclear weapons ambitions has also signalled the geopolitical implications of its growing dependence on major oil producer such as Iran and other Western-perceived 'states of concern'.

China's domestic response

It is increasingly recognised both within and outside China that the sheer scale of the economic transformation underway in that country has profound implications for China and the rest of the world. The environmental impact of China's rapid rise could yet undermine its economic development (Economy 2007). Consequently, environmental issues are becoming increasingly important and feed into energy issues. As such, China has made increasing the use of natural gas a high priority, despite the massive investment costs and the fact that at present gas accounts for less than 3 per cent of its total energy consumption. Although demand for natural gas is increasing by 2020, it is likely to account for a maximum 11 per cent of China's total energy consumption (IEA 2007a).

Simultaneously, however, China's coal consumption has continued to grow. In 2004, China consumed 2.1 billion tons of coal, which represented more than one-third of the global total and an astonishing 46 per cent increase since 2002. In 2005, 69.4 per cent of China's primary energy demand and 78 per cent of its electricity supply had been produced by coal (Chinese State Council 2007; IEA 2007a: 262). Because China possesses the third largest coal reserves in the world (13.9 per cent) behind the United States and Russia (BP 2009: 32), production volumes will further increase because coal projects will probably remain much cheaper than natural gas or other sources in the years ahead. Yet, despite record domestic coal production, China had become temporarily a net importer of coal by 2007. China's appetite for and use of resources like coal not only has profound implications for its natural environment, but it is also affecting its relations with key resources suppliers like Australia, which must attempt to balance potentially competing economic and strategic interests. In short, should countries like Australia privilege relations with a pivotal trade partner, China, or remain close to its traditional strategic ally, the United States? Such questions will become more common and pressing as energy concerns transmute into security issues.

One of the more surprising and positive aspects of the rise of China is that it may actually be playing a key role in developing renewable technologies (Borger and Watts 2009). In 2005, China adopted a National Renewable Energy Law, which envisages that 16 per cent of its primary energy production will be from renewable sources by 2020, up from about 7 per cent at present. For the electricity sector, the target is 20 per cent of the capacity from renewables by 2020. It will include 30 Gigawatts (GW) of wind power, 20 GW of biomass power and 300 GW of hydropower capacity. China's expansion of wind power is dependent on large investments in grid expansion and transmission upgrades. China has already become the world's leader in solar thermal systems for heating and hot water supply with about 75 million m^2 of solar collectors – about half the world total. The national target foresees the expansion to 150 million m^2 for 2010 and 300 million m^2 (IEA 2007a: 356). During the last 2 years, it has even outpaced the United States and the EU by building more efficient and less polluting coal power plants (up to 44 per cent efficiency) – albeit only about 60 per cent of those new plants using newer technologies that are highly efficient, but also more expensive (Bradsher 2009a).

In the longer perspective, however, as China's 'Law on Renewable Energy' of 2006 and administrative decrees indicate, the development of renewable energy sources is being recognised as an important instrument of its national energy supply security strategy that widens and decentralises its national energy mix, reduces the negative effects on the environment the climate and decreases rural energy poverty in China. This laudable goal may not be easy to achieve, however: like a number of other Asian countries (with the exceptions of South Korea, Japan, Singapore and Hong Kong), China has long subsidised energy consumption. The result has been an increasing inefficiency: China consumes up to five times as much energy to produce each dollar of economic output. China's energy efficiency is even lower than that of many other developed countries due to inefficient management, insufficient investment, outdated equipment and poor safety records.

While the picture in China is somewhat mixed as far as its capacity to produce efficient and sustainable energy is concerned, there are a number of points that merit emphasis as they are likely to have a considerable impact on its long-term economic and political development. The legitimacy and even survival of the current political regime in China is heavily dependent on maintaining the rapid growth that has transformed the economy, living standards and expectations of the population as a whole. In such circumstances, securing the energy supplies to underpin continuing growth is a major priority, and one that is likely to influence international as well as domestic politics. In short, energy security is no longer simply a technical problem, but one with major domestic implications and in turn significant geopolitical consequences (Klare 2008).

The future of energy security

Throughout the world integrated solutions to the energy–climate nexus are needed to balance energy security priorities with economic and environmental objectives. While there may be agreement that energy security is a national priority everywhere, there are very different ideas about the best ways of achieving it. Although the EU believes its energy security is threatened primarily by its rising gas import dependence from Russia and Gazprom, it has relied primarily on market-based solutions to its energy needs. There has been a separation of energy questions from political factors and strategic developments in the EU, and energy policies have generally been left to the private sector to determine until very recently when the EU has recognised the need for a common energy foreign policy and to speak increasingly with one voice. This is significant because business interests have been primarily guided by short-term economic concerns in an increasingly competitive environment. As a result, longer-term national interests and energy security issues had been neglected until 2006 by both energy companies and national governments (Umbach 2008a).

China is also very conscious of its energy insecurity and supply vulnerabilities that result from its rising oil imports from the Persian Gulf and Africa. Unlike the EU, however, China has made long-term strategic investments to try and ensure reliability of and control over future energy and resource supplies. Perhaps such policies are entirely predictable in a country that remain notionally 'communist' and where the legitimacy of the ruling elites is almost entirely dependent on maintaining economic growth and development at all costs. Under such circumstances a state-driven rather than market-driven approach to energy and resource security is understandable. The crucial question is whether such an approach will prove more successful as a way of attaining energy security than the EU model, and whether such differences may lead to tensions between different regions as the contest for diminishing supplies intensifies.

The importance attached to energy security, and the potential this has for producing fraught international relations, tendencies of a militarisation of energy policies (Moran/Russell 2008; Russell 2008), if not outright conflict, is very evident in the policy stance of the United States. Despite the rhetorical importance that American policymakers have historically attached to the market as a mechanism for distributing resources (see Beeson, this volume), no country has taken a more interventionist approach to questions of resource and especially energy security, even if they have not always assumed an overt military form (Bromley 2005; Klare 2008). Whatever we may think of the rationale for, or effectiveness of, the United States' attempts to achieve energy security, there is little doubt that ensuring access to energy and other crucial resources has been one of the key drivers of American foreign policy, and there is no reason to suppose that this will change fundamentally under the administration of Barack Obama. What may change, however, is the way such security is pursued. In this regard, there are grounds for cautious optimism as there is finally a recognition that changing domestic consumption patterns and developing alternative sources of energy may actually be part of any potential solution.

Indeed, there is some encouraging evidence that new approaches to energy security questions may be becoming more widespread. Energy organisations like the IEA and the World Energy Council (WEC) have warned that individual states need a new understanding of energy security in the new millennium to cope with the manifold challenges of the energy security–climate change nexus, and that markets alone cannot solve these problems at present or in the future. Instead – in a striking and unexpected convergence of public policy styles – the WEC suggests that high levels of government involvement will be as important as high levels of cooperation and integration for achieving a sustainable energy security in all regions in the developed and developing world (WEC 2007: 4).

In Europe, of course, it remains to be seen whether the EU-27 and its member states have the sufficient political will and necessary financial resources, together with the European energy industry, to implement such projects and policies in the face of powerful vested interests and political resistance. This is an even greater challenge in the United States where the nature of the political system, the dominance of free market rhetoric and the activities of powerful corporations and lobby groups make major changes of policy direction difficult to achieve. Such changes will be even more difficult to achieve in an atmosphere of tense international relations and energy competition with the likes of China. Here, too, there are grounds for cautious optimism as Chinese authorities have clearly realised the importance of energy issues and the potential they have for inflicting enormous environmental damage if they are not well managed. At the level of rhetoric, at least, Beijing has endorsed an environmentally friendly approach to industrialisation, which has given energy conservation and energy efficiency a much more prominent role in the future (Dan 2008). While the new policy approaches have been welcomed in the United States, EU and Japan, doubts remain whether China will be able to reconcile the competing demands of development and sustainability. In that regard, China's challenge is no different than the rest of the world's – simply more urgent, and on a monumental scale. The ability of its leaders to rise to this challenge will shape the course of twenty-first-century history for us all.

Guide to further reading

Yergin's (1991) history of oil, and its economic and geopolitical implications, remains the standout historical work on the topic. American writers produced a range of early works on the geopolitical challenges of energy security in the 1990s and tended to focus particularly on the Asia-Pacific region (Calder 1997; CSIS 2000; Klare 2001; Manning 2000). European experts seemed to be largely unconcerned about this issue until more recent years. For some exceptional examples of European assessments pre-2006, see Umbach (2003), van der Linde (2004) and Godement et al. (2004). For work which makes a foreign policy strategy out of energy security, see Kalicki and Goldwyn (2005). For specific studies of countries and regions, see as follows: China (Andrews-Speed et al. 2002; IEA 2007a), Russia (Larsson 2006; Stern 2005) and the Asia-Pacific region (Wu and Fesharaki 2007). Studies of Asia-Europe energy cooperation can be found in Godement et al. (2004) and Marquina (2008). Excellent sources of reliable empirical data on energy are published annually by the IEA in Paris (e.g., IEA 2008), the EIA in Washington D.C. (e.g., EIA 2009), the WEC in London and the 'Statistical Review of World Energy' of British Petroleum Company (BP) in London (BP 2009).

Chapter 15

Global Financial Crises

TIMOTHY J. SINCLAIR

One of the realities of global politics is that the most important things are often overshadowed by what, on a dispassionate analysis, are really much less significant issues. Financial crises, for example, are increasingly frequent and can pose challenges to the established order of global politics. But even though financial volatility seriously affects governments and the lives of billions, it is typically relegated to the business pages by the drama of terrorism or the high politics of trade negotiations, until it bursts forth in a global financial crisis, such as the one that began in 2007. This is unfortunate because it means that what is happening in the 'engine room' of globalisation is often poorly understood by those in power and by those who wish to change the policies of those in power.

Some of this can be attributed to the cheap thrills of sensationalism. But much of this neglect is a result of the mythic technical character of finance, especially as it is talked about by business people, and written about by most journalists, government officials and even some scholars. Finance and money are discussed as if they are purely technical matters those without the requisite training cannot hope to understand. The widespread propagation and acceptance of this falsehood makes it easy for those with policy control to pursue their objectives without the constraint of informed democratic debate.

An accessible introduction to global financial crises is offered here. I start by examining the competing ways financial crises are understood and comment on the merits of these perspectives, beginning with the market advocates' account of crisis, then moving on to critical views. In the second part I review the renewed financial volatility that followed the end of the Bretton Woods system and the liberalisation of financial regimes in the developed countries starting in the 1980s. This includes the Asian financial crisis of 1997/98 and the Enron bankruptcy of 2001/02. The chapter then considers the global financial crisis that began in 2007, suggesting that the immediate causes for the crisis are quite different from those commonly assumed. After this discussion, I consider the prospects for regulatory reform based on the example of the credit rating agencies case, and then offer a series of conclusions on global financial crises and world politics at the start of the twenty-first century.

Perspectives

It is possible to distinguish between two main ways of understanding financial crises that compete for scholarly and political pre-eminence. The first of these has dominated economic thought about finance for 30 years and has had a major influence on policymakers. This stream of thought I call the exogenous approach to financial crisis. Although invoking Adam Smith, this tradition's modern founders include Friedrich von Hayek and Milton Friedman. Their views are associated with attacks on the mixed economy model of state intervention popular in much of the developed world after the Great Depression of the 1930s. These thinkers took it as axiomatic that markets, when left to their own devices, are efficient allocators of resources. For them, financial crisis is a deviation from the normal state of the market. Given they assume markets work efficiently, this tradition focuses on 'external' causes, especially government failure, as the cause of crisis. Friedman, for example, blamed the Great Depression of the 1930s on what he considered to be incorrect Federal Reserve policy in 1929 and 1930, rather than the effects of the stock market crash in October 1929 (Kindleberger and Aliber 2005: 72).

Exogenous accounts of financial crisis assume that market participants are constantly adjusting their behaviour – for example, whether they buy or sell financial instruments like bonds and stocks – based on new information from outside the market. In this context, market prices are assumed to always reflect what other market participants are prepared to pay. If this is the case, reason exogenous thinkers, prices are never inflated or false. They must always be correct. So the idea of a 'bubble economy', in which assets like houses, stocks and oil futures deviate from true value to a higher, false value, is rejected. There can be no 'true value' other than what the market is prepared to pay.

The endogenous account, by contrast, says that financial crises begin primarily inside finance. For Marx and Polanyi, crises are caused by the internal 'laws of motion' of the capitalist mode of production. These produce constant change and upheaval, not equilibrium between demand and supply. For Keynes, the 'animal spirits' or passions of speculation give rise to risky gambits. Typical of the endogenous perspective is the idea that market traders do not merely integrate information coming from outside the markets in the wider, real economy, but are focused on what other traders are doing, in an effort to anticipate their buy/sell activities, and thus make money from them (or at least avoid losing more money than the market average). Given this, rumours, norms and other features of social life are part of their understanding of how finance works. On this account, finance is subject to the pathologies of social life, like any other activity in which humans engage. This is an image of finance far from the self-regulating conception that characterises the exogenous view.

Keynes provided what remains perhaps the best intuitive illustration of the importance of this internal, social understanding of finance and financial crises in his tabloid beauty contest metaphor, first published in 1936 (Akerlof and Shiller 2009: 133). Keynes suggested that the essence of finance is not, as most supposed, a matter of picking the best stocks, based on an economic analysis of which should rise in value in future. Anticipating what other traders in the market were likely to do was actually more relevant. Keynes compared finance to beauty contests that ran in the popular newspapers of the time. These contests were not, as might be assumed, about picking the most attractive face. Success was achieved by estimating how *others* would vote and voting with them, although as Keynes pointed out, others would be trying to do the same, hence the complexity and volatility of financial markets.

More specifically, in a useful synthesis of some of the writings that fall within what I have termed the endogenous approach to global finance, Cooper has argued that the traditional assumptions made about markets and their tendency to equilibrium between demand and supply do not work for assets like houses, art and financial instruments like stocks, bonds and derivatives (Cooper 2008: 9–13). In the market for goods, greater demand can be met with greater supply or higher prices. But this simple economic logic does not work for assets. Instead, demand often grows in response to price increases for assets. The 'animal spirits' identified by Keynes and elaborated upon by Akerlof and Shiller do not produce stability in the market for assets like they do in the market for goods. In the absence of equilibrium, there is no limit to the expansion of market enthusiasm for financial assets or houses, producing what we have come to call a 'bubble' economy. Unfortunately, as we know, bubbles tend to deflate in an unpredictable manner, with very negative consequences for economic activity.

A brief history of financial crises

The history of financial crises shows that they are always shocking events, as they typically occur after long periods of affluence. Pride comes before the fall. The reversal crises represent seems incomprehensible to those at the centre of things, never mind the general public. The standard against which all financial crises are measured is, of course, the Great Depression of the 1930s. At the height of the Depression a quarter of American workers were unemployed (Galbraith 1997 [1955]: 168). As a quick perusal of the Dow Jones Industrial Average shows, the New York Stock Exchange did not return to its summer 1929 value until the early 1950s, almost a quarter century after the crash of October 1929 (www.djindexes.com). However, financial crises did not start in the twentieth century. The Dutch 'tulip mania' of the 1630s, in which tulip bulbs greatly appreciated in value, is usually cited as the first boom and bust. At the time tulips were exotic imports from the eastern Mediterranean. 'Mass mania' for the bulbs led to massive price inflation, so that some tulip bulbs were worth the equivalent of $50,000 or more each. When the crash came and the bubble deflated 'not with a whimper but with a bang', many who had invested their life savings in tulips lost everything (Galbraith 1993: 4). Mass default ensured a depression in the Netherlands in the years after 1637 (Galbraith 1993: 26–33). More recently, the 1907 financial panic came about after the failure of a trust company at the centre of Wall Street speculation (Bruner and Carr 2007). Calamity was avoided by cooperation between major banks, led by J.P. Morgan, perhaps the world's best known and most powerful financier at the time.

After the Great Depression and the Second World War, the Bretton Woods system was created to bring greater order to the global financial system. As much a political as a financial system, Bretton Woods was intended to avoid rapid and unsettling economic adjustment within countries. The hope was that this would avoid the sort of economic problems which contributed to the Second World War and which would, no doubt, increase support for the communist system in Russia. Although the intent behind Bretton Woods was to avoid crises and the political conflict that followed, despite US assistance, it had few resources at its disposal. Given considerable protectionism in trade after the Second World War, countries were frequently either in considerable surplus or deficit in the national accounts that measured their trade and payments with the rest of the world. This led to crisis-driven efforts to restore balance, often aggravating relations with other states.

The Bretton Woods system, fixed exchange rates and controls over the movement of capital were gradually abandoned in the developed world during the 15 years after 1970. What emerged was a new system in which floating exchange rates were increasingly the norm at least in developed countries, and in which capital could flow freely around the world to find the highest returns. Although a floating exchange rate regime should rapidly and effectively adjust to reflect the changing economic conditions in a country (real interest rates, inflation, profit margins, regulations or political stability), this system proved less than perfect. The 1980s is marked by a series of currency crises, as the values of major currencies like the Japanese Yen appreciated, causing trouble for their trade partners. Perhaps the most dramatic of these crises was the European Exchange Rate Mechanism (ERM) crisis of 1992, in which currency traders, especially George Soros, placed bets on the ability of the British government to keep Pound Sterling within the ERM. At the end of the crisis, the British government abandoned defending Sterling, which depreciated substantially and had to be removed from the ERM.

The Asian financial crisis of 1997/98 was the culmination of a boom in East Asia that led to what in hindsight turned out to be excessive short-term lending and risky pegging of national currencies to the US Dollar, a problem also for Argentina in 2001. Like Holland in the 1630s, the result of the crisis was economic depression in some countries, notably Indonesia, where the price of basic foodstuffs and other costs increased dramatically. The Asian crisis, like the financial crisis that began in 2007, led to criticism of lax regulation, fraud and corruption. In Malaysia, despite a barrage of criticism, controls on the movement of capital were reintroduced until the panic pressures eased.

Global financial crisis

The subprime crisis that began in the summer of 2007 may rank as one of the most traumatic global developments since the Second World War. Unlike wars and famine, this crisis and how it was caused seems to have caught the governing elites in rich countries completely unawares. The crisis and the deep recession it generated have caused dismay and at times panic as the depth of the problem revealed itself, especially in September 2008 with the bankruptcy of investment bank Lehman Brothers. Like most financial crises, the origins of the crisis can be found in the ending of the previous boom, with the bursting of the stock market mania for dot-com stocks in 2000. The US Federal Reserve responded to this market reversal with low interest rate policy intended to make the cost of borrowing cheaper. The policy worked and interest rates fell. But the fall in rates had unanticipated effects. Looking for higher returns in a low-yield environment, bankers sought out financial instruments that would deliver better profits. Structured finance had been around for several years but now it became the financial instrument of choice. Structured finance packages the debt most of us incur – credit card borrowings, car loans and mortgages – into securities that can be traded in financial markets. These securities gave their owners a claim on the revenues that those with the car loans, credit card debt and mortgages repay. In a stroke a whole world of illiquid consumer debt was turned into financial market assets. Traders were then able to trade these new securities in the markets, just as they traded the more traditional bonds issued by corporations, municipalities and national governments.

The usual claim made about securitisation is that it led to a breakdown in the relationship between the originators of mortgages and those in the financial markets creating and trading in the bonds and derivatives that pooled the stream of income from these mortgages. Because people in the financial markets were so distant from the actual credit risk of the individual mortgage payers and may have been poorly advised by credit rating agencies, they underestimated the riskiness of the assets they were buying. This meant the financial system was full of 'toxic assets' and once this was fully appreciated by markets in the summer of 2007 as a result of increasing mortgage defaults by subprime borrowers, panic developed, followed by the collapse of a number of major financial institutions, worldwide government intervention to prop up the markets and the subsequent recession. Many popular accounts such as Baker assert that too much debt was accumulated, and that therefore it was inevitable that the boom would collapse into bust (Baker 2009). These depictions do not typically identify the mechanism through which this took place.

This view suggests that the crisis occurred because some people were not doing their jobs properly, and that if we can just make sure people do what they are supposed to do another financial crisis like this can be avoided. Given that the subprime securities market was worth only $0.7 trillion in mid-2007, out of total global capital markets of $175 trillion, the supposed impact of subprime assets is out of all proportion to their actual weight in the financial system (Bank of England 2008: 20). This strongly suggests that another explanation for the global financial crisis is needed. The 'subprime crisis' is not likely to be a direct consequence of actual subprime mortgage delinquencies given how small they were relative to the system as a whole. The crisis developed not because subprime lending is so important. The paralysis or 'valuation crisis' that came over global finance in 2007–09, in which banks were unwilling to trade with each other or lend money, had no specific relationship to subprime lending. Other bad news might have had the same effect on the markets, as Galbraith shows is typical at the top of a boom (Galbraith 1993: 4).

An interpretation that fits the facts better is that the confidence in financial markets had, prior to 2007, reached such a frenzy that it became an episode of 'irrational exuberance', like so many financial manias before. Like a drunk, the hangover the next day is unpleasant. The 'bad news' about subprime lending was actually quite modest in summer 2007, predicting a higher rate of mortgage foreclosures than anticipated, but not a crisis. But in the context of the preceding mania this was enough to cause panic. The panic, which so typically follows financial expansions, created widespread uncertainty about the quality of financial institutions and their balance sheets. It is this uncertainty or panic that effectively brought the financial markets to a halt, forcing government intervention.

Attributing blame

Since the 1930s, financial crises have almost always been accompanied by public controversy over who was at fault. Before the 1930s, governments were not generally held responsible for economic conditions, but since the 1930s the public have increasingly expected governments to manage problems in the financial system. Inevitably, efforts to defuse or redirect blame develop. During the Asian crisis, corruption in Asian governments and among their business leaders was held responsible, even though just a few years before 'Asian values' were supposedly responsible for the unprecedented growth in the region. During the Enron scandal of 2001/02, auditors were blamed for not revealing the financial chicanery of the corporation. The subprime crisis has been no different, with rating agencies, mortgage lenders, 'greedy' bankers and 'weak' regulators all subject to very strong attacks for not doing their jobs.

The rating agencies have been subject to unprecedented criticism and investigation in the midst of the subprime meltdown. Congressional committees, the Securities and Exchange Commission, the European Parliament and Commission and the Committee of European Securities Regulators all conducted investigations. A very senior rating official has indicated that the crisis over subprime ratings is the most threatening yet experienced by the agencies in their century of activity. This effort to blame the agencies is a curious reaction, given that the rating agency business is now open to greater competition since the passage of the Credit Rating Agency Reform Act of 2006. It suggests that the movement from regulation to self-regulation – from 'police patrol' to 'fire alarm' approaches – has not eliminated the role of the state. Governments are still expected by their citizens to deal with market failure, and when necessary act as lenders of last resort, and they know it.

Three groups seem to have gotten off with little criticism: Politicians them-selves, although responsible as law makers for the design of regulation; the academic discipline of economics, which generally opposed the notion of asset price bubbles and neglected the role of social dynamics such as market confi-dence in the working of financial markets; and consumers and home-owners, who created the debt in the first place and thought it normal for some reason that house values should increase forever at rates well in excess of inflation.

Regulatory reform

Financial crises stimulate demand for new government intervention in markets to prevent a similar problem from occurring again. They also stimulate internal mobilisation as a political strategy on the part of governments to show that they are taking responsibility. The slow development of the central bank role of the Bank of England is an example of these processes over time. The New Deal reforms of the 1930s America are an example of rapid reaction to very threatening conditions. The global financial crisis is likely to see much regulatory action. Whether this will be substantive or not can be gauged by examining the prospects for regulation of the major credit rating agencies, who have, as we have seen, been blamed in part for the development of the crisis.

The activities of rating agencies have been largely free of regulation (Sinclair 2005). Starting in the 1930s, the ratings produced by the agencies in the United States have been incorporated into the prudential regulation of pen-sion funds so as to provide a benchmark for investment. This required pension funds to invest their resources in those bonds rated 'investment grade' and avoid lower rated, 'speculative grade' bonds. Regulation of the agencies them-selves only starts in the 1970s, with the Securities and Exchange Commission's (SEC) Net Capital Rule in 1975. This gave a discount or 'haircut' to issuers whose bonds are rated by National Recognized Statistical Rating Organizations (NRSROs). No criteria were established for NRSROs, and this status was deter-mined by the SEC in a largely informal way. NRSRO designation acted as a barrier to entry until the Rating Agency Reform Act of 2006, passed in the wake of the Enron scandal, created criteria and a recognised path to NRSRO recognition.

Two major sets of concerns have dominated discussions about the rating agen-cies in the wake of the global financial crisis. The first are to do with the competence of the agencies and the effectiveness of their work. The second set of concerns relate to broader, structural issues. Critics have frequently attacked the timeliness of rating downgrades, suggesting that the agencies do not use appropriate methods and fail to ask the sort of forensic questions needed to prop-erly investigate a company. Concerns about staffing, training and resourcing are associated with these problems. Recently and increasingly stridently, critics such as Partnoy have attacked what are perceived to be broader, structural problems in how the agencies do business (Partnoy 2006). These problems, suggest the critics, create poor incentives and undermine the quality of the work the agencies undertake.

The first of these broader structural issues is the legacy of weak competition between rating agencies as a result of the introduction of the NRSRO designation. Although several new agencies were designated NRSRO after the passage of the Rating Agency Reform Act, many critics would like NRSRO status abolished, removing any reference to ratings from law. The view implicit here is that weak competition has led to poor analysis, as the rating agencies have had few incentives to reinvest in their product. In this view, the revenues flowing to rating agencies are rents from a government-generated monopoly.

Concerns about how the agencies are funded became widespread with the onset of the subprime crisis. The idea was that the issuer-pays model, although established for 40 years, was a scandalous conflict of interest because it means that the agencies have incentives to make their ratings less critical than they would if they were paid by investors, the ultimate users of ratings. Like NRSRO status, many critics called for an end to the issuer-pays model of rating agency funding.

A vigorous, if often poorly informed, debate about the merits of regulating rating agencies took place from the onset of the crisis in spring 2007. Behind the rhetoric, it is apparent that both the American SEC and European Commission officials are reluctant to regulate either the analytics of the rating process itself or the business models of the major rating agencies. In amendments to NRSRO rules announced in February 2009, SEC enhanced required data disclosures about performance statistics and methodology and prohibited credit analysts from fee setting and negotiation, or from receiving gifts from those they rate (SEC 2009). How ratings are made and who pays for them are materially unaffected by these changes.

Much the same can be said for European efforts. Hampered by the reality that Moody's and Standard & Poor's (S&P) are both headquartered in the United States, for many years rating agencies were little more than 'recognised' in European states by local regulators who were free-riders on American regulatory efforts. With the Enron crisis concern about rating agencies grew and the industry codes of conduct were increasingly used as a useful form of self-regulation. With the onset of the global financial crisis, European Commission officials have sought to regulate the agencies in Europe with proposed new laws passed by the European Parliament for referral to the Council of Ministers (Commission of the European Communities 2008; European Parliament 2009). This legislation, which is premised on local enforcement, creates a registration process like the NRSRO system and addresses issues of transparency, disclosure and transparency in the rating process. But it does not change rating analytics or challenge the issuer-pays model of rating funding.

It is intriguing that despite the worst financial crisis since the 1930s, and the identification of a suitable culprit in the rating agencies, proposed regulation should be so insubstantial, doing little to alter the rating system that has been in place in the United States since 1909 and Europe since the mid-1980s. Part of this can be put down perhaps to a lack of confidence on the part of regulators and politicians in the efficacy of traditional state-centric solutions to market failure. It may also recognise the apparent weakness of already heavily regulated institutions such as commercial banks, and an understanding that the financial system is, despite the rating crisis, likely to continue to move in a more market- and rating-dependent direction in future.

Conclusions

Two very different understandings of financial crisis compete. The first, the exogenous view, sees finance itself as a natural phenomenon, a smoothly oiled machine that every now and then gets messed up by the government, or events that nobody can anticipate, like war or famine. The other perspective, the endogenous, argues that the machine-like view of finance is mythic. Like all other human institutions, finance is a world made by people, in which collective understandings, norms and assumptions give rise periodically to manias, panics and crashes. On this account, financial crises are normal. What is not normal, concede those who support the endogenous perspective, is the expansion of financial crises into global events that threaten to destabilise world politics, as did the Great Depression of the 1930s.

Whether you adopt an exogenous or endogenous view of financial crises, the necessity for international cooperation to combat them is essential. In the first instance, this probably amounts to no more than ensuring that governments and central banks communicate about their efforts to support vulnerable financial institutions, especially when those institutions operate, as so many do, in multiple jurisdictions. While there is evidence of this in recent times, there was also much unilateral, uncoordinated action intended for national advantage, such as the Irish government's guarantee of all funds deposited in domestic banks. Building up the institutional capacity for cooperation between finance ministries and central banks should be a priority.

Political management will remain at the centre of financial crises. Governments, whether they like it or not, know they have responsibility for financial stability and they have become adept at identifying and disciplining institutions that do not seem to serve their purpose within the financial system. As a result, 'witch hunts' will continue to be a key feature of the fall out of financial crises, as governments attempt to offload as much of the liability for crises as possible.

Substantive regulatory change is likely to be muted by the lack of confidence among law makers in the United States and Europe in the efficacy of regulation in the face of rapid financial change. The weakness of the regulatory response is already evident in the character of the initiatives developed to 'regulate' the credit rating agencies.

Intellectually, recent financial crises do not seem to have had much impact on the assumptions of academic disciplines like economics that provided the justification for the financial innovations at the heart of the subprime crisis. This means that even now the idea of asset price bubbles remains at odds with established thinking in this field, as promoted by financial economists. Inevitably, this means another generation of self-confident financial 'rocket-scientists' is being trained ready to pursue financial innovation once memories of the current crisis fade.

While truly global financial crises are rare, we understand so little about the mechanisms that cause crises that much greater modesty about how finance works seems sensible. I argue we should abandon our assumption that finance is natural like the movements of the planets, and instead embrace the lesson of Keynes's beauty contest and the valuation crisis of 2007 that financial markets are social phenomena in which collective understandings, especially confidence, may be more important than ostensibly technical considerations.

Although many academic assumptions remain resilient to change, it is apparent that, at least for now, the global financial crisis of 2007–09 has created a much greater sense of uncertainty in the world, and challenged the idea that globalisation will deliver us all from want in a riskless way. It turns out that globalisation is something that is unpredictable, that lurches in ways we cannot guess and that, even at the very heart of the global system, can imperil great fortunes.

The relationship between global finance and politics has changed over the past hundred years. Before the twentieth century, governments had an interest in the smooth working of finance to fund the activities of the state, especially in relation to war. After 1929, governments, especially in the developed world, had a new role in preserving financial stability. After the Second World War, because of the absence of leadership between the wars, the United States assumed the central role in the design and implementation of a new global financial architecture of rules and institutions in support of an increasingly liberal order, but also one that, at least in principle, valued stability. After the Bretton Woods system of fixed exchange rates came to an end in the 1970s, the United States played a strong coordinating role in response to the increased financial volatility that went with renewed international capital mobility, especially in relation to exchange rate fluctuations. Given the unprecedented circumstances of the global financial crisis that started in 2007, it is likely that a more activist stance on the part of the United States will be evident in future. Whether US leadership and interstate cooperation will be as effective today as they were in the 1940s and the 1980s remains to be seen.

Unfortunately, the pressure to return to asset price booms (and thus busts) remains very strong. People seem attached to the empirically false proposition that property values only increase in real terms. But given the degree to which Western governments promoted homeownership as a route to prosperity after the Second World War, it is no wonder that people think this way. When we take the likelihood of future asset price bubbles into account, add in perennial developing country crises and note the uncertain nature of market response at the top of bubbles and in busts, it seems almost inevitable that we will be dealing with financial crises on a regular basis in future, as has been the case in the past. Only through cooperation between major governments can we hope to ameliorate their worst effects and minimise their duration.

Guide to further reading

A quick, readable introduction to financial crises is Galbraith's *A Short History of Financial Euphoria* (1993) and his equally readable history of the Great Depression is *The Great Crash 1929* (1955). The standard history of financial crises, soon to be updated, is given in Kindleberger and Aliber (2005). Influential arguments about crisis in capitalism can be found in Polanyi (1957), Schumpeter (1950), Friedman and Schwartz (1963) and Minsky (2008). An excellent review of the economic literature on the Great Depression is Bernanke (2000). On the global financial crisis that started in 2007, the reader should examine Krugman (2008), Cooper (2008) and Akerlof and Shiller (2009). The most readable account for the non-economist is Gamble (2009b). Upton Sinclair's entertaining novel (2001 [orig. 1907]), *The Moneychangers*, based on events leading up to the 1907 panic, is well worth reading for a comparison with things today.

Chapter 16

Governing the Global Economy: Multilateral Economic Institutions

RICHARD HIGGOTT

In the aftermath of the Second World War a number of powerful institutions were created which have influenced the course and nature of global economic policy over the past 60 or so years. The so-called Bretton Woods institutions – the World Bank and the International Monetary Fund (IMF) – and the General Agreement on Tariffs and Trade (GATT) (which eventually became the World Trade Organisation (WTO)) have become central parts of an international order that purports to be multilateral in form and global in scope. Indeed, it is quite difficult to imagine what 'globalisation' might look like without the existence of international organisations generally or of the international economic (financial and trade) institutions (IFTIs or IEIs) in particular. And yet recent events, especially the credit crunch and its aftermath (see Sinclair, this volume), have caused some observers to question whether the international economic institutions are any longer 'fit for purpose': if they are unable to prevent (increasingly recurring) crises or facilitate a more general process of long-term economic collective action problem solving, what are they for? Such superficial readings miss the point. For all their apparent failings the demand for such institutions is unlikely to disappear in an era characterised by higher levels of economic interdependence. While, global economic governance may still be imperfect and, in contrast to the global economy, underdeveloped, if global governance is to evolve, multilateral economic institutions of one kind or another would seem to be key elements of the process.

In order to develop this argument the chapter proceeds as follows. First, it provides some initial clarification of terms and concepts. Second, it sketches the general historical contours and dynamics that have made multilateral institutions quintessential agents of the post-Second World War international system. Third, it outlines the role of the original Bretton Woods institutions and the GATT and explains how their missions have attracted criticism and changed over time. Fourth, it describes some newer multilateral organisational activity and suggests why issues of authority and accountability have become increasingly contested as – often unelected – policymakers (public and private) and economic actors accrue greater decision-making authority. Finally, the chapter assesses the prospects for global economic governance and the ability of multilateral institutions to participate in the management of the complexity and uncertainty that seems an endemic part of the current world order.

Conceptualising multilateralism

In the most influential analyses of multilateralism, Robert Keohane (1990) and John Ruggie (1993: 14) describe it as a process that 'coordinates behaviour among three or more states on the basis of generalised principles of conduct'. While this may seem unambiguous enough, it begs a series of further initial questions that need to be dealt with at the outset: which principles or norms will provide the 'rules of the road' to guide that behaviour which Ruggie thought were key components of coordinated collective state action? According to the theoretical literature, overcoming collective action problems in the absence of enforcement is the key aim of multilateralism (for a review, see Martin 2006). How should the norms that shape behaviour actually be operationalised and how should decision-making authority be allocated? Empirically we can observe that the institutionalisation over time of bodies such as the IMF and the World Bank has seen a greater degree of decision-making autonomy pass to the institution than their membership had almost certainly initially anticipated.

The growth of new state-sponsored and non-governmental organisations has been a defining feature of the international system for decades, and such organisations have played a crucial role in institutionalising particular ideas and practices (Meyer et al. 1997). However, we need to make an initial distinction between organisations and institutions: all organisations are institutions, but not all institutions are organisations (see Higgott 2006). International organisations have a formal identity, staff, budgets and a potential capacity to act in the international system that in some ways mirrors or even stands in for the actions of states. Institutions, by contrast, may also refer to cognitive and regulatory structures that inform more general social behaviour, and which may be carried by cultures and routine patterns of behaviour (Scott 1995). The intersection of formal organisational or state power and more informal cultural or social influences was central to early attempts to theorise emerging practices of 'governance without government' (Rosenau 1992).

A final point to note about multilateral organisations in particular and their potential for exerting influence relates to their composition and role. Some organisations are established to serve a specific purpose, and the IFTIs are especially important illustrations of this possibility. Others may have a circumscribed regional identity; organisations like the North American Free Trade Agreement, the Asia Pacific Economic Cooperation forum and, especially, the European Union (EU) are important in this regard. Thus, an emerging 'conventional wisdom' now has it that international multilateral institutions and organisations provide global public goods, or the sorts of benefits that potentially accrue from effective trade or monetary regimes that states acting alone could simply not provide (Kaul et al. 1999). A brief look at the history of multilateralism suggests why this view prevails.

Economic multilateralism in historical context

The number of international organisations grew dramatically during the course of the twentieth century (for a review, see Armstrong et al. 2004). There was, and is, a strong link between incipient forms of 'globalisation' and the growth of international cooperation and institutionalisation. The fact that what is widely regarded as the first international organisation was the International Telegraph Union (founded in 1865) is reminder also of the enduring links between technological development, functional necessity and political cooperation (Hirst and Thompson 1999). Less happily, the often unsuccessful pursuit of peace has also been a major spur for international cooperation: the Concert of Europe in the nineteenth century and the League of Nations in the first half of the twentieth are sobering reminders of the difficulty of creating lasting and effective institutions. While the links between conflict and cooperation might seem most immediate and obvious, warfare and its aftermath have also been responsible for much more encompassing forms of institutionalised cooperation, including economic policy coordination (Ikenberry 2001).

The most important and enduring example of this possibility is the international order created under the auspices of US 'hegemony' in the aftermath of the Second World War (see Beeson and Higgott 2005). As already suggested, the organisations established at this time were primarily concerned with the management of the international economy. This should not surprise us: the principal lesson that policymakers in the Anglo-American alliance took from history, specifically the period between the two world wars, was that a failure to maintain an 'open', liberal economic order was a recipe for international economic disorder and possibly outright military conflict. Consequently the IEIs were charged with maintaining a stable monetary order, post-war economic rebuilding, liberalising trade via the reduction of tariffs and encouraging economic development more generally. Their obvious wider aggregate welfare-enhancing utility notwithstanding, such policies were seen by some analysts as reflecting the normative preferences of American policymakers and even actively advantaging US-based economic interests (Harvey 2003; Kolko 1988).

There are a number of general points to note about this historical context. First, it is important to reemphasise just how rapidly organisational development has occurred. International Governmental Organisations (IGOs) increased from 37 to well over 400 by the end of the twentieth century (Schiavone 2001). The second point to stress is that there has been a continuing shift of authority from states to non-government or government-sponsored organisations which are assuming greater responsibility for making and enacting policy in their area of presumed competence. Newer bodies, like the International Organization of Securities Commission (IOSCO) or the Bank of International Settlements (BIS), are good examples of organisations that were products of their era and composed of specialist industry representatives or unelected technocrats. Braithwaite and Drahos's review of the growth of business regulation details the way in which new organisations have emerged to address novel problems and issue areas. Unsurprisingly, these organisational activities, like those from an earlier era, reflected the prevailing configurations of power and interest (Braithwaite and Drahos 2000: 583).

The Bretton Woods institutions and the GATT/WTO

Because the Bretton Woods institutions have assumed such a prominent and often contentious place in the history of economic multilateralism and cooperation, it is worth spelling out their roles in more detail. There are two general points to make at the outset. First, the original IFIs were products of specific economic and geopolitical circumstances. They reflected US (and British) desires to rebuild successful capitalist economies in the face of what was then a credible 'communist' competition from the Soviet Union. Second, as the overall post-Second World War geopolitical situation unfolded, the role and mission of the IFIs also underwent a transformation.

From its initial origins, the IMF has undergone a substantial mission change. Originally established to manage and oversee a system of more or less fixed exchange rates, the IMF's entire mandate was fundamentally undermined by the wider, evolving geopolitical context in which it was embedded. The expense of the Vietnam War and intensified international economic competition led to the US 'closing the gold window' in 1971, thus ending the relationship between the US dollar and the value of gold (Gowa 1983) and the system of fixed exchange rates. This in turn led to the growth of international money markets in a new era of 'floating' exchange rates. In this changing context, the IMF reinvented itself in several ways. The 1970s saw its mission transformed from one of the arbiter of global monetary stability to that of arbiter developing country macro-economic rectitude (Elliott and Hufbauer 2002).

This mission evolved throughout the 1980s and 1990s as the IMF became primarily associated with the promotion of a 'neo-liberal' agenda of economic liberalisation – especially policies to enhance asset privatisation, government roll back and capital account liberalisation – and crisis management, two strongly connected roles (Chwieroth 2007) that over time put the IMF at the centre of far-reaching and controversial interventions in the domestic affairs of some of its members. The East Asian crises of the late 1990s marked the apogee of IMF interventionism, which was greatly reinforced by its close relationship with the US government (Wade and Veneroso 1998). Since that time criticism of its role in these crises saw the IMF's influence (both ideational and actual) come under increasing criticism. This criticism spanned the political spectrum from high priests of the anti-globalisation movement (see Bello 1988) through to impeccably credentialed Nobel laureates in economics (see Stiglitz 2002). In effect, the IMF's desired role as the arbiter of global macro-economic rectitude, especially in the developing world, had largely disappeared in the wake of its sub-optimal performance in the financial crises of the late twentieth century, only to return as an instrument of global financial policy in the wake of the 2007–09 crises and the London 2009 G20 summit.

Similarly, the World Bank, over its lifetime, has undergone a process of mission change that has seen a transformation from its initial role as a vehicle for European reconstruction in the post-Second World War era into to a vehicle for supporting developing countries. This transformation had a natural logic to it in the era of decolonisation. While its organisational evolution should not simply be read as a reformulation of the IMF's neo-liberal template (Rodrik 2006), it clearly has supported neo-liberal reform in the developing world. Indeed, one of the reasons the Bank has attracted so much attention has been because its 'structural adjustment' policies – which tied financial assistance to far-reaching reforms designed to reconfigure the political-economies of its client states – complemented IMF policy in the 1980s and early 1990s. Since that time the Bank has undergone a process of self-evaluation and change re-shaped by a changing international environment in which strategic factors and ideas about development have changed over time.

The preoccupation with 'modernisation' and the pursuit of massive, often inappropriate development projects gave way in the late 1990s to a more technocratic approach that stresses its role as a 'knowledge bank' (Stone 2001), with an emphasis on institutional reform, the provision of 'good governance' and a rhetorical commitment to greater inclusiveness and engagement (Stone and Wright 2006). The Bank's intellectual and practical transition, although more widely accepted and less controversial than that of the IMF, has not been without its internal governance failures and critics (see, e.g., Weaver 2008 and Woods 2006). Concerns about their often unaccountable forms of internal organisation, especially with regard to voting rights, continue to reflect the entrenched nature of the political influence of major powers, as indeed is the case in many international organisations more generally (see Keohane et al. 2009).

Consequently, despite the Bank's efforts to differentiate itself from the IMF and respond more effectively to criticisms from 'global civil society' and client states over the decade 1998–2007, there remains a good deal of dissatisfaction with both the ideational and practical roles of the two principal IFIs. The financial crisis of 2007–09 has exacerbated the dissatisfaction in many quarters. Calls for the reform and/or the development of a new institutional architecture continue unabated notwithstanding the G20 summits of November 2008 and April 2009.

The original mandate of the third leg of the post-Second World War international multilateral economic architectural triangle, the GATT, was to reduce those barriers to trade (principally then tariffs) that were seen to have played a destructive role in causing and prolonging the Great Depression of the inter-war years. Not only was increased trade thought likely to spur the reconstruction of the western world's battered economies, but greater economic interdependence was also seen as a way of reducing the prospect of conflict. There was also a broader theoretical agenda emerging on the role of institutions such as GATT as a locus for bargaining trade liberalisation and ensuring compliance (see Martin 2006: 59–65 and WTO 2007: 35–98) And indeed there is strong prima facie evidence that economic interdependence does have pacific effects and is associated with, if not responsible for, higher economic growth (Keohane and Nye 1977; Mousseau 2009). The GATT, through a series of post-Second World War multilateral trade negotiation rounds, successfully and substantially reduced the role of the tariff as an instrument of protection and instilled a series of norms and principles into the multilateral trade regime, most notably the norms of most favoured nation status and national treatment (see Hoekman and Kostecki 2001; Narlikar 2005; WTO 2007: 179–201). It also fulfiled some of the generally unstated, Cold War, geopolitical goals that underpinned its rationale, along with that of the IMF and the World Bank.

As the post-Second World War era progressed, the GATT developed major capacity constraints. The nature of trade evolved (especially with the growth of services as a share of world trade) and the nature of protectionism shifted (from tariff to non-tariff barriers). The reduction in tariffs opened up the US economy more than that of many of its trading partners at the same time as the rise of non-tariff barriers affecting its developing sectors (service and intellectual property) became more difficult to exploit. Throughout the 1970s and early 1980s, the US trade policy community saw that GATT rules and procedures would do nothing to redress these imbalances. This led to the introduction of a policy of 'aggressive unilateralism' intended to prise open markets, especially in the face of mounting trade deficits with Japan, the principal beneficiary in the economic and strategic environment the United States had effectively underwritten (see Bhagwati and Patrick 1990).

While '301' rhetoric exceeded practice, it nevertheless secured an adjustment in the incentive structures of US trading partners and a willingness to contemplate a new trade round to address those interests deemed essential by the United States. Hence, the Uruguay Round commenced in 1985, which resulted a decade later in the creation of the WTO, a new organisation including not only GATT but also agreements on services (GATS), intellectual property (TRIPS) and a dispute settlement mechanism (see Croome 1995) giving the WTO a significantly greater capacity to enforce compliance with its resolutions through its dispute settlement mechanisms. In addition, the ambit of issues that the WTO seeks to manage has expanded significantly in line with the evolving international political economy. The new agreements on services and intellectual property reflected the evolution of the most economically developed countries, especially the United States.

As with the IMF and the World Bank, the life of the WTO is not without difficulties in the contemporary era. It is criticised by analysts across the political spectrum from what we might call 'right nationalists' in the United States and parts of Europe, to the left developmentalist and anti-globalisation movements of the South. Both groups, from their different perspectives, see the WTO as an excessively intrusive, sovereignty challenging and back door to global governance and many would like to have it abolished. The WTO's supporters, however, occupy the pivotal positions in the global policy community (both public and private), although they too do not adopt a uniform position and range across a spectrum from market privileging neoclassicists to interventionist Keynesians. But they too recognise that the WTO faces serious problems in maintaining its global economic institutional salience in the early twenty-first century.

A new institutional architecture?

As argued, discontent over the roles of the IEIs, in both the analytical and policy communities, has been a continuing theme in the post-war period. The East Asian crisis of the late 1990s brought dissatisfaction with the so-called international financial architecture to something of a head. In retrospect this should not surprise us. A number of regional economies, which were formerly objects of admiration because of their economic achievements, were suddenly thrown into chaos and many among their populations were thrown back into poverty from whence they had recently escaped. Observers felt that if the IFIs were not in some way responsible for the crisis by encouraging premature economic liberalisation, they were certainly culpable in failing to manage the impact of and recovery from the crisis. Indeed, one of the big lessons that East Asian economic and political elites drew from the crisis was that the region rapidly needed to develop its own economic institutions if it wanted to be able to respond more effectively to future crises (Grimes 2009). As a consequence, there have been accelerated efforts to develop new, regionally based economic mechanisms (Dieter and Higgott 2003). One of the great paradoxes of globalisation, therefore, has been a noteworthy proliferation of institutions to either encourage regional integration or generate regional responses to specific problems (see Breslin, this volume). Given Ruggie's understanding of multilateralism, as cooperation between two or more states, we should recognise these regional activities for what they also are – exercises in multilateralism.

Indeed, the growth of regional multilateral economic institutions must be seen as the other side of the coin of global multilateralism (see the Warwick Commission 2007: 45–53; Frankel 1997). The growth of regional multilateral institutions is not an exclusively East Asian phenomenon. On the contrary, it is a strong characteristic of post-Second World War international economic relations. Such processes are most fully developed in Western Europe (see Telo 2009) notwithstanding a lack of enthusiasm about the European project among large sections of its own populations at the end of the first decade of the twenty-first century. Indeed, doubts have been expressed about the EU's capacity to survive, much less effectively manage the current global economic crisis (Erlanger and Castle 2009).

Similar doubts about our abilities to provide an appropriate multilateral regulatory framework for the management of the economy at the global level abound in the wake of the great recession of 2007–09 – even by prominent former champions of the free market (Turner 2009; Wolf 2009). Although the arguments of would-be reformers are at least being heard, it is not clear whether the crisis at the end of the first decade of the twenty-first century will lead to major changes in the existent system of regulation. Precisely the same arguments were heard after the Asian crisis when there were widespread calls for institutional reform and tighter control of the activities of banks and financial markets (Armijo 2002; Kenen 2001). In reality, little has changed. Indeed, many of the restrictions that had formerly been put in place to control the activities of banks at a national level were repealed, as policymakers in the Anglo-American economies became locked in a competition to provide 'light touch', business-friendly regulation (see Sinclair, this volume).

The dialectical interaction, broadly conceived, between states and markets has been one of the central dynamics driving the evolution of the international economy, and the institutions that seek to manage it, for the last 60 years. One perennial problem, as economic historian Niall Ferguson opines (2009), seems to be the failure to learn the lessons of history: policymakers in the United States and the United Kingdom in particular have ignored the experiences of the Great Depression, the saving and loans crisis in the United States, the Asian crisis and so on. However, it is important to emphasise that the most recent crisis did not come as a complete surprise to everyone. In addition to the long-standing warnings of some academics (Strange 1998), more institutionalised forms of policy advice were also ignored. The BIS, a key source of independent policy advice for policymakers around the world, despite raising concerns about the dangers associated with the new financial instruments central to the most recent crisis, was continuously ignored (Giles 2009).

That policymakers chose to ignore advice that is unwelcome or at odds with pre-existing ideological prejudices should not surprise us. Nevertheless, it raises important questions about the role that extant or new institutions can actually play in any putative processes of global governance. One key issue, as we have seen, is the unrepresentative nature of existing international institutions. Recently there have been attempts to expand the club of 'developed' economies beyond the confines of the G7 and G8 groupings which have dominated inter-governmental discussions for decades. The prominence achieved by the G20, which includes key actors from the 'global South' such as Brazil, China and India, in the wake of the recent crisis should be seen as part of a genuine push to develop more representative multilateral institutions. An idea developed from an earlier Canadian initiative (see Higgott 2005), the G20, failed to gain momentum until the crises of 2007–09. And yet, it remains far from clear how effective such a group might be in the long term. There remains a reluctance on the part of the major powers, especially the United States, and indeed some declining former major powers (especially in Europe) to concede the need to share power with the new actors from the South (see Beeson and Bell 2009). Indeed, the apparent difficulties of state-based, inter-governmental organisations in securing effective collective action problem solving in times of crisis help to account for the rise of other novel forms of governance.

One of the most striking aspects of what passes for global economic governance at present is just how much of it is becoming increasingly decentralised and network-based. From the closing decades of the twentieth century, we have seen a proliferation in the number of non-state, specialist agencies and organisations playing an increasingly prominent role in international standard setting. Inherently elitist, the principal claim for inclusion in these new informal and often uncoordinated networks of governance is technocratic competence or specialist expertise. The development of the BIS prior to the crises of 2007–09 is a classic example of what we might call a 'transnational executive network' (TEN) and reflects a more generalised ideological preference for light-touch regulation on the parts of many OECD governments, in this case as they delegated responsibility for monetary policy to (unelected) central bankers (Tsingou 2004, 2010). This process is mirrored by a similar, and simultaneous, process of regulatory diffusion occurring in the private sector as different actors develop a responsibility for setting regulatory standards for codes of conduct, production standards and the like (Braithwaite and Drahos 2000). The interesting normative question posed by these developments is the degree to which these actors are contributing to the delivery of global public goods (as public goods theory would have it) or whether they are in fact engaged in the provision of club goods for their respective clientele. The empirical evidence from the financial crises of 2007–09 would suggest that private interest has prevailed over public good.

For some observers, the growth of transnational executive networks is both predictable and appropriate, and marks a functional response to demands for regulation and governance that can no longer be met by states in an era of globalisation (Slaughter 2004.) For others, this is part of a long-running debate between those who see states as taking part in a process in which they have voluntarily ceded power to other actors and those who view state authority as being inexorably undermined by technological developments and intensifying transnational economic and political processes (see Cerny, this volume; Cooper et al. 2008). What is novel and potentially important now, however, is the possibility that the very nature of the 'knowledge economy' is generating new patterns of governance in which informal ties and expertise are generating new networks that help explain the way in which policy is made at the global level (Stone 2008) and, at a more macro-theoretical level for some, even the way the economy is conceived as an object of governance (Haas 1990; Rose 1993).

Of one thing there is little doubt. One effect of the crises of the early twenty-first century is that the state has made a major comeback as a key stakeholder in the unfolding process of economic reform. Although it is too soon to know what the long-term impacts of the current crisis will be, it has challenged the credibility of the hands-off, light-touch style of neo-liberal-inspired economic regulation that characterised the last two decades of the twentieth century and the early years of the twenty-first and especially which justified and actively encouraged the growing role of self-regulation by the private sector in the Anglo-American economies (see Gamble 2009).

The contingent future of multilateral economic governance

Even before the recent economic crisis that has done so much to undermine confidence in, and the influence of, neo-liberal forms of governance and regulation, political legitimacy was an issue for the IFIs and some of the new institutional actors in the global domain. Notwithstanding the argument that some forms of regulation are so specialised that only a handful of experts, practitioners or other insiders can claim to understand their intricacies, this does not overcome fundamental problems that flow from a legitimacy deficit (Hurd 1999). For all their shortcomings, the saving grace of democratically elected polities is that they can claim a popular mandate for their actions. This has never been the case with the multilateral institutions as agents of global governance. They still draw their legitimacy only indirectly from the legitimacy of their member states.

Theoretical endeavours to enhance legitimacy at the global level, emanating from essentially cosmopolitan views of global civil society, have invariably assumed an extension of the 'domestic analogy' to the extra-territorial, or global, context. That is, the extension of the model of democratic accountability that we have come to accept in the advanced countries of the developed world to the wider global context. The weakness of the domestic analogy is that only the most minimal of democratic constraints present within a domestic polity are present at the global level (Dahl 1999.) There is no serious institutionalised system of checks and balances at the global level. Institutional constraints that do exist have little purchase on the behaviour of major powers, especially a hegemon, should it choose to ignore them and to speak of a *global* public sphere or *global* polity, in a legal or a sociological sense, has little meaning (see Ougaard and Higgott 2002).

There are, of course, sophisticated cosmopolitan democratic theories which have problematised the domestic analogy in the attempt to elaborate which elements of 'traditional' democratic theory – that presuppose a national *demos* (people) and a nation-state context – are feasible and desirable on the global level of politics (Archibugi 2000; Archibugi et al. 2000; Held 2002, 2005). But in these theories, which are principally normative, feasibility tends to give way to desirability. Liberal cosmopolitan theorists start from the individual as a member of humanity as a whole, rather than the state, and the idea that we as members deserve equal political treatment. They emphasise the importance of individual rights claims and wish to replace the state-based system of international relations with a new set of cosmopolitan principles, laying out a moral standard that sets limits to what people and political authorities are allowed to do through international institutions. Examples are the principle of inclusiveness and subsidiarity (the all-affected principle), the principle of avoidance of serious harm and the principle of active agency (Held 2002: 23–4). According to David Held, these principles constitute an overarching cosmopolitan law for a multilayered system, specifying the organisational basis of a legitimate public power. Sovereignty, the idea of rightful authority, is thus divorced from the idea of fixed territorial boundaries and thought of as an attribute of basic cosmopolitan law (Held 2002: 32).

But contemporary multilateral institutions and multilateralism as practice do not operate with these normative assumptions. The legitimacy of multilateralism, to the extent that it exists, is embedded in shared norms (usually of elites, rather than wider national publics) and is underwritten by judicial instruments (such as the International Criminal Court (ICC) or the Dispute Settlement Mechanism of the WTO). But contrary to many assumptions in both the scholarly and the policy world that excessively privileges an increasingly dynamic role for civil society and non-state actors, effective multilateral governance at the global level remains with states as the principal (although not exclusive) actors. However, recognising the central role for states does not mean yielding to a purely statist view of legitimacy. States are not the sole actors in global governance. Global institutions involve and reflect the perspectives of individuals as well as states. To have the right to rule means that institutional agents are morally justified in making rules and that people subject to those rules have moral reasons for complying with them or at least not preventing others from doing so (Buchanan and Keohane 2006: 411). Legitimate global governance thus must understand state actions within a global framework of international law and *common norms of action*. Events in the first decade of the twenty-first century, in both the politico-security and the economic domain, have done little to advance the cause of cosmopolitanism. Rather than escaping into pietistic theory, ascribing to states a major role allows us to ask hard questions about the legitimate status of intermediate institutional actors, such as the WTO, in the provision of global public goods in the twenty-first century.

What Keohane (2005) calls the increasingly 'contingent' nature of multilateralism has meant that the multilateral aspirations of the second half of the twentieth century are more muted in the twenty-first century. What can be done multilaterally (in an inclusive sense of the word) is being recast in more restrictive terms. This is clearly a factor behind the emergence of other approaches to and exercises in collective action. This chapter has already identified the growing dynamic towards regional economic cooperation in the rise of preferential trading arrangements.

The growth of regionalism in recent years has clearly been sub-optimal in systemic and political terms in a number of ways. Specifically, regionalism has diverted attention from multilateral negotiations. Governments may believe, or be lulled politically into the conviction, that they can acquire all they need by way of trade policy through regional arrangements. This has led to, and is likely to continue to lead to, neglect of the relative costs and benefits, especially over time, of regional versus multilateral approaches to trade relations. As a consequence, some recent theorising in the trade domain have also led scholars to identify the need, in the words of Richard Baldwin and his colleagues, to 'multilateralise regionalism' (see Baldwin 2006; Baldwin et al. 2007). These calls reflect the reality that while regional preferentialism in trade might be sub-optimal to acting multilaterally through the WTO, it will not be going away, hence the exhortation to multilateralise it. At another level, but related, we are also seeing what Moïses Naim (2009) calls an increasing interest in 'minilateralism'. Minilateralism is a response to a growing recognition that large-scale multilateral agreements – whether they are, for example, in pursuit of trade liberalisation, the attainment of Millennium development goals or the reduction of greenhouse gas (GHG) emissions – have all seen deadlines missed and policy execution stalled. The recognised limits of multilateralism are leading to the advocacy and practice of more targeted approaches at collective action problem solving. The correct number in any given problem area is 'the smallest possible number of countries needed to ensure the largest possible impact'. This number will, of course, vary from issue area to issue area.

The theory has, for example, been developed in the area of trade in the recommendations of the recent Warwick Commission for the development of a process of critical mass decision making at the WTO (Warwick Commission 2007: 27–36; see also Gallagher and Stoler 2009). As is well known, a small number of states (about 20) count for 85–90 per cent of total world trade. A deal made by them – with appropriate safeguards and non-discriminatory access to the deal for latecomer signatories and smaller payers – could offer a way forward in certain contested areas of trade policy without trammelling the consensus decision-making principle that prevails in the organisation. Similarly, the world's top 20 polluters account for 75–80 per cent of the world's GHG emissions. Rather than being thought of as anti-democratic and exclusionary, such minilateral agreements could be thought of as 'deadlock busters' that can be open to other states in an inclusive non-discriminatory fashion after the event. Such approaches are undoubtedly controversial but without such innovations, international collective action decision-making will get progressively more difficult.

Conclusion

The dramatic rise of globalisation in general over the last several decades and the economic crises of the early twenty-first century in particular have challenged the efficacy and legitimacy of multilateralism as both institutional practice and principle. It has also raised more general meta-theoretical questions. One of the most important long-term successes of the twentieth century has been to make market principles an accepted and authoritative part of everyday existence (Hall 2007). A consequence of the most recent crisis has been to damage the authority of both the actors and agencies that had assumed responsibility for managing economic processes, and – more fundamentally – the stability of markets themselves. The rapid transformation of the terms of the debate over economic management in the wake of the crises of 2007–09 must remind us that the processes and practices of governance remain temporally and politically contingent. The economic crises of the early twenty-first century have once again highlighted Harold Lasswell's (1935) perennial questions of modern politics: who gets what and how, governance for whom and in whose interest? These remain essentially contested questions.

The struggle between power and rules-based behaviour continues to be one of the hallmarks of the present system of global economic governance. The challenge

of marrying the two in a meaningful and legitimate manner remains the perennial research question of international political economy. A reformist approach
to the current system is not entirely out of the question, as attempts to marshall
a G20 approach towards global economic cooperation, the growth of minilateralism, multilateral regionalism and transnational network activities identified in this
chapter attest. But we are not yet at a stage where the major players will easily
share power with emerging actors or indeed with various and increasingly active
strata of an emerging global civil society. The generic challenge is to adapt multilateralism to the dynamics of a world battling to come to terms with changing
power balances and emerging policy agendas that do not lend themselves to the
kinds of collective action problem solving that prevailed in the second half of the
twentieth century.

Guide to further reading

For a good historical and analytical introduction to international organisation, see
Armstrong et al. (2004); but see also Schiavone (2001) for an empirical guide.
Ruggie (1993) remains the essential theoretical introduction to multilateralism,
but see also Keohane (1989). On the international economic institutions generally,
see Martin (2006); on the World Bank, see Weaver (2008); on the IMF, see Woods
(2006); and on the WTO, see Hoekman and Koestecki (2001) and Narlikar (2005).
On new forms of international governance, see Slaughter (2004) and Stone (2008).

Chapter 17

Population Movement and Its Impact on World Politics

ANNE HAMMERSTAD

The movement of people has helped shape the trajectory of history for as long as human communities have existed. Since the first groups of modern humans left Africa to populate the world some 60,000 years ago, population movements have brought with them prosperity and devastation, cultural enrichment and annihilation, co-operation and conflict. Mass migration has contributed to the collapse of some empires (the migration of Visigoths, Vandals and other peoples leading to the sacking of Rome in 410 AD) and the construction of others (the mass emigration to the US from Europe in the nineteenth and early twentieth century). More recently, technological innovations have made long-distance relocation cheaper and easier, while the combination of globalisation and inequality has primed the world's working age population to consider migration as a natural path to achieve economic opportunities and betterment. Add to this the political repression and wars that still riddle many parts of the world, ensuring continuing high numbers of refugees, asylum seekers and other forced migrants, and it is safe to say that the movement of people will continue to be a salient feature of global politics in the twenty-first century.

As the dynamics of forced migrants make clear, people do not only move out of desire for a better life. For many the decision to migrate is taken more out of necessity than choice. In the academic literature, there tends to be a distinction between migration studies and forced migration studies – a distinction often strengthened by the fact that research on the two areas tends to be conducted in separate institutes and centres. As has been increasingly recognised over the past decade, the distinction between different categories of migrants (forced/voluntary, legal/illegal, regular/irregular, economic/political, internal/external) has become increasingly blurred. At one end of the voluntary/forced spectrum we find highly educated professionals moving between countries in pursuit of career opportunities, and welcomed by their host country due to the skills and resources they bring with them. At the other end we find poor villagers gathering up their children and fleeing across a border to escape war and ethnic cleansing, who find shelter of a sort in a refugee camp supported by international aid agencies. Between these two extremes (each is a minority among international migrants), are a large group of people who migrate for a varied mix of personal, political, economic and security

238

reasons. The reception these migrants get in their host countries is also mixed, but over the past two decades the trend has been one of increasing unease and even fear over immigration levels.

This chapter will discuss the challenges and opportunities posed by population movement in the twenty-first century. It asks why population movement is such a contentious issue. It addresses this question by investigating whether the present 'age of migration' (Castles and Miller 1998) is indeed characterised by unprecedented migration levels, or whether our understanding of current migration challenges lacks historical depth. It looks at what is old and what is new about migration trends, and argues that today's population movements do pose some unprecedented challenges.

An age of migration?

International migration (the movement of people across sovereign borders) has caused widespread concern among the public and politicians both in the global North and the global South. The topic solicits frequent news coverage, both of the more alarmist and the more supportive kind. According to a recent *Economist* special report, migrants are a 'new force that is reshaping our world' (Roberts 2008). The report, in line with the magazine's liberal outlook, sees this as a challenging but mostly positive force, but documents the widespread backlash against migration, both in terms of public opinion and policy decisions. This hardening of attitudes has been described by migration analysts as well. Luedtke (2009) shows an increasingly restrictive trend in EU policies since 9/11, where EU harmonisation in the immigration sphere has mostly meant adopting the practices of the members with the harshest pre-existing rules and practices. In the US, the events of 9/11 induced a narrower focus on border control, and bolstered, however spuriously, a populist backlash aimed more against Mexican illegal immigrants than Islamist terrorists. Attempts at reforming and liberalising the country's immigration regime in 2006–07 were derailed, and the only policy on which the House of Representatives and the Senate managed to agree was the Secure Fence Act, creating 700 miles of fencing and surveillance along the US–Mexican border (Rosenblum 2009: 13). In the global South, both South Africa and India have put up border fences in recent years in an attempt to keep out illegal immigrants from their poorer and more troubled neighbours, Zimbabwe and Bangladesh, respectively.

How has migration, whether of the voluntary, forced or mixed kind, become such a controversial topic in global politics? In order to assess the challenges and opportunities created by international migration, it is useful to ask first in what ways they differ from earlier eras of migration. Are we indeed living in 'an age of migration' (Castles and Miller 1998), characterised by unprecedented levels of population movement? The answer is both yes and no. Immigration levels are high today compared with recent history, and have accelerated in the past couple of decades. In Europe in modern times, immigration is mostly a post-1945 phenomenon (*emigration*, on the other hand, is an age-old European pursuit). In the 1960s, when Enoch Powell made his infamous reference to 'rivers of blood', less than five per cent of Britain's population was foreign born. By 2001, this proportion had increased to 8.3 per cent (ONS 2005: 133), and by 2007, following the opening of the UK labour market to eastern European EU members, to 10.6 per cent (or 6.3 million people) (ONS 2009: 22).

However, if one takes the long view, there is nothing remarkable about today's levels of migration. As de Haas (2005) points out, in proportion to the world's population, migration levels are no higher today than they were at the height of the last great wave of migrants a century ago. Then as now, international migrants constituted 2.5–3 per cent of the world's population (IOM 2008a: 4). Even after two decades of fast and sustained immigration growth in the US, the foreign-born proportion of the population was still lower in 2007 (12.6 per cent) than at the previous immigration peak in 1910 (14.7 per cent) (MPI 2007). Looking even further back, the era around 300 to 700 AD is known as the Migration Period. It ushered in the Middle Ages in Europe and had a far stronger impact on social, economic and political relations than anything seen in the modern age.

Turning to *forced* migration, there is nothing spectacular about today's levels either. Consider, for instance, the human upheavals during and immediately after Second World War. In May 1945, around 40 million people were displaced in Europe alone. Among them some 13 million ethnic Germans expelled from the Soviet Union, Poland and other eastern European countries, many of whom perished on their march westwards (UNHCR 2000: 13). Added to this came the millions of Chinese displaced by Japan during the war, and the exodus of some 750,000–900,000 refugees from Palestine after the creation of Israel in 1947 and the first Arab–Israeli war in 1947–49. In Europe, by 1951, 400,000 Second World War refugees remained in camps across western Europe – their existence prompting the creation of the United Nations High Commissioner for Refugees (UNHCR 2000: 17). In other words, rapid and large refugee movements are far from a unique phenomenon of the post-Cold War period.

Having provided some historical perspective, there are nevertheless good reasons for arguing that there are distinctive aspects of contemporary migration. The chapter will discuss five ways in which today's migration challenges, and the responses to them, are different. I will look at migration numbers (not proportions); the direction of their flow; issues of migration control and management; the criminalisation of migration; and the rise of a migration security agenda. All are linked to the phenomenon of globalisation, which may be argued to have led to migration challenges of an unprecedented nature – at least in modern history.

Migration numbers

Due to massive population growth over the past 100 years, the actual *number* of migrants is vastly higher now than it was in the early twentieth century. For instance, the 14.7 per cent of the US population that was foreign born in 1910 amounted to 13.5 million people. In 2007, a proportion of 12.6 per cent equalled a foreign-born population of over 38 million people. The cumulative effect of migration in the post-war period has also led to significant demographic changes in some countries, especially in major cities. For instance, in London, one in three residents in 2007 was non-UK born (ONS 2009: 23). In that sense today's mass migration is at an unprecedented level.

Regarding refugee and asylum seeker numbers, the trend has also been upwards, but peaked in the early 1990s. As a proportion of overall international migration figures, forced migration remains small. While there are something like 200 million migrants worldwide, the UNHCR estimated that, in 2007, there were ca. 12 million refugees and asylum seekers (UNHCR 2008: 7). Despite this, the *impact* of displacement on world politics has taken on a new significance. First, although mass and sudden refugee flows are not a new phenomenon, it is nevertheless safe to argue that the frequency with which we have seen such flows in the post-Cold War period is unprecedented. For example, Northern Iraq (1991), Rwanda (1994), Bosnia (1992–95), Kosovo (1999), East Timor (1999), Darfur/Chad (from 2003 and ongoing) and Iraq (from 2003 and ongoing) are just some of the major sources of refugee movements in recent years.

Second, due to the rise of the norm of humanitarian intervention, most recently in the manifestation of a *Responsibility to Protect* (see Bellamy, this volume), forced migration leads more frequently to international interventionism (Roberts 1998). Since the end of the Cold War, refugee movements have been frequently listed in the United Nations Security Council as cause for international action. In the cases of Haiti (1993) and Northern Iraq (1991), refugee situations were determined as a 'threat to international peace and security' and used to justify coercive action under Chapter VII of the UN Charter. Thus, even though the main impact of forced migration continues to be limited to certain regions in the global South, the question of how to respond to this problem has become a dilemma of global politics.

Third, the international refugee regime (consisting of the 1951 UN Convention on the Status of Refugees and its 1967 Protocol, the UNHCR and several regional refugee conventions) asserts the right of individuals to seek asylum and not to be returned to their home country if in danger of persecution (*non-refoulement*). This means, in the developed world, that each asylum application must be treated on an individual basis, and that asylum seekers cannot be controlled in terms of the numbers and background of those arriving. As legal labour migration channels from the global South to the global North have narrowed, the potential loophole provided by cumbersome asylum determination procedures has been seized on as a way into Northern labour markets. This said, the vast majority of the world's asylum seekers come from war-torn or repressive countries. Although economic betterment constitutes an important reason behind many asylum seekers' decision to make the journey to Europe, North America or Australia, often travelling illegally, it does not follow that they do not also have strong political or humanitarian claims to remain in their country of destination.

While the dilemma of how to deal with so-called mixed flows of refugees and labour migrants travelling to the North is not an entirely new phenomenon, its scale and political significance have grown dramatically since the end of the Cold War. As refugees and, particularly, asylum seekers can now be found across the world, they affect a larger number of states in both the North and the South, causing Loescher (1993) to declare a *global* refugee crisis. The early 1990s saw a steep rise in asylum applications in developed countries, especially Europe. From around 20,000 asylum applications in Europe in 1976 (Loescher 1993: 111), numbers started rising more quickly in the late 1980s and exploded in the early 1990s – coinciding with the wars surrounding the collapse of Yugoslavia. Asylum numbers peaked in the European Union in 1992, with 667,770 applications, down to a still high 291,220 in 1998 (UNHCR 1999: Table V1) and, after some fluctuations, 216,300 in 2008 (UNHCR 2009: Table 1). The figure from 2008 covers 'old' EU. If adding the 12 new EU members from Eastern Europe, the figure is 238,100 asylum claims.

To sum up, the world has never before seen so many people on the move, and global migration has accelerated in pace in the past couple of decades. The trend is linked to the long period of economic growth we have seen in many parts of the developing world, especially Asia, since it is generally not the poorest people of the world who become international migrants. In order to make the way from one country to another, some resources are necessary. Thus, part of the migration boom since the end of the Cold War should be seen in conjunction with the success of countries such as China and India in lifting millions of people out of abject poverty in the same period. As these countries continue to develop, global migration levels may continue to rise (Roberts 2008), although as the global economic downturn has hit destination countries such as the UK and US hard, it may make them less attractive for future potential migrants.

Direction of flows – still a regional phenomenon

The rise in asylum requests in the North is an example of how the *direction* of migration flows is changing. In the previous age of migration, those on the move were mostly Europeans resettling in the New World or the colonies. Today, a substantial minority of the world's migrants make their journey from the global South to the global North. The change is particularly visible in Europe, which has gone from a continent of emigration, to one of immigration. As a result, many previously homogenous states in Europe have, at least in their major cities, attained a considerably more multicultural hue.

Despite the picture given by the European media of a relentless flow of rickety boats laden with migrants setting across the Mediterranean from North Africa to Europe, it should, however, be kept in mind that most international migration remains intra-regional. Only a relatively small proportion of migration flows are South–North. For instance, according to an IOM (2008b) presentation, of 8.5 million West African migrants that year, 7.5 million had moved within the region, the remaining 1 million to Europe and the US. We can see the same trend for refugees and asylum seekers. In 2006, the two largest refugee populations originated from Afghanistan (2.1 million) and Iraq (1.5 million). Out of these populations, 1.2 million of the Iraqi refugees settled in neighbouring Jordan and Syria (UNHCR 2007: 7), while almost 2 million of the Afghan refugees lived in Pakistan and Iran. There is a big drop down to the country hosting the third largest Afghani refugee population: the UK, with 23,069 Afghanis (UNHCR 2007: Table 5).

Looking at asylum figures only, in 2006, 19,000 new asylum claims were lodged by Zimbabweans in neighbouring South Africa, compared to 2,100 in the UK (the former colonial power) (UNHCR 2007: 10). Of the six main countries of origin of asylum seekers in 2005 (Burma, Somalia, Serbia and Montenegro, the Russian Federation, the Democratic Republic of Congo and China), only among the Chinese asylum seekers did the majority travel beyond their own region to apply for asylum. Of the rest, most went no further than a neighbouring state (UNHCR 2006a: Tables 1, 2, 6; UNHCR 2006b: 7–8). The only mass flows of refugees and asylum seekers to European countries in the post-Cold War period have come from within the region: from the countries of the former Yugoslavia and, to a lesser extent, Russia.

The only part of the world in which the direction of international migration is mainly South to North is the Americas. Notably, 87 per cent of total migration in the Americas region is from Latin America and the Caribbean to North America (IOM 2008a: 423).

Responses to migration movements: migration management and control

The responses to challenges posed by international migration have also taken some new forms. Here I will first look at domestic politics, before moving on to the increased international interaction and co-operation to attempt to regulate, manage and control migration flows.

Despite the fact that most migrants stay within their region of origin, the sheer number of people on the move, together with growth in South–North migration, have nevertheless made immigration and asylum a highly salient issue in domestic politics across the globe, from South Africa in the South to Scandinavia in the North. In Western Europe, the steep rise in asylum applications in the early 1990s contributed to strong electoral results for far-right parties in countries such as Norway, Denmark, France, the Netherlands and Austria. Consequently, talking 'tough on immigration' has also become a mainstream pursuit, leading some analysts to argue that the mainstream political parties have allowed the far-right too much influence on immigration and asylum agendas (Bralo and Morrison 2005). Across the global North, there has, since the end of the Cold War, been a gradual tightening of legal migration routes: harsher visa regimes and stricter border controls. This has been particularly visible in the case of asylum systems, where preventative (and punitive) measures against asylum seekers have taken the form of detention centres, withdrawal of the right to work while pending application outcomes and distributing benefit payments in vouchers instead of money. Policies like these, combined with a decline in refugee numbers from the peak in the mid-1990s, allowed former British Prime Minister Tony Blair to boast to the Labour party conference in 2003 that his government had halved the number of asylum applications in Britain (Bralo and Morrison 2005: 113). In South Africa, the authorities' inability to stem the influx of Zimbabwean refugees (as well as illegal immigrants from all over southern Africa) contributed to the township riots and xenophobic attacks that left more than 50 people killed in May 2008.

Such national measures can be seen as a series of 'beggar-thy-neighbour' strategies with global effects (Hans and Suhrke 1997: 84), where each country tries to make itself less attractive than its neighbour and thus shifting the burden of hosting refugees, asylum seekers and unwanted migrants onto other states. In terms of protection of the human right to seek asylum, this unilateralism has resulted in a race to the bottom, leading the UNHCR to warn about a crisis in the international refugee protection regime (see, e.g., UNHCR 2004: §5; UNHCR 2001) as asylum practices have become more about migration control, spurred by domestic political and security considerations, than about asylum obligations incurred by international law.

One way of avoiding this race to the bottom is through multilateral co-operation and co-ordination, and particularly strengthening international migration (and forced migration) management regimes and organisations. There has been a flurry of regional and global initiatives in recent years, all with the aim of harnessing the positive aspects of international migration – for migrants themselves and for their host and home communities – and counteracting the negative aspects, especially trafficking and people smuggling. Migration issues are now routinely placed high on the agendas of various regional and global institutions, such as the UN, the EU, the World Bank, the Organization for Security and Co-operation in Europe (OSCE) and the African Union. In addition, migration-specific institutions such as the International Organization for Migration (IOM) have been strengthened and a variety of migration-specific processes have been created to foster international co-operation (Solomon 2005: 1–2).

An overarching international migration regime is difficult to achieve, since states value control over their migration policies in order to be free and flexible to adapt these to the changing demands of economic and political circumstances (Solomon 2005). An added problem is the schism between the perceptions and needs of developed and developing states in migration management. For instance, while the South voices concern about the effect of 'brain drain' on their economies, the North usually welcomes skilled migrants but put pressure on Southern states to stop illegal migration of unskilled workers from the South to the North.

The same North–South tension can be seen in the international refugee regime (an otherwise stronger and more well-established legal regime than what exists for migration). There have been several attempts at serious reform of the refugee regime in the twenty-first century in order to achieve better burden-sharing and deal more efficiently and humanely with so-called mixed flows of forced and economically motivated migration. None of these efforts have had much success. This has to a large extent been due to the mistrust between the North and the South. Attempts by Northern states, especially in the EU, to contain refugees in regions of origin and to negotiate return agreements with so-called safe first countries of asylum, are broadly seen by refugee-hosting countries of the South as attempts at burden-shifting rather than burden-sharing (Hammerstad 2009; Loescher et al. 2008: 62–6). The outcry over asylum seekers in the North is particularly resented in the South, considering that only 14 per cent of the global refugee population leave their own region (UNHCR 2008: 27) and the vast majority remain in the South, to be cared for by some of the world's poorest countries.

Considering these obstacles, combined with the fact that most migration remains intra-regional, it is not surprising that most migration management initiatives have been regional, rather than global. Regional Consultative Processes (RCPs) supported by the IOM have sprung up in all regions of the world. These RCPs are not institutions or organisations, but informal, non-binding and open forums for dialogue with low levels of bureaucracy and rules. Such processes aim to foster common understandings, consider policy options and arrive at consensus views which may lay the foundation for subsequent formal regional agreements (Koppenfels 2001: 9).

Despite difficulties in evaluating achievements of regional and international migration management processes (Koppenfels 2001: 6; Solomon 2005: 4–5), a picture is emerging of an ever denser and more far-reaching web of informal discussion forums, initiatives and Plans of Action. As such, international processes play an increasingly significant role in the migration management strategies of individual states, although there is a long (and probably unrealistic) way to go before it is possible to talk about a global migration regime.

Moving on to *formal* and binding international co-operation on migration policies, the tense climate created by the terror attacks of 9/11 has helped undermine efforts to achieve comprehensive migration management frameworks involving migrant-sending as well as immigrant-receiving states. Instead, recent agreements have focused largely on *immigration control* – with the aim of deterring and preventing asylum seekers, limiting unskilled immigrants and controlling skilled migration. The fate of the EU's Tampere Conclusions is an illustrative example. In 1999, the EU agreed on an ambitious migration policy integration programme. The Tampere Conclusions affirmed the right to seek asylum, the commitment of EU countries to the UN Refugee Convention, the fair treatment of immigrants, their integration into host societies and the provision of equal rights for immigrants. However, Luedtke (2009: 144) argues that this process was derailed by 9/11, and that the EU's substantial integration of immigration policies since 1999 has become an opportunity for member states to withdraw rather than enhance the rights of non-EU immigrants by setting the lowest common denominator as EU-wide standards, and by doing so in the name of national security and the war against terrorism. However, it should be kept in mind that this tightening of non-EU immigration has gone hand in hand with an explosion of intra-EU migration after the admission of nine eastern European countries and Malta into the organisation in 2004.

The pros and cons of international migration – why a backlash?

The EU harmonisation process has in common with other recent national and regional efforts at controlling migration, such as the US, Indian and South African border fences against their poorer neighbours, a particular concern with policing and security aspects of migration management. The focus has been on 'irregular' and 'illegal' migration, 'bogus asylum seekers', 'mixed flows' (of refugees and economic migrants), people smuggling, trafficking and in general what has been termed 'the criminalisation of migration' (Haas 2005: 13). With international terrorism added to this already heady mixture of concern and fear over migration, it can also be argued that there has been a partial *securitisation* of population movements.

The impact of 9/11 was immediately felt by advocates of the rights of refugees and asylum seekers. Only few weeks after the terror attacks on New York and Washington, Erika Feller, UNHCR's Director for Protection (now Assistant High Commissioner for Protection), placed states' anti-terror and security-based efforts to restrict asylum within a broader context of the increasing criminalisation of asylum seekers and refugees, and called for resolute leadership 'to de-dramatise and de-politicise the essentially humanitarian challenge of protecting refugees and to promote better understanding of refugees and their right to seek asylum' (UNHCR 2001). The next section will address the concerns and fears raised by immigration by investigating its impact on economies, culture/identity and political security. Although I will mainly discuss host communities, as the phenomenon has global reach and consequences, it is also necessary to look at effects on sending states, as well as on global politics.

Migration's benefits: an uneven picture

It is not straightforward to determine the economic impact of migration, or to assess whether this impact is mainly of a beneficial or harmful nature. This is partly because migration figures are not accurate, a particular problem in the case of irregular migration (defined by IOM (2008: 203) as 'migrants whose status does not conform, for one reason or another, to the norms of the country in which they reside') – which the International Labour Organization (ILO) estimates constitutes around 10–15 per cent of all international migration (IOM 2008a: 209). The difficulty is also due to the political controversies surrounding immigration, which have made cost-benefits analyses often highly politicised.

What is safe to say is that migration's benefits are uneven (Roberts 2008), whether viewed from the perspective of sending country or host country. Focusing on sending countries first, emigration can be a pressure valve for countries such as the Philippines and Morocco with fast-growing and youthful populations and high unemployment – as indeed it was for European countries such as Ireland and Norway in the nineteenth and early twentieth centuries. On the other hand, since it is often the resourceful and educated who take the leap, it has been argued that emigration can hamper development by tapping developing countries of their most valuable workers and entrepreneurs. The debate continues on whether 'brain drain' hinders development or whether it is underdevelopment and poor economic opportunity, corruption and inefficient bureaucracies that lead the bright and the educated to seek greener pastures elsewhere (Roberts 2008).

The question of the value of remittances is another issue that is high on the migration research agenda. First, it is not straightforward to measure the levels of remittances, since many are not transferred through official channels. This is especially the case for irregular migrants, but regular migrants may also choose cheaper alternatives to official transfer channels. As a consequence, the IOM suggests that the working estimate from 2007 of the size of remittances worldwide at ca. US$318 billion, of which 240 billion goes to developing countries, is probably too low (IOM 2008a: 338). Nevertheless, even on conservative estimates, this is a significant transfer from North to South, dwarfing that of official Overseas Development Aid, which stands at around US$100 billion a year, and outpacing Foreign Direct Investment (FDI) flows globally (World Bank 2006: 1). In many countries remittances are higher than earnings from major export commodities (Page and Plaza 2005: 9).

Early research on remittances tended to dismiss their significance, suggesting that they merely increase immediate consumption among the migrant's friends and family. Today it is clear that remittances can have a strong developmental role. It is a capital flow unhampered by bureaucracy and corruption, which tends to improve nutrition, health and education among recipients, and which can also take the form of highly efficient micro-level direct investment when migrants put money into the businesses of family and friends back home. Due to the size of remittance flows, the question of how to maximise their impact on development is high on the research agenda of the World Bank, IOM and migration research centres across the world. According to the World Bank, the importance of remittances for development will increase due to the global financial crisis, since the level of remittances is predicted to decrease less than other capital flows or overseas aid to the developing world in coming years (World Bank 2008b).

The economic impact on migrants' host countries is also uneven. In the UK, the anti-immigration think tank Migration Watch released a controversial study in 2007 suggesting that the overall economic contribution of immigrants to GDP per capita was almost negligible. While the study agreed that immigration created GDP growth, it argued that because it also increased the population of the country, the very small 'fiscal benefit to the host population' (Migration Watch 2007a) was far outweighed by the social costs of migration on 'already overburdened

infrastructure, housing, health and schools' and 'an increasing impact on employment and added strains on community cohesion' (Migration Watch 2007b). Others
argue that the UK economy would not have boomed in the 1990s and the first half
of the 2000s, were it not for young and dynamic immigrants working in a range of
sectors from construction to banking, and the NHS could not have been reformed
without immigrant health care workers to fill vacant positions. The strain on
infrastructure is mostly a short-term planning problem for local authorities need-
ing to adapt schooling and housing policies to include the new arrivals (Roberts
2008). The fact that even an anti-immigration think tank could not find data to
show an outright *negative* economic cost–benefit analysis of migration into the
UK is a sign that immigration into developed countries have had an overall beneficial impact on host economies, although some groups within those economies
will have benefited more than others and some – especially low-skilled workers –
may have lost out to newcomers.

From identity concerns to national security

Migration Watch's comments point to the fact that concerns over immigration
levels often relate to identity and culture more than to the economy. The perceived unmanageability of immigration adds to this unease, as it is difficult
for states' border authorities to distinguish between 'deserving' and desired
immigrants and 'bogus' and unwanted ones. Both in political and academic
debates (see Wæver et al. 1993) there have been concerted and partly successful
attempts at elevating both economic migration and forced migration onto states'
broader security agenda. Huysmans (2006), for instance, has shown how a language of threat and unease permeates EU discourse on immigration. Migration
has usually been categorised as a 'societal security' threat, defined by Buzan
(1991: 19) as 'the sustainability, within acceptable conditions for evolution, of
traditional patterns of language, culture and religious and national identity and
custom'.

Anxieties over immigration have heightened after 9/11 due to fears over let-
ting in international terrorists through a country's immigration or asylum system
(Givens et al. 2009). Such fears have been constantly fuelled by high-profile
arrests, such as when 11 Pakistani nationals in the UK, ten of which were on
student visas, were arrested in April 2009 in a dramatic police action on suspicion
of plotting a major terrorist act. The 11 were released without charge and deported
with much less fanfare a few weeks later (BBC 2009a). As global recession hits
most of the world's economies, security-related anxieties are likely to be com-
pounded by economic concerns and protectionist instincts. In South Africa, which
descended into recession in 2009, xenophobic attacks continue to take place, and
human rights groups argue that it will take little to spark violence on a par with the
deadly riots of 2008 (Evans and Ncana 2009). In the UK, prime minister Gordon
Brown's ill-considered phrase 'British jobs for British people' came back to haunt
him when employees at an oil refinery staged wildcat strikes to protest against the

hiring of Portuguese and Italian workers for a construction project on the site (BBC 2009b).

Mixed motives are not a prerogative of immigrants

The above discussion makes clear how difficult it is to separate out concerns raised by the economic, cultural/identity and national security impact of migration. While it is analytically useful to attempt to separate these concerns, in reality the political discourse on immigration tends to include a mix of all types of concerns, where cultural/identity fears provide a vaguely formulated but pervasive background atmosphere to more clearly articulated and specified concerns relating to the national security of the state and the economic welfare of its citizens.

Neither in the case of immigration nor in the case of asylum was 9/11 the starting point for such securitisation of population movements. An emerging trend could be seen already in the 1980s, where immigrants, asylum seekers and refugees became increasingly subsumed within a discourse of unease and fear (Huysmans 2006: 63; and on the particular securitisation of forced migration, see Hammerstad 2009). This is important for understanding the way in which international migration and international terrorism were quickly grouped together in the aftermath of 9/11. This happened almost automatically and without substantial political debate as the ground had already been laid for perceiving immigrants and asylum seekers within a security perspective.

Conclusion: immigration challenges and opportunities for twenty-first century world politics

Migration challenges are not likely to abate in the coming years. Immigration controls have gone some way to reduce some inflows into some developed countries, but, as Harris (2002 mentioned in Haas 2005) points out, immigration correlates more strongly with economic growth than with migration control policies. Complete immigration control in a world with an increasingly globalised labour market (IOM 2008a: 24) is not possible without creating a politically authoritarian and economically autarkic state disregarding both the rights of the individual and the logic of the market.

On the other hand, as Harris suggests, the global financial crisis may lead to somewhat reduced migration flows as labour markets contract and provide fewer opportunities for those seeking economic betterment abroad. We may also see some reversals of migration flows. There are, for instance, signs of eastern European migrants to the UK returning to more promising prospects in their home countries (Pollard et al. 2008). Most migrants, however, are likely to stay, and this may lead to a further backlash against immigrants during the global downturn. The administrative war against (certain types of) immigration fought by states in terms of ever stricter border controls and bureaucratic measures continues unabated, often in the name of national security.

The welcome immigrants receive has always ebbed and flowed. Migration trends are to some extent cyclical, where immigration booms are followed by increasing concern and fear among host populations and ensuing political back-lashes. The reaction following the mass influxes of economic migrants to the US in the late nineteenth and early twentieth century was more severe, and more xenophobic and racist, than anything we have seen in recent years. The back-lash then started with the recession in the 1890s, and by 1930 'the doors to the new world were effectively closed' (Hatton and Williamson 2005: 160). The glob-alised nature of twenty-first century politics and economics makes such draconian reactions less likely today. A combination of demographic trends and economic realities will ensure that international migration remains a central feature of world politics. Considering the inequalities of the world economy, not even the global financial crisis will stop motivated individuals from wanting to relocate to improve their prospects. In terms of demographics, the combination of youthful and fast-growing populations in many parts of the global South, and an ageing population in many parts of the North, will ensure that a relatively high level of migration remains desirable for both sending and host countries for the foreseeable future.

Guide to further reading

Migration and forced migration studies are fast-growing academic fields. Because of the policy salience of the topic, a lot of recent research come out in the form of reports and policy papers from migration organisations such as IOM (www.iom.int) and UNHCR (www.unhcr.org), and think tanks and research centres such as the Migration Policy Institute (www.migrationpolicy.org); the Center for Immigration Studies (www.cis.org); and Oxford University's Centre on Migration Policy and Society (www.compas.ox.ac.uk) and Refugee Studies Centre (www.rsc.ox.ac.uk). Hatton and Williamson (2005) provide an impressive overview of the economics and history of international migration over the past two centuries, giving the reader a much-needed sense of perspective on today's challenges. Huysmans (2006) employs and critiques the securitisation perspec-tive of the Copenhagen School in his analysis of 'Fear, Migration and Asylum in the EU', and several post-9/11 volumes cover the topic of security and migration (e.g., Guild and van Selm 2005; and Givens et al. 2009). Loescher et al. (2008) provide a useful overview of the state of the international refugee regime and the organisation mandated to oversee it, that is, the UNHCR.

References

Abrahamian, Ervand (2003) 'The Media, Huntington, and September 11', *Third World Quarterly*, 24(3): 529–44.

Acharya, Amitav (2001) *Constructing a Security Community in Southeast Asia: ASEAN and the Problem of Regional Order* (London and New York: Routledge).

Ackerly, B., Stern, M. and True, J. (eds) (2006) *Feminist Methodologies for International Relations* (Cambridge: Cambridge University Press).

Adamson, F.B. (2005) 'Globalisation, transnational political mobilisation, and networks of violence', *Cambridge Review of International Affairs*, 18(1): 31–49.

Adler, Emanuel (1997) 'Imagined (Security) communities: Cognitive regions in international relations', *Millennium*, 26(2): 249–77.

Adler, Emanuel and Barnett, Michael (1998) *Security Communities* (Cambridge: Cambridge University Press).

AFP (2008a) 'Asia's migrant workers fear losing jobs in global crisis', Agence France Presse, 12 October.

AFP (2008b) 'World jobless total could rise by 25 million: OECD chief', Agence France Presse, 22 December.

AFP (2008c) 'World must manage water carefully: Experts', Agence France Presse, 24 June.

Agnew, J. (2005) *Hegemony: The New Shape of Global Power* (Philadelphia: Temple University Press).

Agnew, J. and Corbridge, S. (1995) *Mastering Space: Hegemony, Territory and International Political Economy* (London: Routledge).

Akerlof, George A. and Shiller, Robert J. (2009) *Animal Spirits: How Human Psychology Drives the Economy and Why It Matters for Global Capitalism* (Princeton, NJ: Princeton University Press).

Alagappa, Muthiah (1988) 'Comprehensive security: Interpretations in ASEAN countries', in Robert Scalapino et al. (eds), *Asian Security Issues Regional and Global* (Institute of East Asian Studies, University of California, Berkeley).

Alagappa, Muthiah (1998) *Asian Security Practice: Material and Ideational Influences* (Stanford: Stanford University Press).

Albert, M. (1993) *Capitalism vs. Capitalism* (New York: Four Wall Eight Windows).

Ali, Tariq (2002) *The Clash of Fundamentalisms: Crusades, Jihads and Modernity* (London: Verso).

All Africa (2008a) 'About 50 million more hungry people in 2007', 4 July.

All Africa (2008b) 'World is 40 percent prepared for pandemic, UN official says', 20 November.

Allen, C. (1999) 'Warfare, endemic violence & state collapse in Africa', *Review of African Political Economy*, 26(81): 367–84.

Altman, R.C. (2009) 'The great crash of 2008: A geopolitical setback for the west', in *Foreign Affairs*, January/February.

Al-Zawahiri, Ayman (2005) English translation of a letter from Ayman al-Zawahiri to Abu Musab al-Zarqawi, http://www.weeklystandard.com/Content/Public/Articles/000/000/006/203gpuul.asp?pg_1 (accessed 5 November 2007).

251

America.gov (2009) 'U.S. tells China climate change is national security priority', http://www.america.gov/st/energy-english/2009/July/20090728121912esnamfuak0.5545465.html#ixzz0OcwrxiOP (accessed 20 August 2009).

Anderson, B. (1991) *Imagined Communities: Reflections on the Origin and Spread of Nationalism* (London: Verso).

Anderson, Dorothy (1998) 'David Mitrany (1888–1975): An appreciation of his life and work', *Review of International Studies*, 24(3): 577–92.

Andrews-Speed, P., Liao, X. and Dannreuther, R. (2002) *The Strategic Implications of China's Energy Needs*, IISS-Adelphi Paper 346 (Oxford University Press).

Andrews-Speed, Philip and Xin Ma (2008) 'Energy production and social marginalization in China', *Journal of Contemporary China*, 17(55): 247–72.

Angstrom, J. (2005) 'Introduction: Debating the nature of modern war', in I. Duyvesteyn and J. Angstrom (eds), *Rethinking the Nature of War*, 1st edn (London, New York: Frank Cass), pp. 1–27.

Annan, Kofi (1999) 'Annual Report of the Secretary-General to the United Nations General Assembly', 20 September, available at http://www.un.org.ezproxye.bham.ac.uk/News/Press/docs/1999/19990920.sgsm7136.html.

Archibugi, D. (2000) 'Cosmopolitan democracy', *New Left Review*, 4: 137–50.

Archibugi, D., Balduini, S. and Donati, M. (2000) 'The United Nations as an agency of global democracy', in B. Holden (ed.), *Global Democracy* (London: Routledge).

Archibugi, Daniele (2008) *The Global Commonwealth of Citizens: Toward Cosmopolitan Democracy* (Princeton, NJ: Princeton University Press).

Arend, A.C. and Beck, R.J. (1993) *International Law and the Use of Force: Beyond the UN Charter Paradigm* (London: Routledge).

Armijo, L.E. (ed.) (2002) *Debating the Global Financial Architecture* (New York: New York State University).

Armstrong, D., Lloyd, L. and Redmond, J.B (2004) *International Organisation in World Politics* (Basingstoke: Palgrave Macmillan).

Armstrong, Karen (2000) *The Battle for God* (New York: Alfred A. Knopf).

Arrighi, G. (1994) *The Long Twentieth Century: Money, Power, and the Origins of Our Times* (London: Verso).

Associated Press Newswires (2008) 'UN official: Financial crisis could harm food aid', 24 September 2008.

Ayson, R. (2007) 'The changing character of warfare', in R. Devetak, A. Burke and J. George (eds), *An Introduction to International Relations: Australian Perspectives* (Cambridge, UK: Cambridge University Press), pp. 167–78.

Badie, Bertrand and Birnbaum, Pierre (1983) *The Sociology of the State* (Chicago: University of Chicago Press).

Baker, Dean (2009) *Plunder and Blunder: The Rise and Fall of the Bubble Economy* (Sausalito, CA: PoliPoint Press).

Baldwin, R. (2006) 'Multilateralising regionalism: Spaghetti bowls as building blocs on the path to global free trade', *The World Economy*, 29(11): 1451–518.

Baldwin, R., Evenett, S. and Low, P. (2007) 'Beyond tariffs: Multilaterising deeper RTA commitments', *Multilateralizing Regionalism Conference*, Geneva, 10–12 September 2007, at www.wto.org/english/tratope/regione/consep07e/ Baldwin_evenett_low_e.pdf.

Balsdon, J.P.V.D. (1979). *Romans and Aliens* (Chapel Hill, NC: University of North Carolina Press).

Bank of England. *Financial Stability Report*. London: April 2008.

Barber, B.R. (2001) *Jihad vs. McWorld* (New York: Ballantine Books).

Barkawi, Tarak (2004) 'On the pedagogy of "Small Wars" ', *International Affairs*, 80(1): 19–37.

Barker, Sir Ernest (ed.) (1962) *Social Contract: Essays by Locke, Hume and Rousseau* (New York: Oxford University Press).

Barma, N., Ratner, E. and Weber, S. (2007) 'A world without the West', *The National Interest* (July/August): 23–30.

Barnes, J. and Myers Jaffe, A. (2006) 'The Persian Gulf and the geopolitics of oil', *Survival*, 48(1) (Spring): 143–62.

Barnett, M. and Finnemore, M. (2004) *Rules for the World: International Organizations in Global Politics* (Ithaca: Cornell University Press).

Barton, Barry, Redgwell, Catherine, Ronne, Anita and Zillman, Donald N. (2004) *Energy Security: Managing Risk in a Dynamic Legal and Regulatory Environment* (Oxford: Oxford University Press).

Bass, Gary J. (2008) *Freedom's Battle: Humanitarian Intervention in the Nineteenth Century* (London: Knopf).

BBC (2009a) 'No charges after anti-terror raid' (BBC Online News, 22 April 2009). Accessed on 7 May 2009 at http://news.bbc.co.uk/2/hi/uk_news/8011341.stm.

BBC (2009b) 'Refinery strikes spread across UK' (BBC Online News, 30 January 2009). Accessed on 7 May 2009 at http://news.bbc.co.uk/2/hi/uk_news/7859968.stm.

BBC Monitoring Asia Pacific (2008) 'Singapore PM declines to rule out nuclear power in long term', 8 December.

Bedford, K. (2007) 'The imperative of male inclusion: How institutional context influences World Bank gender policy', *International Feminist Journal of Politics*, 9(3): 289–311.

Beeson, M. (2007) *Regionalism and Globalization in East Asia: Politics, Security, and Economic Development* (Palgrave Macmillan).

Beeson, M. (2009) 'Hegemonic transition in East Asia? The dynamics of Chinese and American power', *Review of International Studies*, 35(1): 95–112.

Beeson, M. and Bell, S. (2009) 'The G-20 and international economic governance: Hegemony, collectivism, or both?', *Global Governance*, 15(1): 67–86.

Beeson, M. and Higgott, R. (2005) 'Hegemony, institutionalism and US foreign policy: Theory and practice in comparative historical perspective', *Third World Quarterly*, 26(7): 1173–88.

Beeson, M. and Islam, I. (2005) 'Neo-liberalism and East Asia: Resisting the Washington Consensus', *Journal of Development Studies*, 41(2): 197–219.

Beier, J.M. (2006) 'Outsmarting technologies: Rhetoric, revolutions in military affairs, and the social depth of warfare', *International Politics*, 43(2): 266.

Bell, C. (2007) *The End of the Vasco da Gama Era: The Next Landscape of World Politics*, Lowy Institute Paper No. 21 (Sydney: Lowy Institute for International Policy).

Bellamy, Alex J. and Williams, Paul D. (2009) *Understanding Peacekeeping*, 2nd edn (Cambridge: Polity Press).

Bellin, Eva (2000) 'Contingent democrats: Industrialists, labor, and democratization in late-developing countries', *World Politics*, 52(2): 175–205.

Bello, W. (1998) 'East Asia: On the eve of the great transformation?', *Review of International Political Economy*, 5(3): 424–44.

Bendix, Reinhard (1964) *Nation-Building and Citizenship* (Garden City, NY: Anchor Books).

Berdal, M. (2003) 'How "New" are "New Wars"? Global economic change and the study of civil war', *Global Governance*, 9(4): 477–502.

Berdal, M. and Malone, D. (eds) (2000) *Greed & Grievance: Economic Agendas in Civil Wars* (Boulder, CO: Lynne Rienner).

Bergeron, S. (2004) *Fragments of Development: Nation, Gender and the Space of Modernity* (Ann Arbor, MI: University of Michigan Press).

Bergsten, C.F. (2005) 'Rescuing the Doha Round', *Foreign Affairs*, 84(7) (December). [Online] Available at: http://www.foreignaffairs.org/20051201faessay84702/c-fred-bergsten/r.

Berman, Paul (2003) *Terror and Liberalism* (New York: Norton).

Bernanke, Ben S. (2000) *Essays on the Great Depression* (Princeton, NJ: Princeton University Press).

Bernstein, M.D. and Adler, D.E. (1994) *Understanding American Economic Decline* (Cambridge: Cambridge University Press).

Bhagwati, J. (2004) *In Defence of Globalization* (Oxford: Oxford University Press).

Bhagwati, J. (2005) 'From Seattle to Hong Kong', *Foreign Affairs*, 84(7) (December). [Online] Available at: http://www.foreignaffairs.org/20051201faessay84701/jagdish-bhagwati/from-seattle-to-hong-kong.html.

Bhagwati, J. and Patrick, H.T. (1990) *Aggressive Unilateralism: America's 301 Trade Policy and the World Trading System* (Ann Arbor, MI: Michigan University Press).

Bigo, Didier (2005) 'From foreigners to "Abnormal Aliens": How the faces of the enemy have changed following September the 11th', in Elspeth Guild and Joanne van Selm (eds), *International Migration and Security: Opportunities and Challenges* (Abingdon: Routledge).

Bilmes, Linda and Stiglitz, Joseph (2008) *The Three Trillion Dollar War: The True Cost of the Iraq Conflict* (New York: Norton).

Binder, D. and Crossette, B. (1993) 'As ethnic wars multiply, U.S. strives for a policy'. *New York Times* (7 February). [Online] Available at: http://query.nytimes.com/gst/fullpage.html?res=9F0CEFD9113AF934A35751C0A965958260&sec=&spon=&pagewanted=all.

Bisley, N. (2007) *Rethinking Globalization* (Basingstoke: Palgrave Macmillan).

Black, Jeremy (2005) War and international relations: A military-historical perspective on force and legitimacy, *Review of International Studies*, 31 (Supplement): 127–42.

Blair, Tony (1999) 'Doctrine of the International Community', speech to the Economic Club of Chicago, Hilton Hotel, Chicago, 22 April.

Blanche, E. (2002) 'Terror attacks threaten Gulf's oil routes', *Jane's Intelligence Review (JIR)* (December): 6–11.

Blankley, Tony (2005) *The West's Last Chance: Will We Win the Clash of Civilizations?* (Washington, DC: Regnery Pubishing).

Blum, D.W. (2007) *National Identity and Globalization: Youth, State, and Society in Post-Soviet Eurasia* (Cambridge: Cambridge University Press).

Blyth, M. (2002) *Great Transformations: Economic Ideas and Institutional Change in the Twentieth Century* (Cambridge: Cambridge University Press).

Bobbitt, P. (2002) *The Shield of Achilles: War, Peace, and the Course of History* (New York: Random House).

Bolton, John (2007) *Surrender Is Not an Option: Defending America at the United Nations and Abroad* (New York: Threshold Editions).

Bond, Brian (1996) *The Pursuit of Victory: From Napoleon to Saddam Hussein* (Oxford: Oxford University Press).

Booth, D. (1985) 'Marxism and development sociology: Interpreting the impasse', *World Development*, 13(8): 761–87.

Borger, J. and Watts, J. (2009) 'China launches green power revolution to catch up on west', *The Guardian*, 10 June.

Bowle, J. (1964) *Politics and Opinion in the 19th Century* (New York: Oxford University Press).

Bowles, Paul (1997) 'ASEAN, AFTA and the "New Regionalism" ', *Pacific Affairs*, 70(2): 219–34.

Boyarin, J. (1994) 'Introduction', in J. Boyarin (ed.), *Remapping Memory: The Politics of TimeSpace* (Minneapolis: University of Minnesota Press).

Boyer, M., Urlacher, B., Hudson, N.F., Niv-Solomon, A., Janik, L.L., Butler, M.J., Brown, S.W. and Ioannou, A. (2009) 'Gender and negotiation: Some experimental findings from an international negotiation simulation', *International Studies Quarterly*, 53(1): 23–47.

Bradsher, Keith (2009a) 'China outpaces U.S. in cleaner coal-fired plans', *The New York Times*, 11 May 2009 (Online version).

Bradsher, Keith (2009b) 'China vies to be world's leader in electric cars', *The New York Times*, 2 April 2009 (Online version).

Bradsher, K. (2009c) 'Manufacturing slump sends fear across Asia', *International Herald Tribune*, 22 January 2009.

Braithwaite, J. and Drahos, P. (2000) *Global Business Regulation* (Cambridge: Cambridge University Press).

Braithwaite, John (2008) *Regulatory Capitalism: How It Works, Ideas for Making It Work Better* (Cheltenham, Gloucestershire: Edward Elgar).

Bralo, Zrinka and Morrison, John (2005) 'Immigrants, refugees and racism: Europeans and their denial', in Elspeth Guild and Joanne van Selm (eds), *International Migration and Security: Opportunities and Challenges* (Abingdon: Routledge).

Brandon, H. (1973) *The Retreat of American Power* (London: Bodley Head).

Bremmer, I. (2008) 'The return of state capitalism', *Survival*, 50(3): 55–64.

Brenner, Neil (2004) *New State Spaces: Urban Governance and the Rescaling of Statehood* (Oxford: Oxford University Press).

Brenner, Neil, Jessop, Bob, Jones, Martin and MacLeod, Gordon (eds) (2003) *State/Space: A Reader* (Oxford: Blackwell).

Breslin, Shaun (2009) 'Understanding China's regional rise: Interpretations, identities and implications', *International Affairs*, 85(4): 779–813.

Breslin, Shaun, Higgott, Richard and Rosamond, Ben (2002) 'Regions in comparative perspective', in Shaun Breslin, Christopher Hughes, Nicola Phillips and Ben Rosamond (eds), *New Regionalisms in the Global Political Economy: Theories and Cases* (London: Routledge), pp. 1–19.

British Petroleum (BP, 2009) Statistical Review of World Energy, June.

Bromley, S. (2005) 'The Unites States and the control of world oil', *Government and Opposition*, 40(2): 225–55.

Bronson, Rachel (2006) *Thicker than Oil: America's Uneasy Partnership with Saudi Arabia* (Oxford and New York: Oxford University Press).

Brooks, S.G. and Wohlforth, W. (2002) 'American primacy in perspective', *Foreign Affairs*, 81(4): 20–35.

Brown, Michael et al. (eds) (2004) *New Global Dangers: Changing Dimensions of International Security* (Cambridge, MA: MIT Press).

Brown, M.E. (2003) *Grave New World: Security Challenges in the Twenty-First Century* (Washington, DC: Georgetown University Press).

Brownlie, Ian (1974) 'Humanitarian intervention', in John N. Moore (ed.), *Law and Civil War in the Modern World* (Baltimore: Johns Hopkins University Press), pp. 217–21.

Bruner, Robert F. and Carr, Sean D. (2007) *The Panic of 1907: Lessons Learned from the Market's Perfect Storm* (New York: Wiley).

Buchanan A. and Keohane, R.O. (2006) 'The legitimacy of global governance institutions', *Ethics & International Affairs*, 20(4): 405–38.

Bull, Benedicte (1999) ' "New regionalism" in Central America', *Third World Quarterly*, 20(5): 957–70.

Bull, H. (1977) *The Anarchical Society: A Study of Order in World Politics* (London: Macmillan).

Burchell, Graham, Gordon, Colin and Miller, Peter (eds) (1991). *The Foucault Effect: Studies in Governmentality* (Chicago: University of Chicago Press).

Burrows, M. and Treverton, G.F. (2007) 'A strategic view of energy futures', *Survival*, 49(3): 79–90.

Burton, Michael and Higley, John (1987) 'Elite settlements', *American Sociological Review*, 52(3): 295–307.

Burton, Michael, Gunther, Richard and Higley, John (1991) 'Introduction: Elite transformations and democratic regimes', in John Higley and Richard Gunther (eds), *Elites and Democratic Consolidation in Latin America and Southern Europe* (Cambridge: Cambridge University Press), pp. 1–37.

BusinessDay (2008) 'France sets up sovereign wealth fund' (24 October). [Online] Available at: http://www.businessday.com.au/business/france-sets-up-sovereign-wealth-fund-20081024-57m1.html.

Butler, J. (1993) *Bodies that Matter: On the Discursive Limits of 'Sex'* (London: Routledge).

Butler, J. (1994) 'Contingent foundations: Feminism and the question of postmodernism', in S. Seidman (ed.), *The Postmodern Turn: New Perspectives on Social Theory* (Cambridge: Cambridge University Press), pp. 153–70 [orig. 1990, presented at the Greater Philadelphia Philosophy Consortium].

Butler, J. (1999) *Gender Trouble*, rev. edn (London: Routledge).

Buzan, B. (2008) *People, States and Fear* (New York: Columbia University Press).

Buzan, Barry (1991) *People, States and Fear: An Agenda for International Security Studies in the Post-Cold War Era*, 2nd edn (Hemel Hempstead: Harvester Wheatsheaf).

Byers, Michael (2005) 'High ground lost', *Winnipeg Free Press*, 18 September 2005, p. B3.

Caballero-Anthony, Mely (2006) 'Combating infectious diseases in East Asia: Securitisation and global public goods for health and human security', *Journal of International Affairs* (Spring/Summer): 105–27.

Caballero-Anthony, Mely and Koh, Collin (2008) 'The Way Forward for Energy Security', *Policy Brief*, Centre for Non-Traditional Security (NTS) Studies, December.

Caballero-Anthony, Mely, Emmers, Ralf and Acharya, Amitav (eds) (2006), *Non-Traditional Security in Asia: Dilemmas in Securitisation* (London: Ashgate).

Calder, K. (1997) *Asia's Deadly Triangle. How Arms, Energy and Growth Threaten to Destabilize Asia-Pacific* (London-Sonoma: Nicholas Brealey Publishing).

Cameron, David (1991) 'The 1992 initiative: Causes and consequences', in Alberta M. Sbragia (ed.), *Euro-Politics: Institutions and Policymaking in the New European Community* (Washington, DC: Brookings), pp. 23–74.

Campbell, D. (1998) *Writing Security: United States Foreign Policy and the Politics of Identity*, rev. edn (Minneapolis, MN: University of Minnesota Press).

Caney, Simon (1997) 'Human rights and the rights of states: Terry Nardin on non-intervention', *International Political Science Review*, 18(1): 27–37.

Canwest News Service (2008) 'Migrant workers casualties in economic slowdown', 13 November.

Caprioli, M. (2000) 'Gendered conflict', *Journal of Peace Research*, 37(1): 51–68.

Caprioli, M. and Boyer, M. (2001) 'Gender, violence and international crisis', *Journal of Conflict Resolution*, 45(4): 503–18.

Carment, D. (2003) 'Assessing state failure: Implications for theory and policy', *Third World Quarterly*, 24(3): 407–27.

Carothers, Thomas (2002) 'The end of the transition paradigm', *Journal of Democracy*, 13(1): 5–21.

Carothers, Thomas (2006) 'The backlash against democracy promotion', *Foreign Affairs*, March/April.

Carter, N. (2007) *The Politics of the Environment: Ideas, Activism, Policy*, 2nd edn (Cambridge: Cambridge University Press).

Carver, T. (1996) *Gender Is Not a Synonym for Women* (London and Boulder, CO: Lynne Rienner).

Case, William (2002) *Politics in Southeast Asia: Democracy or Less* (Richmond, UK: Curzon).

Castles, Stephen and Miller, Mark (1998) *The Age of Migration: International Population Movements in the Modern World*, 2nd edn (Basingstoke: Palgrave Macmillan).

Center for Strategic and International Studies (CSIS) (2000) *The Geopolitics of Energy in the 21st Century, 3 Vol.* (Washington, DC: CSIS Press).

Cerny, P.G. (1996) 'What next for the state?', in E. Kofman and G. Youngs (eds), *Globalization: Theory and Practice* (London: Pinter).

Cerny, P.G. (2003) 'Globalization and other stories: Paradigmatic selection in international politics', in A. Hülsemeyer (ed.), *Globalization in the Twenty-First Century: Convergence or Divergence?* (New York: Palgrave Macmillan).

Cerny, Philip G. (1990) *The Changing Architecture of Politics: Structure, Agency and the Future of the State* (London: Sage).

Cerny, Philip G. (2000a) 'Globalization and the disarticulation of political power: Toward a new middle ages?', in Henri Goverde, Philip G. Cerny, Mark Haugaard and Howard H. Lentner (eds), *Power in Contemporary Politics: Theories, Practices, Globalizations* (London: Sage), pp. 170–86.

Cerny, Philip G. (2000b) 'Restructuring the political arena: Globalization and the paradoxes of the competition state', in Randall D. Germain (ed.), *Globalization and Its Critics: Perspectives from Political Economy* (London: Macmillan), pp. 117–38.

Cerny, Philip G. (2006) 'Dilemmas of operationalizing hegemony', in Mark Haugaard and Howard H. Lentner (eds), H*gemony and Power: Consensus and Coercion in Contemporary Politics* (Lanham, MD: Lexington Books on behalf of the International Political Science Association, Research Committee No. 36 [Political Power]), pp. 67–87.

Cerny, Philip G. (2009a) 'Some pitfalls of democratisation: Thoughts on the 2008 Millennium conference', *Millennium: Journal of International Studies*, 37(3) (May): 763–86.

Cerny, Philip G. (2009b) 'The competition state today', *Policy Studies*, 31(1), pp. 5–21.

Cerny, Philip G. (2009c) 'Crisis and renewal: Saving capitalism from the capitalists?', *Naked Punch: The Engaged Review of Contemporary Art and Thought* (Spring).

Cerny, Philip G. (2010) *Rethinking World Politics: A Theory of Transnational Neoplural-ism* (New York and Oxford: Oxford University Press).

Chan, S. (2008) *China, the US, and the Power-Transition Theory* (London: Routledge).

Chandler, David (2005) 'The responsibility to protect: Imposing the liberal peace', in Alex J. Bellamy and Paul D. Williams (eds), *Peace Operations and Global Order* (London: Routledge), pp. 59–82.

Chang, H.-J. (2002) *Kicking Away the Ladder: Development Strategy in Historical Perspective* (London: Anthem Books).

Charrier, Philip (2001) 'ASEAN's inheritance: The regionalisation of Southeast Asia', *The Pacific Review*, 14(3): 331–8.

Chesterman, Simon (2001) *Just War or Just Peace? Humanitarian Intervention and International Law* (Oxford: Oxford University Press).

China, Government of (2005) 'Position Paper of the People's Republic of China on the United Nations Reforms', 8 June.

Chinese State Council (2007) *White Paper on Energy*, Beijing: 26 December.

Chomsky, Noam (2003) *Hegemony or Survival: America's Quest for Global Dominance* (New York: Metropolitan Books).

Chwieroth, J.M. (2007) 'Testing and measuring the role of ideas: The case of neo-liberalism in the International Monetary Fund', *International Studies Quarterly*, 51(1): 5–30.

Clapp, J. and Dauvergne, P. (2005) *Paths to a Green World: The Political Economy of the Global Environment* (Cambridge, MA: MIT Press).

Clarke, Richard A. (2004) *Against all Enemies – Inside America's War on Terror* (New York: Free Press).

Clausewitz, Carl von (1976) *On War*. Translated by M. Howard and P. Paret (Princeton, NJ: Princeton University Press).

Cockett, R. (1994) *Thinking the Unthinkable: Think-Tanks and the Economic Counter-Revolution 1931–1983* (London: Harper Collins).

Cohen, Jean L. (2006) 'Sovereign equality vs. imperial right: The battle over the "New World Order"', *Constellations*, 13(4): 485–505.

Cohn, C. (1987) 'Sex and death in the rational world of defense intellectuals', *Signs*, 12(4): 687–718.

Coleman, William and Underhill, Geoffrey (eds) (1998) *Regionalism and Global Economic Integration: Europe, Asia, and the Americas* (London: Routledge).

Collier, P. (2007) *The Bottom Billion: Why the Poorest Countries Are Failing and What Can Be Done about It* (Oxford: Oxford University Press).

Collier, P., Elliott, V., Håvard, H., Hoeffler, A., Reynal-Querol, A. and Sambanis, N. (2003) *Breaking the Conflict Trap: Civil War and Development Policy* (Oxford: Oxford University Press for the World Bank).

Collins, Alan (2007) 'Forming a security community: Lessons from ASEAN', *International Relations of the Asia-Pacific*, 7(2): 203–35; 218–19.

Commission of the European Communities (2008) 'Proposal for a Regulation of the European Parliament and of the Council on Credit Rating Agencies', Brussels, 11 November.

Connor, W. (1993) *Ethnonationalism: The Quest for Understanding* (Princeton, NJ: Princeton University Press).

Connor, W. (1996) 'Beyond reason: The nature of the ethnonational bond', in J. Hutchinson and A.D. Smith (eds), *Ethnicity* (Oxford: Oxford University Press).

Conversi, D. (2004) 'Conceptualizing nationalism: An introduction to Walker Connor's work', in D. Conversi (ed.), *Ethnonationalism in the Contemporary World: Walker Connor and the Study of Nationalism* (London: Routledge).

Cooper, Andrew, Hughes, Christopher and De Lombaerde, Philippe (eds) (2007) *Regionalisation and Global Governance: The Taming of Globalisation?* (London: Routledge).

Cooper, George (2008) *The Origin of Financial Crises: Central Banks, Credit Bubbles and the Efficient Market Fallacy* (Hampshire: Harriman House).

Cooper, S., Hawkins, D., Jacoby, W. and Nielson, D. (2008) 'Yielding sovereignty to international institutions: Bringing system structure back in', *International Studies Review*, 10(3): 501–24.

Corrêa, S. and Jolly, S. (2008) 'Development's encounter with sexuality: Essentialism and beyond', in A. Cornwall, S. Corrêa and S. Jolly (eds), *Development with a Body: Sexuality, Human Rights and Development* (London: Zed), pp. 22–44.

Cox, M. (2001) 'Whatever happened to American decline? International relations and the new United States hegemony', *New Political Economy*, 6(3): 311–40.

Cox, M. (2003) 'The Empire's back in town: Or America's imperial temptation – Again', *Millennium: Journal of International Studies*, 32(1): 1–27.

Crenshaw, Martha (1981) 'The causes of terrorism', *Comparative Politics*, 13(4): 379–99.

Cronin, Audrey (2002/03) 'Behind the curve: Globalization and international terrorism', *International Security*, 27(3): 30–58.

Croome, J. (1995) *Reshaping the World Trading System: A History of the Uruguay Round* (Geneva: World Trade Organisation).

Dahl, R. (1999) 'Can international organisations be democratic?', in I. Shapiro and C. Hacker Gordon (eds), *Democracy's Edge* (Cambridge: Cambridge University Press), p. 17.

Dahl, Robert (1971) *Polyarchy: Participation and Observation* (New Haven: Yale University Press).

Dahl, Robert (1999) 'Can international organizations be democratic?' in Ian Shapiro and Casiano Hacker-Cordon (eds), *Democracy's Edges* (Cambridge: Cambridge University Press), pp. 19–36.

Dalby, S. (2009) *Security and Environmental Change* (Cambridge: Polity Press).

Dan, S. (2008) 'China's energy policy and its development', in Antonio Marquina (ed.), *Energy Security: Visions from Asia and Europe* (Houndmills–Basingstoke–Hampshire–New York: Palgrave Macmillan), pp. 135–46.

Declassified Key Judgements of the National Intelligence Estimate: 'Trends in Global Terrorism: Implications for the United States' April 2006 [cited 6 November 2007]. Available from http://www.dni.gov/press_releases/Declassified_NIE_Key_Judgments.pdf.

Deiter, H. and Higgott, R. (2003) 'Exploring alternative theories of economic regionalism: From trade to finance in Asian co-operation', *Review of International Political Economy*, 10(3): 430–54.

Deng, Francis M. et al. (1996) *Sovereignty as Responsibility: Conflict Management in Africa* (Washington, DC: The Brookings Institution).

Deudney, D. (2006) 'Security', in A. Dobson and R. Eckersley (eds), *Political Theory and the Ecological Challenge* (Cambridge: Cambridge University Press), pp. 516–58.

Di John, J. (2008) 'Conceptualising the Causes and Consequences of Failed States: A Critical Review of the Literature', *Development as State-Making*, no 25 (January), Crisis States Research Centre [Online] Available at: http://se1.isn.ch/serviceengine/FileContent?serviceID=ISN&fileid=E23CB.

Diamond, Larry (1999) *Developing Democracy: Toward Consolidation* (Baltimore: Johns Hopkins University Press).

Diamond, Larry (2008) *The Spirit of Democracy: The Struggle to Build Free Societies Throughout the World* (New York: Times Books).

Diamond, Larry, Linz, Juan J., Lipset, Seymour Martin (eds) (1990) *Politics in Developing Countries: Comparing Experiences with Democracy*, 2nd edn (Boulder, CO: Lynne Rienner).

Doran, Michael Scott (2002) 'Somebody else's civil war', *Foreign Affairs*, 81(1): 22–42.

Dow Jones International News (2008) 'IEA sees global oil production peaking in 2020 – Report', 15 December.

Downs, E.S. (2007) 'The fact and fiction of Sino-African energy relations', *China Security*, 3 (Summer): 42–68.

Doyle, Michael W. and Nicholas Sambanis (2000) 'International peacebuilding: A theoretical and quantitative analysis', *American Political Science Review*, 94(4): 779–801.

Drezner, D.W. (2001) 'Globalization and policy convergence', *International Studies Review*, 3(1): 53–78.

Drezner, Daniel W. (2007) *All Politics Is Global: Explaining International Regulatory Regimes* (Princeton, NJ: Princeton University Press).

Duffield, M. (2000) 'Globalisation, transborder trade and war economies', in M. Berdal and D. Malone (eds), *Greed & Grievance: Economic Agendas in Civil Wars* (Boulder, CO: Lynne Rienner), pp. 69–90.

Dupont, A. (2001) *East Asia Imperilled: Transnational Challenges to Security* (Cambridge: Cambridge University Press).

Durch, William J. (ed.) (2006) *Twenty-First-Century Peace Operations* (Washington, DC: US Institute of Peace).

Duyvesteyn, I. and Angstrom, J. (eds) (2005) *Rethinking the Nature of War* (London and New York: Frank Cass).

Economy, E.C. (2007) 'The great leap backwards: The costs of China's environmental crisis', *Foreign Affairs*, 86(5): 38–59.

Edgecliffe-Johnson, A. (2009) 'Wen and Putin lecture western leaders', *Financial Times*, 29 January.

Edwards, Michael (2004) *Civil Society* (Oxford: Polity Press).

Eichenberg, E.C. (2003) 'Gender difference in public attitude toward the use of force by the United States, 1990–2003', *International Security*, 28(1): 110–41.

Elhefnawy, N. (2008) 'The impending oil shock', *Survival*, 50(2) (April–May): 37–66.

Elliott, K. and Hufbauer, G. (2002) 'Ambivalent multilateralism and the emerging backlash: The IMF and the WTO', in S. Patrick and F. Shephard (eds), *Multilateralism and US Foreign Policy: Ambivalent Engagement* (Boulder, CO: Lynn Reinner)

Elliott, L. (2004) *The Global Politics of the Environment* (New York: NYU Press).

Emmott, B. (2008) *Rivals: How the Power Struggle between China, India and Japan Will Shape Our Next Decade* (London: Allen Lane).

Energy Information Administration (EIA) (2009) *International Energy Outlook 2009*, Washington, DC, May.

Enloe, C. (2000) *Bananas, Beaches and Bases: Making Feminist Sense of International Politics*, 2nd edn (London and Berkeley, CA: University of California Press).

Environmental Politics (2008) *Perspectives on Justice, Democracy and Global Climate Change*, Special Issue, 17(4).

Epsing-Anderson, G. (1990) *The Three Worlds of Welfare Capitalism* (Princeton: Princeton University Press).

Erlanger, S. and Castle, S. (2009) 'Growing economic crisis threatens the idea of one Europe', *New York Times*, 2 March.

Etzioni, A. (1992–93) 'The evils of self-determination', *Foreign Policy*, 89 (Summer): 21–35.

EU Energy (2008) 'Climate change a greater risk than financial crisis: Barroso', Issue 196, 28 November.

European Commission (2005) *Green Paper on a European Programme for Critical Infrastructure Protection*, COM(2005) 576 final, Brussels.

European Commission (2008) *An EU Energy Security and Solidarity Action Plan. Second Strategic Energy Review.* Communication from the Commission to the European Parliament, the Council, the European Economic and Social Committee of the Regions, Brussels, November.

European Council (2007) *Presidency Conclusions*, Brussels, 8–9 March 2007.

European Council (2009a) *Presidency Conclusions*, CONCL 1 7880/09, Brussels, 20 March 2009.

European Council (2009b) *Presidency Compromise Proposal for Financing of the Infrastructure Projects Put Forward by the Commission as Part of the EERP [European Economic Recovery Plan]*, 7848/1/09 REV 1, Brussels, 20 March 2009.

European Parliament and European Council (2009) *Directive 2009/28/EC on the Promotion of the Use of Energy from Renewable Sources and Amending and Subsequently Repealing Directives 2001/77/EC and 003/30/EC*, Brussels, 2 April 2009.

European Parliament. Committee on Economic and Monetary Affairs (2009) 'Draft Report on the Proposal for a Regulation of the European Parliament and of the Council on Credit Rating Agencies', Strasbourg: 13 January.

Evans, Gareth (2008) *The Responsibility to Protect: Ending Mass Atrocity Crimes Once and for All* (Washington, DC: The Bookings Institution).

Evans, Mark G. (2005) *Policy Transfer in Global Perspective* (London: Ashgate).

Evans, Sally and Nkululeko Ncana (2009) 'Xenophobic attacks return', *The South African Times* (22 July). http://www.thetimes.co.za/News/Article.aspx?id=1037748.

Evans-Pritchard, Ambrose (2009) 'World faces hi-tech crunch as China eyes ban on rare metal exports', *Telegraph*, 24 August 2009 (Online Version).

Falk, Richard (2003) 'Humanitarian Intervention: A Forum', *Nation*, 14 July.

Fawcett, Louise and Hurrell, Andrew (eds) (1996) *Regionalism in World Politics: Regional Organization and International Order* (Oxford: Oxford University Press).

Feinstein, Lee (2007) 'Darfur and Beyond: What Is Needed to Prevent Mass Atrocities', Council on Foreign Relations Special Report, Washington, DC.

Ferguson, N (2009) Interview, *The New Statesman*, 2 July, 2009.

Ferguson, N. (2004) *Colossus: The Rise and Fall of the American Empire* (London: Allen Lane).

Ferguson, N. (2005) 'Sinking globalization', *Foreign Affairs*, 84(7) (December): 64–77.

Ferguson, Y.H. and Mansbach, R.W. (2004) *Remapping Global Politics* (Cambridge: Cambridge University Press).

Financial Times (2008) 'Energy: The dawn of a disturbing new reality', 3 November.

Fine, B. (2003) 'Neither the Washington nor the post-Washington consensus', in B. Fine, C. Lapavitas and J. Pincus (eds), *Development Policy in the Twenty-First Century: Beyond the Washington Consensus* (London: Routledge), pp. 1–27.

Finnemore, Martha (2003) *The Purpose of Intervention: Changing Beliefs about the Use of Force* (Ithaca: Cornell University Press).

Foreign Policy (2008) 'The Failed State Index 2008', no. 167 (July/August), pp. 64–68.

Fortna, Virginia Page (2003) 'Inside and out: Peacekeeping and the duration of peace after civil and interstate wars', *International Studies Review*, 5(4): 97–114.

Fortna, Virginia Page (2004) 'Does peacekeeping keep peace? International intervention and the duration of peace after civil war', *International Studies Quarterly*, 48(2): 269–92.

Fortna, Virginia Page (2008) *Does Peacekeeping Work? Shaping Belligerents' Choices after Civil War* (Princeton, NJ: Princeton University Press).

Foucault, Michel (2007) *Security, Territory, Population: Lectures at the Collège de France, 1977–1978,* translated by Graham Burchell (London: Palgrave Macmillan; French edition 2004).

Foucault, Michel (2008) *The Birth of Biopolitics: Lectures at the Collège de France, 1978–1979,* translated by Graham Burchell (London: Palgrave Macmillan; French edition 2004).

Frank, A.G. (1969) *Capitalism and Underdevelopment in Latin America* (New York: Monthly Review Press).

Frankel, Jeffrey (1997) *Regional Trading Blocs in the World Economic System* (Washington, DC: Institute for International Economics).

Freedman, L. (1994) *War* (Oxford, New York: Oxford University Press).

Freedman, L. (1998) 'The changing forms of military conflict', *Survival*, 40(4): 39–56.

Freedom House (2009) Freedom in the World 2009: Global Data, at http://www.freedomhouse.org/uploads/fiw09/FIW09_Tables&GraphsForWeb.pdf.

Friedberg, A.L. (1989) 'The strategic implications of relative economic decline', *Political Science Quarterly*, 104(3): 401–31.

Friedman, Milton and Schwartz, Anna Jacobson (1963) *A Monetary History of the United States, 1857–1960* (Princeton, NJ: Princeton University Press).

Friedman, T.L. (2006) 'The first law of petropolitics', *Foreign Policy* (May–June): 28–36.

Fukuyama, F. (1989) 'The end of history?' *The National Interest*, 16 (Summer): 3–18.

Fukuyama, F. (1992) *The End of History and the Last Man* (New York: Free Press).

Fukuyama, F. (1998) 'Women and the evolution of world politics', *Foreign Affairs*, 77(5): 24–40.

Fukuyama, Francis (2004) *State-Building: Governance and World Order in the 21st Century* (Ithaca: Cornell University Press).

Galbraith, John Kenneth (1993) *A Short History of Financial Euphoria* (London: Penguin).

Galbraith, John Kenneth (1997 [1955]) *The Great Crash 1929* (New York: Mariner)

Gallagher, P. and Stoler, A. (2009) 'Critical mass as an alternative framework for multilateral trade negotiations', *Global Governance*, 15(3): 375–92.

Gallarotti, Giulio M. (2000) 'The advent of the prosperous society: The rise of the guardian state and structural change in the world economy', *Review of International Political Economy*, 7(1) (January): 1–52.

Gallarotti, Giulio M. (2009) *The Power Curse: Influence and Illusion in World Politics* (Boulder, CO: Lynne Rienner).

Gamble, A. (2009a) 'The western ideology', *Government and Opposition*, 44(1): 1–19.

Gamble, A. (2009b) *The Spectre at the Feast: Capitalist Crisis and the Politics of Recession* (Basingstoke: Palgrave Macmillan).

Gamble, Andrew and Payne, Anthony (eds) (1996) *Regionalism and World Order* (New York: St Martin's Press).

Garnaut, R. (2008) *The Garnaut Climate Change Review* (Cambridge: Cambridge University Press).

Garvey, J. (2008) *The Ethics of Climate Change* (London: Continuum).

Gat, A. (2007) 'The return of authoritarian great powers', *Foreign Affairs*, 86(4): 59–69.

Gawdat, B. (2008) 'Sovereign wealth funds: Dangers and opportunities', *International Affairs*, 84(6): 1189–204.

Geddes, Barbara (1999) 'What do we know about democratization after twenty years?', *Annual Review of Political Science*, 2 (June): 115–44.

Gellner, E. (1983) *Nations and Nationalism* (Ithaca: Cornell University Press).

German Advisory Council on Global Change (WBGU), *Climate Change as a Security Risk.* Summary for Policy Makers, Berlin, 29 May 2007.

German Ministry of Interior (2008) *Protecting Critical Infrastructures – Risks and Crisis Management. A Guide for Companies and Government Authorities*, Berlin, January 2008.

Giddens, A. (2009) *The Politics of Climate Change* (Cambridge: Polity Press).

Giles, C. (2009) 'BIS calls for global financial reforms' *Financial Times*, 29 June.

Gill, Stephen (2003) *Power and Resistance in the New World Order* (London: Palgrave Macmillan).

Giry, S. (2006) 'France and its Muslims', *Foreign Affairs*, 85(5) (September/October): 87–104.

Givens, Terry, Freeman, Gary P. and Leal, David L. (eds) (2009) *Immigration Policy and Security: US, European, and Commonwealth Perspectives* (Abingdon: Routledge).

Godement, F., Nicolas, F. and Yakushiji, T. (eds) (2004) *Asia and Europe. Cooperating for Energy Security.* A Council for Asia-Europe Cooperation (*CAEC*)-Task Force Report (Paris: Institut Francais des Relations Internationals/ IFRI).

Goldman Sachs (2001) *Building Better Global Economic BRICs* (New York: Goldman Sachs Global Economic Group).

Goldman Sachs (2007) *BRICs and Beyond* (New York: Goldman Sachs Global Economic Group).

Gopinath, Meenakshi (2007) 'Gender and NTS Formulations in South Asia', Policy Brief presented at the NTS-Asia Inaugural Meeting, 8–9 January, Singapore.

Gordon, Philip H. and Shapiro, Jeremy (2004) *Allies at War: America, Europe, and the Crisis over Iraq* (New York: McGraw-Hill).

Gowa, J. (1983) *Closing the Gold Window: Domestic Politics and the End of Bretton Woods* (Ithaca: Cornell University Press).

Gray, C. (1999) 'Clausewitz rules, OK? The future is the past – With GPS', *Review of International Studies*, 25(5): 161–82.

Gray, Colin S. (2007) *War, Peace and International Relations: An Introduction to Strategic History* (London: Routledge).

Grieco, Joseph (1995) 'The Maastricht Treaty, Economic and Monetary Union and the Neo-Realist Research Programme', *Review of International Studies*, 21(1): 21–40.

Grieco, Joseph (1999) 'Realism and regionalism: American power and German and Japanese institutional strategies during and after the Cold War', in Ethan B. Kapstein and Michael Mastanduno (eds), *Unipolar Politics: Realism and State Strategies after the Cold War* (New York: Columbia University Press), pp. 107–31.

Gries, Peter Hays (2005) 'China eyes the hegemon', *Orbis: A Journal of World Affairs*, 49(3): 401–12.

Griffin, P. (2007) 'Sexing the economy in a neo-liberal world order: Neo-liberal discourse and the (Re)production of heteronormative heterosexuality', *British Journal of Politics and International Relations*, 9(2): 220–38.

Griffin, P. (2009) *Gendering the World Bank: Neoliberalism and the Gendered Foundations of Global Governance* (Basingstoke and New York: Palgrave Macmillan).

Grimes, Scott (2002) 'San Diego-Tijuana: Microregionalism and metropolitan spillover', in Shaun Breslin and Glenn Hook (eds), *Microregionalism and World Order* (Basingstoke: Palgrave Macmillan), pp. 23–41.

Grimes, W.W. (2009) *Currency and Contest in East Asia: The Great Power Politics of Financial Regionalism* (Ithaca: Cornell University Press).

Grugel, Jean (2002) *Democratization: A Critical Introduction* (Houndmills: Palgrave Macmillan).

Grugel, Jean (2006) 'Regionalist governance and transnational collective action in Latin America', *Economy and Society*, 35(2): 209–31.

Gunaratna, Rohan (2003) 'Sri Lanka: Feeding the Tamil Tigers', in K. Ballentine and J. Sherman (eds), *The Political Economy of Armed Conflict – Beyond Greed and Grievance* (London: Lynne Rienner).

Gunther, Richard (1991) 'Spain: The very model of the modern elite settlement', in John Higley and Richard Gunther (eds), *Elites and Democratic Consolidation in Latin America and Southern Europe* (Cambridge: Cambridge University Press), pp. 38–80.

Gurr, T.R. (1996) *Minorities at Risk: A Global View of Ethnopolitical Conflicts* (Washington, DC: United States Institute of Peace Press).

Haas, E.B. (1990) *When Knowledge Is Power: Three Models of International Organizations* (Berkley: University of California Press).

Haas, Ernst (1958) *The Uniting of Europe* (Stanford: Stanford University Press).

Haas, Ernst (1975) *The Obsolescence of Regional Integration Theory* (Berkeley: Institute of International Studies Working Paper).

Haas, Hein de (2005) 'International migration, remittances and development: Myths and fact', *Global Migration Perspectives No. 30* (Geneva: Global Commission of International Migration, April 2005).

Haas, P. (1990) *Saving the Mediterranean* (New York: Columbia University Press).

Haass, R.N. (2008) 'The age of nonpolarity – What will follow US dominance', *Foreign Affairs*, May/June.

Hafner-Burton, E. and Pollack, M.A. (2002) 'Mainstreaming gender in global governance', *European Journal of International Relations*, 8(3): 339–73.

Haggard, S. (2004) 'Institutions and growth in East Asia', *Studies in Comparative International Development*, 38(4): 53–81.

Hale, D. (2004) 'China's growing appetites', *The National Interest*, 76: 137–47.

Hall, P.A. (1989) *The Political Power of Economic Ideas: Keynesianism across Nations* (Princeton: Princeton University Press).

Hall, P.A. and Soskice, D. (eds) (2001) *Varieties of Capitalism: The Institutional Foundations of Comparative Advantage* (Oxford: Oxford University Press).

Hall, R.B. (1999) *National Collective Identity: Social Constructs and International Systems* (New York: Columbia University Press).

Hall, R.B. (2007) 'Explaining "market authority" and liberal stability: Toward a sociological-constructivist synthesis', *Global Society*, 21(3): 319–42.

Hall, S. (1985) 'Signification, representation, ideology: Althusser and the post-structuralist debates', *Critical Studies in Mass Communication*, 2(2): 91–114.

Halliday, F. (2009) 'International relations in a post-hegemonic age', *International Affairs*, 85(1): 37–51.

Hammerstad, Anne (2009) 'The securitisation of refugees and its impact on the international refugee regime'. Paper presented at the International Studies Association Annual Conference. New York: 16 February 2009.

Hampson, Fen Osler et al. (2001) *Madness in the Multitude: Human Security and World Disorder* (Oxford: Oxford University Press).

Hans, Asha and Suhrke, Astri (1997) 'Responsibility sharing', in James Hathaway (ed.), *Reconceiving International Refugee Law* (The Hague: Kluwer Law International).

Hanson, Victor Davis (2002) 'Defending the West', *City Journal*, 25 February.

Hanson, V.D. (2003) *Mexifornia: A State of Becoming* (San Francisco: Encounter Books).

Hardin, G. (1968) 'The tragedy of the commons', *Science*, 162: 1243–8.

Harmon, Christopher C. (2001) 'Five strategies of terrorism', *Small Wars & Insurgencies*, 12(3): 39–66.

Harvey, D. (2003) *The New Imperialism* (Oxford: Oxford University Press).

Harvey, D. (2007) *A Brief History of Neoliberalism* (Oxford: Oxford University Press).

Hatton, Timothy and Williamson, Jeffrey (2005) *Global Migration and the World Economy: Two Centuries of Policy and Performance* (Cambridge, MA: MIT Press).

Hegel, G.W.F. (1969) 'Philosophy of law', in W. Ebenstein (ed.), *Great Political Thinkers*, 4th edn (New York: Holt, Rinehart & Winston).

Heginbotham, E. and Samuels, R.J. (1998) 'Mercantile realism and Japanese foreign policy', *International Security*, 22(4): 171–203.

Held, D. (1995) *Democracy and the Global Order: From the Modern State to Cosmopolitan Governance* (Cambridge: Polity Press).

Held, D. (1999) 'The transformation of political community: Rethinking democracy in the context of globalization', in Ian Shapiro and Casiano Hacker-Cordon (eds), *Democracy's Edges* (Cambridge: Cambridge University Press), pp. 84–111.

Held, D. (2002) 'Law of states, law of peoples: Three models of sovereignty', *Legal Theory*, 8(1): 1–44.

Held, D. (2005) *Democracy and the Global Order: From the Modern State to Cosmopolitan Democracy* (Cambridge: Polity Press).

Held, D., McGrew, A., Goldblatt, D. and Perraton, J. (1999) *Global Transformations: Politics, Economics and Culture* (Stanford: Stanford University Press).

Helleiner, E. (1994) *States and the Reemergence of Global Finance* (Ithaca: Cornell University Press).

Henry, Laurence (2007) 'The ASEAN way and community integration: Two different models of regionalism', *European Law Journal*, 13(6): 857–79.

Herd, Graeme P. and Ella Akerman (2002) 'Russian strategic realignment and the post-post Cold War era?', *Security Dialogue*, 33(3): 357–72.

Herrmann, R.K., Tetlock, P.E. and Diascro, M.N. (2001) 'How Americans think about trade: Reconciling conflicts among money, power, and principles', *International Studies Quarterly*, 45(2): 191–218.

Hettne, Björn, Sapir, Andras and Sunkel, Osvaldo (eds) (1999) *Globalism and the New Regionalism* (New York: St. Martin's Press).

Heupel, Monika (2008) 'Combining hierarchical and soft modes of governance: The UN Security Council's approach to terrorism and weapons of mass destruction proliferation after 9/11', *Cooperation and Conflict*, 43(7): 7–29.

Higgott, R.A. (2000) 'Contested globalization: The changing context and normative challenges', *Review of International Studies*, 26: 131–53.

Higgott, R.A. (2005) 'Old and new economic multilateralism: The WTO, IMF and the G20', in John English, Ramesh Thakur and Andrew Fenton Cooper (eds), *A Leaders 20 Summit: Why, How, Who and When?* (Tokyo, United Nations University Press).

Higgott, R.A. (2006) 'International political institutions', in R. Rhodes, S. Binder and B. Rockman (eds), *The Oxford Handbook of Political Institutions* (Oxford: Oxford University Press).

Hill, Christopher (1994) 'Europe's international role', in Simon Bulmer and Andrew Scott (eds), *Economic and Political Integration in Europe: Internal Dynamics and Global Context* (Oxford: Blackwell), pp. 103–26.

Hinsley, F.H. (1966) *Sovereignty* (London: Watts).

Hirst, P. and Thompson, G. (1999) *Globalization in Question*, 2nd edn (Oxford: Polity Press).

Hirst, P. and Thompson, G. (2003) 'Globalization – A necessary myth?', in A.G. McGrew and D. Held (eds), *The Global Transformations Reader: An Introduction to the Globalization Debate*, 2nd edn (Cambridge, UK; Malden, MA: Polity Press), pp. 98–106.

Hlaing, Kyaw Yin (2009) 'Setting the rules for survival: Why the Burmese military regime survives in an age of democratization', *The Pacific Review*, 22(3): 271–91.

Hobsbawm, E.J. (1983) 'Introduction: Inventing traditions', in E. Hobsbawm and T. Ranger (eds), *The Invention of Tradition* (Cambridge: Cambridge University Press).

Hobsbawm, E.J. (1990) *Nations and Nationalism since 1780: Programme, Myth, Reality* (Cambridge: Cambridge University Press).

Hoekmann, B. and Kostecki, M. (2001) *The Political Economy of the World Trading System* (Oxford: Oxford University Press).

Hoffman, Bruce (1998) *Inside Terrorism* (New York: Columbia University Press).

Hoffman, Brucs (2002) 'Defining terrorism', in R.D. Howard and R.L. Sawyer (eds), *Terrorism and Counter-terrorism: Understanding the New Security Environment* (New York: McGraw-Hill).

Hollingsworth, J.R. and Boyer, R. (eds) (1997) *Contemporary Capitalism: The Embeddedness of Institutions* (Cambridge: Cambridge University Press).

Homer-Dixon, T. (1999) *The Environment, Scarcity and Violence* (Princeton, NJ: Princeton University Press).

Homer-Dixon, T. (2006) *The Upside of Down: Catastrophe, Creativity, and the Renewal of Civilization* (Washington: Island Press).

Hooper, C. (2001) *Manly States: Masculinities, International Relations and Gender Politics* (Chichester and New York: Columbia University Press).

Horowitz, D.L. (2000) *Ethnic Groups in Conflict*, 2nd edn (Berkeley: University of California Press).

Howard, M.E. (1983) *Clausewitz* (Oxford, New York: Oxford University Press).

Hoyos, C. (2007) 'The new seven sisters: Oil and gas giants dwarf western rivals', *Financial Times*, 11 March, www.ft.com/indepth/7sisters.

Huang, Y. (2008) *Capitalism with Chinese Characteristics: Entrepreneurship and the State* (Cambridge: Cambridge University Press).

Hulme, M. (2009) *Why We Disagree about Climate Change* (Cambridge: Cambridge University Press).

Human Rights Watch (2009) *Troops in Contact: Airstrikes and Civilian Deaths in Afghanistan*, Human Rights Watch, http://www.hrw.org/sites/default/files/reports/afghanistan0908web_0.pdf, 8 May.

Human Security Centre (2005) *Human Security Report 2005: War and Peace in the 21st Century* (New York: Oxford University Press).

Huntington, Samuel P. (1984) 'Will more countries become democratic?', *Political Science Quarterly*, 99(2): 193–218.

Huntington, Samuel P. (1991) *The Third Wave: Democratization in the Late Twentieth Century* (Norman, OK: University of Oklahoma Press).

Huntington, Samuel P. (1991–92) 'How countries democratize', *Political Science Quarterly*, 106(4): 579–616.

Huntington, Samuel P. (1996) *The Clash of Civilizations and the Remaking of World Order* (New York: Simon & Schuster).

Huntington, S.P. (1989) 'The US – Decline or renewal?', *Foreign Affairs*, 62(2): 76–96.

Huntington, S.P. (2005) *Who Are We? The Challenges to America's National Identity* (New York: Simon & Schuster).

Hurd, I. (1999) 'Legitimacy and authority in international politics', *International Organization*, 53(2): 379–408.

Hurrell, Andrew (1995) 'Explaining the resurgence of regionalism in world politics', *Review of International Studies*, 21(4): 331–58.

Hurrell, Andrew (2007) *On Global Order: Power, Values and the Constitution of International Society* (Oxford: Oxford University Press).

Huysmans, Jef and Buonfino, Alessandra (2008) 'Politics of exception and unease: Immigration, asylum and terrorism in parliamentary debates in the UK', *Political Studies*, 56(4) (December): 766–88.

Huysmans, Jef (2006) The Politics of Insecurity: Fear Migration and Asylum in the EU (Abingdon: Routledge).

International Energy Agency (IEA) (2007a) *World Energy Outlook 2007: China and India Insights* (Paris: IEA-Publications).

IEA (2007b) *Energy Security and Climate Policy: Assessing Interactions* (Paris: IEA Publications).

International Energy Agency (IEA) (2008a) *World Energy Outlook 2008* (Paris: IEA-Publications).

IEA (2008) *The European Union: IEA Energy Policies Review* (Paris: IEA-Publications).

Ikenberry, G.J. (2001) *After Victory: Institutions, Strategic Restraint, and the Rebuilding of Order after Major Wars* (Princeton, NJ: Princeton University Press).

Ikenberry, G.J., Mastanduno, M. and Wohlforth, W.C. (2009) 'Unipolarity, state behaviour and systemic consequences', *World Politics*, 61(1): 1–27.

Indo-Asian News Service (2008) 'Climate change adding to hunger, illnesses worldwide', 12 December.

Institute for Global Environmental Strategies (IGES) (2009) 'CDM Project Base', http://www.iges.or.jp/en/cdm/report_cdm.html (accessed 20 August 2009).

Intergovernmental Panel on Climate Change (IPCC) (2007) *Climate Change 2007: The Physical Science Basis. Summary for Policymakers. Contribution of Working Group I to the Fourth Assessment Report of the IPCC* (Geneva).

Inter Press News Service (2008) 'Environment: Health – A victim of climate change', 3 December.

Inter Press Service (2008) 'Sanitation: Millions eat vegetables irrigated with raw sewage', 20 August.

Intergovernmental Panel on Climate Change (IPCC) (2007) *Climate Change 2007: Impacts, Adaptation, and Vulnerability* (Fourth Assessment, Cambridge).

International Commission on Intervention and State Sovereignty (ICISS) (2001) *The Responsibility to Protect* (Ottawa: IDRC).

International Crisis Group (2008) *China's Thirst for Oil*. Asia Report No. 153. Brussels, 9 June.

International Food Policy Research Institute (2008) *Global Hunger Index: The Challenge of Hunger 2008*. Available at http://www.ifpri.org/pubs/cp/ghi08.pdf.

International Organisation for Migration (IOM) (2008a) World Migration 2008: Managing Labour Mobility in the Evolving Global Economy (Geneva: IOM).

International Organisation for Migration (IOM) (2008b) 'Addressing Mixed Migration Flows'. Presentation to the International Dialogue on Migration. Accessed on 15 January 2009 at: http://www.iom.int/jahia/webdav/shared/shared/mainsite/about_iom/en/council/96/Mixed_Migration_Flows_FINAL.pdf.

Jackson, R.H. (1993) 'The weight of ideas in decolonization: Normative change in international relations', in J. Goldstein and R.O. Keohane (eds), *Ideas and Foreign Policy: Beliefs, Institutions and Political Change* (Ithaca: Cornell University Press).

Jackson, Robert H. (2002) *The Global Covenant: Human Conduct in a World of States* (Oxford: Oxford University Press).

Jakobson, Linda (2008) 'Does China have an "energy diplomacy"? Reflections on China's energy security and its international dimensions', in Antonio Marquina (ed.), *Energy Security. Visions from Asia and Europe* (Hampshire–New York: Palgrave Macmillan), pp. 121–34.

James, A. Baker III Institute for Public Policy of Rice University (2007) *The Changing Role of National Oil Companies in International Energy Markets*, Baker Institute Policy Report, No. 35 (Houston: James Baker III Institute, March).

James, Alan (1986) *Sovereign Statehood: The Basis of International Society* (London: Allen & Unwin).

Japan Institute of International Affairs (JIIA) (2001) *In Quest of Human Security* (Tokyo: Japan Institute of International Affairs).

Jayasuriya, Kanishka (ed.) (2004) *Governing the Asia Pacific: Beyond the 'New Regionalism'* (Basingstoke: Palgrave Macmillan).

Jensen, Richard Bach (2004) 'Daggers, rifles and dynamite: Anarchist terrorism in nineteenth century Europe', *Terrorism and Political Violence*, 16(1): 116–53.

Jervis, Robert (1999) 'Realism, neoliberalism, and cooperation: Understanding the debate', *International Security*, 24(1): 42–63.

Johnson, Chalmers (2002) *Blowback – The Costs and Consequences of American Empire* (London: Little, Brown, and Company).

Johnston, A.I. (2003) 'Is China a status quo power?', *International Security*, 27(4): 5–56.

Johnson, C. (2004) *The Sorrows of Empire: Militarism, Secrecy and the End of the Republic* (New York: Holt).

Jolly, S. (2000) ' "Queering" development: Exploring the links between same-sex sexualities, gender and development', *Gender and Development*, 8(1): 78–88.

Kabeer, N. (1994) *Reversed Realities: Gender Hierarchies in Development Thought* (London: Verso).

Kaldor, M. (2006) *New & Old Wars* (Stanford: Stanford University Press).

Kalicki, J.H. and Goldwyn, D.L. (eds) (2005) *Energy and Security. Toward a New Foreign Policy Strategy* (Baltimore: Johns Hopkins University Press).

Kalyvas, S.N. (2001) ' "New" and "old" civil wars: A valid distinction?', *World Politics*, 54(1): 99–118.

Katz, R. (1998) *Japan: The System that Soured* (Armonk: M.E. Sharpe).

Katzenstein, Peter (2002) 'Regionalism in Asia', in Shaun Breslin, Christopher Hughes, Nicola Phillips and Ben Rosamond (eds), *New Regionalisms in the Global Political Economy: Theories and Cases* (London: Routledge), pp. 104–18.

Kaul, I., Grunberg, I. and Stern, M. (eds) (1999) *Global Public Goods: International Cooperation in the 21st Century* (New York: Oxford University Press).

Keane, J. (2003) *Global Civil Society?* (Cambridge: Cambridge University Press).

Keane, John (1988) *Democracy and Civil Society* (London: Verso).

Keegan, J. (1994) *A History of Warfare* (New York: Alfred A. Knopf).

Keidel, A. (2007) 'The limits of a smaller, poorer China', *Financial Times*, 13 November.

Kenen, P.B. (2001) *The International Financial Architecture: What's New? What's Missing* (Washington: Institute for International Economics).

Kennedy, Paul (1987) *The Rise and Fall of the Great Powers: Economic Change and Military Conflict from 1500 to 2000* (New York: Random House).

Keohane, R.O. (1984) *After Hegemony: Cooperation and Discord in the World Political Economy* (Princeton, NJ: Princeton University Press).

Keohane, R.O. (1989) *International Institutions and State Power: Essays in International Relations Theory* (Boulder, CO: Westview Press).

Keohane, R.O. (1990) 'Multilateralism: An agenda for research', *International Journal*, 45(4): 731–64.

Keohane, R.O. (2005) 'The Contingent Legitimacy of Multilateralism', *Working Paper, No. 9*, Warwick University: EU FP6 Network of Excellence on Global Governance, Regionalisation and Regulation: The Role of the EU.

Keohane, R.O. and Nye, J.S. (1977) *Power and Interdependence: World Politics in Transition* (Boston: Little, Brown & Co).

Keohane, R.O., Macedo, S. and Moravcsik, A. (2009) 'Democracy-enhancing multilateralism', *International Organization*, 63(1): 1–31.

Keohane, Robert (1988) 'International institutions: Two approaches', *International Studies Quarterly*, 32(4): 379–96.

Keohane, Robert and Nye, Joseph (1977) *Power and Interdependence: World Politics in Transition* (Boston: Little, Brown and Company).

Keohane, Robert O. and Nye, Joseph S. Jr. (1977) *Power and Interdependence: World Politics in Transition* (Boston: Little, Brown and Company).

Kepel, Gilles (2003) 'The origins and development of the Jihadist movement: From anti-communism to terrorism', *Asian Affairs*, 34(2): 91–108.

Keppeler, J.H. (2007) *International Relations and Security of Energy Supply: Risks to Continuity and Geopolitical Risks*. External Study for the Directorate-General for External Policies of the Union. Policy Department (Brussels: European Parliament, February).

Kiely, R. (2007a) 'Poverty reduction through liberalization, or intensified uneven development?: Neo-liberalism and the myth of global convergence', *Review of International Studies*, 33(4): 415–34.

Kiely, R. (2007b) *The New Political Economy of Development* (Basingstoke: Palgrave Macmillan).

Kilcullen, David (2005) 'Countering global insurgency', *The Journal of Strategic Studies*, 28(4): 597–617.

Ki-moon, Ban (2009) 'Implementing the responsibility to protect', Report of the UN Secretary-General', A/63/677, 12 January.

Kimmitt, R.M. (2008) 'Public footprints in private markets: Sovereign wealth funds and the world economy', *Foreign Affairs*, 87(1): 119–30.

Kindleberger, C.P. (1973) *The World in Depression 1929–1939* (Berkeley: University of California Press).

Kindleberger, Charles P. and Aliber, Robert Z. (2005) *Manias, Panics and Crashes: A History of Financial Crises*, 5th edn (London: Palgrave Macmillan).

King, G. and Zeng, G.L. (2001) 'Improving forecasts of state failure', *World Politics*, 53(4) (July): 623–58.

Klaebel, A. (2007) *Unity and Separation in World Politics: Rethinking the Question of International Society* (Copenhagen: Department of Political Science, University of Copenhagen).

Klare, M.T. (2001) *Resource Wars – The New Landscape of Global Conflict* (New York: Metropolitan Books).

Klare, M.T. (2008) *Rising Powers, Shrinking Planet: The New Geopolitics of Energy* (New York: Metropolitan Books).

Kohli, Atul (ed.) (2004) *The Success of India's Democracy* (Cambridge: Cambridge University Press).

Kohn, Hans (1955) *Nationalism: Its Meaning and History* (Princeton, NJ: Van Nostrand).

Kolko, G. (1988) *Confronting the Third World: United States Foreign Policy* (New York: Pantheon Book).

Koppenfels, Amanda Klekowski von (2001) 'The Role of Regional Consultative Processes in Managing International Migration', *IOM Migration Research Series no. 3* (Geneva: IOM)

Kothari, U. (2005) 'Authority and expertise: The professionalisation of international development and the ordering of dissent', *Antipode*, 37(3): 425–46.

Kozul Wright, R. and Rayment, P. (2004) 'Globalization reloaded: An UNCTAD perspective, UNCTAD Discussion Papers no. 167, pp. 1–50.

Krain, M. (2005) 'International intervention and the severity of genocides and politicides', *International Studies Quarterly*, 49(2): 363–87.

Krasner, S.D. (1999) *Sovereignty: Organized Hypocrisy* (Princeton, NJ: Princeton University Press).

Krasner, Stephen D. (1999) *Sovereignty: Organized Hypocrisy* (Princeton, NJ: Princeton University Press).

Krugman, Paul (2008) *The Return of Depression Economics and the Crisis of 2008*, 2nd edn (London: Penguin).

Kruk, Margaret (2007) 'Global public health and biosecurity: Managing twenty-first century risks,' *Coping with Crisis Working Paper Series*, International Peace Academy, New York, March; available at http://www.ipacademy.org/our-work/coping-with-crisis/working-papers.

Kubicek, Paul (2009) 'The commonwealth of independent states: An example of failed regionalism?', Special Issue of *Review of International Studies*, 35: 237–56.

Lacy, M. (2005) *Security and Climate Change* (London: Routledge).

Lampton, D.M. (2008) *The Three Faces of Chinese Power: Might, Money, and Minds* (Berkeley: University of California Press).

Lardy, N.R. (1998) *China's Unfinished Economic Revolution* (Washington, DC: Brookings Institution Press).

Larner, W. (2003) 'Neoliberalism? Guest Editorial', *Environment and Planning D: Society and Space*, 21: 509–12.

Larosière, Jacques de (2009) *The High-Level Group on Financial Supervision in the EU*, chaired by Jacques de Larosière (Brussels, 25 February 2009), http://ec.europa.eu/internal_market/finances/docs/de_larosiere_report_en.pdf.

Larsson, R.L. (2006) *Russia's Energy Policy: Security Dimensions and Russia's Reliability as an Energy Supplier* (Stockholm: Swedish Defence Research Agency/FOI).

Lasswell, H. (1935) *Politics: Who Gets What, When, How* (Chicago: Chicago University Press).

Latham, R. (1997) *The Liberal Moment: Modernity, Security, and the Making of Postwar International Order* (New York: Columbia University Press).

Leiken, R.S. (2005) 'Europe's angry Muslims', *Foreign Affairs*, 84(4) (July/August): 120–35.

Leverett, F. and Noel, P. (2006) 'The new axis of oil', *National Interest* (Summer): 62–70.

Levy, J. (1998) 'The causes of war and the conditions of peace', *Annual Review of Political Science*, 1(1): 139–65.

Lijphart, Arend (1969) 'Consociational democracy', *World Politics*, 21(2): 207–25.

Lincoln, E.J. (2001) *Arthritic Japan: The Slow Pace of Economic Reform in Japan* (Washington: Brookings Institute Press).

Lind, M. (1994) 'In defense of liberal nationalism', *Foreign Affairs*, 73(3) (May/June): 87–99.

Lindberg, Todd (2005) 'Protect the people', *Washington Post*, 27 September.

Linz, Juan J. (1990) 'Presidents vs. parliaments: The virtues of parliamentarism', *Journal of Democracy*, 1(4): 84–91.

Lipset, Seymour Martin (1959) 'Some social requisites of democracy: Economic development and political legitimacy', *American Political Science Review*, 53: 69–105.

Lisowski, M. (2002) 'Playing the two-level game: US President Bush's decision to repudiate the Kyoto Protocol', *Environmental Politics*, 11(4): 101–19.

Little, Richard (2007) *The Balance of Power in International Relations: Metaphors, Myths and Models* (Cambridge: Cambridge University Press).

Loescher, Gil (1993) *Beyond Charity: International Cooperation and the Global Refugee Crises* (Oxford: Oxford University Press).

Loescher, Gil, Betts, Alexander and Milner, James (2008) *The United Nations High Commissioner for Refugees: The Policy and Practice of Refugee Protection in the 21st Century* (Abingdon: Routledge).

Luck, Edward (2006) *UN Security Council: Practice and Promise* (London: Routledge).

Luedtke, Adam (2009) 'Fortifying fortress Europe? The effect of September 11 on EU immigration policy', in Givens et al. (eds), *Immigration Policy and Security: US, European and Commonwealth Perspectives* (Abingdon: Routledge).

Lynch, T.J. and Singh, R.S. (2008) *After Bush: The Case for Continuity in American Foreign Policy* (Cambridge: Cambridge University Press).

Mack, Andrew (2007) *Global Political Violence: Explaining the Post Cold War Decline* (New York: International Peace Academy, Coping with Crisis Working Paper).

Maddison, A. (2001) *The World Economy: A Millennial Perspective* (Paris: Development Centre of the OECD).

Mahbubani, K. (2008) *The New Asian Hemisphere: The Irresistible Shift of Global Power to the East* (New York: Public Affairs).

Maizels, A., Palaskas, T. and Crowe, T. (1998) 'The Prebisch singer hypothesis revisited', in D. Sapford and J. Chen (eds), *Development Economics and Policy* (Basingstoke: Palgrave Macmillan), pp. 45–70.

Mandel, R. (2001) 'The privatization of security', *Armed Forces & Society*, 28(1): 129.

Mankiw, N.G. and Swagel, P.L. (2005) 'Antidumping: The third rail of trade policy', *Foreign Affairs*, 84(4) (July/August): 107–19.

Mann, M. (1993) *The Sources of Social Power: The Rise of Classes and Nation-States, 1760–1914*, vol. II (Cambridge: Cambridge University Press).

Mann, M. (2003) *Incoherent Empire* (London: Verso).

Manning, R. (2000) *The Asian Energy Factor, Myths and Dilemmas of Energy, Security and the Pacific Future* (New York: Palgrave).

Mansfield, Edward and Milner, Helen (1999) 'The new wave of regionalism', *International Organization*, 53(3): 589–627.

Mansfield, Edward and Milner, Helen (eds) (1997) *The Political Economy of Regionalism* (New York: Columbia University Press).

Marchand, M. (2000) 'Gendered representations of the global: Reading/Writing globalization', in R. Stubbs and G. Underhill (eds), *Political Economy and the Changing Global Order*, 2nd edn (Oxford: Oxford University Press), pp. 218–27.

Marquina, A. (ed.) (2008) *Energy Security: Visions from Asia and Europe* (Hampshire– New York: Palgrave Macmillan).

Martin, Lisa (2006) 'International economic institutions', in R. Rhodes, S. Binder and B. Rockman (eds), *The Oxford Handbook of Political Institutions* (Oxford: Oxford University Press), pp. 613–34.

Marx, K. (1913) *The Eighteenth Brumaire of Louis Bonaparte* (Chicago: Charles Kerr).

Mason, D.S. (2008) *The End of the American Century* (Lanham, MD: Rowman and Littlefield).

Mattli, Walter (1999) *The Logic of Regional Integration: Europe and Beyond* (Cambridge: Cambridge University Press).

Mayall, J. (1990) *Nationalism and International Society* (Cambridge: Cambridge University Press).

McDonald, A. (2008) '*Hors de Combat*: Post-September 11 challenges to the rules', in H.M. Hensel (ed.), *The Legitimate Use of Military Force: The Just War Tradition and the Customary Law of Armed Conflict* (Aldershot, UK; Burlington, VT: Ashgate), pp. 219–62.

McInnes, C. (2002) *Spectator-Sport War: The West and Contemporary Conflict* (Boulder, CO: Lynne Rienner).

McLeod, Ross (2000) 'Soeharto's Indonesia: A better class of corruption', *Agenda*, 7(2): 99–112.

McLuhan, Marshall (1964) *Understanding Media: The Extensions of Man* (New York: McGraw Hill).

Mearsheimer, J.J. (2001) *The Tragedy of Great Power Politics* (New York: W.W. Norton).

Mearsheimer, J.J. (2006) 'China's unpeaceful rise', *Current History* (April): 160–2.

Mendelsohn, Barak (2009) *Combating Jihadism: American Hegemony and Interstate Cooperation in the War on Terrorism* (Chicago: University of Chicago Press).

Mera, Laura Gomez (2005) 'Explaining Mercosur's survival: Strategic sources of Argentine–Brazilian convergence', *Journal of Latin American Studies*, 37(1): 109–40.

Meyer, J.W., Boli, J., Thomas, G.M. and Ramirez, F.O. (1997) 'World society and the nation-state', *American Journal of Sociology*, 103(1): 144–81.

Migdal, Joel (1988) *Strong States and Weak States: State-Society Relations and State Capabilities in the Third World* (Princeton, NJ: Princeton University Press).

Mignolo, Walter (2005) *The Idea of Latin America* (Oxford: Blackwell).

Migration Watch (2007a) *Submission to the House of Lords Select Committee on Economic Affairs on 'The Economic Impact of Immigration'* (London: Migration Watch UK, Economic Briefing Paper 1.18). Accessed at www.migrationwatchuk.com/ Briefingpapers/economic/1_18_submission_to_the_hol.asp.

Migration Watch (2007b) *Migration Benefit 'Equal to a Mars Bar a Month'*. Press Release (London: Migration Watch UK, 3 January 2007). Accessed at www.migrationwatchuk. com/pressreleases/pressreleases.asp?dt=01-January-2007.

Milanovic, B. (2007) 'Globalization and inequality', in D. Held and A. Kaya (eds) *Global Inequality* (Cambridge: Polity Press), pp. 11–32.

Minsky, Hyman P. (2008) *John Maynard Keynes* (New York: McGraw-Hill).

Mitrany, David (1943) *A Working Peace System* (London: Royal Institute for International Affairs).

Modood, T. (1997) 'Introduction: The politics of multiculturalism in the New Europe', in T. Modood and P. Werbner (eds), *The Politics of Multiculturalism in the New Europe: Racism, Identity and Community* (London: Zed Books).

Mohan, C. Raja (2007) 'Towards safe nuclear energy in Asia', *NTS-Asia Alert*, July.

Molden, David, de Fraiture, Charlotte and Rijsberman, Frank (2007) 'Water scarcity: The food factor', *Issues in Science & Technology*, 23(4) (1 July): 1–7.

Moore, Barrington (1966) *Social Origins of Dictatorship and Democracy: Lord and Peasant in the Making of the Modern World* (Boston: Beacon Press).

Moore, Thomas (2008) 'Racing to integrate, or cooperating to compete? Liberal and realist interpretations of China's new multilateralism', in Guoguang Wu and Helen Lansdowne (eds), *China Turns to Multilateralism: Foreign Policy and Regional Security* (London and New York: Routledge), pp. 35–50.

Moran, Daniel and Russell, James A. (2008) 'The militarization of energy security', *Strategic Insights*, 7(1) (February): 13.

Moravcsik, Andrew (1993) 'Preferences and power in the European Community: A liberal intergovernmentalist approach', *Journal of Common Market Studies*, 31(4): 473–524.

Mostov, Julie (2008) *Soft Borders: Rethinking Sovereignty and Democracy* (London: Palgrave Macmillan).

Mousseau, M. (2009) 'The social market roots of democratic peace', *International Security*, 33(4): 52–86.

Mousseau, Michael (2002/03) 'Market civilization and its clash with terror', *International Security*, 27(3): 5–29.

Moynihan, D.P. (1993) *Pandaemonium: Ethnicity in International Politics* (New York: Oxford University Press).

Moyo, Dambisa (2009) *Dead Aid: Why Aid Is Not Working and How There Is a Better Way for Africa* (New York: Farrar, Straus and Giroux).

MPI (Migration Policy Institute) (2007) 'Foreign-Born Population and Foreign Born as Percentage of the Total US Population, 1850 to 2007', *MPI Data Hub: Migration Facts,*

Stats and Maps. www.migrationinformation.org/datahub/charts/final.fb.shtml (accessed 22 April 2009).

Münkler, H. (2005) *The New Wars* (Oxford: Polity Press).

Murphy, C.N. (2000) 'Global governance: Poorly done and poorly understood', *International Affairs*, 76(4): 789–803.

Naim, M. (2009) 'Minilateralism: The magic number to get real international action', *Foreign Policy*, 173 (July/August): 136–35.

Narlikar, A. (2005) *The World Trade Organisation: A Very Short Introduction* (Oxford: Oxford University Press).

National Energy Policy Development Group (2001) *National Energy Policy* (Washington: White House).

National Intelligence Council (NIC) (2008) *Global Trends 2025: A Transformed World* (Washington, DC: National Intelligence Council).

Nau, H. (1990) *The Myth of America's Decline: Leading the World Economy in the 1980s* (Oxford: Oxford University Press).

Naughton, B. (2007) *The Chinese Economy: Transitions and Growth* (Cambridge, MA: MIT Press).

Ness, L. (2006) *Securing Utility and Energy Infrastructures* (Hoboken/New Jersey: John Wiley & Sons).

Netherlands Environmental Assessment Agency (2007) *Global Fossil CO_2 Emissions for 2006*, Den Hague, 21 June.

Newman, E. (2004) 'The "new wars" debate: A historical perspective is needed', *Security Dialogue*, 35(2): 173–89.

Nichols, Thomas M. (2005) 'Anarchy and order in the new age of prevention', *World Policy Journal*, 22(3): 1–23.

Nies, S. (2008) *Oil and Gas Delivery to Europe: An Overview of Existing and Planned Infrastructures* (Paris–Brussels: French Institute for International Relations).

Nye, J.S. (1990) *Bound to Lead: The Changing Nature of American Power* (New York: Basic Books).

Nye, Joseph S. Jr. (2004) *Soft Power: The Means to Success in World Politics* (New York: Public Affairs).

O'Donnell, Guillermo (1999) *Counterpoints: Selected Essays on Authoritarianism and Democracy* (Notre Dame: University of Notre Dame Press).

O'Donnell, Guillermo and Schmitter, Philippe C. (1986) *Transitions from Authoritarian Rule: Tentative Conclusions about Uncertain Democracies* (Baltimore: Johns Hopkins University Press).

O'Tuathail, G. and Agnew, J. (1992) 'Geopolitics and discourse: Practical geopolitical reasoning in American foreign policy', *Political Geography*, 11(2): 190–204.

Oakeshott, Michael (1976) 'On misunderstanding human conduct: A reply to my critics', *Political Theory*, 4(2) (August): 353–67.

Obama, B. (2009) 'From peril to Progress', White House address, 26 January, at http://www.whitehouse.gov/blog_post/Fromperiltoprogress/.

Oberthür, S. and Roche Kelly, C. (2008) 'European Union leadership in international climate policy: Achievements and challenges', *The International Spectator*, 43(3): 35–50.

O'Brien, R., Goetz, A.M., Scholte, J.A. and Williams, M. (2000) *Contesting Global Governance: Multilateral Economic Institutions and Global Social Movement* (Cambridge: Cambridge University Press).

Ohmae, K. (1990) *The Borderless World: Power and Strategy in the Interlinked Economy* (New York: Harper Business).

Ohmae, Kenichi (1995) *The End of the Nation-State: The Rise of Regional Economies* (New York: Simon and Schuster).

Olcott, Martha Brill (2005) 'The great powers in Central Asia', *Current History*, 104(684): 331–5.

ONS (Office for National Statistics) (2005) *Focus on People and Migration 2005* (London: ONS).

ONS (Office for National Statistics) (2009) *Populations Trends*, no. 135 (London: ONS, Spring).

Orwell, George (1949) *Nineteen Eighty-Four: A Novel* (London: Secker & Warburg).

Osborne, David and Gaebler, Ted (1992) *Reinventing Government: How the Entrepreneurial Spirit Is Transforming the Public Sector, from Schoolhouse to Statehouse, City Hall to the Pentagon* (Reading, MA: Addison-Wesley).

Osiander, A. (2001) 'Sovereignty, international relations, and the Westphalian myth', *International Organization*, 55(2) (Spring): 251–87.

Ostrom, Vincent, Tiebout, Charles M. and Warren, Robert (1961) 'The organization of government in metropolitan areas: A theoretical inquiry,' *American Political Science Review*, 55(3) (September): 831–42.

Ougaard, M. and Higgott, R. (eds) (2002) *Towards a Global Polity?* (London: Routledge).

Owens, P. (2008) 'Distinctions, distinctions: "Public" and "private" force?', *International Affairs*, 84(5): 977–90.

Oxford Research Group (2006) Global Response to Global Threats: Security for the 21st Century, Briefing Paper.

Page, John and Plaza, Sonia (2005) 'Migration Remittances and Development: A Review of Global Evidence', World Bank Draft Paper presented at the Plenary Session of the African Economic Research Consortium, 29 May, 2005.

Panagariya, A. (2005) 'Liberalizing agriculture', *Foreign Affairs*, 84(7) (December). [Online] Available at: http://www.foreignaffairs.org/20051201faessay84706/arvind-panagariya/liberalizing-agriculture.html.

Panagariya, A. (2008) *India: The Emerging Giant* (Oxford: Oxford University Press).

Panagariya, Arvind (1999) 'The regionalism debate: An overview', *The World Economy*, 22(4): 477–511.

Panitch, L. and Gindin, S. (2004) 'Finance and American empire', in L. Panitch and C. Leys (eds), *The Socialist Register: The Empire Reloaded* (London: Merlin Press), pp. 46–80.

Pape, R.A. (2009) 'Empire falls', *The National Interest* (January/February): 21–34.

Parekh, Bhikhu (1997) 'Rethinking humanitarian intervention', *International Political Science Review*, 18(1): 49–69.

Paris, R. (2001) 'Human security: Paradigm shift or hot air?', *International Security*, 26(2): 87–102.

Parpart, J. (1995) 'Deconstructing the gender "expert": Gender, development and the "vulnerable groups" ', in M. Marchand and J.L. Parpart (eds), *Feminism/Postmodernism/Development* (London: Routledge), pp. 221–43.

Parpart, J. and Zalewski, M. (eds) (2008) *Rethinking the 'Man' Question: Sex, Gender and Violence in International Relations* (London: Zed).

Partnoy, Frank (2006) 'How and why credit rating agencies are not like other gatekeepers', in Yasuyuki Fuchita and Robert E. Litan (eds), *Financial Gatekeepers: Can They Protect Investors?* (Washington, DC: Brookings).

Paterson, M. (1996) *Global Warming and Global Politics* (London: Routledge).

Paterson, M. (2009) 'Post-hegemonic climate politics', *British Journal of Politics and International Relations*, 11(1): 140–58.

Peck, J. and Tickell, A. (2002) 'Neoliberalizing space', *Antipode*, 34(3): 380–404.

Peet, R. (2003) *Unholy Trinity: The IMF, World Bank and WTO* (London: Zed Books).

Peterson, V.S. and Runyan, A.S. (1999) *Global Gender Issues*, 2nd edn (Oxford and Boulder, CO: Westview Press).

Peterson, V.S. (1999) 'Sexing political identities/nationalism as heterosexism', *International Feminist Journal of Politics*, 1(1): 34–65.

Pew Global Attitudes Project (2005) 'Islamic extremism: Common concern for Muslim and western publics' (14 July) [Online] Available at: http://pewglobal.org/reports/display.php?ReportID=248.

Pew Global Attitudes Project (2006) 'Muslims in Europe: Economic worries top concerns about religious and cultural identity' (6 June) [Online] Available at: http://pewglobal.org/reports/display.php?ReportID=254.

Phillips, Andrew (2009) 'How Al Qaeda lost Iraq', *Australian Journal of International Affairs*, 63(1): 64–84.

Phillips, M. (2006) *Londonistan* (New York: Encounter Books).

Pierson, P. (2000) 'Increasing returns, path dependence, and the study of politics', *American Political Science Review*, 94(2): 251–67.

Pijl, Kees van der (1998) *Transnational Classes and International Relations* (London: Routledge).

Plender, John (2008) 'The return of the State: How government is back at the heart of economic life,' *Financial Times* (22 August).

Podhoretz, Norman (2007) *World War IV: The long struggle against Islamofascism*, 1st edn (New York: Doubleday).

Pogge, T.W. (2002) *World Poverty and Human Rights: Cosmopolitan Responsibilities and Reforms* (Molden, MA: Blackwell).

Polanyi, Karl (1957 [1944]) *The Great Transformation: The Political and Economic Origins of Our Time* (Boston: Beacon).

Polidano, C. (2000) 'Measuring public sector capacity', *World Development*, 28(5): 805–22.

Pollard, Naomi, Latorre, Maria and Sriskandarajah, Dhananjayan (2008) *Floodgates or Turnstiles? Post-EU Enlargement Migration Flows to (and from) the UK* (London: Institute for Public Policy Research, 30 April 2008).

Pollard, Sidney (2006) *The Integration of the European Economy since 1815* (London: Taylor and Francis).

Power, Samantha (2002) 'Raising the cost of genocide', *Dissent*, 49(2): 69–77.

Prebisch, R. (1959) 'Commercial policy in the underdeveloped countries', *American Economic Review*, 44: 251–73.

Przeworski Adam, Michael Alvarez, Jose Antonio Cheibub, and Fernando Limongi (1996) 'What makes democracies endure', *Journal of Democracy*, 7(1): 39–55.

Putnam, Robert D. (1988) 'Diplomacy and domestic policy: The logic of two-level games', *International Organization*, 42(3) (Summer): 427–60.

Rabushka, Alvin and Shepsle, Kenneth (1972) *Politics in Plural Societies* (Stanford: Stanford University Press).

Radice, H. (2000) 'Globalization and national capitalisms: Theorizing convergence and differentiation', *Review of International Political Economy*, 7(4): 719–42.

Rai, S. (2008) *The Gender Politics of Development: Essays in Hope and Despair* (London: Zed).

Raine, Sarah (2009) *China's African Challenges* (Oxon/London/New York: IISS/ Routledge).

Ramo, J.C. (2004) *The Beijing Consensus* (London: The Foreign Policy Centre).

Ramsey, Paul (2002) *The Just War: Force and Political Responsibility* (Lanham: Rowman and Littlefield).

Rapoport, David C. (2001) 'The fourth wave: September 11 in the history of terrorism', *Current History*, 100(650): 419–24.

Read, R. (2004) 'The implications of increasing globalization and regionalism for the economic growth of small island states', *World Development*, 32(2): 365–78.

Record, J. (2003) *Bounding the Global War on Terrorism*, Strategic Studies Institute, US Army War College, December, available at http://www.strategicstudies institute.army.mil/pubs/display.cfm?pubID=207.

Record, Jeffrey (2004) *Dark Victory: America's Second War against Iraq* (Annapolis, MD: Naval Institute Press).

Reddy, Sanjay and Pogge, Thomas (2002) 'How not to count the poor', www. socialanalysis.org. Unpublished mimeo.

Reddy, S. and Pogge, T. (2003) 'Unknown: The extent, distribution and trend of global income poverty', www.socialanalysis.org. Unpublished mimeo.

Reilly, Benjamin (2001) *Democracy in Divided Societies: Electoral Engineering for Conflict Management* (Cambridge: Cambridge University Press).

Reinert, E.S. (2007) *How Rich Countries Got Rich ... and Why Poor Countries Stay Poor* (New York: Carroll & Graf).

Renan, E. (1994) 'Qu'est-ce qu'une nation?', in J. Hutchinson and A.D. Smith (eds), *Nationalism* (New York: Oxford University Press).

Reus-Smit, C. (1999) *The Moral Purpose of the State* (Princeton, NJ: Princeton University Press).

Reus-Smit, C. (2002) 'Imagining society: Constructivism and the English School', *British Journal of Politics and International Relations*, 4(3): 487–509.

Reuters News (2008a) 'Update 1 – Nearly 1 bln people hungry, food prices still high', 9 December.

Reuters News (2008b) 'UPDATE 2 – Poor accuse rich of meanness in UN climate fight', 13 December.

Reuters News (2008c) 'Interview – Food crisis, silent famine to continue: World Bank', 3 September.

Reuters (2009) 'China climate change report sets out options', http://www.reuters.com/ article/GCA-GreenBusiness/idUSTRE57G34W20090817 (accessed 20 August).

Risk Management (2007) 'Japanese earthquake renews nuclear energy safety concerns', 54(9) (1 September), http://www.allbusiness.com/environment-natural-resources/ environmental/8911215-1.html.

Roberts, A. (2003) 'Law and the use of force after Iraq', *Survival*, 45(2): 31.

Roberts, A. (2005) 'The "War on Terror" in historical perspective', *Survival*, 47(2): 101–30.

Roberts, Adam (1993) 'Humanitarian war: Military intervention and human rights', *International Affairs*, 69(3): 429–49.

Roberts, Adam (1998) 'More refugees, less asylum: A regime in transformation', *Journal of Refugee Studies*, 11(4): 375–95.

Roberts, Adam (2008) 'Open up'. Special Report in the *Economist* Magazine (London: The *Economist* Magazine, 3 January 2008).

Rodrik, D. (2001) *The Global Governance of Trade as if Development Really Mattered* (Geneva: United Nations Development Programme).

Rodrik, D. (2006) 'Goodbye Washington consensus? Hello Washington confusion? A review of the World Bank's economic growth in the 1990s: Learning from a decade of reform', *Journal of Economic Literature*, 44(4): 973–87.

Rodrik, D. (2007) *One Economics, Many Recipes: Globalization, Institutions, and Economic Growth* (Princeton: Princeton University Press).

Rosamond, Ben (2000) *Theories of European Integration* (Basingstoke: Palgrave Macmillan).

Rosamond, Ben (2007) 'The political sciences of European integration: Disciplinary history and EU studies', in Knud Erik Jørgensen, Mark A. Pollack and Ben Rosamond (eds), *The Handbook of European Union Politics* (London: Sage), pp. 7–30.

Rosand, Eric (2003) 'Security council resolution 1373, the counter-terrorism committee, and the fight against terrorism', *The American Journal of International Law*, 97(2): 333–41.

Rose, N. (1993) 'Government, authority and expertise in advanced liberalism', *Economy and Society*, 22(3): 283–99.

Rosecrance, R. (ed.) (1976) *America as an Ordinary Country: US Foreign Policy and the Future* (Ithaca: Cornell University Press).

Rosenau, J.N. (1992) 'Governance, order, and change in world politics', in J.N. Rosenau and E.-O. Czempiel (eds), *Governance Without Government: Order and Change in World Politics* (Cambridge: Cambridge University Press), pp. 1–29.

Rosenau, J.N. (1995) 'Governance in the twenty-first century', *Global Governance*, 13: 13–43.

Rosenau, J.N. (2003) *Distant Proximities: Dynamics beyond Globalization* (Princeton, NJ: Princeton University Press).

Rosenau, James N. (2003) *Distant Proximities: Dynamics Beyond Globalization* (Princeton, NJ: Princeton University Press).

Rosenblum, Marc (2009) 'Immigration and U.S. national interests: Historical cases and the contemporary debate' in Terry Givens, Gary Freeman and David Leal (eds), *Immigration Policy and Security: U.S., European, and Commonwealth Perspectives* (Abingdon, Oxon: Routledge).

Ross, George (1995) *Jacques Delors and European Integration* (New York: Oxford University Press).

Ross, M.L. (2001) 'Does oil hinder democracy?', *World Politics*, 53(3) (April): 325–61.

Ross, M.L. (2004a) 'How do natural resources influence Civil War: Evidence from thirteen cases', *International Organization*, 58 (Winter): 35–67.

Ross, M.L. (2004b) 'What do we know about natural resources and Civil War?', *Journal of Peace Research*, 41(3): 337–56.

Ross, R.S. (2006) 'Balance of power politics and the rise of China: Accommodation and balancing in East Asia', *Security Studies*, 15(3): 355–95.

Rossi, V. (2008) *Decoupling Debate Will Return: Emergers Dominate in Long Run*, Chatham House Briefing Note IEP BN 08/01 (London: Royal Institute for International Affairs).

Rostow, W. (1960) *The Stage of Economic Growth* (Cambridge: Cambridge University Press).

Rothberg, R.I. (2003) 'The failure and collapse of Nation-States: Breakdown, prevention, and repair', in R.I. Rothberg (ed.), *When States Fail: Causes and Consequences* (Princeton, NJ: Princeton University Press).

Roy, Olivier (2007) *Secularism Confronts Islam* (New York: Columbia University Press).

Roy, Ravi, Denzau, Arthur T. and Willett, Thomas D. (eds) (2007) *Neoliberalism: National and Regional with Global Ideas* (London: Routledge).

Rueschemeyer, Dietrich, Evelyne Huber and Stephens, John D. (1992) *Capitalist Development and Democracy* (Chicago: University of Chicago Press).

Ruggie, J.G. (1982) 'International regimes, transactions and change: Embedded liberalism in the postwar economic order', *International Organization*, 36(2): 379–415.

Ruggie, J.G. (1993) 'Multilateralism: The anatomy of an institution', in J.G. Ruggie (ed.), *Multilateralism Matters: The Theory and Praxis of an Institutional Form* (New York: Columbia University Press), pp. 3–47.

Ruggie, J.G. (1998) 'What makes the world hang together? Neo-utilitarianism and the social constructivist challenge', *International Organization*, 52(4): 855–85.

Ruggie, John Gerard, Katzenstein, Peter, Keohane, Robert and Schmitter, Philippe (2005) 'Transformations in world politics: The intellectual contributions of Ernst B. Haas', *Annual Review of Political Science*, 8: 271–96.

Rummel, R.J. (1994) *Death by Government* (London: Transaction Press).

Runyan, A.S. (2003) 'The place of women in trading places: Gendered global/regional regimes and inter-nationalized feminist resistance', in E. Kofman and G. Youngs (eds), *Globalization: Theory and Practice*, 2nd edn (London: Continuum), pp. 139–56.

Rupert, M. (2000) 'Globalization and American common sense: Struggling to make sense of a post-hegemonic world', in B.K. Gills (ed.), *Globalization and the Politics of Resistance* (London: Macmillan), pp. 171–88.

Russell, James A. (2008) 'The militarization of energy security', *Strategic Insights*, 7(3) (July): 7.

Rustow, Dankwart A. (1970) 'Transitions to democracy: Toward a dynamic model', *Comparative Politics*, 2(3): 337–63.

Sachs, J.D. (2008) 'A users guide to the coming century', *The National Interest* (July/August): 8–15.

Sachs, Jeffrey (2008) 'Land, water and conflict; As drylands get drier and violence grows, new crises resembling Darfur will arise', *Newsweek International*, 14 July.

Sassen, Saskia (ed.) (2007) *Deciphering the Global: Its Scales, Spaces and Subjects* (London and New York: Routledge).

Schedler, Andreas (2002) 'Elections without democracy: The menu of manipulation', *Journal of Democracy*, 13(2): 36–50.

Schedler, Andreas (2006) *Electoral Authoritarianism: The Dynamics of Unfree Competition* (Boulder, CO: Lynne Rienner).

Scheuer, Michael (2007) *Imperial Hubris: Why the West Is Losing the War on Terror* (Washington, DC: Brassey's).

Schiavone, G. (2001) *International Organizations: A Dictionary and a Directory*, 5th edn (Basingstoke: Palgrave Macmillan).

Schlosstein, S. (1989) *The End of the American Century* (New York: Congdon and Weed).

Schmidl, E.A. (2000) 'The evolution of peace operations from the nineteenth century', in E.A. Schmidl (ed.), *Peace Operations Between War and Peace* (London: Frank Cass), pp. 4–20.

Schmitter, Philippe C. (1995) 'Transitology: The science or art of democratization?', in Joseph S. Tulchin and Bernice Romero (ed.), *The Consolidation of Democracy in Latin America* (Boulder, CO: Lynne Rienner), pp. 11–41.

Schmitter, Philippe C. and Karl, Terry Lynn (1991) 'What democracy is ... and is not', *Journal of Democracy*, 2(3): 75–88.

Schnabel, A. (2001) 'Preventing the plight of refugees', *Peace Review*, 13(1): 109–14.

Schreuder, Y. (2009) *The Corporate Greenhouse: Climate Change Policy in a Globalizing World* (London: Zed Books).

Schreurs, M. and Tiberghien, Y. (2007) 'Multi-level reinforcement: Explaining European Union leadership in climate change mitigation', *Global Environmental Politics*, 7(4): 19–46.

Schuman, Robert (1950) 'The Schuman Declaration', available at http://europa.eu/abc/symbols/9-may/decl_en.htm.

Schumpeter, Joseph R. (1950[1942]) *Capitalism, Socialism and Democracy* (New York: Harper and Row).

Scott, W.R. (1995) *Institutions and Organizations* (London: Sage).

Securities and Exchange Commission (2009) '17 CFR Parts 240, 243, and 249b Re-Proposed Rules for Nationally Recognized Statistical Rating Organizations; Amendments to Rules for Nationally Recognized Statistical Rating Organizations; Final Rule and Proposed Rule', *Federal Register*, 74(25) (9 February): 6456–84.

Seybolt, T. (2007) *Humanitarian Military Intervention: The Conditions for Success and Failure* (Oxford: Oxford University Press for SIPRI).

Sharma, J. (2008) 'The language of rights', in A. Cornwall, S. Corrêa and S. Jolly (eds), *Development with a Body: Sexuality, Human Rights and Development* (London: Zed), pp. 67–76.

Shawcross, W. (2000) *Deliver Us from Evil: Peacekeepers, Warlords, and a World of Endless Conflict* (New York: Simon & Schuster).

Sheehan, James J. (2008) *Where Have All the Soldiers Gone? The Transformation of Modern Europe* (Boston: Houghton Mifflin).

Shepherd, L.J. (2008) *Gender, Violence and Security: Discourse as Practice* (London: Zed).

Simmons, B.A. and Elkins, Z. (2004) 'The globalization of liberalization: Policy diffusion in the international political economy', *American Political Science Review*, 98(1): 171–89.

Simmons, M.R. (2005) *Twilight in the Desert. The Coming Saudi Oil Shock and the World Economy* (Hoboken/New Jersey: John Wiley & Sons).

Sinclair, Timothy J. (2005) *The New Masters of Capital: American Bond Rating Agencies and the Politics of Creditworthiness* (Ithaca: Cornell University Press).

Sinclair, Upton (2001[1908]) *The Moneychangers* (New York: Prometheus Books).

Singer, H. (1950) 'The distribution of gains from trade between investing and borrowing countries', *American Economic Review*, 40: 473–85.

Sjoberg, L. and Gentry, C.E. (2007) *Mothers, Monsters, Whores: Women's Violence in Global Politics* (London: Zed).

Sklair, Leslie (2000) *The Transnational Capitalist Class* (Oxford: Blackwell).

Skons, Elisabeth (2007) 'Analysing risks to human lives', in *SIPRI Yearbook 2007: Armaments, Disarmament and International Security* (Stockholm: Stockholm International Peace Research Institutes; Oxford: Oxford University Press).

Slaughter, A.M. (2009) 'America's edge: Power in the networked century', *Foreign Affairs*, 88(1) (January/February): 94–113.

Slaughter, A.-M. (2004) *A New World Order* (Princeton, NJ: Princeton University Press).

Smith, A.D. (1986) *The Ethnic Origins of Nations* (New York: Basil Blackwell).

Smith, A.D. (2001) *Nationalism: Theory, Ideology, History* (Cambridge: Polity Press).

Snyder, Craig A. (ed.) (2008) *Contemporary Security and Strategy*, 2nd edn (Basingstoke: Palgrave Macmillan).

Søderbaum Fredrik and Van Langenhove, Luk (2005) 'The EU as a global actor and the role of interregionalism', Special Issue of *Journal of European Integration*, 27(3): 365–80.

Soederberg, Susanne, Menz, George and Cerny, Philip G. (eds) (2005) *Internalizing Globalization: The Rise of Neoliberalism and the Erosion of National Varieties of Capitalism* (London and New York: Palgrave Macmillan).

Solomon, Michele Klein (2005) International Migration Management through Inter-State Consultation Mechanisms: Focus on Regional Consultative Processes on Migration, IOM's International Dialogue on Migration and the Berne Initiative. Paper prepared for the United Nations Expert Group Meeting on International Migration and Development (Geneva: IOM, 6–8 July).

South China Morning Post (2007) 'Woefully ill-prepared for natural disasters', 12 March.

Spruyt, Hendrik (1994). *The Sovereign State and Its Competitors: An Analysis of Systems Change* (Princeton, NJ: Princeton University Press).

Stares, P.B. (ed.) (2000) *Rethinking Energy Security in East Asia* (Tokyo: The Japan Center for International Exchange/JCIE).

Stepan, Alfred and Cindy Skach (1993) 'Constitutional frameworks and democratic consolidation: Parliamentarism versus Presidentialism', *World Politics*, 46(1): 1–2.

Stern, J.P. (2005) *The Future of Russian Gas and Gazprom* (Oxford: Oxford University Press).

Stern, N. (2007) *The Economics of Climate Change* (Cambridge: Cambridge University Press).

Stern, N. (2009) *A Blueprint for a Safer Planet* (London: Bodley Head).

Stiglitz, J.E. (2002) *Globalization and Its Discontents* (New York: Norton).

Stiglitz, J.E. (2006) *Democratizing Globalization* (New York: Norton).

Stone, D. (2008) 'Global public policy, transnational policy communities and their networks,' *Policy Studies Journal*, 36(10): 19–38.

Stone, D. (ed.) (2001) *Banking on Knowledge: The Genesis of the Global Development Network* (London: Routledge).

Stone, D. and Christopher Wright (eds) (2006) *The World Bank and Governance* (London: Routledge).

Stracke, N. (2007) 'Economic Jihad: A security challenge for global energy security', in Gulf Research Center (ed.), *Energy Security* (Security & Terrorism Research Bulletin, Issue No. 6, Dubai), August, pp. 26–32.

Straits Times (2007) 'US will take lead in climate change fight', 28 September.

Straits Times (2008) 'Watch out for those living in the shadows', 24 November.

Strange, S. (1987) 'The persistent myth of declining hegemony', *International Organization*, 41(4): 551–74.

Strange, S. (1998) *Mad Money: When Markets Outgrow Governments* (Ann Arbor: University of Michigan Press).

Streeck, W. (1997) 'German capitalism: Does it exist? Can it survive?', *New Political Economy*, 2(2): 237–56.

Sukma, Rizal (2007) 'Thoughts from Indonesia: National nuclear plants needs re-thinking', in *NTS-Asia Alert*, July.

Sullivan, Andrew (2001) 'This *is* a religious war', *New York Times*, 7 October.

Sumner, A. (2004) 'Epistemology and "evidence" in development studies: A review of Dollar and Kraay', *Third World Quarterly*, 25(6): 1160–74.

Sutherland, P.D. (2005) 'Correcting misperceptions', *Foreign Affairs*, 84(7) (December). [Online] Available at: http://www.foreignaffairs.org/20051201faessay84705/peter-d-sutherland/correcting-misperceptions.html.

Sylvester, C. (1994) *Feminist Theory and International Relations in a Postmodern Era* (Cambridge: Cambridge University Press).

Sylvester, C. (1996) 'The contributions of feminist theory to international relations', in S. Smith, K. Booth and M. Zalewski (eds), *International Theory: Positivism and Beyond* (Cambridge: Cambridge University Press), pp. 254–78.

Szporluk, R. (1998) 'Thoughts about change: Ernest Gellner and the history of nationalism', in J.A. Hall (ed.), *The State of the Nation: Ernest Gellner and the Theory of Nationalism* (Cambridge: Cambridge University Press).

Tamir, Y. (1993) *Liberal Nationalism* (Princeton, NJ: Princeton University Press).

Telo, M. (2009) *International Relations: A European Perspective* (London: Ashgate).

Tesón, Fernando R. (1997) *Humanitarian Intervention: An Inquiry into Law and Morality*, 2nd edn (New York: Transnational Publishers).

Tesón, Fernando R. (2003) 'The liberal case for humanitarian intervention', in J.L. Holzgrefe and Robert O. Keohane (eds), *Humanitarian Intervention: Ethical, Legal and Political Dilemmas* (Cambridge: Cambridge University Press).

Thakur, Ramesh (2004) 'Iraq and the responsibility to protect', *Behind the Headlines*, 62(1): 1–16.

The Economist (2008) 'Obama's world', 8 November.

The Jakarta Post (2008) 'Water: Needed but still taken for granted', 30 September.

The National Security Strategy of the United States of America (2002) cited 30 October 2007. Available from http://www.whitehouse.gov/nsc/nss/2002/nss.pdf.

Thompson, Mark (1995) *The Anti-Marcos Struggle: Personalistic Rule and Democratic Transition in the Philippines* (New Haven: Yale University Press).

Tickell, O. (2008) *Kyoto2* (London: Zed Books).

Tickner, J.A. (1999) 'Why women can't run the world: International politics according to Francis Fukuyama', *International Studies Review*, 1(3): 3–11.

Tickner, J.A. and Sjoberg, L. (2007) 'Feminism', in T. Dunne, M. Kurki and S. Smith (eds), *International Relations Theories: Discipline and Diversity* (Oxford: Oxford University Press), pp. 185–202.

Tilly, C. (1975) 'Reflections on the history of European state-making', in C. Tilly (ed.), *The Formation of National States in Western Europe* (Princeton, NJ: Princeton University Press), pp. 3–83.

Tilly, C. (1990) *Coercion, Capital, and European States, A.D. 990–1990* (Oxford, UK; New York, NY: Blackwell).

Tonelson, A. (2006) 'The Real Lessons in the Doha Round's Failure', *AmericanEconomicAlert* (15 August). [Online] Available at: http://www.americaneconomicalert.org/view_art.asp?Prod_ID=2537.

Tow, William, Ramesh Thakur and In-Tyaek Hun (2000) *Asia's Regional Order: Reconciling tradition and human security* (Tokyo: UN University Press).

Townsend, M.E. (1941) *European Colonial Expansion since 1871* (Chicago: Lippincott).

Traub, James (2006) *The Best of Intentions: Kofi Annan and the UN in an Era of American World Power* (London: Bloomsbury).

Treasury, Department of (US) (2008) *Final Monthly Treasury Statement* (Washington, DC: USGPO).

True, J. (2009) 'Feminism', in S. Burchill et al. (eds), *Theories of International Relations*, 4th edn (Basingstoke and New York: Palgrave Macmillan), pp. 237–59.

True, J. and Mintrom, M. (2001) 'Transnational networks and policy diffusion: The case of gender mainstreaming', *International Studies Quarterly*, 45(1), 27–57.

Tsai, K.S. (2007) *Capitalism Without Democracy: The Private Sector in Contemporary China* (Ithaca: Cornell University Press).

Tsingou, E. (2010) 'Transnational governance networks in the regulation of finance – The making of global regulation and supervision standards in the banking industry', in Morten Ougaard (ed.), *Theoretical Perspectives on Business and Global Governance: Bridging Theoretical Divides* (London: Routledge).

Tsingou, E. (2004) *Policy Preferences in Financial Governance: Public-Private Dynamics and the Prevalence of Market-Based Arrangements in the Banking Industry*, University of Warwick: Centre for the Study of Globalisation and Regionalisation, Working Paper 131/04.

Tu, J. (2008) 'China's new National Energy Commission and energy policy', *China-Brief*, 8(7) (28 March). http://www.jamestown.org/programs/chinabrief/single/?tx_ttnews%5Btt_news%5D=4820&tx_ttnews%5BbackPid%5D=168&no_cache=1.

Tuastad, Dag (2003) 'Neo-Orientalism and the new Barbarism thesis: Aspects of symbolic violence in the Middle East conflict(s)', *Third World Quarterly*, 24(4): 591–9.

Turner, A. (2009) *The Turner Review: A Regulatory Response to the Global Banking Crisis* (London: FSA): at http://www.fsa.gov.uk/pages/Library/Corporate/turner/index.shtml.

Umbach, F. (2003) *Globale Energiesicherheit. Herausforderungen für die europäische und deutsche Außenpolitik* (Munich: Oldenbourg Verlag).

Umbach, F. (2006) 'Europe's next Cold War', *Internationale Politik (Global Edition)* (Summer): 64–71.

Umbach, F. (2007) 'The legs of the triangle – The EU-China relations', in W. Jung (ed.), *The New Strategic Triangle: China, Europe and the United States in a Changing International System*, Konrad-Adenauer-Stiftung, KAS-Schriftenreihe No. 76 (Beijing: KAS), pp. 36–45.

Umbach, F. (2008a) 'German debates on energy security and impacts on Germany's 2007 EU presidency', in Antonio Marquina (ed.), *Energy Security: Visions from Asia and Europe* (Hampshire-New York: Palgrave Macmillan), pp. 1–23.

Umbach, F. (2008b) 'Diversifizierung statt Protektorat. Energiepartnerschaft zwischen Russland und der EU', *Die politische Meinung* (September): 25–30.

Umbach, F. (2008c) 'China's energy insecurity in context of growing geopolitical competition: Implications for the future EU-China relations', in Klaus Lange (ed.), *European-Chinese Security Cooperation: Possibilities and Limits* (Konferenzband), Munich: Akademie für Akademie für Politik und Zeitgeschehen der Hanns-Seidel-Stiftung (HSS), Studies & Comments 6, pp. 43–59.

Umbach, F. (2009) 'Global energy security and the implications for the EU', *Energy Policy*, March 2009 edition.

UNCTAD (2002a) *Trade and Development Report 2002* (Geneva: UNCTAD).

UNCTAD (2002b) *World Investment Report 2002* (Geneva: UNCTAD).

UNCTAD (2007) *World Investment Report 2007* (Geneva: UNCTAD).

UNDP (2001) *Human Development Report* (New York: Oxford: Oxford University Press).

UNHCR (1999) 'Refugees and others of concern to UNHCR: 1998 statistical overview' (Geneva: UNHCR, July).

UNHCR (2000) *The State of the World's Refugees 2000* (Oxford: Oxford University Press).

UNHCR (2001) 'Care urged in balancing security and refugee protection needs'. *Press Release* (Geneva: UNHCR, 1 October).

UNHCR (2004) *Proposal to Establish an Assistant High Commissioner (Protection) Post in UNHCR* (Geneva: EXCOM 55th session, A/AC.96/992/Add.1, 2 September 2004).

UNHCR (2006a) 'Asylum Levels and Trends in Industrialized Countries, 2005: Overview of Asylum Applications Lodged in Europe and None-European Industrialized Countries in 2005' (Geneva: UNHCR, 17 March 2006).

UNHCR (2006b) '2005 Global Refugee Trends: Statistical Overview of Populations of Refugees, Asylum-Seekers, Internally Displaced Persons, Stateless Persons, and Other Persons of Concern' (Geneva: UNHCR, 9 June 2006).

UNHCR (2007) '2006 Global Trends: Refugees, Asylum-Seekers, Returnees, Internally Displaced and Stateless Persons' (Geneva: UNHCR, 16 July 2007).

UNHCR (2008) 'Statistical Yearbook 2007: Trends in Displacement, Protection and Solutions' (Geneva: UNHCR, December 2008).

UNHCR (2009) 'Asylum Levels and Trends in Industrialized Countries 2008: Statistical Overview of Asylum Applications Lodged in Europe and selected Non-European Countries' (Geneva: UNHCR, 24 March).

United Nations (2000) *The World's Women 2000: Trends and Statistics* (New York: United Nations Publications).

United Nations (2004) *A More Secure World: Our Shared Responsibility.* Report of the High-level Panel on Threats, Challenges and Change. New York. http://www.un.org/secureworld/report.pdf.

United Nations Commission of Experts on Reforms of the International Monetary and Financial System (2009) *Recommendations* (19 March 2009), http://www.un.org/ga/president/63/letters/recommendationExperts200309.pdf.

Urbatsch, R. (2009) 'Interdependent preferences, militarism and child gender', *International Studies Quarterly*, 53(1): 1–21.

Van Creveld, M.L. (1991) *The Transformation of War* (New York, Toronto: Free Press).

van der Linde, C. (2004) *Study on Energy Supply Security and Geopolitics* (The Hague: Institute for International Relations 'Clingendael').

Vayrynen, Raimo (2003) 'Regionalism: Old and new', *International Studies Review*, 5(1): 25–52.

Verkuyten, M. (2005) *The Social Psychology of Ethnic Identity* (East Sussex, UK: Psychology Press).

Victor, D. (2004) *The Collapse of the Kyoto Protocol and the Struggle to Slow Global Warming* (Princeton, NJ: Princeton University Press).

Victor, D.G., Jaffe, A.M. and Hayes, M.H. (eds) (2006) *Natural Gas and Geopolitics* (Cambridge and New York: Cambridge University Press).

Vogel, S.K. (2006) *Japan Remodeled: How Government and Industry Are Reforming Japanese Capitalism* (Ithaca: Cornell University Press).

Vogler, J. and Bretherton, C. (2006) 'The European Union as a protagonist to the United States on climate change', *International Studies Perspectives*, 7: 1–22.

von Clausewitz, C., Howard, M.E. and Paret, P. (1984) *On War* (Princeton, NJ: Princeton University Press).

Wade, R. (2000) 'Wheels within wheels: Rethinking the Asian crisis and the Asian model', *Annual Review of Political Science*, 3: 85–115.

Wade, R. and Veneroso, F. (1998) 'The Asian crisis: The high debt model versus the Wall Street-Treasury complex', *The New Left Review*, 228 (March–April): 3–23.

Wade, Robert (2003) 'The disturbing rise in poverty and inequality: Is it all a "Big Lie"?', in David Held and Mathias Koenig-Archibugi (eds), *Taming Globalization* (Cambridge: Polity Press), pp. 18–46.

Wade, Robert (2004) *Governing the Market: Economic Theory and the Role of Government in East Asian Industrialization* (Princeton, NJ: Princeton University Press).

Wæver, Ole Barry Buzan, Morten Kelstrup and Pierre Lemaitre (1993) *Identity, Migration and the New Security Agenda in Europe* (London: Pinter).

Walker, R.B.J. (1992) *Inside/Outside: International Relations as Political Theory* (Cambridge: Cambridge University Press).

Wallace, Helen (2002) 'Europeanisation and globalisation: Complementary or contradictory trends?', in Shaun Breslin, Christopher Hughes, Nicola Phillips and Ben Rosamond (eds), *New Regionalisms in the Global Political Economy: Theories and Cases* (London: Routledge), pp. 137–49.

Waltz, K.N. (2000) 'Structural realism after the Cold War', *International Security*, 25(1): 5–41.

Waltz, Kenneth (1979) *Theory of International Politics* (Reading, MA: Addison-Wesley).

Warwick Commission (2007) *The Multilateral Trade Regime: Which Way Forward?* University of Warwick, at http://go.warwick.ac.uk/go/warwickcommission.

Waylen, G. (1996) *Gender in Third World Politics* (Buckingham: Open University Press).

Weaver, K. (2008) *The Hypocrisy Trap: The World Bank and the Poverty of Reform* (Princeton, NJ: Princeton University Press).

Weber, M., Gerth, H.H. and Mills, C.W. (1991) *From Max Weber: Essays in Sociology* (London: Routledge).

Weiner, Myron (1987) 'Empirical Democratic Theory', in Myron Weiner and Ergun Ozbudun (eds), *Competitive Elections in Developing Countries* (Durham: Duke University Press), pp. 3–36.

Weiss, Meredith (2006) *Protest and Possibilities: Civil Society and Coalitions for Political Change in Malaysia* (Stanford: Stanford University Press).

Weiss, Thomas G. (2004) 'The sunset of humanitarian intervention? The responsibility to protect in a unipolar era', *Security Dialogue*, 35(2): 135–53.

Weiss, Thomas G. (2007) *Humanitarian Intervention: Ideas into Action* (Cambridge: Polity Press).

Welsh, Jennifer (ed.) (2004) *Humanitarian Intervention and International Relations* (Oxford: Oxford University Press).

Wheeler, Nicholas J. (2000) *Saving Strangers: Humanitarian Intervention in International Society* (Oxford: Oxford University Press).

Wheeler, Nicholas J. (2001) 'The legality of NATO's intervention in Kosovo', in Ken Booth (ed.), *The Kosovo Tragedy: The Human Rights Dimensions* (London: Frank Cass).

White, D.W. (1996) *The American Century: The Rise and Decline of the United States as a World Power* (New Haven, CT: Yale University Press).

White House (2002) 'The National Security Strategy of the United States of America', *The White House Website*, 17 September.

Whitworth, S. (2004) *Men, Militarism and UN Peacekeeping* (London and Boulder, CO: Lynne Rienner).

WHO (2008) 'Cumulative Number of Confirmed Human Cases of Avian Influenza A/(H5N1) Reported to WHO', as of 12 December. http://www.who.int/csr/disease/avian_influenza/country/cases_table_2008_12_12/en/index.html.

Wichterich, C. (2000) *The Globalized Woman* (London: Zed).

Williams, M.C. (2004) 'Why ideas matter in international relations: Classical realism, and the moral construction of power politics', *International Organization*, 58: 633–65.

Williamson, J. (1994) 'In search of a manual for Technopols', in J. Williamson (ed.), *The Political Economy of Policy Reform* (Washington: Institute for International Economics), pp. 11–28.

Wilson, W. (2006) 'Appeal for support of the League of Nations at Pueblo, Colorado', in M. DiNunzio (ed.), *Woodrow Wilson: Essential Writings and Speeches of the Scholar-President* (New York: NYU Press).

Wolf, M. (2004) *Why Globalization Works* (New Haven: Yale University Press)

Wolf, M. (2009) 'The cautious approach to fixing banks will not work', *Financial Times*, 30 June.

Woods, N. (2000) 'The challenge of good governance for the IMF and the World Bank themselves', *World Development*, 28(5): 823–41.

Woods, N. (2006) *The Globalizers: The IMF, the World Bank and Their Borrowers* (Ithaca: Cornell University Press).

World Bank (1997) *World Development Report 1997: The State in a Changing World* (New York: Oxford University Press).

World Bank (1999) *World Development Report 1999* (Oxford: Oxford University Press).

World Bank (2002) *Globalization, Growth and Poverty* (Oxford: Oxford University Press).

World Bank (2008a) *State and Trends of the Carbon Market 2008* (Washington, DC: World Bank).

World Bank (2008b) 'Remittances may buoy developing countries caught in financial crisis'. World Bank news item (Washington: World Bank, 24 November). Accessed at http://web.worldbank.org/WBSITE/EXTERNAL/NEWS/0,contentMDK: 21996712~pagePK:64257043~piPK:437376~theSitePK:4607,00.html.

World Bank, Development Prospects Group, Migration and Remittances Team (2006) *Migration and Development Trends Brief 2: Remittance Trends 2006* (Washington: World Bank). Accessed at http://siteresources.worldbank.org/INTPROSPECTS/ Resources/334934-1110315015165/MigrationDevelopmentBriefingNov2006.pdf.

World Economic Council (WEC) (2007) *Deciding the Future: Energy Policy Scenarios to 2050* (London: WEC).

World Economic Forum (WEF) (2006) 'Global Risks 2006', World Economic Forum, Davos (Switzerland), January 2006, available at http://www.weforum.org/ pdf/CSI/Global_Risk_Report.pdf.

World Energy Council (WEC) (2008) *Europe's Vulnerability to Energy Crisis: Executive Summary* (London: WEC).

Wright, M.W. (2006) *Disposable Women and Other Myths of Global Capitalism* (London: Routledge).

WTO (2005) *International Trade Statistics* (Geneva: WTO).

WTO (2007) *World Trade Report: Six Decades of Multilateral Trade Cooperation – What Have We Learned?* (Geneva: WTO).

Wu, Kang and Fesharaki, F. (eds) (2007) *Asia's Energy Future: Regional Dynamics and Global Implications* (Honolulu: East-West Center).

Yergin, D. (1991) *The Prize: The Epic Quest for Oil, Money and Power* (New York–London–Toronto: Simon & Schuster).

Yergin, D. (2006) 'Ensuring energy security', *Foreign Affairs*, 85(2) (March–April): 69–82.

Zakaria, F. (2003) *The Future of Freedom: Illiberal Democracy at Home and Abroad* (New York: W.W. Norton).

Zakaria, F. (2008) *The Post-American World* (New York: W.W. Norton).

Zalewski, M. (1992) 'Well, what is the feminist perspective on Bosnia?', *International Affairs*, 71(2): 339–56.

Zalewski, M. and Parpart, J. (eds) (1998) *The 'Man' Question in International Relations* (Oxford and Boulder, CO: Westview Press).

Zheng, Z. (2002) 'China's terms of trade in world manufactures, 1993–2000' (UNCTAD Discussion Paper no. 161), pp. 1–61.

Zweig, D. and Jianhai, B. (2005) 'China's global hunt for energy', *Foreign Affairs*, 84(5): 25–38.

Zysman, J. (1983) *Governments, Markets, and Growth: Financial Systems and the Politics of Industrial Change* (Ithaca: Cornell University Press).

Index

absolute poverty, 194, 196
absolute war, 128
acid rain, 52
Afghanistan, 10, 27, 72, 77, 116–17, 125,
    133–4, 138, 140, 142–4, 243
Africa, 27
  and colonialism, 67
  democratisation in, 23, 93, 95, 104
  and energy security, 203, 208–9, 211
  and nationalism, 116–17, 121–2
  north, *see* north Africa
  population movement in, 238
  regional integration in, 34, 37–8, 50
  sub-Saharan, 93, 151, 197
  and terrorism, 139, 146
  and underdevelopment, 190, 195
African Union, 244
Ahmadinejad, Mahmoud, 96
Akerlof, George, 216
Alagappa, Muthiah, 164
Albania, 108
Algeria, 207
  independence of, 139
alliances, 28
Allied South-East Asia Command, 37
  see also south-East Asia
Al-Qa'ida, 7, 132, 138, 140, 142–3
the Americas, *see* Latin America
Andean Community of Nations, 38
Anderson, Benedict, 110
Angola, 152
Annan, Kofi, 159–60
anti-globalisation movements, 228, 230
apartheid, 43
Arafat, Yasser, 139
Argentina, 96, 98, 121, 197, 217
Armenia, 108–14
Asia, 37, 87, 106
  Central, *see* Central Asia
  and China, 48
  democratisation in, 93
  financial crisis in, 43, 164, 171, 214, 217,
    228, 232

food security in, 169–71 *passim*
in history, 69
human security in, 162–7 *passim*, 169
and nationalism, 115, 116–17
and Pacific, 42
regional integration in, 34, 44, 48
rise of, 67, 70–1, 73, 78–9
and terrorism, 139, 146
water security in, 169–70 *passim*
ASIAATOM, 174
Asian Development Bank, 196
Asian tigers, 69, 90
  see also Asia, rise of
Asia-Pacific, 43
Asia-Pacific Economic Cooperation (APEC),
  38, 43, 226
Asia-Pacific Partnership on Clean Environment
  and Climate (2005), 58
Association of South East Asian States
  (ASEAN), 34, 38, 42–4, 47–8, 50, 100
  Plus Three, 38, 43
asylum, 242–5
Augustus (the Emperor), 110
Australasia, 38
Australia, 43, 50, 67, 78, 85, 241
  and energy security, 209–10
  and environment, 56–8, 65
Australia-New Zealand Close Economic
  Relations (CER), 50
Austria, 60, 207, 243
Austria-Hungarian Empire, 114
authoritarianism, 23, 26, 28, 30, 105–6
  electoral, 104–5
authority, the, 8, 10, 22, 28, 55, 225, 227,
  234, 236
  political, 28, 111, 114–15, 127, 130, 187
  of the state, 40–3 *passim*, 49, 111,
    131, 233
Ayman al-Zawahiri, 140

Baader-Meinhof Group, 139
Bahrain, 70
Baker, Dean, 218

Keohane, Robert, 235
Keynesianism, 31, 83, 84
Keynes, John Maynard, 83, 215, 216, 223
Kieli, Ray, 71
Ki-moon, Ban, 160, 161
Korea, 43, 97, 100
    see also South Korea
Kosovo, 74, 150, 152, 155, 158, 159, 241
Kossuth, Lajos, 112
Kurds, 111
Kuwait, 70
Kyoto
    mechanisms, 57
    Protocol, 52, 54–65

Labour Party conference in 2003, 244
Lansing, Robert, 114
Laos, 38
Lasswell, Harold, 236
Latin America, 23, 27, 37, 38, 39, 44, 46, 47, 50,
    67, 83, 86, 93, 100, 105, 190, 192, 195,
    197, 198, 201, 243
Latvia, 109
law and the state, 25–6
leadership
    by example, 60
    of international system, 5
League of Nations, 151, 227
Lebanon, 96, 106, 116
Lehman Brothers, 1, 171, 218
Leiken, Robert, 117
Lenin, Vladimir Ilyich, 139
Levy, Jack, 126
liberal capitalism, *see* neoliberalism
liberal institutionalism, 44
liberalisation
    anti-, 120
    financial, 87, 194, 195, 200, 214, *see also*
        neoliberalism
    of investment, 87, 194, 195
    political, 9, *compare* civil liberties
    of trade, *see* trade, liberalisation of
liberalism, 3, 5
    and regionalism, 42, 43, 44
    triumph of, 67
Liberation Tigers of Tamil Eelam (LTTE), 138
Liberia, 130, 149, 155
Lijphart, Arend, 96
Lindberg, Todd, 160
Lipset, Seymour Martin, 96
Lithuania, 207
lobbying, 42
London, 142, 241

the London Conference (1908), 128
'Londonistan', 117
Los Angeles, 119
Luck, Edward, 160

Maastricht Treaty (1992), 42, 47
Madrid, 117, 142
Mahathir bin Mohammad, 100, 105
Malaysia, 70, 95, 96, 98, 100, 105, 171, 217
Mali, 63
'Manhattan Raid', 136
    see also 9/11 terrorist attack
Mao Zedong, 139
Marcos, Ferdinand, 97, 105
'market failure', 85
'market state', 120
Marrakesh Conference (COP-7), 59
Marseilles, 118
Marx, Karl, 4, 215
masculinity, 177, 181, 182
    see also gender
Mattli, Walter, 41
Mayall, James, 112
Mazzini, Giuseppe, 112
Mc Innes, Colin, 129
McLeod, Ross, 101
McLuhan, Marshall, 26
Mekong River, 170
Mercosur, 38, 42, 50
Mexicans, 119
Mexico, 38, 39, 46, 47, 62, 98, 105, 109,
    182, 197
    gulf of, 203
Mezoamerica, 38, 39
    see also Central America
Microsoft, 6
Middle East, 23, 55, 58, 66, 67, 89, 105, 116,
    117, 118, 122, 139, 140, 141, 142, 143,
    144, 145, 150, 151, 203, 205, 208
migration
    international, 239, 244
    management of, 243–6 *passim*, 249
Migration Period, 240
Migration Watch, 247, 248
Milan, 118
Millenium Development Goals (MDGs), 194,
    196, 236
Milosevic, Slobodan, 113
Milton, John, 108
miniliteralism, 235
Mintrom, Michael, 183
Mission de l'Organisation des Nations Unies en
    RD Congo (MONUC), 150